Education in Australia, New Zealand and the Pacific

Education in Australia, New Zealand and the Pacific

Edited by Michael Crossley,

Greg Hancock and Terra Sprague

Education Around the World

Bloomsbury Academic
An imprint of Bloomsbury Publishing Plc

B L O O M S B U R Y
LONDON · OXFORD · NEW YORK · NEW DELHI · SYDNEY

Bloomsbury Academic

An imprint of Bloomsbury Publishing Plc

50 Bedford Square	1385 Broadway
London	New York
WC1B 3DP	NY 10018
UK	USA

www.bloomsbury.com

BLOOMSBURY and the Diana logo are trademarks of Bloomsbury Publishing Plc

First published 2015 by Bloomsbury Academic
Paperback edition first published 2016 by Bloomsbury Academic

British Library Cataloguing-in-Publication Data
A catalogue record for this book is available from the British Library.

ISBN: HB: 978–1–6235–6785–9
PB: 978–1–4742–7051–9
ePub: 978–1–4725–0357–2
ePDF: 978–1–4725–0358–9

Library of Congress Cataloging-in-Publication Data
Education in Australia, New Zealand and the Pacific / edited by Michael Crossley, Greg Hancock,
and Terra Sprague. pages cm. – (Education around the world) ISBN 978-1-62356-785-9 (hardback)
1. Education–Australia. 2. Education–New Zealand. 3. Education–Islands of the Pacific. I.
Crossley, Michael. LA2102.E385 2015 370.9730994–dc23 2014030474

Series: Education Around the World

Typeset by Newgen Knowledge Works (P) Ltd., Chennai, India
Printed and bound in Great Britain

For KC and Lindsay
F, Z, A and E
and Helen

Contents

Series Editor's Preface

This series comprises 19 volumes, between them looking at education in virtually every territory in the world. The initial volume, *Education Around the World: A Comparative Introduction*, aimed to provide an insight to the field of international and comparative education. It looked at its history and development and then examined a number of major themes at scales from local to regional to global. It is important to bear such scales of observation in mind because the remainder of the series is inevitably regionally and nationally based.

The identification of the 18 regions within which to group countries has sometimes been a very simple task, elsewhere less so. Europe, for example, has 4 volumes and more than 50 countries. National statistics vary considerably in their availability and accuracy, and in any case date rapidly. Consequently, the editors of each volume point the reader towards access to regional and international datasets, available online, that are regularly updated. A key purpose of the series is to give some visibility to a large number of countries that, for various reasons rarely, if ever, have coverage in the literature of this field.

The region, if such it is, with which this book is concerned is not an easy one to delimit or to name. We have settled on Australia, New Zealand and the Pacific, but are aware that it will not satisfy everyone. Likewise, it has not been an easy one for the co-editors to determine the contents, especially with regard to the 'Pacific' dimension, as there are so many countries and territories therein. So they, and I, are most grateful to those members of staff from institutions in that area, especially from The University of the South Pacific, who have contributed.

I would like to thank the co-editors Michael Crossley, Greg Hancock and Terra Sprague for all their hard work, leading to a valuable contribution to the literature of comparative and international education, and of the region.

Colin Brock
Series Editor

Foreword

This book brings the research of many leading scholars in education in the Australia, New Zealand and Pacific region together. In doing so it strengthens ongoing linkages and collaboration, and makes a valuable contribution to our understanding of the contemporary educational challenges, issues and priorities that are faced throughout the region as a whole.

I am delighted to have been asked to provide a Foreword but cannot really do full justice to the range and depth of the analyses that are so effectively and insightfully presented here. Together, the chapters help greatly in revealing the common challenges that are faced across the region, at the same time as they demonstrate sensitivity to the historical, cultural and contextual differences that generate distinctive educational priorities. The issues of the quality of education, and its relevance, accessibility and inclusivity stand out in all systems, along with increased attention to the place of language, culture and the potential of information and communication technologies to enhance the reach and impact of educational reform. The importance of balance between national and regional plans, and the priorities articulated by external agencies, is also well argued, as is the need for mutual trust in successful educational development partnerships and cooperation.

From my own vantage point, this is a book that rightly prioritizes well-informed and locally grounded analyses, and contributions that are carried out by researchers from, or working within, some of the least well-documented contexts and cultures within the region. Importantly, this raises the international visibility of the achievements and the challenges faced by the Pacific Island Countries that are so often overlooked in the international literature.

I congratulate the authors for their contributions, and am truly grateful to the book's editors, Michael Crossley, Greg Hancock and Terra Sprague, for the opportunity to support this timely initiative.

Akanisi Kedrayate
Dean, Faculty of Arts, Law and Education
The University of the South Pacific
Suva
Fiji Islands

Notes on Contributors

Robert Andreas is a Professor of Education at the College of Micronesia (COM), Pohnpei. He was a teacher, an educational administrator in government and a professor at the COM. Among other roles in FSM, he is an author and a community leader. He has a Master's degree in Linguistics from the University of Hawaii and a Bachelor's degree in Education from the University of Guam.

Salanieta Bakalevu is Senior Lecturer at the School of Education, The University of the South Pacific, Fiji, where she teaches graduate and undergraduate courses and supervises graduate students' work. Her teaching areas are mathematics education, assessment and gender and education. She taught in several secondary schools in Fiji before enrolling at the University of Waikato, New Zealand, to do a doctoral degree in mathematics education. She spent 1 year as Advisor in Mathematics at the Curriculum Development Unit of the Ministry of Education before moving on to head the Centre for Professional Development at the Fiji Institute of Technology, a position she held for 4 years. She worked as an instructional designer at The University of the South Pacific's Centre for Flexible Learning for 3 years before joining the School of Education.

Gerald Burke is Adjunct Professor at the Monash University, Australia. He has engaged in research and consulting in Australia and internationally on the financing of education and training and on education and employment. He was director of the Centre for the Economics of Education and Training at Monash University Melbourne, Australia, from 1994 to 2008. Appointments include chair of the Victorian Qualifications Authority and member of the Victorian Learning and Employment Skills Commission. From 2008 to 2013, he was a member of Skills Australia and later the Australian Workforce and Productivity Agency (AWPA) which advises the Australian government on skill needs and workforce development.

Subhas Chandra is Associate Professor in Education and former Head of School of Education at The University of the South Pacific, Fiji. He coordinates postgraduate and undergraduate courses in educational measurement and evaluation, educational psychology and is also the team manager for the developmental psychology and special and inclusive education staff and programmes. Subhas

has extensive teaching, research, consultancy and management experience in both education and psychology. He has worked in three universities in Australia as well as in private and public schools and government departments of health and community care in Canberra and New South Wales. He was also Professor of Education and Head of the School of Education at the Fiji National University. He graduated with a BA degree in psychology from the University of New South Wales, Australia, an MA degree in psychology from Sydney University, Australia and a PhD in psychology from The University of the South Pacific, Fiji.

Glenys Collard is a South-West Nyungar woman, mother of six, grandmother of 30, great-grandmother of 3 and a matriarch within her family of over 280 people. Glenys has pioneered the development of the Nyungar Language Project and understanding surrounding the use of Aboriginal English in the non-Aboriginal world. Glenys holds a degree in Community Development and has in a wide range of experience working in the public sector and in particular in training teachers on Aboriginal English. She has co-authored numerous educational publications and academic papers, including two books written in Nyungar and Aboriginal English: *Kura* and *Kwobba Keip Boya*. Glenys's experience in Nyungar language, Aboriginal English, culture and education have enabled her to contribute significantly to developments in policy and planning within many government and non-government agencies throughout Western Australia. Glenys has played a leading role in the West Australian Department of Education's *ABC of Two-Way Literacy and Learning* project which she co-managed with Patricia Konigsberg since 1996.

Steven J. Coombs is Head of the School of Education and Professor of Teacher Education at The University of the South Pacific, Fiji. Previously, he was Head of the Continuing Professional Development department at Bath Spa University, UK, since 2002. Steve also previously worked as Professor of Educational Technology at Sonoma State University in California, USA, and for another 3 years as Assistant Professor of Instructional Technology at the National Institute of Education, Singapore. He is a life member of the Educational Research Association of Singapore and a member of the International Professional Development Association (IPDA). Steve has published many books, journal articles and conference papers covering a wide field of education. Currently, he is engaged in a shared book project introducing the concept and practice of the emerging field of 'Living Global Citizenship'. He is an external examiner for the postgraduate professional development programmes at the University of the West of Scotland, UK, Vice Chair of the IPDA and Teaching Fellow at Bath Spa University, UK.

Eve Coxon is Associate Professor in the School of Critical Studies and Director of the Research Unit in Pacific and International Education (RUPIE) in the Faculty of Education, University of Auckland, Australia. For many years, she has been involved in a wide range of research and research-based teaching and consultancy relating to education in the Pacific region and other parts of the 'developing' world. A central focus of this work has been on the role of educational aid in enhancing sustainable and equitable education development, including recent shifts in aid donor policy and modes of aid delivery.

Michael Crossley is Professor of Comparative and International Education, Director of the Research Centre for International and Comparative Studies at the Graduate School of Education and Director of the Education in Small States Research Group, University of Bristol, UK. Previously, he was Associate Dean for Planning and Research at the University of Papua New Guinea and he is currently Adjunct Professor of Education at The University of the South Pacific, Fiji. Key research interests relate to: theoretical and methodological scholarship on the future of comparative and international education; the international transfer of educational policy and practice; educational research and evaluation capacity and international development cooperation and educational development in small states. In 2005, he was elected as an Academician by the UK Academy for the Social Sciences (AcSS).

Jeremy Dorovolomo is Lecturer at the School of Education, The University of the South Pacific, Fiji. He taught in high schools in the Solomon Islands for several years where he held various positions including School Principal. He was also a lecturer at the Solomon Islands College of Higher Education (SICHE) that is now the Solomon Islands National University (SINU). He joined the School of Education, The University of the South Pacific, Fiji, in 2004. His research interests are physical education and sport pedagogy, physical activity and health, outdoor education and Solomon Islands and Melanesia issue.

Kisione Finau has been the director of Information Technology Services at The University of the South Pacific, Fiji for the last 15 years. He has a Bachelor's and Master's degree in Computer Science and an MBA. He has over 30 years of experience in the area of information and communication technologies. His area of interests is Network and IT Strategies.

Greg Hancock has worked as an Australian Schools Commissioner, the Chief Education Officer of the Australian Capital Territory and most recently at AusAID as Human Resources Development Specialist for the Pacific and at The World Bank. He has a PhD from the University of Chicago, USA and his involvement in comparative studies dates back to the 1960s when he was responsible for planning and research functions in the NSW Education Department. He shifted to the federal sphere in the early 1970s when the national government became seriously involved in school level education. At the OECD, he took a particular interest in the education of special populations.

Garry Hornby is Professor of Education at the University of Canterbury, New Zealand. He was born in England and emigrated to New Zealand in 1971. He worked as a mainstream and special class teacher in Auckland and then trained and worked as an educational psychologist until 1986, when he returned to England to work at the Universities of Manchester and Hull, with 2 years at the University of the West Indies in Barbados, before moving back to New Zealand. His teaching and research is in the areas of educational psychology, inclusive and special education, teacher education and parental involvement in education.

Te Kawehau Hoskins (Ngāti Hau, Ngāpuhi) is Lecturer in Te Puna Wānanga (School of Māori Education) in the Faculty of Education, University of Auckland, New Zealand. Her primary interest is the sociology of education with a particular focus on the politics and ethics of indigenous–settler relations, and multicultural and bicultural education. Her research focus to date has concerned the Treaty of Waitangi in educational governance, policy and practice; and Māori community participation in school governance and educational decision making.

Seu`ula Johansson-Fua is Director for the Institute of Education, at The University of the South Pacific, Fiji. She received her PhD and MA in Educational Administration from the Ontario Institute of Education (OISE) at the University of Toronto, Canada. Her research interests include: educational leadership, policy and planning development, educational evaluation and promotion of Pacific indigenous languages. She has carried out work in the Cook Islands, Fiji, Kiribati, Marshall Islands, Niue, Nauru, Palau, Solomon Islands, Samoa, Tuvalu and Tonga.

Patricia Konigsberg is Principal Consultant, Leadership, Teaching and Support, EAL/EAD at the Institute for Professional Learning, Western Australia. She is a linguist and a teacher with extensive experience in both the adult and the school sectors, with a strong interest in diversity of language and its effect on teaching and learning. Patricia grew up as a dialect speaker herself and is fluent in four languages. She has worked with Aboriginal people from across Australia. Involved in collaborative linguistic research in the area of Aboriginal English since 1994, Patricia (with Glenys Collard) managed the ABC of Two-Way

Literacy and Learning Project. Patricia has co-authored *Bee Hill River Man*, a book written in Aboriginal English, with the late Jack McPhee, a Nyamal Elder from the Pilbara Region and numerous other educational publications. More recently, Patricia managed the West Australian Aboriginal Literacy Strategy.

Guy Le Fanu is Programme Development Advisor (Education) for Sightsavers, an international non-governmental organization working in the fields of health, education and social inclusion. He is responsible for establishing, overseeing and providing technical assistance for education programmes for young people with disabilities across sub-Saharan Africa, India and South Asia. He has 13 years of experience working in international development, including 4 years supporting inclusive and integrated education in Bangladesh and 6 years lecturing in special and inclusive education at the University of Goroka in Papua New Guinea. Before working in international development, he taught in comprehensive and special schools in the United Kingdom.

Gregory Lee is Professor of History of Education and Education Policy in the School of Educational Studies and Leadership, College of Education, The University of Canterbury, New Zealand. Gregory was Head of this School from 2009 until mid-2011. He has published extensively in his specialist field of educational history and is the author of several books and large-scale academic monographs. Gregory's more recent publications include analysis of comprehensive models of post-primary schooling; secondary education in Aotearoa/New Zealand and internationally; knowledge and subject contestation within a national curriculum framework; national standards and testing regimes; academic and practical intersections between philosophy and history of education and managerialist orientations within universities. He is on the editorial board of several education journals, was joint editor of the *New Zealand Journal of Educational Studies* from 2000 to 2005, and *Teachers and Curriculum*. Gregory has written, edited and co-authored some 350 articles in his 33-year academic career.

Howard Lee is Professor of Education Policy and History of Education at Massey University College (now Institute) of Education, New Zealand, where from 2008 to 2013 he also was Head of the School of Educational Studies. Throughout his 33-year academic career, Howard has authored and co-authored four books and monographs and written more than 250 book chapters, journal articles, archival articles, reviews, opinion pieces and conference papers. In December 2006, Howard was one of ten academic staff members who received the Outstanding Thesis Supervisor of the Year award from The University of

Otago. Howard is on the editorial boards of several journals and is a regular reviewer for many national and international journals.

Alfred Liligeto sadly passed away in October 2014, and the Editors of this book wish to acknowledge his significant contribution to Chapter 12 and to this field of study. Dr Liligeto was a Lecturer at The School of Education, The University of the South Pacific, Fiji, where he had worked for over 20 years. He taught both graduate and undergraduate courses and supervised graduate students' work. His special area was Technology education. He taught in Solomon Islands secondary schools for several years and was also head of department. At the time, he was chair of the technology education curriculum panel for the Ministry of Education and Human Resources Department in the Solomon Islands. Alfred's qualifications include a Master of Arts in Education from The University of the South Pacific, Fiji, a Master of Science (Construction Technology) from the Loughborough University of Technology, UK and a PhD from Waikato University, New Zealand.

Govinda Ishwar Lingam is Associate Professor and Deputy Head of the School of Education at The University of the South Pacific, Fiji. Previous experience includes secondary school teaching in Fiji, rising to the position of Head of Department for Mathematics, before serving at the Lautoka Teachers' College which is now part of the Fiji National University as Senior Lecturer in Education and later as Head of the School for Education. He obtained his Bachelor's and Master's degrees from The University of the South Pacific, Fiji, and his Doctoral degree from Griffith University, Australia.

Kapa Kelep-Malpo is Executive Dean of the School of Education at the University of Goroka, Eastern Highlands Province, Papua New Guinea. She oversees several divisions of the school of which the Special and Inclusive Education Division is one. This division is responsible for preparing teachers in Special and Inclusive Education from primary and secondary schools in PNG and the neighbouring countries of Solomon Islands and Vanuatu. The school closely works with the Special & Inclusive Education arm of the PNG National Department of Education.

Phillip McKenzie is Research Director of the Teaching, Learning and Transitions programme at the Australian Council for Educational Research (ACER). He is a former Director of the ACER Centre for the Economics of Education and Training (CEET), at the Monash University, Australia and spent 5 years as a senior analyst at the Organisation for Economic Co-operation and Development (OECD). He works on a range of projects on the costs, financing and labour market outcomes of education and training, and on education policy issues.

Elizabeth McKinley (Ngāti Kahungunu, Ngāi Tahu) is a professor in Te Puna Wānanga (School of Māori Education), and Director of the Starpath Project for Tertiary Participation and Success at the University of Auckland, New Zealand. The Starpath Project is a Partnership for Excellence between the University of Auckland and the New Zealand Government. Her current research interest is focussed on increasing the access, participation and achievement of students from groups currently under-represented in degree level study.

Unaisi Nabobo-Baba's career as a teacher, teacher educator, researcher and scholar spans some 28 years in various institutions in Fiji and in the wider Pacific region (Micronesia, Polynesia, Melanesia and New Zealand) as well as with an Australian Teacher Education Project. She is currently Associate Professor in Education and Chair of the University of Guam's Institutional Research Review Board (IRB). Unaisi has done reviews for five journals over the last 10 years and is currently the editor for *Micronesian Educator*. She is author of over 100 articles, book chapters, books and other professional development materials, articles, reports, curriculum and programme evaluation reports, papers and peer-reviewed conference presentations.

Shikha Raturi is Assistant Lecturer in Education and co-manager of Teachers' Education Resource and Elearning Centre at The University of the South Pacific, Fiji. For 20 years, she worked as a researcher and teacher integrating technology in Senior High School (A-level) and Undergraduate Chemistry interacting with learners from diverse backgrounds from Africa to Pacific Island Countries. She made a transition to the education field 6 years ago, studying and researching the learning environments and use of technology in higher education. She is a certified online instructor with specialization in online pedagogy and administration.

Judith Rochecouste is Adjunct Senior Lecturer at Monash University, Australia and an independent consultant. She has worked extensively in Western Australia and nationally researching issues relating to Aboriginal education in the primary, secondary, vocational and university sectors. In particular, she has studied the comprehension of Aboriginal English by non-Aboriginal educators and Aboriginal English story structure. Judith has co-authored numerous academic papers and book chapters on Aboriginal English and has extensive experience in the development of print and electronic instructional materials across all educational sectors and within the health sector.

Manueli Sagaitu is former Lecturer in Technical and Vocational Education and Training at The University of the South Pacific, Fiji. He was a double gold medalist when he graduated from The University of the South Pacific,

Fiji, with a Bachelor of Education in 1987. In 1992, he obtained his Master of Science degree in Engineering Design from Loughbourough University of Technology, UK.

Akhila Nand Sharma is Associate Professor in Education and a former Head of School of Education at The University of the South Pacific, Fiji. He coordinates Postgraduate Certificate in Tertiary Teaching, Educational Management and Curriculum Studies courses. Akhila was previously a teacher, vice principal and principal in various primary and secondary schools in Fiji. He graduated with a BA degree from The University of the South Pacific, Fiji, in 1974, a Postgraduate Diploma in Education from Massey University, New Zealand, in 1982, a MEd degree (with honours) from the University of New England, UK, in 1989 and a Doctor of Education degree from the University of Bristol, UK, in 1995.

Terra Sprague is Research Fellow at the Research Centre for International and Comparative Studies and a core member of the Education in Small States Research Group at the Graduate School of Education, University of Bristol, UK. She is Convenor for the UKFIET International Conference on Education and Development. Terra's professional experience includes education consultation, teacher training, special education and teaching English as a Foreign Language in the small state of Armenia. Her current research investigates the concepts of Environmental Resilience and Education for Sustainable Development (ESD) in Small Island Developing States (SIDS).

Konai Helu Thaman is a Professor of Pacific Education and Culture, and UNESCO Chair of Teacher Education and Culture at The University of the South Pacific, Fiji. She is a Tongan national and has led numerous research and consultancy projects, and has published widely in the areas of teacher education, curriculum development and culture and education. Konai has held senior administrative positions at The University of the South Pacific, Fiji, including Director of the Institute of Education, Head of the School of Humanities and Pro Vice Chancellor. She is a Fellow of Asia-Pacific Programme of Educational Innovation for Development (APEID) and a member of several international and professional organizations including UNESCO's Global Monitoring and Evaluation Committee for the Decade of Education for Sustainable Development.

Hilary Tolley recently graduated with her PhD in Development Studies from The University of Auckland, New Zealand. Her thesis developed a complexity-focussed analytical framework to examine sector-wide approaches (SWAp) in education in two Pacific Island contexts: Solomon Islands and Tonga. Her Master's thesis (2004) focussed on the rise of Basic Education as a development approach with case studies in Samoa and Fiji. Hilary has lived in numerous developing countries and worked mainly in education, starting as a secondary science teacher in Botswana and more latterly as an independent researcher and consultant in the Pacific and New Zealand.

Robert Underwood is the President of the University of Guam. He is a honourable former Member of Congress, Professor Emeritus at the University of Guam and is a distinguished educator with many publications and major presentations to his credit. He has served as a classroom teacher, curriculum writer, school administrator, School Board member, Dean of the College of Education and Academic Vice President of the University of Guam. He served five terms as Guam's Congressional Delegate and was a senior member of both the Armed Services and Resources Committees in the US House of Representatives. He authored major pieces of legislation for Guam, served as Chair of the Congressional Asian Pacific American Caucus and was ranking member of several panels and subcommittees. His public service and professional record reflect his passion for his homeland, his commitment to high educational standards and his devotion to issues of justice and equity.

Anthony Welch is Professor of Education, University of Sydney, Australia. As a policy specialist, he has consulted to state, national, and international agencies, governments and US institutions and foundations. Project experience includes East and South-East Asia, particularly in higher education. His work is translated into numerous languages, and he has been Visiting Professor in the United States, United Kingdom, Germany, France, Japan and Hong Kong, China. A Fulbright New Century Scholar (2007–2008), his most recent books are *The Professoriate: Profile of a Profession* (2005), *Education, Change and Society* (2007), *ASEAN Industries and the Challenge from China* (2011), *Higher Education in Southeast Asia. Changing Balance, Blurring Borders* (2011) and *Counting the Cost: Financing Higher Education for Inclusive Development in Asia* (2012). He also directs the national project, The Chinese Knowledge Diaspora.

Paul Weldon is Research Fellow in the Teaching, Learning and Transitions programme at the Australian Council for Educational Research (ACER). Prior to joining ACER in 2010, he was Research Associate at Independent Schools Victoria, Australia. His recent work includes managing the Staff in Australia's Schools Survey, evaluating teacher education programmes and analysing trends in teacher supply and demand.

Introduction

Education in Australia, New Zealand and the Pacific: Challenges, Issues and Priorities

Terra Sprague, Michael Crossley and Greg Hancock

There are many ways of considering the geographical area encompassing Australia, New Zealand and the Pacific. The countries covered in this volume make up part of the region, sometimes referred to as Oceania. The sub-regions of Australasia, Melanesia, Micronesia and Polynesia help to further delineate among the countries and territories. However one chooses to refer to this geographical area, the countries involved represent a great diversity of cultures, languages and approaches to education. This volume provides an up-to-date and well-grounded analysis of educational provision, focusing upon contemporary educational challenges, issues and priorities. It does so by drawing upon ongoing empirical research and contributions from leading scholars across the region. The detailed studies of specific educational systems, sectors and developments are considered in the context of broader comparative analyses. In this way, this book bridges theoretical scholarship with recent empirical research relating to the implementation of educational policy in context.

This introduction provides a conceptual framework for the volume by reflecting upon key themes that emerge from the collective analysis of education in Australia, New Zealand and the Pacific (hereafter ANZP). We begin by introducing the region as covered here, including an explanation of the sub-regions therein. We then explain the general approach to the volume's organization, including a discussion of what has not been covered. Following this, a synopsis of each chapter is presented before addressing the broad, cross-cutting themes that emerge.

Before continuing, it is helpful to consider the nature of the *Education Around the World* series and how this book sits within it. Consistent with the spirit of the series as a whole, this book reflects elements of the traditional approach to comparative education that focuses upon accounts of education in nation states and regions. Here, large international datasets can be helpful resources, such as those providing up-to-date educational data for all Commonwealth countries (Menefee and Bray, 2012), and others which annually report on global progress towards internationally agreed targets and goals (UNESCO, 2014). This book is further infused throughout with an analytical approach that identifies key arguments, themes and issues that emerge from contemporary research and scholarship. These analyses are thoroughly grounded in context, and in planning this book every effort was made to identify authors who are from, or working in, the countries and systems concerned. Building upon contemporary developments within the field of Comparative and International Education, we remain keenly aware of the influence of both globalization and postcolonial sensitivities to difference (Crossley and Watson, 2003) and to influences that run within and beyond the region in multiple directions. For example, while the power of Australia and New Zealand is of major significance throughout the region, numerous chapters and arguments here demonstrate why and how much can be learned from the smaller states themselves (Crossley et al., 2011).

The regional context

The ANZP region, as covered in this book, includes 30 countries, territories and dependencies varying greatly in size, population, language, culture and educational provision. What will quickly become apparent to readers is the diversity of geographical and population characteristics within the region. This ranges from the Pitcairn Islands (a British Overseas Territory [BROT] located south-east of Tahiti), at 47 square kilometres and a population of 48 (Central Intelligence Agency, 2014a), to Australia at 7,741,220 square kilometres with a population of 22.5 million (Central Intelligence Agency, 2014b). Some of the countries covered here are multi-island nations with sparse land mass but with vast sea area. The educational challenges generated by size and scale are addressed further later. What is important to emphasize here is that while certain characteristics unite these countries, and while many of them may be classed as small or micro states, the cultural and linguistic characteristics in particular remain highly diverse. Much has been written about this elsewhere (see, e.g. Crocombe, 2001; Teaero, 2010).

Table 0.1 lists the countries and territories by sub-region, while Figure 0.1 visually represents the sub-regional categorizations.

Aside from these geographical categorizations, the small states in the Pacific are referred to by a variety of socio-economic and geo-political designations. One such example is the term Small Island Developing States (SIDS), a classification of the United Nations. Classifications denoting different levels of national autonomy include Pacific Island Countries (PICs), Pacific Island Nations (PINs) and Pacific Island Countries and Territories (PICTs). The term most commonly used in this book to describe the autonomous island states is PICs. Referring to Table 0.1, readers can see that while many are independent nations in their own right, others are territories or in forms of dependency. As noted in the key to the table, these include BROT, Special Territory of Chile, Overseas Collectivity of France, and Self Governing in Association with New Zealand.

Table 0.1 Countries and territories in the ANZP area by sub-region

Australasia	Melanesia	Micronesia	Polynesia
Australia, Christmas Island (AUST), Cocos [Keeling] Islands (AUST), **New Zealand***, Norfolk Island (AUST)	**Fiji Islands**, New Caledonia (FRORD), Papua (Indonesia), **Papua New Guinea, Solomon Islands, Vanuatu**	**Federated States of Micronesia**, Guam (SGUT), **Kiribati, Marshall Islands, Nauru**, Northern Mariana Islands (SGCUS), **Palau**, Wake Island (UST)	American Samoa (UST), Cook Islands (SGNZ) Easter Island (STC), French Polynesia (FROC), Hawaii (US State), Niue (SGNZ), Pitcairn Islands (BROT), **Samoa**, Tokelau (NZSAT), **Tonga, Tuvalu**, Wallis and Futuna (FROC)

Abbreviations: AUST: Australian Territory Administered from Canberra; BROT: British Overseas Territory; FROC: French Overseas Collectivity; FRORD: French Overseas Regions and Department; NZSAT: New Zealand Administering Territory; SGNZ: Self Governing in Association with New Zealand; SGCUS: Commonwealth in Political Union with USA; SGUT: Self-Governing Unincorporated Territory of the USA; STC: Special Territory of Chile; UST: Unincorporated territory and administered by the USA Office of Insular Affairs.

Notes: The table does not include uninhabited islands. Countries in **bold** are UN member states.
*New Zealand is sometimes classified as Australasia and other times as Polynesia.

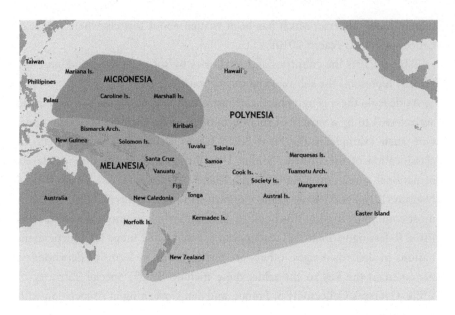

Figure 0.1 Pacific Islands by sub-regional category.

This diversity of classifications is reflective of one characteristic common to nearly all constituent bodies of this region – European colonization. With the exception of Tonga, officially the Kingdom of Tonga, a country that has historically maintained its sovereign status and never been formally colonized, all other countries in the ANZP region have experienced colonial rule. In some cases, this has been with one ruling power and in others by a succession of colonizers. A number of Pacific states still remain in some form of dependency as shown in Table 0.1. Territorial dependencies are largely not covered in this volume, except by brief mention in a number of the chapters. In some cases, such territories are covered elsewhere in this series of books, within chapters dealing with former colonial powers and their ongoing political affiliations in the Pacific. Nor has it been possible to cover Nauru and Palau.

Territories and dependencies aside, with so many independent countries in the region, this volume could not set out to provide a separate chapter for each. This book is, therefore, divided into three main sections: Australia, New Zealand and the Pacific Island Countries. The Australia and New Zealand sections each open up with an overview chapter, followed by additional chapters on specific aspects of education. This is followed by a chapter on Aid to Pacific Education, which serves as a bridge to the PIC chapters. It discusses the region as a whole with respect to international assistance, specifically that from Australia and

New Zealand to PICS in the education sector. This leads to an overview chapter on education in PICs, before moving into specific countries and sub-regions: Papua New Guinea, Fiji, Melanesia, Polynesia and parts of Micronesia (see Figure 0.1). This book concludes with a further regionally framed and thematic analysis that explores the potential of Information and Communication Technologies (ICT) in PICs, and for ongoing linkages and connectivity across the region as a whole.

The following section describes briefly each chapter in turn.

Overview of chapters

In Chapter 1, McKenzie and Weldon offer a comprehensive overview of educational provision in Australia. They show Australia as a dynamic society with high levels of immigration and population growth, and an open economy subject to considerable change. There is much debate about the role of education in preparing people for an uncertain future, and education's contribution to reducing social disadvantage. Educational provision is highly differentiated with a large and growing non-government sector, and policy development is complicated by the federal system of government within which education sits.

Education systems have been expanding rapidly for several decades and there has been a large increase in spending, particularly on schools. Yet despite these efforts, Australia's performance in international tests of literacy and numeracy – although still relatively high – has declined in absolute terms since 2000, the achievement gaps between social groups have not narrowed, and the status of teaching appears to have declined. These disappointing results have focused even more attention on education and its reform, and each new election of governments at national and state levels is accompanied by vigorous debate, and some wide policy swings.

In Chapter 2, Welch examines political federalism in Australian education, particularly from a fiscal perspective. The original division of powers between the national (federal) government and the states under the Commonwealth of Australia Constitution is outlined; and the gradual extension of federal (Commonwealth) powers at the expense of the states is traced. The fact that the Commonwealth has long held sole control over income taxation has led to a significant imbalance: the Commonwealth collects the bulk of revenue while the States deliver actual services, including education. The increasing use by the Commonwealth of conditional tied grants to the states has further strengthened its hand.

The author explains the evolving character of Australian political federalism through a case study of the changing pattern of public funding of non-government ('private') schools. He shows how the initial reticence of the Commonwealth has been supplanted by enthusiastic intervention via various states' grants, often for specific purposes or programmes, and usually with conditions attached. Rising neo-liberalist populism in Australian politics is argued to have somewhat mollified federal/state tensions, though effective coordination remains problematic. The recent 'Gonski' review of school funding highlights the complexities of federal/ state relations in education and the trend at both levels of government to support private schools at the expense of government ones.

Postsecondary education in Australia is taken to embrace vocational education and training (VET) and higher education, and in Chapter 3, Burke considers the postsecondary education policy context and offers an overview of students, courses and institutions. Attention is given to funding as it affects students' participation and course quality. While participation rates are rising, there is increasing concern about the quality of provision, especially in VET. Despite there being nationally agreed goals for increased participation and social inclusion, disadvantaged students are worryingly underrepresented in higher education. VET enrolments are much larger and more socially diverse.

The author outlines the Commonwealth (national) government's grants to universities so as to partially subsidise tuition costs, and its financial grants to low-income full-time students. University fees are substantial but Australian domestic students can be assisted via income-contingent loans. The publicly (largely state) subsidised VET sector has, until recently, charged relatively low fees. Universal entitlement for all Australians to a publicly supported place in postsecondary education is being gradually introduced. In higher education, such access is restricted to public universities with a set maximum fee schedule. In VET, this access is available in both public and private institutions, and in some states, there is no cap on chargeable fees. The chapter concludes with a summation of the outcomes sought from the postsecondary education sector and a listing of issues in need of attention in the near future.

Chapter 4 by Welch et al. reminds us that Aboriginal education, arguably the longest-lived form of structured learning worldwide, was largely disrupted as a result of the European occupation of Australia from the end of the eighteenth century. The authors sketch some of the principles and practices informing traditional patterns of instruction and set out key ideologies underpinning the British-imported colonial education meted out to Aboriginal people – which bedevilled black–white relations. The authors then deal with current dimensions of Aboriginal education, including more reciprocal and respectful forms designed to engage Aboriginal people and to address the wide performance gap with mainstream Australia. The chapter concludes with a case study of Two-Way Bidialectical Education in the State of Western Australia.

Chapter 5 begins the section on New Zealand at which point Lee and Lee delineate institutional arrangements for education in New Zealand and focus on the passage by the New Zealand national parliament in 2008 of the Education (National Standards) Amendment Act. This legislation compelled schools to provide specific information to parents regarding the literacy and numeracy progress of their children enrolled in Years 1–8. The authors show that the collection and publication of such comparative data generated intense debate and divisiveness among stakeholders – parents, politicians, the media, school staff, teachers' unions, academics and the general public. It is then argued that the so-called new National Standards are not 'national' and do not constitute a 'standard'.

After explaining the origins and subsequent development of National Standards, the chapter considers school principals' responses to these Standards, explores the research evidence about them and critiques the New Zealand Prime Minister's insistence that the information be published online despite admitting that it was 'very ropey'. The authors conclude that those intent on applying 'quick fix' solutions (such as the ideological mantra of National Standards) to intractable educational concerns actually exacerbate problems.

Hornby addresses the contentious issue of inclusive education in New Zealand in Chapter 6 where the focus is upon children with special educational needs (SEN), particularly those with social, emotional and behavioural difficulties (SEBD). He critiques policies and practices concerning educational provision for SEN children and the special implications for SEBD children. A case study is made of two follow-up studies involving former students of a residential special school for SEBD children. Students with significant SEBD reported very positively about their residential special school but generally experienced break-down when transferred to a mainstream school. The author deduces that mainstream schools need to be much better prepared for SEBD students if they are to be effectively provided for and concludes with a call for more attention to be given to key factors such as: adaptation of successful strategies used in residential special schools; organizational modification in mainstream schools; professional development of mainstream teachers; transition planning for the relocation of SEBD students to mainstream schools; support to mainstream schools from ongoing residential special schools; and external/community support for teachers, parents and families.

The last chapter dealing with education in New Zealand, Chapter 7, focuses on Māori education in Aotearoa, New Zealand. Hoskins and McKinley set the scene by reminding us of the colonial legacy and introduce three key contexts: the Treaty of Waitangi, educational achievement and self-managing schools. The chapter continues by exploring current challenges facing Māori student achievement, including the imperative to support Māori students to live and learn 'as Māori' and to contribute to their nation. The challenges facing Māori students in English medium schools are discussed before moving on to issues of quality teaching and learning, and school leadership. Priority areas in addressing the disparities between Māori students and their non-Māori peers are identified, to include better data usage, improving instructional leadership and stronger parental engagement.

As Australia and New Zealand continue to be the main contributors to aid for education in PICs, Chapter 8 transitions this book to the chapters on PICs. Tolley and Coxon bring us to the topic of Aid to the Pacific by way of an analysis of the use of the sector-wide approaches, or SWAPs. The chapter is centred on the concept of 'partnership', which has become a dominant discourse in aid and development, and as the authors explain, is linked to the push for improved aid effectiveness and supported by the Paris Declaration. The authors introduce the concept of SWAPs before moving into a description of SWAPs within the Pacific as used by Australia and New Zealand international aid agencies. Two case studies from original and independent research are presented which describe and analyse the progress of SWAPs in Tonga and Solomon Islands. The analysis is presented by way of discussing SWAPs in each country in the following areas: the ownership/leadership by host country; the comprehensiveness of programme and budget frameworks; the harmonization/coordination of development partners; the alignment with and use of local funding systems; and the institutional capacity and management. Through their analysis, Tolley and Coxon conclude that while the Solomon Islands may have started from a 'lower base' of education management and service delivery, the progress seen in SWAP components was stronger than that in Tonga. They comment on the fact that this goes against expectations and describe why they see Solomon Islands as having beaten the trend.

Chapter 9 brings us firmly to the section of this book covering PICs, with an overview of education in the region presented by Thaman. While she also comments on the delivery of international aid from Australia and New Zealand to

PICs, Thaman's chapter first describes educational provision by way of examples drawn from a number of countries. All formal education levels from early childhood and elementary to secondary and higher education are highlighted, including achievements and challenges at these different levels in the region. The Pacific Education Development Framework (PEDF) 2009–2015 is then introduced, including the six priority areas and eight cross-cutting themes of this framework which help to coordinate the regional education vision. An analysis of the progress made by many PICs in relation to the framework is then presented by addressing the areas of: access and equity; quality; efficiency and effectiveness and regional initiatives. While acknowledging the many challenges to education in the region, Thaman draws upon her 30 years' experience as a teacher, teacher educator and curriculum adviser to conclude that recent emphases in the region have failed to address the underlying question of the purposes for education in the Pacific. She urges a reconsideration of the question of what education is meant to provide for Pacific peoples, their cultures and livelihoods; one that relies less upon Western psychology and addresses what she describes as the current educational paradox faced in the region. Thaman then offers a 'framework for shifting educational focus' based on the Delors Report and the four pillars of learning to know, learning to do, learning to live together and learning to be as it applies to PICs. Finally, the chapter suggests how learning institutions can respond to this framework, urging action over 'business as usual' in order to meet the challenges facing PICs today.

Chapter 10 focuses upon Education in Papua New Guinea, with particular reference to its inclusiveness. Taking a broad definition of inclusive education as an 'Education for All of good quality and in mainstream settings,' Le Fanu and Kelep-Malpo offer a deeply researched account of the inclusiveness of education in Papua New Guinea at all levels and from both qualitative and quantitative perspectives. They begin with an outline of the contextual background including a brief description of the history of education in Papua New Guinea, before providing an account of the present day education system including recent reforms. The inclusiveness of education is then assessed both in terms of access and quality. They describe how access has expanded dramatically over the last two decades, while acknowledging some of the challenges that have come with this, and come to a conclusion that, in general, teaching and learning in Papua New Guinea lacks inclusiveness on these two counts. The current picture is then addressed in terms of supply and demand perspectives as a way to further investigate the factors shaping current provision. The chapter continues with a case study of the exclusion of girls from schools in the Highlands and concludes with a critique of the recent curriculum reform, and cross-sectoral, multi-level programme of work undertaken with AusAID. Despite these recent developments, the authors express their doubts about the future development of a more inclusive education system in Papua New Guinea.

In Chapter 11, Sharma et al. examine education in Fiji including its evolution from colonial to modern times. It opens with a description of the origins and development of the Fijian education system two centuries ago, then focuses upon the changing nature of education and schooling that includes the management of schools, the assessment system and vocational education opportunities. In doing so, the authors provide clear insights into some of the key challenges facing this education system. These include the difficulties of the urban and rural divide, disparities in wealth across the country and inequalities among ethnic groups. Education policies put in place to deal with these challenges are examined, including the use of affirmative action. School community partnerships in Fiji, the demands made upon teacher education, in embedding Fijian culture within the curriculum are also given special attention in terms of what they have to offer for the improvement of educational quality. The case of Technical and Vocational Education and Training (TVET) is then taken up in some detail before concluding that the overarching aim of recent reforms across the different sectors of education has been to help widen participation in education and to meet the diverse needs of the Fijian learners.

Chapter 12 is the first of three chapters focusing on the sub-regional groupings of PICs: Melanesia, Polynesia and Micronesia (see Figure 0.1). The chapter by Bakalevu et al. clearly identifies the educational challenges and priorities in Melanesia. Opening with a description of the sub-region, the authors remind us that Melanesia is both an ethnic and a geographical grouping whose people are faced with the 'conflicts between the old and the new, the traditional and the modern, indigenous and Western'. The challenges to education in Melanesia are discussed, including geographical issues, language dilemmas, teacher quality, political issues and educational aid, all rooted within larger questions about the purposes of education. The chapter then moves into an account of recent educational reforms, taking in turn Vanuatu, Fiji, Papua New Guinea and the Solomon Islands. Finally, the authors raise questions about the ways forward for education in the sub-region. A regional approach for development, higher education capacity building and an approach that blends the old with the new are proposed priories.

Polynesia is addressed in Chapter 13 by Johansson-Fua who puts educational quality at the centre of attention as she uses the PEDF to examine the background, educational systems and priority educational issues of the Cook Islands, Tonga and Tuvalu. In each country section, drawing upon a range of official sources, statistics are provided to describe educational provision at the levels of Early Childhood Education and Care (ECED), formal schooling, TVET, non-formal education and teacher development. The priority issues addressed for each country include curriculum relevance and Education for Sustainable Development (ESD). The chapter concludes with a critical commentary on the nature of educational quality for the region as characterized by relevancy – that is education which is 'meaningful, worthwhile and useful for the Polynesian child' and which focuses on the total system and the Polynesian way of life.

Chapter 14 focuses on Micronesia, paying particular attention to the Federated States of Micronesia, its distinctive colonial and postcolonial history and the challenges, issues and priorities that this has generated. Once again the importance of the quality and cultural relevance of education emerges strongly from the analysis.

Finally, Chapter 15 brings us back to PICs as a whole with an examination of the improvement of educational reach via Information Communications Technology (ICT). With the potential to transform educational provision and the regional economy, Lingam et al. describe the rapid growth of ICT developments in the region. PIC targets and goals for ICT are identified, before moving to accounts of recent projects, including partnerships with One Laptop Per Child at the school level, and distance education and 'elearning' projects at the tertiary level with The University of the South Pacific. The chapter focuses on the physical infrastructure that is necessary to make ICT-supported education a realistic possibility for the region. Putting this in place has been a major hurdle, and understandably a main focus over recent years. For these authors, the PIC context is a unique 'Sea of Islands', where challenges to infrastructure are considerable. It is these very challenges of scale and isolation, as faced by small island states elsewhere, that ICTs promise to help overcome by bringing educational services to those who would otherwise not be able to access them.

Connections and cross-cutting themes

A number of cross-cutting themes emerge from the collection of chapters. Especially pertinent to the PICs in this volume is the literature on education in small states, which has been alluded to earlier. A body of work specifically on education in small states began to emerge in the 1980s (see Brock and Crossley, 2013). The introductory volume to this book series (Brock and Alexiadou, 2013) devotes a chapter to the particularities of scale, including a discussion on small state characteristics and their impact on education. The chapters in the present volume not only draw upon this literature, but also make a significant contribution to it. Some frequently cited characteristics of small states with particular implications for education include: challenges of working to economies of scale, for example, in terms of educational assessment (Bray and Steward, 1998), and higher education quality assurance (Martin and Bray, 2011), in part addressed by regional initiatives (Mayo, 2008); the response to external economic and environmental shocks (Crossley et al., 2011); and the importance of working regionally. Of particular note, and picked up by authors across this volume, are the challenges of remoteness faced by many PICs and efforts to overcome these in part by innovations in ICTs; and the impact of the small human resource pool in respect of teacher supply and aid dependency. Some of these are elaborated as follows.

The most prevalent cross-cutting theme is the clear emphasis that emerges throughout the volume on the importance of educational quality. This ranges from quality assurance mechanisms in the higher education sector to improved teacher performance. In Chapter 3 on Australian post-secondary education, quality is highlighted in terms of the diversion of funds from teaching to research, and the impact of the recent influx of students with English as a second language. The issue of teacher quality emerges especially strongly in Chapter 4 on Aboriginal education in Australia and Chapter 7 on Māori education in New Zealand. Suggested measures to improve teacher quality include enhancing teacher training entry standards, raising the quality of initial teacher training, providing and strengthening ongoing professional development and reconsidering remuneration and career structures.

The concepts of equity, equality, inclusivity and participation also feature strongly across the chapters. Chapter 4, for example, makes particular reference to the disparity seen in participation rates and assessment outcomes between Aboriginal and non-Aboriginal students. Of particular concern is the growing disparity in learning outcomes between different groups, the resulting educational competition and the knock-on effect of social inequalities that arise from this. Attention is therefore paid to the importance of inclusiveness in terms of social, cognitive and cultural justice. Inclusiveness is also emphasized in the chapters on New Zealand and Papua New Guinea where participation rates differ significantly between communities and genders. In some instances, the discussion of equality is embedded in historical analyses of colonial rule. Chapter 11 on Fijian education, for example, focuses on the inequalities that persisted for many years as a result of colonial education and that continued into recent times. It is argued here that these were systemic and embedded, with the effect that some educational policies between 1800 and the early 1900s 'favoured and thereby reinforced ethnically divided education.'

While the theme of external aid for education is the main focus of Chapter 8, this issue emerges strongly across several other chapters, with that on Papua New Guinea in particular developing a strong critique of the influence of aid in the region, and the way in which the Australian international aid agency has been seen to exercise a strong hand in policy development. It should be noted that during the course of writing, AusAID underwent a restructuring and is now part of the Australian Government Department for Foreign Affairs and Trade (DFAT), resulting in the combined usage of AusAID and DFAT across the chapters.

Quality and equality, two previously identified themes that run throughout this book, can be seen as currently dominating the international development focus in the education sector. This is particularly true within the debates relating to a successor for the Millennium Development Goals, and is also reflected in the Global Thematic Consultation on Education in the Post-2015 Development Agenda (UNICEF and UNESCO, 2013). This raises questions about how educational systems in the ANZP region can benefit from a global focus upon educational quality, social equity and equality of opportunity in ways that remain sensitive to their own local realities, aspirations and priorities.

Conclusions

A first priority area for future consideration that emerges throughout this volume points to the need for more explicit attention to be given to the nature of international development assistance relationships. Currently there is much international discourse about donor–recipient partnerships as the preferred mode of international development. Evidence throughout the chapters suggests that these partnerships must be more genuine with a strengthened sense of balance between the influence of regional/national priorities on one hand and the agendas of external aid agencies on the other. Many chapters here suggest that the building or strengthening of mutual trust is essential for the future of successful development cooperation in the region. This is particularly well argued in Chapter 12 where the authors recognize the importance of both self-determination and external collaboration.

Of specific relevance in this respect is the *Cairns Compact on Strengthening Development Coordination in the Pacific*. This Compact was agreed to by Pacific leaders at the 2009 Pacific Islands Forum. The initiative arose from concerns that the Pacific region was off-track in attaining the UN Millennium Development Goals by the 2015 target date. The twin aims of the Cairns Compact are the promotion of best development practice in the region and the better deployment of all available resources towards national priorities. Key features include country reporting and peer review of national development plans; and development partner reporting on aid coordination and effectiveness. The signing of the Compact was followed soon after by regional Ministers of Education endorsing the PEDF 2009–2015, a scheme for cooperation among ANZP partners in providing quality education for all in PICs.

A second consideration brings us back to the priority of quality and to ways in which some contributors, notably Chapter 13, have conceptualized educational quality in terms of relevance to local contexts, values and culture. A third consideration focuses on the dilemmas faced in balancing national goals and system priorities with the perceived cost effectiveness of institutional autonomy. Historically, educational provision in ANZP aimed to deliver equality of opportunity through centralized systems based on uniformity – training and employing teachers, setting syllabuses, prescribing textbooks, determining class sizes and conducting examinations. Increasing costs and student participation rates, coupled with the growing bargaining power of the education sector workforce, led to overstretched and locked-up budgets which in turn invoked rising community dissatisfaction expressed especially by influential elites. Stimulated by evolving social norms and enhanced community expectations, these factors contributed to the push for educational reform across the region, albeit at differing speeds and intensities. This can be characterized by moves to devolve decision making and to grant institutional autonomy in varying degrees. Concomitants are greater choice and diversity and, consequently, heightened competition and inequality among institutions. The residualization of students in underperforming establishments is of major concern. Accordingly, the quest for many is now to rebalance the situation by formulating rules, incentives and sanctions, supported by equitable funding arrangements and effective performance monitoring measures.

Finally, it is argued here that if the implementation of educational reform is to be more successful in practice, there is much to be gained from the strengthening of collaborative partnerships across the region as a whole, in ways that are informed by well-grounded analyses involving researchers from, and working within, the distinctive communities and contexts concerned. Looking to future educational priority areas for regional collaboration and cooperation, significant opportunities also lie in the arena of ESD (Crossley and Sprague, 2013; Sprague, 2013). While this does not receive sizeable coverage in the chapters of this book, it is argued that this as an emergent and collective priority, and a space where the international community can learn much from this distinctive region.

References

Bray, M. and Steward, L. (1998), *Examinations Systems in Small States: Comparative Perspectives on Policies, Models and Operations.* London: Commonwealth Secretariat.

Brock, C. and Alexiadou, N. (2013), *Education Around the World: A Comparative Introduction.* London and New York: Bloomsbury.

Brock, C. and Crossley, M. (2013), 'Revisiting scale, comparative research and education in small states', *Comparative Education* 49, 388–403.

Central Intelligence Agency (2014a), 'Pitcairn Islands'. *CIA World Factbook.* Available at: https://www.cia.gov/library/publications/the-world-factbook/geos/pc.html (Accessed: 30 March 2014).

— (2014b), 'Australia'. *CIA World Factbook.* Available at: https://www.cia.gov/library/publications/the-world-factbook/geos/as.html (Accessed: 30 March 2014).

Crocombe, R. (2001), *The South Pacific.* Suva, Fiji: The University of the South Pacific.

Crossley, M., Bray, M. and Packer, S. (2011), *Education in Small States: Policies and Priorities.* London: Commonwealth Secretariat.

Crossley, M. and Sprague, T. (2013), 'Education for Sustainable Development: Implications for Small Island Developing States (SIDS)', *International Journal of Educational Development* 35, 86–95. doi:10.1016/j.ijedudev.2013.03.002.

Crossley, M. and Watson, K. (2003), *Comparative and Internaional Research in Education: Globalisation, Context and Difference.* London: Routledge.

Martin, M. and Bray, M. (eds) (2011), *Tertiary Education in Small States. Planning in the Context of Globalization.* Paris: UNESCO International Institute for Educational Planning (IIEP).

Mayo, P. (ed.) (2008), 'Education in Small States: Global imperatives, Regional Initiatives and Local Dilemmas'. Special issue of *Comparative Education* 44.

Menefee, T. and Bray, M. (2012) *Education in the Commonwealth: Towards and Beyond Internationally Agreed Goals.* London: Commonwealth Secretariat. Available at: http://files.eric.ed.gov/fulltext/ED538725.pdf (Accessed: 13 May 2014).

Sprague, T. (2013), 'Education for Sustainable Development: Examples from Commonwealth Small States', in A. Robertson and R. Jones-Parry (eds), *Commonwealth Education Partnerships 2012–14*. Cambridge: Commonwealth Secretariat, pp. 80–82.

Teaero, T. (2010), 'Weaving a Living from Our Cultures: Challenges and Opportunities', in U. Nabobo-Baba, C. F. Koya and T. Teaero (eds), *Continuity and Survival in the Pacific*. Suva, Fiji: The University of the South Pacific, pp. 149–165.

UNESCO (2014), *Education for All Global Monitoring Report 2013/14: Teaching and Learning: Achieving Quality for All*. Paris: UNESCO. Available at: http://www.unesco.org/new/en/education/themes/leading-the-international-agenda/efareport/reports/2013/ (Accessed: 13 May 2014).

UNICEF and UNESCO (2013), 'Envisioning Education in the Post-2015 Development Agenda: Executive Summary of the Global Thematic Consultation in the Post-2015 Development Agenda'. New York and Paris: UNICEF and UNESCO.

1

Australia: An Overview

Phillip McKenzie and Paul Weldon

Population

Australia is a large island continent of 7.7 square kilometres located close to south-east Asia and the South Pacific. The population is around 23.5 million, having increased by over 50 per cent in the past 20 years (ABS, 2013a). More than half of this population growth is due to net overseas migration, including many people from Asia and smaller though increasing numbers from the Middle East and Africa. The rapid increase in population and changing ethnic mix are leading to major changes in education and society.

The original inhabitants, the Aboriginal and Torres Strait Islander or Indigenous peoples have been living in Australia for at least 40,000 years. In 2014, their population was about 0.7 million or 3 per cent of the total. Indigenous people have long been marginalized, and experience much worse education, health and employment outcomes than other Australians. Improving Indigenous access to, and success in, education have been major priorities of Australian governments for the past two decades; and although there have been some achievements, much remains to be done. Chapter 4 deals in-depth with these issues.

The rest of the population are migrants or descendants of migrants who have arrived in Australia from some 200 countries since Britain established a penal colony at Sydney in 1788 and gradually colonized the rest of the country. In 1945, Australia's population was around 7 million people and was mainly Anglo-Celtic in background. At that time, the country was relatively isolated from external influences and the basic framework was essentially British in character. Since then, over 7 million migrants have settled in Australia, significantly broadening its social and cultural mix. The 2011 Census showed that over a quarter (26%) of Australia's population was born overseas and a further one-fifth (20%) had at least one overseas-born parent (ABS, 2012). The proportion of migrants born in Asia increased from 24 per cent of the overseas-born population in 2001 to 33 per cent in 2011.

Educational opportunities have been a major attraction for immigrants and a significant vehicle of social advancement for them and their children. Australia is one of the few OECD countries where immigrant school students achieve at similar levels as native-born students (OECD, 2012), although the weighting of immigration criteria in recent decades towards educational qualifications and English proficiency is undoubtedly a major contributor to this situation.

English is the language of education and virtually all official activities. There is extensive provision of English language programmes for immigrants from non-English-speaking countries and support for non-English speakers in education. Nevertheless, languages other than English continue to play an important role among some immigrant groups – particularly older immigrants and refugees – and Indigenous people. The 2011 Census indicated that more than 300 languages are spoken in Australian households, and that 23 per cent of the population speak a language other than English at home (ABS, 2012).

The population is highly concentrated in relatively small areas of the continent and Australia is a highly urbanized society, especially in the south-east, east and south-west of the country. Two-thirds of the people live in cities of over 100,000 people, and about 40 per cent of all Australians live in either Sydney or Melbourne (ABS, 2012). The large majority of immigrants settle in urban centres, and population growth is particularly rapid in the outer suburbs of the large cities – social services and infrastructure, including for education, are struggling to meet demand.

Most of the country, though, is arid and sparsely populated and many rural areas have declining populations. Nevertheless, geography continues to influence the character of Australian education: the need during the nineteenth and twentieth centuries to provide schooling in large numbers of small rural communities separated by vast distances led to each colony (and, after federation in 1901, each State) establishing centralized and government-led education systems, and there are perennial concerns about how to provide quality, affordable educational opportunities for those Australians living in rural and remote locations.

Government

By 1850, six major colonies had been established across the country. Each colony was administered directly from the United Kingdom until 1901 when they federated as the Commonwealth of Australia. The six former colonies became states and the country gained substantial independence that through legislation and convention increased during the twentieth century. Nevertheless, although Australia is an independent nation, Queen Elizabeth II of Great Britain is also formally Queen of Australia. The Queen appoints a Governor-General (on the advice of the elected Australian Government) to represent her. The Governor-General has wide powers, but by convention acts only on the advice of ministers on virtually all matters. Each State has a Governor representing the Queen, who is appointed on the advice of the state government concerned. Large numbers of people support Australia becoming a republic and ceasing all links to the British Crown, but as yet there has been insufficient support to change the Constitution, which requires a referendum.

Although the states transferred a number of powers to the new federal government in 1901, they retained responsibility for education. There are also two territories with educational powers similar to the states. There is no single Australian education system as such. However, there are few major differences in the structure and focus of education between the states and territories; the increasing financial power and policy influence of the national Australian government, and moves towards national education frameworks, suggest that these differences will further narrow in the future. Nevertheless, differing policy emphases and budget circumstances between the national Australian government and state governments, and among state governments, can lead to disputes and fragmented responses to educational problems. Chapter 2 examines federal-state relations in detail.

Over the past 20 years, there has been broad political consensus about opening up the economy to greater competition, reduction of tariff barriers, sale of public enterprises and deregulation of much of the labour market. These policies have also been evident in the education system, particularly in vocational education and training (VET) and higher education. Training providers and universities now compete openly within each sector and across sectors for fee-paying students from overseas and within Australia, a substantial proportion of research funds are allocated on a competitive basis and public funding of education and training institutions is increasingly tied to performance measures. Such changes have generated considerable opposition within the education sector, but they are unlikely to be revoked no matter which political party is in power. There has also been strong bipartisan support for lifting educational participation and completion rates and a number of national partnership agreements have been reached between different levels of government to give effect to these goals.

Australian politics tends to be highly adversarial. This, combined with short electoral cycles of 3–4 years, an increasing number of small parties and independents and a still-dominant role for governments in funding education, means that shifts in education policy look like they are becoming more abrupt.

For example, from 2007 to about 2010 there were Labor governments at national level and in most states these tended to emphasize social democratic values of improving educational access and equity and increased funding, albeit combined with an uneasy mix of centralized decision making and encouraging more non-government schools and private VET providers. From about 2010 onwards the political pendulum started to swing towards coalitions of Liberal and National governments at state level, and in 2013 at national level. Such governments include strong elements of both social conservative and free market values. In 2014, major government reviews have been launched into school curricula, teacher preparation and funding of higher education, and steps have been taken to increase school autonomy within government school systems. Concerns about Australia's relative decline in educational performance have been key drivers of these initiatives. (These concerns are discussed later.) These reviews are all likely to lead to substantial – and highly contested – changes in educational provision.

Economy and labour market

In 2012 the Australian economy was the twelfth largest in the world, with a GDP of around US$1 trillion in Purchasing Power Parity terms (World Bank, 2014). Australia is also a wealthy country, with GDP per capita of US$44,400 (PPP) – the sixth highest among OECD countries (OECD, 2013a). The fact that Australia is a relatively wealthy country is a further factor underpinning the demand for education and the growth in education participation rates.

There is evidence, though, that income inequality in Australia has increased relative to the OECD average between 1995 (when income inequality was close to the OECD average) and 2010, when Australia was ranked tenth among OECD countries in the extent of income inequality (Fletcher and Guttmann, 2013). Broadly speaking, two countervailing trends are evident: employment growth has tended to help reduce wage inequality, while growth in investment income (at least up until the GFC in 2008) has tended to improve the relative position of those with higher income levels.

Australia has not experienced an economic recession since the early 1990s, and continued to grow even during the global financial crisis of 2008 and 2009, albeit at a slower rate (ABS, 2012). In 2012–2013 GDP grew by 3 per cent, which was just below the long-term average growth rate of 3.5 per cent that has been experienced since 1960. In early 2014 the unemployment rate was 6 per cent, which was relatively low by OECD standards. However, unemployment among groups such as early school leavers, people living in rural areas and Indigenous Australians was much higher than the national figure – and has been much higher for a long time.

Much of Australia's economic success has been due to its abundance of agricultural and mineral resources, large capital investments in those industries and the opening up of substantial export markets in rapidly growing economies – such as Japan from the 1950s onwards, and China and Korea since the 1980s. The exports have not all been in primary production – over the last 20 years, exports of education services (in the form of fee-paying students from overseas, particularly from Asia), in-bound tourism and financial services have all broadened Australia's export base.

In recent years, the booming export sector has been associated with an increased exchange rate that has sharpened competition for import-competing industries. Australia's terms of trade are highly volatile which makes the economy vulnerable to external factors. The Australian economy is very open: as assessed by the International Chamber of Commerce (2013), Australia is one of only four G20 countries which record an above average level of openness (the others being Canada, Germany and the United Kingdom). This, combined with a small domestic market that makes it hard to obtain scale economies, and the privatization of many government enterprises, has been associated with substantial occupational change and job losses over the past decade, particularly in manufacturing and utilities, and among low-skilled workers.

Since the 1980s there has been a decline in the relative contribution to GDP from goods-producing industries, particularly manufacturing, and a rise in the contribution from service industries. During this period, the mining, manufacturing and electricity, gas and water supply industries experienced declining employment, along with outsourcing of some activities, particularly support services (ABS, 2012).

Australia's economy and employment are now dominated by its services sector (ABS, 2012). From an industry perspective, in 2011 the health care and social assistance industry employed the greatest number of people (1.3 million persons or just over 11.4% of total employment). The next largest industry was retail trade (10.9%), followed by construction (9.1%) and manufacturing (8.6%).

As one indicator of the employment changes that have been underway for a long time in Australia, about 16 per cent of the working-age population changes residence each year, which is high by international standards (Productivity Commission, 2013). The emphasis on mobility has been associated with initiatives in the education and training system focusing on improving educational qualifications, enhancing flexibility including generic skills and the capacity of individuals to navigate their way through increasingly complex pathways.

In 1996, just 5.8 million people aged 15–64 years (42%) had at least one post-school qualification (trade qualification, certificate, diploma or degree). By 2011, this number had increased by 45 per cent to 8.4 million people or 57 per cent of 15 to 64-year-olds (ABS, 2012). These numbers underline the rapid growth in education that Australia has achieved in recent years, and the deepening of skills associated with economic and social change. Nevertheless, modelling by the Australian Workforce and Productivity Agency indicates that there is a widening gap between the expected supply of higher level skills and projected demand: it estimates that by 2025 Australia could be 2.8 million short of the number of higher-skilled workers that industry will need (AWPA, 2013).

Structure of education and training

Depending on the state or territory concerned, the compulsory years of schooling commence in primary school at age 5 or 6 years. Prior to 2010, the minimum school leaving age in most jurisdictions was 15 or 16 years. In 2010, all governments agreed on a mandatory requirement for all students to participate in schooling until they complete Year 10 and to participate full time in education, training or employment, or a combination of these activities until the age of 17 years. Before commencing primary school, large numbers of 3- and 4-year-olds participate in some form of structured learning in diverse settings variously described as pre-school, pre-primary or early childhood. In practice, almost all students complete at least Year 10 of schooling (secondary education runs until Year 12). Post-school educational provision is very diverse

Table 1.1 Structure of education and training

Level and type	Theoretical starting age (years)	Duration (number of years)	ISCED level	Qualifications usually issued
Pre-school	3–4	1–2	0	None
Primary education	5–6	6–7	1	None
Secondary education	12–13	5–6	2–3	Certificate at end of Year 12
Vocational education and training (Technical and Further Education colleges, and other Registered Training Organisations)	16–17	0.5–1	2–3	Certificates I and II
	16–17	1–2	3	Certificate III
	17–18	0.5–2	4B	Certificate IV
	18–19	1–2	5B	Diploma
	20–21	1.5–2	5B	Advanced diploma
Higher education (Universities)	18–19	3–4	5A	Bachelor degree
	18–19	4	5A	Bachelor honours
	21–22	1–2	5A	Graduate diploma
	22–23	1–2	6	Masters
	22–23	3–4	6	Doctorate
Adult and community education	*17–18*	*Generally short courses*	*2–4*	*Formal qualifications not usually issued*

Sources: Derived from OECD (2013b) and AQFC (2013).

and involves many different types of courses, qualifications and institutions. Post-compulsory education and training is regulated within the Australian Qualifications Framework Council (AQFC, 2013), a unified system of national qualifications in schools, VET and the higher education sector (principally universities).

Table 1.1 outlines the levels and types of education and training in Australia. It indicates typical starting ages, durations, the relevant International Standard Classification of Education (ISCED) and the names of any qualification(s) usually issued at each level. The table does not include all the variations by state or territory, but rather outlines the overall picture. Subsequent sections provide details on the types of institutions, curricula, enrolments, financing and outcomes at the levels concerned.

Chapter 3 provides a detailed analysis of VET and higher education sectors in terms of students, courses, institutions, courses, funding and quality. The chapter therefore focuses on the other levels listed in Table 1.1: pre-school; primary education; secondary education and adult and community education (ACE).

Pre-school programmes

There is a range of pre-school programmes provided for children in a year or two before they start full-time schooling. Such programmes are usually provided on a sessional or part-time basis. Programmes are delivered by various government and non-government organizations and there is a great variety of locations involved including child care centres, stand-alone pre-schools, kindergartens and primary schools.

A pre-school programme is defined as a structured play-based programme delivered by a degree-qualified teacher (Productivity Commission, 2014). In order to receive funding, support programmes have to be accredited and meet minimum standards. Programmes for children in the year before schooling (i.e. usually when they are 4-years-old) receive a high level of government funding and most parents need to pay only low fees. Programmes for 3-year-olds are usually not subsidised and parents pay full fees.

The wide range of provider types and differences among states and territories in the age at which children start school have made it difficult until fairly recently to develop a comprehensive picture of pre-school programmes. Nevertheless, this is an area which governments have made a major national priority, including through the National Childhood Development Strategy (Council of Australian Governments, 2009). The overall objective is to build a more effective and better coordinated national early childhood development system and to better support families, including by universal participation in the year before commencing school. The initiative covers children from birth to 8 years, particularly those who are socio-economically disadvantaged. As a result, there is now a much improved information base as well as enhanced funding, teacher training, professional development and quality assurance.

In 2012, there were about 250,000 children enrolled in pre-school programmes, most of whom were aged 4 years (Productivity Commission, 2014). Around 75 per cent of 4-year-olds attended a pre-school in the reference week, compared to just 60 per cent in 2008, and the gaps in participation rates of children from disadvantaged backgrounds appear to have narrowed. The majority of children (63%) attended for at least 15 hours per week.

In the financial year 2012–2013, total government expenditure on early childhood education and care services, including pre-school, was A$6.8 billion. Nationally, the annual average growth rate of real expenditure was 8 per cent between 2008–2009 and 2012–2013. Pre-school is a rapidly expanding level of education in Australia.

Primary education

A number of the issues concerning primary education also apply to secondary education and so this discussion includes material that is also relevant to the next section and is not replicated there.

Schools and enrolments

The six states and two territories have constitutional responsibility for primary education, as they do for other forms of education. The scale of the primary sector varies widely by jurisdiction, reflecting population differences: from about 25,000 students in the Northern Territory (NT) to around 650,000 students in New South Wales (NSW). Primary education lasts for either 6 or 7 years, depending on the jurisdiction concerned, although the broad trend is towards 7 years. In 2013, there were 2.1 million primary students enrolled in around 7,600 schools, an average enrolment of about 280 students per school (ABS, 2014). The scattered population in many rural areas means that Australia has a large number of very small primary schools: one in eight schools enrolled less than 35 students in 2013, and one in four had fewer than 100 students.

There are a number of special schools that enrol students with physical, intellectual or other disabilities. Such schools tend to be very small and have low student–teacher ratios. The long-term trend is for higher proportions of students with disabilities to be integrated into mainstream schools and to receive additional support in that environment.

All government primary schools and most non-government primary schools are coeducational. Over 80 per cent of the institutions that provide primary education are stand-alone primary schools; the remainder are part of a combined primary–secondary school, a model that is more common in the non-government sector.

Within each state and territory the government schools operate as a single system, and have common organizational features, curricula and staffing conditions. Until the 1980s government school systems were generally managed in a highly centralized manner, but there is a clear trend towards greater school-based management. In a number of jurisdictions, government schools now have community-based governing councils, considerable budget autonomy and the capacity to select their teachers. These developments have led to greater diversity within government systems and many initiatives to enhance the leadership and management capacity of principals and other senior teachers.

Non-government schools

A key feature of Australian schooling is the large number of non-government or private schools. In 2013, 31 per cent of primary students were enrolled in a non-government school (ABS, 2014), and this proportion has been steadily increasing – in 2003, it was 28 per cent while in 1993, 25 per cent. The non-government schools are not-for-profit institutions, and need to meet minimum standards to be able to enrol students and receive government funding. Compared to government schools, they have a high level of operational autonomy.

Currently about 63 per cent of non-government schools are affiliated to the Catholic Church, and the others are classified as Independent. In the main, the Catholic schools operate as part of systems of Catholic schools in each state and territory, with similar curriculum and staffing features to each other. The Independent schools by their nature are much more diverse, and include schools linked to non-Catholic religious denominations and schools that focus on particular philosophies. Independent schools have been increasing relatively rapidly in number, particularly those that charge comparatively low tuition fees and that emphasize different religious or educational philosophies.

The reasons for the increasing share of enrolments in non-government schools are complex, and include rising incomes in Australia (all such schools charge some tuition fees), government subsidies that bring the cost of non-government schools within the reach of more families, concerns in some quarters about the quality of government schools and parental desires for programmes they feel are better suited to their children's needs. The provision of government funds to non-government schools has long been a contentious issue in Australian education.

School funding

In 2009–2010, total expenditure (recurrent plus capital) per government school student was A$17,700 compared to A$16,400 per non-government school student (ACARA, 2012). Expenditure per primary student was about 10 per cent lower than per secondary student. In total, Australia spent about 3 per cent of GDP on primary and secondary education in 2009–2010. Real expenditure per primary student increased by about 10 per cent between 2005–2006 and 2009–2010.

The funding of schools in Australia is complex, and is in an uncertain state of transition to new arrangements. Government schools in each jurisdiction are principally funded by state and territory governments (about 90% of their expenditure, OECD, 2013b), with the national Australian government providing additional funds to support improved service delivery and reform to meet nationally agreed outcomes including for students with particular needs (e.g. Indigenous students and students from disadvantaged communities). The national Australian government provides about 10 per cent of the expenditure on government schools. There are no tuition fees in government schools (except for a small number of overseas students who come to Australia on specific visas), although parents usually pay levies for some books and materials, computers, excursions and so on.

Non-government schools do charge tuition fees; such fees are unregulated and vary widely between schools, ranging from around A$3,000 per annum to over A$20,000 although with many exemptions and scholarships. In 2010, the fees and charges per student in non-government schools averaged around A$5,100 for Australia as a whole (ACARA, 2012). Tuition fees in Catholic schools tend to be lower than in Independent schools although there is much variation within sectors. All non-government schools also receive government funding, principally from the national Australian government (which provides about 70 per cent of government expenditure on non-government schools, OECD, 2013b) and also from state and territory governments (about 30%).

Broadly speaking, the extent of national Australian government funding of non-government schools has been determined by two main factors: the average cost of educating a student in a government school (the more spent on government schools the more is provided to non-government schools) and a measure of the socio-economic background of the students enrolled at the non-government school. State and territory governments have used variety of criteria to determine their level of funding for non-government schools, including flat per capita payments and some needs-based funding. The net effect is that all non-government schools receive some government funding. In the schools that enrol a high proportion of students assessed as disadvantaged government funding comprises most of their income.

Along with many Australian analysts, the OECD (2013b) has concluded that funding for schools lacks transparency and coherence, and that this prompts concerns about efficiency and equity in education, particularly given the high proportion of non-government schools (which generally have proportionally fewer disadvantaged students than government schools).

A major review of school funding has advocated substantial reform to funding arrangements and levels (Gonski, 2011). It recommended that all public recurrent funding for schooling, whether provided by the national Australian government or state and territory governments, be based on a new resource standard that would apply to students in all government and non-government sectors. The new standard would involve a base level of funding per student plus loadings based on the additional costs of meeting certain educational needs, and reflect the actual resources used by schools already achieving high educational outcomes over a sustained period of time.

The Gonski review also recommended increasing governments' recurrent funding by about A$5 billion or 15 per cent in order to commence implementing the new approach from 2014 onwards, with the transition arrangements and cost sharing to be negotiated between the national government, and the States and Territories and non-government school sectors. The review was commissioned by the former Labor government which had not completed implementation negotiations with all school authorities when it lost office in 2013. While the incoming Coalition government has committed to the general directions of school funding reform, the arrangements and levels are not yet clear.

Curriculum

Until recent years, there was no common school curriculum across the country. Each state and territory had its own curriculum, and although there was a number of joint curriculum initiatives and many aspects were common, there were growing concerns about the difficulties that differing curricula posed for students moving between jurisdictions, the costs of each jurisdiction developing its own material and the need to revise curricula to reflect national agreements about educational priorities. As a result, in 2008 all governments agreed to establish the Australian

Curriculum, Assessment and Reporting Authority (ACARA) to lead national collaboration to produce the Foundation to Year 12 Australian Curriculum.

The Australian Curriculum has three dimensions: learning areas; general capabilities and cross-curriculum priorities (ACARA, 2014). Primary education (and lower secondary education) comes within the Foundation to Year 10 Australian Curriculum. There are eight learning areas: English; mathematics; science; humanities and social sciences; the arts; technologies; health and physical education; and languages. The seven general capabilities built into the curricula are: literacy; numeracy; ICT capability; critical and creative thinking; personal and social capability; ethical understanding; and intercultural understanding. The three cross-curriculum priorities are: Aboriginal and Torres Strait Islander histories and cultures; Asia and Australia's engagement with Asia; and Sustainability.

By 2014, national curricula have been developed in most of the learning areas and endorsed by Education Ministers. The process of implementation, which is the responsibility of states and territories, commenced in 2013. Credentialing and related assessment requirements and processes remain the responsibility of states and territories. Thus, as it is early days, it is not yet completely clear just how common the Australian Curriculum will actually be. The curricula and associated processes are still subject to considerable debate, and the picture has been potentially complicated by the national Australian government in 2014 establishing a review of the Australian Curriculum to evaluate 'the robustness, independence and balance of the Australian Curriculum, examining the content and development process', and emphasizing 'restoring the focus on a back to basics approach' (Department of Education, 2014, p. 1).

Assessment and reporting

The establishment of ACARA in 2008 led to two other significant developments that have changed the national discussion about education:

- The introduction of the National Assessment Program encompassing annual tests of literacy and numeracy. The tests were first introduced in 2008 and are now sat annually by almost all students in Years 3, 5, 7 and 9 through the National Assessment Program – Literacy and Numeracy (NAPLAN). There are also sample assessments every 3 years in science literacy, civics and citizenship and ICT literacy. These national assessments, along with Australia's long-standing participation in international achievement studies, means that much of the debate is now focused on student outcome data.

- The establishment in 2010 of the *My School* website. This website enables public access to the profiles of every Australian school. School-level data for NAPLAN are presented for each school, shown against the national average and the average of statistically similar schools, using an Index of Community Socio-Educational Advantage (ICSEA). Also included on the website is information about each school's objectives, programmes and finances. There is widespread media reporting and discussion of the annual updates of data on the website. *My School* has led to a greater focus on each school's performance and increased the accountability pressures on school systems, schools and teachers.

Teachers

Primary school teachers must have a 4-year university qualification in order to be registered to teach. Teacher registration is the responsibility of each state and territory although they work within a common framework. In another indication of the increasingly national character of Australian education, in 2010 the Australian Institute for Teaching and School Leadership (AITSL) was established to develop promoting national professional standards for teachers and school leaders, and since 2011 there has been a national approach to the accreditation of initial teacher education programmes.

There are around 135,000 full-time equivalent (FTE) teaching staff in primary schools, which means that the student to teacher ratio is 15.6 (ABS, 2014). The student–teacher ratio has been declining over a long period of time (in 2003 it was 16.6, and in 1993 it was 18.4). This is one of the major reasons for the trend of increased real expenditure per school student (other contributors to this trend include growth in spending on non-teaching staff, ICT and, since 2008, on school buildings).

Primary teaching is highly feminized: females comprised about 80 per cent of the primary teaching workforce in 2010 and constituted the large majority of recent entrants to the profession (McKenzie et al., 2011). Around 23 per cent of primary teachers are employed on a part-time basis. The average age of primary teachers in 2010 was 42 years and it has been gradually increasing over time. The current trends suggests that large numbers of primary as well as secondary teachers will need to be recruited in the next few years to meet projected growth in student enrolments and replace teachers who retire (Productivity Commission, 2012).

One of the main challenges in recruiting sufficient numbers of well-qualified teachers is that teaching appears to have declined in attractiveness as a career.

There is evidence that the average academic standards of those entering initial teacher education programmes in universities have declined, and that teachers' salaries have not kept pace with comparable professions (Productivity Commission, 2012). Teachers' salaries in Australia have increased more slowly than in OECD countries as a whole (OECD, 2013b). This situation has led to proposals to reform teachers' career structures and increase investment in professional standards and staff development (e.g. Dinham et al., 2008; Ingvarson, 2013). The national Australian Government in 2014 established a major review of initial teacher education programmes.

Learning outcomes

A major reason for initiating the Gonski review of school funding, and the other reviews outlined in this chapter, is the concern that, although by international standards Australian student still perform well, the country's relative performance has slipped. In regard to primary school students' performance in international studies of mathematics and science, this general view is broadly supported by the detailed review of achievement studies by Ainley and Gebhardt (2013). They found that it was not so much that Australia had declined in absolute terms on such measures between the mid-1990s and 2010 (during which time several international studies were conducted), but that its average scores had not improved. Other countries had improved, and thus Australia's relative position had fallen somewhat. (An analogous study of primary students' reading achievement was not possible because Australia had only participated in one such study, in 2010).

In terms of national achievement measures, the NAPLAN tests conducted annually since 2008 provide extensive data. Ainley and Gebhardt (2013) found that reading performance at both Year 3 and Year 5, on the one hand, improved steadily between 2008 and 2012. On the other hand, there was little or no improvement in numeracy performance by Year 3 and Year 5 students at national level, although the pattern varies between jurisdictions.

Secondary education

Schools and enrolments

Students progress to secondary education on the basis of having completed the final year of primary school. Except in the case of a relatively small number of academically selective schools, students do not have to sit any examination to enter or transfer between secondary schools.

Secondary schools operate for 5-year levels from Year 8 to Year 12 in three jurisdictions (Queensland, South Australia and Western Australia) and for 6-year levels from Year 7 to Year 12 in the other five jurisdictions. The long-term trend is towards secondary education comprising 6-year levels. In the Australian Capital Territory (ACT) and Tasmania, government secondary education has two institutional types: high schools that cover Years 7 to 10 and colleges that enrol students in Years 11 and 12. In the other jurisdictions, the most common pattern is for all secondary year levels to be provided in the one institution – either in a stand-alone secondary school or in a combined primary–secondary school.

Secondary schools and colleges are generally bigger than primary schools, although still not large by international standards. In 2013 there were 1.51 million FTE secondary students enrolled in 2,700 schools, an average enrolment of around 560 FTE students per school (ABS, 2014). (Almost all secondary students – 99% – are enrolled full time.) Stand-alone secondary schools had an average enrolment of 760 students whereas the secondary component of combined primary–secondary schools enrolled 340 secondary students on average. Only 15 per cent of all the institutions that provide secondary education enrolled more than 1,000 secondary students, and 35 per cent had fewer than 300 students. These relatively small sizes increase the costs of provision and make it difficult to offer students a diverse curriculum.

Non-government schools are more prominent in secondary education than in primary education. In 2013, 41 per cent of secondary students were enrolled in a non-government school (ABS, 2014), which is a marked increase from 20 years earlier (32%). The greater propensity of parents to enrol their children in non-government secondary schools is attributable to a mix of factors, including the higher age of secondary students (which makes them more likely to be able to travel greater distances to school), the capacity of many non-government secondary schools to be able to offer a wide range of programmes and facilities and perceptions that non-government schools improve the chances of high scores in final school examinations and thus entrance to university. Longitudinal data suggest that the latter perception has some empirical basis: while the impact of individual student characteristics is dominant with regard to their final school results, school characteristics (including being a non-government school) do have an influence, other factors equal (Gemici et al., 2013).

School completion rates

Secondary school enrolments have been rising because of an increasing population of school-aged children in Australia and also because of a greater propensity for students to continue to Year 12, the final year of secondary education. In 2013, the apparent retention rate of full-time students from Year 7/8 to Year 12 was 82 per cent (ABS, 2014). (The rate is termed 'apparent' because it is based on aggregate enrolments at the beginning and end of secondary school rather than tracing individual students.) In 2003, the corresponding rate was 75 per cent. In the mid-1970s, the apparent retention rate to Year 12 was only 33 per cent. Completing secondary school is now the experience of most young people whereas formerly it was largely for the more socially and academically advantaged.

Improving school completion rates and education participation rates more generally has long been an objective of governments in Australia. This is because of the substantial evidence accumulated over many years that completing Year 12 or a vocational qualification that is broadly equivalent assists considerably in young people's transition to tertiary education and training and to employment, but that completion rates have historically been much lower for disadvantaged groups including Indigenous people, people living in remote locations and people from low-income backgrounds.

In 2009, the focus on this area was sharpened by all governments committing to *The National Partnership on Youth Attainment and Transitions* that included a suite of initiatives to support the achievement of two main goals – to increase the proportion of young people completing their Year 12 or equivalent qualification, and to halve the gap in the proportion of Indigenous young people completing Year 12 or an equivalent qualification.[1] This National Partnership operated from 2010 to 2013 and involved around A$700 million in funding. The independent evaluation concluded that while the Partnership has been effective, and participation and attainment rates have increased, the number of young people disengaged from education, training or employment remains high, many of the issues that led to the formation of the Partnership have not been resolved and Australia needs a continuing collaborative approach among governments and other stakeholders to achieve sustainable outcomes (Dandolo Partners, 2014). It is not yet clear what, if any, ongoing inter-governmental arrangements to improve youth attainment and transitions will be put in place.

Curriculum and certification

Secondary schools in Australia are comprehensive in the sense that each school generally provides a broad curriculum. Although there is a growing number of schools that specialize in a particular area (such as mathematics and science, or the performing arts), such schools currently enrol only a small proportion of students. There are no specialist technical or vocational schools at secondary level; such schools existed in several jurisdictions up until the 1980s. There are some schools, though, that place a particular emphasis on vocational subjects in the senior secondary year levels, but such programmes normally exist alongside more academically oriented subjects, and students often do studies from the different programme types concurrently.

The first 1 or 2 years of secondary education are generally a common programme taken by all students in the school concerned (with some differences between schools and jurisdictions). In later years, students usually take a core group of subjects and electives. Core subjects usually include English, mathematics, science, society and environment, languages other than English, technological and applied studies, creative arts and health and physical education (Australian Education International, 2012). Some subjects are offered at different levels of depth to reflect students' interests and capacities, but there is little formal streaming of students by ability. As noted in the previous section, implementation of the Foundation to Year 10 Australian Curriculum commenced in 2013.

At Years 11 and 12, students specialize in courses and subjects accredited by the relevant state and territory authority, and at the end of Year 12 are issued with a qualification that is part of the AQF (Australian Education International, 2012). The final Year 12 certificate provides access to university and other tertiary education, and generally requires meeting the requirements of a combination of external and school-based assessment. Year 12 students who apply to enter university and some other tertiary courses normally require an Australian Tertiary Admission Rank (ATAR) that is based on their final assessments.

The initiation during the 1990s of VET in Schools has been a major strategy for introducing greater differentiation to upper secondary education, and catering to a wider range of students' interests. The fact that VET in Schools programmes are linked to the AQF means that they provide the early stages of pathways to employment and vocational training. The possibility in some jurisdictions for VET subjects to form part of the final Year 12 certificate also gives them currency for tertiary education. VET programmes are assessed using industry-endorsed competency standards endorsed under the AQTF. School students generally take AQF Certificate I and II courses but there is an increased emphasis on encouraging participation in AQF III and above, especially for school-based apprentices and trainees. Most secondary schools now offer some form of VET, and in 2012 over 240,000 students took at least one VET in Schools unit, including around 35 per cent of 16- and 17-year-old students (NCVER, 2013).

In terms of the development of the Senior Secondary Australian Curriculum, 15 secondary subjects across English, mathematics, science, history and geography have been endorsed by Education Ministers (ACARA, 2014). State and territory authorities are responsible for how the Australian Curriculum content and achievement standards will be integrated into their courses. Some jurisdictions commenced implementation of integrated courses in 2014, while others are still determining implementation guidelines.

Teachers

Secondary teachers are also required to have a 4-year university qualification in order to be registered to teach. Secondary teachers are more likely than primary teachers to do an initial degree in a discipline such as science, commerce or arts and then a postgraduate qualification in education. This reflects the fact that secondary teachers are more likely than primary teachers to work as subject specialists in schools.

In 2013, around 125,000 FTE teachers were employed in secondary schools (ABS, 2014). This means that the secondary student to teacher ratio (12.0) was markedly lower than the primary ratio.

Secondary teaching is a feminized career (57% in 2010) although not to the extent of primary teaching (McKenzie et al., 2011). Around 82 per cent of secondary teachers work on a full-time basis. The average age of secondary teachers in 2010 was 45 years and it has also been gradually increasing over time. Secondary teachers on average are paid slightly more than primary teachers; this mainly reflects the fact that secondary schools are generally larger and have more positions of responsibility. There tends to be little explicit differentiation in teachers' pay according to performance or in response to shortages in particular subject areas (Productivity Commission, 2012).

There are more reported shortages of secondary teachers than primary teachers, especially in areas such as mathematics, sciences and languages (McKenzie et al., 2011). Such shortages tend to be more pronounced in schools serving low socio-economic status (SES) communities, and those located in rural and remote areas. One of the rationales behind the new approach to school funding recommended by Gonski (2011) was to provide schools in disadvantaged communities with more capacity to attract well-qualified teachers.

One consequence of staffing difficulties is that secondary schools often require teachers to teach in fields where they may not have had much university study and/or pedagogical training. Such pressures tend to be more acute in small secondary schools (of which Australia has many) and at times such as the present when substantial curriculum changes are underway.

Learning outcomes

The results of the OECD's Programme for International Assessment (PISA) of 15-year-olds have been influential in Australia. Australia participated in all five cycles of PISA from 2000 to 2012 and is participating in PISA 2015. The differences between cycles in the major fields assessed provide different reference points for assessing change over time.

Ainley and Gebhardt (2013) note that although reading literacy achievement by Australian 15-year-olds in the first cycle was considered high compared to most other OECD countries, there was a small but significant decline in average achievement from 2000 to 2009. In addition, they concluded that:

- The decline was more pronounced at the upper part of the achievement distribution.
- The spread of reading scores is relatively large among Australian students compared to other countries, and the spread did not change between 2000 and 2009.
- The gaps in reading achievement by students from low and high SES backgrounds, and by Indigenous and non-Indigenous Australians, did not appear to change between 2000 and 2009.
- There was an increase in the percentage of the variation in student scores which was associated with differences among schools.
- A decline in reading achievement was not experienced by all jurisdictions, which suggests that organizational and curricular differences may be playing a part.

Thomson et al. (2013) reached broadly similar conclusions about the pattern of change in mathematical literacy of 15-year-old Australians between PISA 2003 and 2012 although in this case the absolute decline in performance was more marked than in reading literacy.

Thomson et al. (2013) also examined changes in Australia's relative performance in scientific literacy between PISA 2006 and PISA 2012. In this field Australia's mean score did not change significantly, and the proportions of top performers and low performers remained stable between those two cycles. However, because a number of other OECD countries recorded improved performance in scientific literacy between 2006 and 2012, Australia – while still a high performer – has slipped slightly in relative terms.

Such results have stimulated much debate in Australia, particularly given that spending on schools has increased over the past decade and much priority has been given to literacy and numeracy, and to closing Indigenous and socio-economic achievement gaps.

Adult and community education

ACE is not so much a 'level' of education in Australia, but rather a diverse sector that sits at the nexus of education and community development (Thomson, 2011). The ACE sector comprises about 1,200 not-for-profit organizations, of which about 800 are Registered Training Organisations (ibid.). The distinctions between ACE and other types of education and training include its decentralized, community-based nature and a focus on non-formal learning across the lifespan rather than on the provision of specific qualifications – although it does much of that as well. For example, the proportion of ACE learners taking accredited AQF courses almost doubled (from 25% to 47%) between 2002 and 2009 (Skills Australia, 2011).

ACE organizations are diverse in size and focus. Thomson (2011) provides a classification based on where they sit on the social capital/human capital spectrum. At the 'social capital' end are small community development organizations that provide mainly non-formal and non-accredited programmes in settings such as neighbourhood houses, libraries and men's sheds (a recent development in Australia). The types of activities such organizations provide are very diverse and include personal development and enrichment, hobbies, language support for non-English speakers and initiatives to re-engage learners who are not well suited to formal education. Such organizations rely heavily on volunteers, supplemented by low fees, donations and some government subsidies. At the 'human capital' end of the spectrum are the large Adult Education institutions that exist in most state capitals (supplemented by regional networks) and Community Colleges that exist in some jurisdictions such as NSW. These types of organizations tend to deliver significant amounts of accredited VET training, and fee-for-service learning activities, and receive government financial support. Such distinctions, though, are not easily drawn in practice as most ACE organizations engage in a wide range of different activities.

Despite the challenges in conceptualizing and measuring ACE, there is growing recognition of the role and potential of the ACE sector in contributing to social and economic development in Australia (Allen Consulting Group, 2008; Skills Australia, 2011).

There are certainly substantial numbers of adults involved in some form of learning. About 8 million people, or just under half of Australia's working age population, undertook some form of training or study in 12 months to April 2013 (ABS, 2013b). These numbers included 1.4 million people (8% of the relevant population) who undertook non-formal study for personal interest, and about 4.6 million (27%) who undertook non-formal work-related training. Many of those in these groups would have been involved in ACE activities, as would a number of the 3.7 million adults (22%) engaged in formal study during those 12 months.

There are some significant differences in the extent of participation in adult learning (ABS, 2013b). Participation in personal interest learning was more prevalent among women (10%) than men (7%), and among those living in high SES communities (12%) than in disadvantaged locations (5%). In regard to work-related training, people who have completed a post-school qualification are much more likely to participate than those who lack such qualifications (35% compared with 16%). For people who wanted to participate in non-formal learning but did not, or who wanted to participate more, ABS (2013b) reported that the main barriers to participation were: too much work or no time (48%); financial reasons (24%); personal reasons (12%) and course not available (5%).

Data from the OECD's Programme for the International Assessment of Adult Competencies (PIAAC) show that Australians aged 16–65 years have above average proficiency in literacy and problem solving in technology-rich environments compared with adults in the other countries participating in the survey (OECD, 2013c). Nevertheless, as in most countries, relatively large proportions of the adult population in Australia have low literacy, problem solving and (especially) numeracy skills. Given the strong evidence about the link between adult literacy and numeracy and employment and health outcomes, such results are focusing attention in Australia on the need to lift the skill levels of significant numbers of adults, particularly in the context of rapid economic change and an ageing population.

Note

1 Other National Partnerships have focused on improving teacher quality, education in low SES communities and literacy and numeracy.

References

Ainley, J. and Gebhardt, E. (2013), *Measure for Measure: A Review of Outcomes of School Education in Australia*. Melbourne: Australian Council for Educational Research (ACER).

Allen Consulting Group (2008), *The Economic Benefit of Investment in Adult Community Education in Australia*. Melbourne: Department of Planning and Community Development.

Australian Bureau of Statistics (ABS) (2012), *Year Book Australia 2012* (3101.0). Canberra: ABS.

— (2013a), *Australian Demographic Statistics* (3101.0). Canberra: ABS.

— (2013b), *Work-Related Training and Adult Learning, Australia* (4234.0). Canberra: ABS.

— (2014), *Schools Australia 2013* (4221.0). Canberra: ABS.

Australian Curriculum, Assessment and Reporting Authority (ACARA) (2012), *National Report on Schooling in Australia 2010*. Sydney: ACARA.

— (2014), *Foundation to Year 12 Australian Curriculum*. Sydney: ACARA.

Australian Education International (2012), *Country Education Profiles: Australia*. Canberra: Australian Government, AEI.

Australian Qualifications Framework Council (AQFC) (2013), *Australian Qualifications Framework Second Edition*. Adelaide: AQFC.

Australian Workforce and Productivity Agency (AWPA) (2013), *Future Focus, 2013 National Workforce Development Strategy*. Canberra: AWPA.

Council of Australian Governments (COAG) (2009), *Investing in the Early Years – A National Early Childhood Development Strategy*. Canberra: COAG.

Department of Education (2014), *Strengthening the Curriculum*. Canberra: Australian Government Department of Education. www.studentfirst.gov.au

Dandolo Partners (2014), *Evaluation of the National Partnership on Youth Attainment and Transitions*. Canberra: Department of Education.

Dinham, S., Ingvarson, L. and Kleinhenz, E. (2008), *Investing in Teacher Quality: Doing What Matters Most*. Melbourne: Business Council of Australia.

Fletcher, M. and Guttmann, B. (2013), *Income Inequality in Australia*. Canberra: Australian Treasury.

Gemici, S., Lim, P. and Karmel, T. (2013), *The Impact of Schools on Young People's Transition to University, Longitudinal Surveys of Australian Youth Research Report 61*. Adelaide: National Centre for Vocational Education Research (NCVER).

Gonski, D. (Chair) (2011), *Review of Funding for Schooling – Final Report*. Canberra: Department of Education, Employment and Workplace Relations.

Ingvarson, L. (2013), *Reforming Career Paths for Australian Teachers*. Melbourne: Australian Council for Educational Research (ACER).

International Chamber of Commerce (2013), *ICC Open Markets Index*. Paris: ICC.

McKenzie, P., Rowley, G., Weldon, P. and Murphy, M. (2011), *Staff in Australia's Schools 2010: Main Report on the Survey*. Melbourne: ACER.

NCVER (2013), *Young People in Education and Training*. Adelaide: NCVER.

Organisation for Economic Co-operation and Development (OECD) (2012), *Untapped Skills: Realising the Potential of Immigrant Students*. Paris: OECD.

— (2013a), *OECD Factbook 2013*. Paris: OECD.

— (2013b), *Education Policy Outlook: Australia*. Paris: OECD.

— (2013c), *Survey of Adult Skills, First Results: Australia*. Paris: OECD.

Productivity Commission (2012), *Schools Workforce Research Report*. Melbourne: Productivity Commission.

— (2013), *Geographic Labour Mobility*. Melbourne: Productivity Commission.

— (2014), *Report on Government Services 2014*. Melbourne: Productivity Commission.

Skills Australia (2011), *Skills for Prosperity, A Roadmap for Vocational Education and Training*. Sydney: Skills Australia.

Thomson, S. (2011), *New Directions for the Adult and Community Education (ACE) Sector*. Melbourne: Adult Learning Australia.

Thomson, S., De Bortoli, L. and Buckley, S. (2013), *PISA 2012: How Australia Measures Up*. Melbourne: ACER.

World Bank (2014), *GDP 2012*. Washington DC: The World Bank.

2

Federalism in Australian Education

Anthony Welch

Without understanding the specific (some might say peculiar) form of Australian federalism, it is hard to understand the realities of Australia's education system. The current chapter sketches the mainsprings of Australian federalism, its key provisions and its evolution, and then examines its impact on education, using government funding of non-government schools as a case study that illuminates both increasing federal intervention and state resistance, as well as the key social implications. While jurisdictional elements are treated, the emphasis on funding is used to reveal key changes in federal state intervention and control over education.

Resulting from Constitutional Conventions held in 1891 and 1897–1898, the Australian federation came into being in 1901, replacing a system of individual British colonies that had been established for a century or so. Constitutional provisions were ultimately agreed to by voters in the various Australian colonies, and then passed into law by the British Parliament.

Like other federations (Brazil, Germany, Canada, the United States), a critical issue of longstanding is the division of powers between the national government and states or provinces, and how the two levels coordinate (The existence of a third tier of Australian government, local Councils, is beyond the remit of the current analysis and is of no substantial relevance to education.) (Fenna, 1994). The existence of both state and federal authorities affects education quite directly, and can be a source of contest and division. At times, (constitutional) courts must arbitrate between national and other levels of jurisdiction. This has meant that the division of powers, including over education, has not been static but has rather evolved. In the Australian case, this resulted in an uneven evolution in the direction of enhanced federal (in Australia, the term used is Commonwealth) authority over education: 'The power of the Commonwealth waxes and that of the States wanes, as approving High Court judges have affirmed' (APH, 2001: p. 28). But even this is not uniform, with some sectors (schooling, and vocational–technical education) being administered and funded largely by the states, while higher education has traditionally been administered and largely funded by the Commonwealth.

The foundations of federalism

The basic principles behind Australian federalism, as set out in the Constitution, were that Commonwealth powers should be restricted to areas governing the national economy and foreign relations. In practice, this meant defence, customs and excise, external trade and commerce and the post office.

These broad founding principles, however, were given more specific expression in various sections of the Constitution. Under §106 and §107, for example, states retain rights and powers except where otherwise stipulated. This also means that states should retain rights to their own internal matters, whereas the Commonwealth retains powers with respect to matters that go beyond any single state (i.e. that cross state boundaries). An example is industrial relations, where state Acts of parliament govern workplace relations, including the employment conditions of teachers in public schools across the state. It is important to point out that Australia has one of the largest private schooling sectors in the Organisation for Economic Co-operation and Development (OECD), but private teachers' working conditions are generally negotiated with either the large Catholic system, or their own school.

Under §51, and in one or two other places, the Commonwealth has power to legislate over certain areas. This includes taxation, money supply, trade between states and dealing with overseas entities and financial borrowing. Its Corporations powers, however, have proved more contentious. Under §51 (xx), the Commonwealth may legislate with respect to 'Foreign corporations, and trading or financial corporations formed within the limits of the Commonwealth'. Also under §51 (xxiii), the Commonwealth was given power over 'invalid and old-age pensions', while the costs of World War One led to the introduction of modest national income tax provisions. War again provided a significant impetus, when the Commonwealth government passed uniform tax legislation in 1942, during World War Two, a decision that was subsequently upheld by the High Court, in the first *Uniform Tax* case, of that same year. The decision withstood further challenge in the High Court in the *Second Uniform Tax* case, of 1957 (APH, 2001: pp. 23–24). The effect of these decisions was to vest and then consolidate monopoly power to collect income tax in the Commonwealth government, a move with far-reaching implications that still echo today, as seen later. A state premier and trenchant critic of the process of increased centralization of (fiscal) power in the hands of the Commonwealth argued in 2000 that the blame lay largely with the High Court, and its liberal interpretation of the External Affairs power:

> The resulting increase in the range and scope of the Commonwealth Parliament's powers has enabled Commonwealth legislation to govern and regulate almost all aspects of Australian life. (Court cited APH, 2001: p. 23)

In general terms then, we can say that the states were given broad residual powers (but no defined powers), while the Commonwealth was given some specific powers, and the power to legislate with respect to those arenas only. This principle had already been clearly articulated in 1891, by Henry Parkes, one of federalism's founding fathers:

> ... the powers and privileges and territorial rights of the several existing colonies shall remain intact, except in respect to such surrenders as may be agreed upon as necessary and incidental to the power and authority of the National Federal Government. (APH, 2001: p. 7)

In practice, many policy arenas are governed by shared arrangements – Commonwealth powers are often held concurrently with the states. The only significant policy power exclusive to the Commonwealth is the power to impose customs duties and excises (§90).

Adjudicating conflicts

This raises a key problem – what to do when state and Commonwealth interests conflict? Here, §109 of the Constitution holds that, wherever state and Commonwealth legislation conflicts, 'the latter shall prevail, and the former shall, to the extent of the inconsistency, be invalid' (APH, 2001; see also Fenna, 2004: p. 169). §51 (xxix) further specifies that where Commonwealth legislation refers to international commitments (the so-called External Powers provision), it over-rides any conflicting state legislation (by virtue of §109).

An example of how different jurisdictions interact is in the area of industrial relations, where the Commonwealth was given authority to legislate in the area of conciliation and arbitration (workplace relations), but only where a dispute crossed state borders. Thus, as indicated earlier for example, there are different state and federal Acts governing industrial relations, but here again the *Moore v Doyle* case established the precedent that, where state and Commonwealth legislation clashed, the latter took precedence (McClelland, 1991; Hose, 2003).

The actual details, however, were not for the Commonwealth itself to decide, but were adjudicated on a case-by-case basis by the High Court, Australia's supreme legal authority. Thus the role of the High Court of Australia is particularly significant in interpreting the actualities of federalism and the respective roles of the state and federal governments. Unlike lower courts, the High Court is not bound by principles of *stare decisis* (precedent), so it can – and has – changed course, at various times, and reverse an earlier decision. While its decisions in the first decade or so after federation were more in the spirit of states' rights, subsequent interpretations have tended to defend and extend federal intervention and/or the power of the Commonwealth.

Examples of High Court decisions have included the following extensions of Commonwealth powers:

- That the Commonwealth be the single agent of income tax collection (and bar states from doing so). This was not the case before 1942 – when both levels of government levied income taxes.
- That the Commonwealth may attach (unlimited) conditions to state grants, under §96.
- That the Commonwealth can gain further powers under §51.
- That the Commonwealth may exert control over goods for export and the conditions under which these were made.
- That the Commonwealth may use the *Racial Discrimination Act* to over-ride state authority and legislation.
- That the Commonwealth may protect the environment and over-ride state decisions on land use, by reference to §51 (xxix).

Use of external affairs powers

While the above largely exhaust the ways in which the Commonwealth has been able to extend its powers over many aspects of policy, the key mechanism referred to in §51 (xxix) has proved quite contentious. It gives to the Commonwealth power to legislate with respect to 'external affairs', something it has used to leverage greater control over the states. Although this section has not been used to over-ride state-specific legislation in education, it was applied in 1975, for example, when the *Racial Discrimination Act* was invoked to over-ride discriminatory Queensland legislation that outlawed the state *Aboriginal Land Fund* from purchasing grazing properties. The basis for federal intervention in this case was that Australia had become a signatory to UN *Declaration of Human Rights* in 1960. The External Affairs power was famously again invoked in 1983, when the new *World Heritage Properties Protection Act* was passed, and then used to list the Franklin River, Tasmania with UNESCO as a protected site, thereby preventing the construction of a hydro-electric plant. In both cases, while the relevant authority (over land use) was clearly vested in the state, Commonwealth external affairs powers were deployed to over-ride state powers. In both cases, Australia's formal status as a signatory to an external treaty (which, unlike some other countries, is a Cabinet decision, and requires no parliamentary or other mandate) formed a sufficient base for the invocation of Commonwealth powers. Such powers can prove to be a double-edged sword, however: in an era of increasing globalization, '. . . the Commonwealth might gain power at the expense of the States within the domestic arena, while at the same time losing sovereignty in the international arena' (APH, 2001: p. 28).

Fiscal levers and the special case of education

So, what does this mean for education? Curiously perhaps, the Australian Constitution is largely silent with respect to education. It is only briefly mentioned in §51, and is generally defined as a state matter – yet intriguingly, higher education, and universities, are, as seen earlier, administered by the Commonwealth. Why is this the case? The answer lies in the fact that, notwithstanding that universities are established by Acts of state parliaments,[1] the Commonwealth supplies the lion's share of universities' resources, (although, as vice chancellors never tire of pointing out, this proportion has declined significantly over the past two decades or so: from an average of perhaps over 80% of their budgets, to half or less, for all Australian universities).[2] In this case, then, it is fiscal, rather than legislative authority, that is responsible for the allocation of power: s/he who pays the piper, calls the tune. In general terms, this phenomenon is termed in Australia *Vertical Fiscal Imbalance* (VFI) – that is, the Commonwealth occupies a superior financial position, by virtue of holding the bulk of revenue (around 80%). A recent Victorian report succinctly summarized the peculiar paradox of Australian federalism:

> In Australia, the Commonwealth collects the vast majority of taxes, and in particular has exclusive power to impose duties of customs and of excise, and has been solely responsible for collection of income tax since 1942. The states and territories on the other hand are responsible for delivering a majority of services, such as in the areas of education and health. (Victorian Parliament, 2012: p. 15)

While most federations have a degree of VFI, the rate in Australia is significantly higher than in comparable countries such as the United States, Canada and Germany (Victorian Parliament, 2012: p. 17). There are somewhat different processes at work here. On the one hand, the Australian system deliberately aims to equalize levels of service, notably including education, across the different states, via a mechanism termed horizontal fiscal equalization (HFE), which compensates those states with weaker revenue streams. On the other hand, special purpose grants (see later) are made to states on the basis of relative service levels, irrespective of their different fiscal strengths.

But since the Commonwealth is responsible for only around 50 per cent of total government spending, much of the remainder is allocated to the states, often as Specific Purpose Payments (SPPs), commonly known as tied grants. SPPs, as their name implies, are for specific purposes, and the Commonwealth may invoke §96 to impose 'restrictive policy conditions' as a condition of accepting the grant (APH, 2001: p. 24). The use of these instruments grew dramatically during the Whitlam Labor government (1972–1975) (especially in the areas of education and health). The instruments were used as a means to enhance Commonwealth powers to make national policy, effectively using financial levers as a means to circumvent constitutional division of powers. According to former Prime Minister Gough Whitlam, the relevant section of the Constitution (§96) 'was Labor's "charter of public enterprise" because it enabled the Commonwealth to use its fiscal dominance to invade major policy areas of State jurisdiction' (APH, 2001: p. 25). As a result, tied grants rose from 2.0 per cent to 5.5 per cent of GDP, almost tripling their overall proportion. Although the subsequent (1976–1983) Liberal[3] (conservative) government reversed this process, it has continued since that era to the point where:

> ... tied grants became a distinctly coercive element in Australian federalism, a way for governments in Canberra to establish uniform national policies despite recalcitrant state governments. (Fenna, 2004: p. 174)

During the 1980s and 1990s, SPPs (tied grants) averaged around half of all Commonwealth grants, but the introduction of a form of value-added tax, the Goods and Services Tax (GST) (a reform to which the states assented in 1999, and which came into effect in July 2000), has meant that this proportion declined. (Nonetheless, the 2012 Victorian inquiry into Commonwealth funding found that a little over half of Commonwealth revenues supplied to the state was in the form of tied grants [Victorian Parliament, 2012: pp. 18–19]). GST revenue was to be transferred directly to the states, but in line with the principle of HFE, as outlined earlier. This has proved contentious with wealthier states such as Western Australia complaining that they are in effect, subsidising fiscally weaker states, such as South Australia and Tasmania.

In 2002–2003, some $21.6 billion were in the form of SPPs, of a total of $53 billion of Commonwealth transfers. Over $7 billion was for education, and closer to $8 billion for medical benefits. Such transfers have included conditions such as the following, which while selectively applied can be effective ways of enforcing national policy development(s):

- That states must expend the funds on the purpose for which they were designated.
- That states must match the Commonwealth grant, from their own treasuries.
- That state policies must conform to Commonwealth policies.
- That states must agree, for example, to the national blood alcohol limit, in order to receive road funding (so-called 'Piggy-back' requirements).

Funds are dispersed via the Commonwealth Grants Commission.

State premiers, and treasurers, while continuing to rail against such Commonwealth controls, have according to some,

> . . . learnt to manipulate the system in ways that help retain aspects of State power. To an extent the States collude in the ongoing fiscal arrangements that deliver them large grants of money for which they have no responsibility for collecting as taxes. They reap the political benefits of spending money without attracting the odium of raising it, which makes a certain political sense even if it offends good public finance principles. (APH, 2001: p. 25)

All in all, the evidence about the use and abuse of tied grants is mixed. While reforms introduced from 2007 by the Rudd-Gillard Labor government (2007–2013) were intended to usher in a new era of 'cooperative federalism', one contemporary analyst characterized tied grants as a '. . . fragile and uncertain policy-making instrument, consistently open to political opportunism, ideological fluctuation and policy and implementation resistance from the states and local stakeholders' (Ramamurthy, 2013: p. 117). At the same time, the same author acknowledged their role in '. . . assisting states to overcome local resistance to controversial policy reforms such as greater (school) principal autonomy, and performance pay (for teachers)' (Ramamurthy, 2012: p. 128).

Cooperative federalism?

So, how are things to be managed, given that state and federal interests often do not coincide, and political power at state level may be vested in the hands of one political party, while a different party is in power at the federal level?

Ministerial Councils are used to manage specific policy arenas, or particular issues/problems. The main one that has operated in the area of education is the (former) Ministerial Council on Employment, Education, Training and Youth Affairs (MCEETYA), founded in June 1993 by the Council of Australian Governments (COAG) who amalgamated several existing councils to increase policy coordination across the interrelated portfolios. Three previous councils were merged – the Australian Education Council (AEC), the Council of Ministers of Vocational Education, Employment and Training (MOVEET) and the Youth Ministers Council (YMC) – to form the MCEETYA. In July 2009, the Council was re-named MCEEDYA (Ministerial Council for Education, Early Childhood Development, and Youth Affairs). In January 2012, this was replaced with the Standing Council on School Education and Early Childhood (SCSEEC).

The latest re-organization of the Commonwealth Public Service, consequent upon the election of the Abbott conservative government in 2013, saw the previous Department of Employment, Education and Workplace Relations split into different departments, one of which became the Department of Education, responsible for childcare, early childhood education, school education, post-school, higher education, international education and academic research. At the time of writing, the initiation of an *Education Council* (EC) had been announced, with transition arrangements to be named during 2014 (COAG, 2013b). While membership of the foreshadowed EC had yet to be announced, the principles of federalism are likely to dictate a similar membership to that of its preceding councils. MCEETYA, for example comprised state, territory, Australian Government and New Zealand ministers with relevant responsibilities (portfolios of education, employment, training and youth affairs), with Papua New Guinea and Norfolk Island having observer status. Functions of the impending EC, too, are likely to be similar to its preceding councils, such as MCEETYA:

- coordination of strategic policy at the national level,
- negotiation and development of national agreements on shared objectives and interests (including principles for Australian Government/State relations) in the Council's areas of responsibility,
- negotiations on scope and format of national reporting on areas of responsibility,
- sharing of information and collaborative use of resources towards agreed objectives and priorities and
- coordination of communication with, and collaboration between, related national structures.

COAG – an umbrella coordinating body

Specific councils, such as MCEETYA, MCEEDYA or the foreshadowed EC, operate under the umbrella of the COAG. Founded in 1992, the COAG is the peak Commonwealth/state government relations forum in Australia, with ten members: the prime minister, state premiers, territory chief ministers and the president of the Australian Local Government Association (ALGA). The prime minister chairs COAG, which usually meets once a year, although the recent COAG communiqué foreshadowed bi-annual meetings (COAG, 2013b). Its Secretariat is situated within the Department of the Prime Minister and Cabinet (PM and C).

COAG's role is to initiate, develop and monitor the implementation of policy reforms that are of *national* significance and which require cooperation by Australian governments (examples include National Competition Policy, water reform, environmental regulation, a National Education Agreement, the use of human embryos in medical research, counter-terrorism arrangements, gun regulations, etc.). Issues may arise from, among other things, Ministerial Council deliberations; international treaties which affect the states and territories; or major initiatives of one government (particularly the Commonwealth Government) which impact on other governments or require the cooperation of other governments.

COAG meets on an as-needed basis. However, former Prime Minister John Howard stated after the April 1999 Premiers' Conference that, since there would be no further Premiers' Conferences following the landmark *Intergovernmental*

Agreement on the Reform of Commonwealth–State Financial Relations, COAG would meet at least once a year from 2000. Alternatively, COAG may settle particular issues out-of-session by correspondence. In recent years, a number of issues have been settled in this manner. The outcomes of COAG meetings are contained in communiqués released at the end of each meeting. Where formal agreements are reached, these may be embodied in Intergovernmental Agreements.

Some have argued that notwithstanding a promised new era of 'cooperative federalism' heralded by a perhaps overly ambitious incoming prime minister (Kevin Rudd), and the initiation of an *Intergovernmental Agreement on Federal Financial Relations* that promised collaboration on policy development and service delivery as well as facilitated implementation of priority social and economic reforms, the ensuing breakdown in trust between the state and Commonwealth governments has inhibited the effectiveness of COAG in recent years. A new format must be found that encourages both cooperation and competition and gives the states more initiative to introduce items and issues (Keating, 2009: pp. 34–39; Gallop, 2012: p. 44; Kildea, 2012). It has been argued that an end to forms of dysfunctional and biased 'top-down bargaining behavior' on the part of Commonwealth authorities is needed, in order to make federalism work more effectively (Ramamurthy, 2012: pp. 119–127). Twomey is only one of many to point to the 'inefficiency, duplication and waste' of the current system (Twomey, 2007: p. 1), while others have argued for strengthening of both the various Ministerial Councils, and COAG (BCA, 2006), and for more cooperation between state and federal governments: '. . . a more collective approach based upon mutual interest and less scope for "passing the buck"' (Matthews, 2009: p. 66). Criticism has been also voiced by some state leaders that the increasingly burdensome Commonwealth reporting requirements associated with National Partnerships was against the spirit of cooperative federalism (Kildea, 2012).

Case study: federalism and school funding

The case of school funding provides a rich tapestry that illustrates how federalism has evolved in Australian education. The separate systems of colonial schooling that emerged during the early part of the nineteenth century were often sites of sectarian rivalry and dispute; it was not until 1848 in New South Wales, for example, that the Denominational Schools Board was created, to respond to and mediate between the competing claims of the major Christian denominations for support. (Non-Christian schools were ignored, although a few existed). Subsequently, the passage of Free, Compulsory and Secular Acts in the various colonies during the final decades of the nineteenth century effectively removed state support for sectarian (called Denominational) schools (Proctor and Sriprakash, 2013; Campbell and Proctor, 2014; Sherington and Hughes, 2014). The passage of the various Acts in different colonies reflected the temper of the times, in particular, a climate of efficiency, and rising secularism (seen by many Catholics as a cloak for Protestantism) (Wilkinson et al., 2007; Sherington and Hughes, 2014). There was a sense that '. . . public education would serve public interests by creating responsible citizens, while widening educational opportunities' (Sherington and Hughes, 2014). But wasteful duplication of limited resources, and in particular, the fact that schools from different denominations, each of which gained state support, competed for limited numbers of pupils, was also a major concern: '. . . In many districts there were three competing schools, all receiving aid, with an average of 75 children in the district attending school . . . (Hogan, 2005: pp. 113–114; Sherington and Hughes, 2014).

This settlement, whereby private denominational schools continued, but without state support, endured for some 80 years, until the 1960s, when it came under substantial challenge. During the decades without state support, both Protestant and Catholic sects concentrated their resources on developing single sex, denominational schools, that often charged high fees, although the much larger and more socially comprehensive Catholic system made a more systematic effort to limit these, and to contain costs. (This was helped by the fact that until the 1960s, Catholic schools were largely staffed by priests, brothers and nuns, often members of teaching orders.) The expansion of the public schooling systems imposed significant demands on individual state finances – even during the interwar years, state spending on education rose substantially (by almost 50%), as a proportion of their overall budgets, at least until the Great Depression of the 1930s. This proportion of the state budget doubled again from 1938 to 1958 (Sherington and Hughes, 2014). In part this reflected the major expansion of secondary schooling in the post World War Two era, a response to rising aspirations, the post war baby boom and Australia's vigorous post-war migration scheme that saw many new migrant children entering the schooling system (Welch, 2013b: pp. 105–115).[4] Yet, although as was seen earlier, education had constitutionally been reserved as a matter for the states, World War Two saw minor interventions by the Commonwealth which, impelled by fears unleashed by war's advent, provided grants to the states, for example, for the purpose of improving the fitness of schoolchildren (Sherington and Hughes, 2014). As well, in 1952, changes to the taxation regime saw school fees of up to £50, and gifts to schools for school building, become tax deductible (Wilkinson et al., 2007: p. 24; Sherington and Hughes, 2014). Again, the benefits accrued overwhelmingly to families whose children attended non-government schools.

At the state level, the 'Goulburn school strike' of 1962, by Catholic authorities who 'closed' their schools temporarily, sending some 2,000 to enrol in public schools, was designed to push the New South Wales state government to pledge support for the non-government sector, a tactic that ultimately succeeded with the state government assenting to per-capita grants for such schools. In Victoria, the next most populous state, interest rate subsidies had been introduced for non-government schools in 1965 on borrowings for school buildings. In 1967 these were doubled and per capita grants made available. The Victorian decision on per-capita grants was then swiftly followed by all other states (Wilkinson et al., 2007: p. 36).

But arguably the first breach in the federal wall came in 1964, with the *States Grants (Science Laboratories and Technical Training)* bill that provided modest Commonwealth funds for science education (just as the United States and the United Kingdom had done somewhat earlier, and at least in part for the same reason – the anxiety among the capitalist West, after the Soviet Sputnik space launch of late 1957, that their assumed technological lead was being threatened). Given that the scheme was announced a matter of days before the 1963 federal election was held, some argued that it was a none-too-subtle bid for the Catholic vote. Support for this view was evident in the response of some Protestant groups not to accept such funds, although the pattern was diffuse (Wilkinson et al., 2007: pp. 33–34). May 1964 also saw the introduction of Commonwealth secondary scholarships that provided both reimbursement of fees and a living allowance to support recipients in completing the final 2 years of secondary school. The decision became contentious when it was shown that three times the proportion of non-government pupils were successful at gaining such scholarships compared to pupils from government schools, whose parents were almost certainly much poorer (Wilkinson et al., 2007: p. 33). Federal grants for the construction of school libraries were finally introduced in 1968, somewhat delayed by the prime minister's drowning, just days after having received the submission in 1966 (Wilkinson et al., 2007: pp. 35–40, table 2.1). Per capita grants of $35 per primary pupil and $50 per secondary pupil were introduced by the Federal government in 1970, with a total of $24.2 million being allocated in the scheme's first year of operation. Promised federal support to non-government schools then swiftly grew to $60 million (Wilkinson et al., 2007: p. 41).

A watershed initiative occurred in 1973 with the establishment of the Australian Schools Commission. The Commission, pledged by the federal Australian Labor Party prior to the 1972 election that brought it to government, was in significant part a response to changes in federal-state financial relations. As indicated earlier, the fact that the Commonwealth government had acquired the sole right to levy an income tax meant that it amassed the lion's share of income. Economic expansion of the late 1960s and early 1970 ensured that federal government coffers grew, and hence pressure for funding support for non-government schools was directed at the federal government rather than at the more impecunious states. After surveying the state of schools around the country, and documenting substantial and ongoing inequities, the *Schools in Australia* (Karmel) Report of 1973 recommended that standards needed to be improved in general, and resources increased, especially for schools in disadvantaged communities, and that government support was necessary for all schools, both government (where, then as now, disadvantage was concentrated) and non-government. Although it had been initially proposed that non-government schools that received substantial support would have reciprocal obligations, this was quickly rejected: indeed, to the contrary, '. . . although the Church and other corporate schools willingly accepted the largesse of both Commonwealth and State grants, they were also determined to be "independent"' (Sherington and Hughes, 2014).

Subsequent (Hawke) federal government proposals to phase out support to the wealthiest schools were also soon abandoned, and by the 1980s non-government schools were receiving more federal government support than government schools (Dudley and Vidovich, 1995). In 1996, the incoming Howard federal government removed any limits on the expansion of the private sector, and instituted subsidy schemes to non-government schools, both the initial enrolment benchmark adjustment (EBA) and its 'socio-economic status' (SES) successor, that were widely criticised as inequitable (including the insertion of a 'no-losers' provision into the latter, in response to pressure from the non-government sector) (Proctor and Sriprakash, 2013: p. 230; Welch, 2013a: pp. 208–209). The socially regressive logic of the latter scheme was pilloried by a well-known economist:

The average Australian has fewer than two legs. Not many fewer but, as the number of one-legged people far exceeds the number of three-legged people, there is no doubt about the end result. Not surprisingly though, designers of products, from pants to staircases, don't focus on the average. Rather they tend to focus on the characteristics of the majority. Not so the Federal Government, though. Its attempt to explain why exclusive private schools are to receive millions of dollars in additional funding have relied squarely on the confusion that blind reference to averages can create. (Gittins in Welch, 2013a: p. 208)

By now any pretence that government funding to non-government schools was needs-based, as had been recommended by the Karmel Schools Committee report in 1973, or that recipients of such largesse might have reciprocal obligations, had been abandoned. Both state and federal governments were shovelling funds to private schools, with no strings attached. The effects were predictably fissiparous: state schools were becoming residualized as more and more parents expressed nervousness at the prospect of sending their children to the local government school, while the private sector expanded unchecked (Campbell et al., 2014). The years from 2001–2002 to 2008–2009, for example, saw combined federal and state government funding to government schools increase by 48 per cent, but 64 per cent to Catholic schools and 82 per cent to 'Independent' schools (ACARA, 2011; *The Australian*, 2012).

In the face of this unregulated expansion, and its socially regressive effects, the federal Labor government of Julia Gillard commissioned the first systematic review of school funding in 40 years, the so-called Gonski Review (*Review of Funding for Schooling*), which consulted widely before proposing in 2011 that a substantial increase in funding was warranted and that the largest component be directed at government schools, where disadvantage was concentrated. Government support, it argued, whether from state or Commonwealth sources, should be on the basis of need according to a base resource standard that was guaranteed to all schools, and which would be supplemented in the case of schools with higher proportions of disadvantage (such as high proportions of indigenous, poor or recently arrive migrant pupils). Such schools are, overwhelmingly, public schools. This clear re-articulation of a needs-based approach to funding was also an important re-articulation of the need to coordinate government funding across state and federal boundaries.

The politics surrounding the report and its recommendations were predictable and intense. Despite widespread support from virtually all quarters, including the non-government sector, the conservative federal opposition criticised it, claiming (in defiance of the evidence) that there was nothing wrong with existing funding arrangements (see earlier).[5]

But the debate also crossed political boundaries, with some conservative states expressing their support for a Labor federal government initiative. Indeed, the Commonwealth government moved to conclude deals with several state governments, including in the two most populous states, each headed by a conservative government. At least two other conservative state governments, however, refused to sign an accord with the Commonwealth.

In one sense, the state-federal concord, at least with the majority of states, was no surprise: the deals were to result in billions of dollars of additional school funding over the ensuing few years to hard-pressed state governments that signed on to such arrangements with the Commonwealth. But it was instructive that several conservative states expressed support for the principles of the Gonski funding scheme. As the Premier of the most populous state reportedly said:

> I think it would be disappointing if the opportunity that Gonski has presented wasn't accepted . . . [I]t's a formula that benefits both public education and non-government education . . . that we would dismiss at our own peril. (The Conversation, 2012)

In the febrile atmosphere of an impending federal election, this left the federal opposition nowhere to hide: in the face of strong community support, including premiers and ministers of education in state government from its own side of politics, it performed an abrupt *volte face*, promising to support the Gonski proposals, albeit with significantly less funding in the final 2 years of the scheme. This promise proved short-lived, however: upon coming to power in the subsequent federal election, it attempted to go back on its pledge (The Conversation, 2013). Once again, widespread community resistance made it perform yet another *volte face*, reverting to its previously promised support. At the time of writing, a by-now-skeptical community awaits implementation.

Conclusion

Federal systems of government have their strengths and weaknesses; and coordination across the different levels of government is critical to the effectiveness and efficiency of any federation and any policy arena, including education. This is by no means always easy, especially when political ideologies collide, with one party in government at the federal level and another at state level. The Australian example is characterized by the need to equalize service provision across a vast terrain and very uneven population distribution, as well as across states with very different fiscal profiles. This too has not proved easy, including in education. The evolution of federal arrangements, including via critical interpretations at various junctures by the High Court, has seen power transfer from the states to the federal arena. This has gradually drawn the Commonwealth government to intervene more and more, despite initial reluctance based on the premise that education was, constitutionally, a state matter.

Now, in a more neo-liberal era, arguments about individual rights and choice (including of school) are tending to supplant earlier priorities of state-building, citizenship and communalism, of which the local state school was an important pillar. Such neo-liberal principles are increasingly transcending former party-political differences, although this does not necessarily mean that state-federal coordination automatically becomes easier.

Clearly, however, the peculiar paradox of Australian federalism – that the Commonwealth collects by far the bulk of income (by virtue of its sole right to levy income tax), while states are responsible for delivering the bulk of services, including schools and technical education – remains a work in progress. In education, the Commonwealth has a leading role in higher education, and is assuming a greater role in the school sector, by virtue of its greater fiscal leverage. This has become a more commonly wielded instrument of federal power, via the increasing use of tied grants, and other such instruments that made federal funds to states conditional on acceptance of specific terms. This has included in recent years, for example, the provision of Commonwealth funds to the states for education that were made conditional upon acceptance of the public reporting of school performance data by state authorities.

The example of school funding underlines several of these elements: growing assertion of federal authority, after initial reluctance premised on the basis that education was a 'state matter'; the increasing use of federal funding as a lever to impose conditions on at times reluctant state governments (who, as argued earlier, have learned to manipulate the system); and the ongoing need for improved state-federal coordination, via reforms to instruments such as MCEEDYA (and the foreshadowed CE), as well as COAG. Improved efficiency and coordination on their own, however, are not enough; the basis for government intervention is also critical. Commonwealth and state government support for fissiparous policies that residualize the government sector, while promoting the interests of the non-government sector based on spurious arguments about choice, will, if left unchallenged, undermine the health and overall performance of the Australian education system. Such divisiveness would be anathema to the founding fathers of the Australian federation, intent upon welding a nation together.

Notes

1   The principal exception being the Australian National University, established in the Australian Capital Territory.

2   This was by no means always the case, of course: the 'Murray' Report into Universities (1957) reported that in 1956, states had provided 50.3 per cent of universities' recurrent budgets for general purposes and 5.8 per cent for specific purposes, compared with Commonwealth proportions of 29.2 per cent and 2.0 per cent, respectively (table 4, Murray Report, p. 24). The report also pointed to a Commonwealth agreement to provide support for state funding for universities on a £1 per £3 basis; the support was capped, but had more than doubled over the years 1951–1957. Further Commonwealth funding was in the form of Commonwealth scholarships that paid the fees of approximately one-third of full-time students at university. In addition, the Australian National University and Canberra University College, both in Australia's national capital, were fully funded by the Commonwealth. The committee proposed the initiation of an Australian University Grants Committee to advise on 'the financial needs of universities' (p. 109). A subsequent inquiry into the future of universities (the Martin Report) led to, *inter alia*, Commonwealth funding being provided to build teachers colleges (Martin Report, 1964).

3   In the Australian context, Liberal refers to conservative parties, of which the largest holds the title Liberal.

4   Secondary enrolments more than tripled from 1955 to 1975 (Proctor and Sriprakash, 2013: p. 228).

5   Although by no means the first time that governments put politics over policy, it was a particularly egregious example of the triumph of ideology over evidence. For another example, see Welch (2014).

References

Australian (The) (2012), 'Public schools "lose out" on funds as rises favour wealthy'. 9 January.

Australian Curriculum, Assessment and Reporting Authority (ACARA) (2011), *National Report on Schools in Australia*. Sydney, ACARA. Available at: http://www.acara.edu.au/verve/_resources/National Report_on_Schooling_in_Australia_2011.pdf (Accessed: 28 March 2014).

Australian Parliament (APH) (2001), *Parliament's Development of Federalism* (Research Paper No. 26). Available at: http://www.aph.gov.au/About_Parliament/Parliamentary_Departments/Parliamentary_Library/pubs/rp/rp0001/01RP26 (Accessed: 28 March 2014).

Business Council of Australia (BCA) (2006), *Reshaping Australia's Federation. A New Contract for Federal State Relations.*

Caldwell, B. (2011), 'Educational Reforms and School Improvement in Australia', in J. Lee and B. Caldwell (eds), *Changing Schools in an Era of Globalization.* London: Routledge, pp. 67–84.

Campbell, C. and Proctor, H. (2014), *A History of Australian Schooling.* Sydney: Allen & Unwin.

Campbell, C., Proctor, H. and Sherington, G. (2014), *School Choice: How Parents Negotiate the New School Market in Australia.* Sydney: Allen & Unwin.

Committee on the Future of Tertiary Education [Martin Report] (1964), Canberra: Government Printer.

Conversation (The) (2013), *Back to the Drawing Board on Gonski: No Logic in Abandoning School Reforms.* Available at: https://theconversation.com/back-to-the-drawing-board-on-gonski-no-logic-in-abandoning-school-reforms-20725 (Accessed: 28 March 2014).

Council of Australian Governments (COAG) (2013a), *Lessons for Federal Reform: COAG Reform Agenda 2008–2013.* COAG Reform Council. Available at: http://www.coagreformcouncil.gov.au/reports/reform-progress/lessons-federal-reform-coag-reform-agenda-2008–2013 (Accessed: 28 March 2014).

— (2013b), *COAG Communique.* COAG Reform Council. Available at: http://www.coag.gov.au/node/516 (Accessed: 28 March 2014).

Dudley, J. and Vidovich, L. (1995), *The Politics of Education: Commonwealth Schools Policy 1973–95.* Melbourne: ACER.

Fenna, A. (1994), 'Federalism and Public Policy in Australia', in *Australian Public Policy.* Sydney: Pearson, pp. 164–189.

Gallop, G. (2012), 'The COAG Reform Council. A View from the Inside', in P. Kildea, A. Lynch and G. Williams (eds), *Tomorrow's Federation.* Sydney: Federation Press, pp. 43–52.

Hogan, M. (2005), *A Lifetime in Conservative Politics: Political Memoirs of Sir Joseph Carruthers.* Sydney: UNSW Press.

Hose, K. (2003), 'Structural Change in Australian Trade Unionism, 1969–1996: A Structural Events Approach', *Australian Bulletin of Labour* 29 (2), 177–193.

Inside Story (2012), *'Gonski Again'.* Available at: http://inside.org.au/gonski-again/ (Accessed: 28 March 2014).

Keating, J. (2009), *A New Federalism in Australian Education. A Proposal for a National Reform Agenda.* R.E. Ross Trust and Education Foundation. Available at: www.fya.org.au/media-links/a-new-federalism-in-australian-education/ (Accessed: 28 March 2014).

— (2011), *Federalism in the Real World.* Melbourne: University of Melbourne.

Kildea, P. (2012), 'We need to talk about COAG', The Conversation. Available at: http://inside.org.au/we-need-to-talk-about-coag/ (Accessed: 28 March 2014).

Matthews, M. (2009), 'Fostering Creativity and Innovation in Cooperative Federalism – The Uncertainty and Risk Dimensions', in J. Wanna (ed.), *Critical Reflections on Australian Public Policy*. Canberra: ANU EPress, pp. 59–70.

McClelland, R. (1991), 'Moore v Doyle: A Legend Larger than Life?' *Australian Journal of Labour Law* 4 (3), 256–260.

Parliamentary Library (2013), *Australian Government Funding for Schools Explained: 2013 Update*. Available at: http://www.aph.gov.au/About_Parliament/Parliamentary_ Departments/Parliamentary_Library/pubs/BN/2012-2013/schoolfunding (Accessed: 28 March 2014).

Proctor, H. and Sriprakash, A. (2013), 'School Choice', in R. Connell et al. (eds), *Education Change and Society*. Oxford University Press, pp. 213–233.

Ramamurthy, V. (2012), 'Tied Grants and Policy Reform in Public Hospitals and Schools', in P. Kildea, A. Lynch and G. Williams (eds), *Tomorrow's Federation*. Sydney: Federation Press, pp. 114–130.

Report of the Committee on Australian Universities [Murray Report] (1958), Canberra: Government Printer.

Review of Funding for Schooling: Final Report [Gonski Report] (2011), Canberra: Department of Education Employment and Workplace Relations.

Schools in Australia; Report of the Interim Committee for the Australian Schools Commission [Karmel Report] (1973), Canberra: Australian Schools Commission.

Sherington, G. and Hughes, J. (2014), 'Money Made Us': A Short History of Government Funds for Australian Schools', in H. Proctor, P. Brownlee and P. Freebody (eds), *New and Enduring Controversies in Education: Orthodoxy and Heresy in Policy and Practice*. New York/Amsterdam: Springer (In Press).

Twomey, A. (2007), 'Federalism – Options for Reform. National Industrial Relations'. September Conference Paper.

Victorian Parliament (2012), *Inquiry into Commonwealth Payments to Victoria*. Available at: http://www.parliament.vic.gov.au/images/stories/documents/council/ SCEI/CPTV/cptv_finalreport.pdf (Accessed: 28 March 2014).

Welch, A. (2013a), Making Policy, Making Democracy, in R. Connell et al. (eds), *Education Change and Society*. Oxford University Press, pp. 186–212.

— (2013b), Cultural Difference and Identity, in R. Connell et al. (eds), *Education Change and Society*. Oxford University Press, pp. 99–130.

— (2014), 'Evidence Based Policy: Epistemologically Dubious, Ideologically Unsound', in H. Proctor, P. Brownlee and P. Freebody (eds), *New and Enduring Controversies in Education: Orthodoxy and Heresy in Policy and Practice*. New York/Amsterdam: Springer (2014).

Wilkinson, I. R., Caldwell, B. J., Selleck, R. J. W., Harris, J. and Dettman, P. A. (2007), *A History of State Aid to Non-Government Schools in Australia*. Canberra Department of Education, Science and Training (DEST).

Australia: Finance, Quality and Participation in Postsecondary Education

Gerald Burke

Introduction

This chapter considers 'postsecondary' education in Australia. Major attention is given to funding especially as it affects participation and the quality of courses. The policy context is considered first and then an overview of institutions, students and courses. Research is only considered in passing as it relates to teaching.

The term postsecondary is used in this chapter to include courses taken by persons who have left secondary school. Its main components are higher education and vocational education and training (VET). Postsecondary education is broader than that considered as tertiary education under the International Standard Classification of Education (ISCED). Courses for a bachelor degree or higher (ISCED 5A and 6) are provided in higher education. Courses for diploma and advanced diploma (ISCED 5B) are largely provided in VET. The main VET provision is in Certificates I–IV. Certificate IV is rated ISCED 4B 'Post-secondary non-tertiary'. Certificates I–III are rated by ISCED at secondary level. VET institutions also provide second chance courses which would be considered as secondary level.

Higher education and VET are usually reviewed separately in Australia even though there is considerable and increasing interaction between them. More persons participate in VET than in higher education, especially the less advantaged. VET provides vocationally oriented education and training for young and older persons and provides a pathway to higher education. Joint consideration of the sectors helps draw attention to anomalies in funding and quality assurance.

Policy context

From the mid-1980s, government policy exposed the Australian economy to greater international competition and there was a reduction in regulation in financial and labour markets within the country. Education and skills were seen as increasingly important for the economy though their expansion was to be provided in part by private funding and by efficiencies prompted by increased competition among education and training providers (Burke, 2000; Davis, 2013).

Key statements on higher education were made in the Bradley report, the Australian government's most recent comprehensive review of higher education (Bradley, 2008). Its advice included that: the nation will need more well-qualified persons; achieving this will require greater enrolment by the less advantaged; more support was needed for the less advantaged; the quality of the educational experience was declining and additional funding was needed for improved quality and for greater quantity of higher education. It advocated that *all* Australian students in bachelor degree courses and some postgraduate courses be provided with a government-supported place.

Current statements about the VET sector are set out in the National Agreement for Skills and Workforce Development among the state, territory and Australian governments (COAG, 2012a). The Agreement advocated developing the skills of all persons of working age to enable effective participation in the labour force and to improve social inclusion. A major plank was the introduction of an entitlement for all to a government-supported place at least to Certificate III level.

There is a range of benefits from expanding postsecondary education, many acknowledged in governmental statements on higher education and VET. Social benefits include better health, effects on the next generation, greater civic responsibility and reduced welfare dependency. The economic benefits include the effects on labour force participation of those who would not otherwise obtain qualifications. Higher education qualifications and VET qualifications at Certificate III and higher levels have much the same additional effect on employment (ABS, 2013b). These employment benefits alone are likely to exceed the costs of the proposed additional education and support services (AWPA, 2013). There are also the higher relative earnings of those with qualifications.

These relative earnings have held up over time despite the considerable growth in the number of employed persons with qualifications. Rates of return tend to be quite high for many higher education qualifications. Rates of return for VET qualifications on average are good when consideration is given to lower costs and lower earnings foregone (Long and Shah, 2008; Lee and Coelli, 2010). Lower-level VET qualifications obtained by early school leavers are associated with a notably higher rate of employment and can provide a pathway to higher and more rewarding qualifications.

Earnings are an indicator of the contribution of a more educated workforce to productivity. There are good grounds too for the case that more educated workers facilitate the introduction of new technology and the productivity of other workers.

Institutions, students and courses

Institutions and governance

In 1960, Australia had 10 universities growing to 19 in 1975. Several technological colleges were converted into colleges of advanced education which progressed to bachelor degree awarding status. In the 1970s, teacher training colleges which had been part of the state government education systems became colleges of advanced education.

The Commonwealth government in 1974 assumed the public funding of the colleges and of the universities. It had previously shared public funding responsibility with the states. At the same time, it supported the formation into state systems of remaining technical colleges which became known as Technical and Further Education (TAFE), the major component of the VET sector (Goozee, 2001).

From 1988, colleges of advanced education were required by the Australian government to merge with universities or with other colleges to form universities with more than 5,000 students leading to the current total of 37 universities and the Batchelor Institute of Indigenous Tertiary Education which together enrol nearly 95 per cent of all higher education students. Alongside these are 3 private universities, over 100 private institutions including 2 overseas universities with at least some self-accrediting capacity and another 30 or so non-self-accrediting institutions.

In the early 1990s, the Commonwealth and the states agreed on the establishment of the Australian National Training Authority (ANTA) to develop policy for the VET system and to allocate a temporarily growing Commonwealth contribution of funds. Under ANTA, national competency standards were developed for qualifications grouped by industry sectors. These were later developed into 'Training Packages' discussed later. This period also saw the beginnings of provision of public funding for private VET providers, initially for the training of apprentices and trainees and now extended in some states to virtually all nationally recognized courses.

The public universities, which are established under state legislation though receiving public funds and policy guidance from the Commonwealth government, have considerable autonomy in matters of courses, capital development and international ventures. The TAFE institutions have less autonomy but this varies across states.

Davis (2013) has observed that Australian universities have for a long time been similar in their structure and functions though this may change considerably with increased private funding and the use of new technologies. All the universities are associated in Universities Australia which lobbies on their behalf. The major research-oriented universities have formed the Group of Eight and others have grouped to support their particular interests.

Four universities in Victoria were formed from colleges which had contained large VET components and they retained these. They are known as dual sector institutions. Charles Darwin University in the Northern Territory is also a dual sector institution and Central Queensland University is moving to that status. Other universities offer VET courses in some areas. Some VET institutions have also registered as higher education providers and offer degree courses without Australian government funding. Holmesglen Institute, primarily a VET provider, has obtained direct Australian government funding for some of its degree programmes and works in partnership with the University of Canberra to deliver several of that university's publicly supported degrees. Federation University has arranged for the delivery of part of several of its degree programmes to be delivered by public VET providers. Examples of these relationships are becoming more common.

Public funding is provided very largely to the 37 public universities and with only small exception is not available to the 140 or so private providers. As mentioned, the public universities provide for nearly 95 per cent of all higher education students and this proportion has not changed greatly in recent years.

There were over 2,100 VET providers receiving public money in 2012 to provide courses (NCVER, 2013b). A further 2,500 providers were registered to provide nationally accredited VET courses but do not receive public funds. Reliable data on their activities are not available.

In 2012, 68 per cent of VET delivery was by public providers, a large fall from 84 per cent in 2008 (NCVER, 2013b). The largest VET providers are the public TAFE institutions, usually with several campuses each. There are over 60 TAFEs and the largest 50 of them average about 25,000 students each. Some not-for-profit providers catering for less advantaged groups are known as Community Education Providers. They currently provide less than 5 per cent of delivery. Other registered providers, who now deliver approaching 30 per cent of all VET, are mainly for-profit private companies. There are around a dozen with more than 3,000 students but over a thousand private providers receiving public funds have less than 100 publicly supported students.

Students

About 80 per cent of students persist to the end of secondary school and 60 per cent of school leavers move directly into higher education or VET. With later age enrolments, the total eventually entering postsecondary is in excess of 80 per cent. Australia ranks among the highest in the world in participation in any form of education by persons 40 and over (OECD, 2013).

To enter higher education, students are generally expected to have completed secondary schooling or its equivalent. School leavers will usually require achievement in the top half of the age group, higher for the prestigious institutions. Entry requirements for VET vary with the course and are generally lower and for those seeking remedial and second chance courses there may be no entry requirements.

The overall standard of school leavers in Australia is roughly indicated by Australia's good ranking in the Programme for International Student Assessment (PISA) tests for 15 year olds though the average scores have fallen somewhat absolutely and relatively in recent years. Australia is ranked 'high quality and high equity' though a larger proportion of the scores are explained by socio-economic background than the OECD average (Thomson et al., 2013).

On the one hand, less than half the commencing students in higher education in any year is admitted on secondary school results. About one-quarter is admitted on the basis of prior higher education and about one in ten on VET qualifications, and the latter figure is rising (Guthrie et al., 2011).

On the other hand, a considerable number of higher education graduates later take courses in the VET sector. In 2009, persons with degrees made up 7 per cent of all VET students (Guthrie et al., 2011).

Table 3.1 shows that persons enrolled in postsecondary education, full or part time, equal 20 per cent of the population aged 15 to 64 and 12 per cent of the population aged 25–64.

Overall, 60 per cent of students are in VET though 85 per cent of these are part time compared with 30 per cent in higher education. VET has many older enrolments with 20 per cent aged 45 or more compared with 6 per cent of higher education students. A much higher proportions of VET students are Indigenous, have a disability, are from areas outside the major cities or are male. There are nearly 700,000 domestic students from the lowest two SES quintiles in VET compared with less than 200,000 in higher education. The lowest SES students in VET tend to be disproportionately in the lower level courses.

About 55 per cent of higher education students are female compared with 20 per cent 60 years ago. Increased completion of secondary schooling by females

Table 3.1 Students by sector and demographic characteristics, Australia 2010

	VET	Higher education	Total
Total students including international thousands	1,799	1,193	2,992
Students as % of Australian population aged 15 to 64	12	8	20
Domestic students	1,753	845	1,219
Domestic students in two most disadvantaged SES quintiles thousands	691	191	882
	%	%	%
Bachelor degree or higher	–	86	37
Diploma, advanced diploma and associate degree	13	7	9
Certificate	67		40
Other	20	7	13
Female	47	56	51
Part time	85	30	63
Indigenous	5	1	3
With a disability	6	3	5
Main language at home Non-English	15	17	16
25 and over	57	37	49
Major cities	56	77	63

Notes: Most international students in VET are enrolled with private providers and not counted in the NCVER data. Over one-third of international students in higher education are *off-shore* studying with overseas campuses or partners of Australian universities.

Source: NCVER (2012).

(now much higher than for males), the shift of nursing and teacher training to higher education, the abolition of fees for the years 1974 to 1987 and improved income support grants contributed to the change. These factors had less influence in VET sector.

About a quarter of VET students are on 'contracts of training' involving both employment and the provision of training and take courses at Certificate III level. Nearly half of these are in apprenticeships in the skilled trades such as electricians, carpenters and plumbers.

Data available from 2006 to 2011 show a constant proportion of VET students from the lowest SES quintile (NCVER, 2013b; NVEAC, 2013). For higher education, data from 1989 show some fluctuations in the share of the lowest SES background though they have benefited in share and number in years of rapid expansion of the system, discussed further later in relation to fees and loans.

Domestic students in higher education increased rapidly in the early 1990s, slowly until the late 2000s and fast again in recent years. The average growth rate in the decade to 2011 was 2.6 per cent per annum. Student numbers in VET after rapid growth in the 1990s were roughly constant for most of the recent decade but increased strongly the last years for an average growth of 1 per cent. Overall, total postsecondary students grew at 1.5 per cent per annum, about the same rate as the adult population but faster than the population aged 15–45 which grew about 1.1 per cent per annum. The participation rate of younger persons increased in this period and that of older declined.

In 2011, for the whole population aged 25–64, 64 per cent held a non-school qualification: 36 per cent held VET and 28 per cent higher education. In the 25–34 age group, the number with higher education qualifications held outnumbered VET qualifications. This reflects the faster growth in higher education enrolments in the last decade (including the effect of international students remaining in Australia) and also that the VET students are relatively older and more of them complete courses later in life.

Rates of graduation from higher education are among the highest in the OECD though once international students are removed the rate falls considerably and for 'first time' domestic higher education graduates is slightly below the OECD average (OECD, 2013).

International students

International students are a much greater proportion of total tertiary students as defined by OECD than in any other country. Australia, with 7 per cent of all international students, ranks third in total number behind the United States and United Kingdom and around the numbers of France and Germany (OECD, 2013).

The number of onshore higher education international students peaked in 2010 at over 240,000 and were 5 per cent lower in 2013. The number of VET students peaked in 2009 at over 200,000 but was 35 per cent lower in 2013 (AEI, 2013). One factor in the fall was the increase in the value of the Australian dollar from well below to above that of the US dollar. Another was change in migration regulations. From 2009, the number of occupations (and related courses) leading to independent skilled migration was reduced, particularly affecting VET. This change was made on assessment of employment outcomes and because of some sub-standard training (Knight, 2011). Visa restrictions were eased in 2013 for higher education graduates to allow them to work in Australia for a year or more after graduation and with the recent fall in the value of the Australian dollar to around 89 US cents this is likely to see higher numbers at least in higher education.

Courses

The largest field of study in both higher education and VET is Management and Commerce with nearly one-quarter of the total enrolments. In higher education, Society and Culture is almost as large but in VET the second field is Engineering and Related Technologies which includes many skilled trades (NCVER, 2013b; DE, 2013b).

Some 85 per cent of higher education students are in bachelor or higher level courses. Research students make up a little less than 10 per cent of all higher education students. About 15 per cent of VET students are in diploma or higher diploma courses, the large majority are in certificate courses and about 15 per cent in other courses including specifically secondary school courses (NCVER, 2013b).

Half the international students in higher education are in Management and Commerce and they roughly equal in number the domestic students in that field (DE, 2013b). This dependence of some faculties – and some universities – on this field was seen as a potential risk by Bradley (2008).

Some 35 per cent of onshore international students at universities are at higher degree level compared with 20 per cent of all students. Eighty per cent of VET onshore students are at Certificate IV or above compared with only 13 per cent of the total of VET in public institutions.

Course differences, higher education and VET

Higher education, on the one hand, is seen to be concerned with knowledge and, at least in universities, teaching is seen to be informed by research. The idea of teaching-only universities has been raised though the Bradley committee firmly supported the continuation of the teaching/research nexus and indeed to strengthen it in higher education institutions with the name 'university'. The growth in the use of casual staff and in the outsourcing by some universities of delivery of at least part of their degree programmes tend to weaken the nexus in practice.

VET, on the other hand, is seen as providing skills for employment. Karmel (2011) says this distinction of VET between university and VET courses does not hold across the board, and a considerable proportion of university teaching is directed at meeting the requirements of professional bodies.

The sectors differ in the design and delivery of their courses and this has some effect on the transition between them. It could be a factor in the lack of credit and great variation in credit, given for VET graduates seeking entry to higher education (Watson et al., 2013).

Courses delivered in VET and higher education classified as 'nationally recognized' have to comply with the Australian Qualifications Framework (AQF). This was one of the first such frameworks when developed in the 1990s and has recently been substantially revised (AQFC, 2013). It has ten levels from Certificate I to doctorate, based on complexity.

Public universities accredit their own courses against the AQF though they are subject to overall regulation by the Tertiary Education Quality and Standards Agency (TEQSA) established in 2011. Private higher education providers may obtain self-accrediting status for one or more courses and the majority has done so.

Prior to the 1990s, courses in VET were delivered by public providers in separate state systems. A need for registration of providers emerged with the increase in private providers following their access to public funds and the growth of the international student market. VET providers are now registered and audited largely by the Australian Skills Quality Authority (ASQA), a national body set up in 2011, against standards developed by the National Skills Standards Council (NSSC, 2013). The registration allows VET providers to deliver specific qualifications. VET providers cannot self-accredit courses for national recognition. Most national qualifications in VET are set out in 'training packages' which indicate competencies to be achieved for particular qualifications and the assessment methods to be used (Karmel, 2011).

The training packages are developed by national Industry Skills Councils, with employer and union membership but not training provider representation. An objective in developing training packages was to increase the influence of industry on the content of vocational training, seem to have been determined too much in the past by public providers. Training packages were also designed to facilitate training carried out in the workplace and for assessment to occur in the workplace or in a simulated workplace.

The training packages do not specify a normal time taken to complete training. Under the revised AQF, 'volume of learning' is included as an integral part of the descriptor for each qualification type. For example, the volume of learning of a diploma is typically 1–2 years. However, there are myriad examples of courses being provided with a much smaller volume than that indicated in the AQF. Industry Skills Councils are deliberating this issue. ASQA (2013) has recently voiced its concern about this.

There has been a range of criticisms of training packages. They are regularly revised, though not quickly enough for some critics who argue that the skills needed are changing rapidly. Recently, particular importance has been given to embedding foundation studies and employability skills within them. A further issue is the extent to which they put emphasis on doing and neglect the underpinning knowledge that provides a basis for continued learning. Along with a continued reduction in funding per hour of training, discussed later, training packages are seen by critics to strip delivery to basic skills (Bannikoff, 2013). In defence, the Skills Councils can argue that they are specifying competencies and not the curriculum or the way to teach, and they are not responsible for funding levels.

Funding

Funding in international context

The OECD reports spending on tertiary education across member countries. For Australia, this covers higher education and diploma and advanced diplomas in VET. Tertiary spending in Australia as a percentage of GDP lies close to the 'OECD average' (OECD, 2013). Australia lies below the 'OECD total', the weighted average. Australian is below average in public spending and above in private spending.

It is arguable that the OECD approach to estimating private and public expenditures leads to an exaggeration of the importance of private relative to public spending in Australia. The OECD treats all spending from income contingent student loans as private spending whereas perhaps one-third of the loan outlays in Australia should be counted as a cost to government for the exemption from repayment for those who earn low incomes, are resident overseas or who die and also the waiver of real interest. The OECD includes the expenditures of international students as private spending. However, one form of private spending is omitted from both OECD and Australian statistics and that is the domestic private spending on private providers of VET.

Three of the top four OECD countries in total spending, the United States, Korea and Chile, have very high private spending and Canada, the third highest in total, has above average private and public spending. Finland and Sweden which have the highest *public* spending rank well below the top four in total spending as a share of GDP. Where the high fee is compensated with loans or grants to students, the rates of entry are higher than in countries without well-developed student support systems (OECD, 2013).

This means that we cannot draw inferences about equity or the quality of provision from a study of one element of funding such as fees. In summary, access is affected by:

- government grants relative to fees as components of tuition costs,
- availability of (income contingent) loans,
- capped or unlimited access to a subsidized place,
- support for additional learning needs,
- support for living costs.

The quality and quantity of postsecondary education is affected by:

- funding levels,
- costs of provision,
- efficiency and responsiveness of the system including effective quality assurance.

Revenues in Australia

Table 3.2 shows the revenues of the higher education and VET sectors. The higher education sector has revenues almost three times of the VET sector.

Public funding for higher education is very largely provided by the Australian government which exercises policy control over the sector. VET is mainly the responsibility of the six states and two territories. Recently, about 30 per cent of all

Table 3.2 VET and higher education institutional revenues, Australia 2011 $ million

Higher education

Australian government research funding	1,977	8%
Australian government grants scheme, capital grants and other assistance	8,088	34%
States financial assistance	821	3%
Australian government loans (HELP) (for domestic student fees)	3,276	14%
Fee paying overseas students	4,124	17%
Upfront domestic student contributions (fees)	543	2%
Other fees	1,325	6%
Consultancies royalties	1,085	5%
Investment income	872	4%
Bequests and related	701	3%
Other	888	4%
TOTAL	23,659	100%

VET

Total Commonwealth recurrent and capital	2,414	29%
Total States recurrent and capital	4,150	50%
Government agencies fees	226	3%
Overseas students fees and contracts	323	4%
Domestic student fees and charges	314	4%
Other fee for service	518	6%
Other income	304	4%
TOTAL	8,249	100%

Note: Excludes grants for living expenses such as Youth Allowance and grants to employers of apprentices; excludes private incomes of private providers.

Sources: Based on NCVER (2013a) and DE (2013a).

public funds for tuition in VET have been provided by the Australian government mainly as grants to the state and territory governments who pool it with their own funds for allocation to training providers. There are intergovernmental agreements about the Australian government funds and through them it has considerable policy influence on VET.

Table 3.2 shows that in higher education a little over 40 per cent of total funds are Australian government grants though an additional 15 per cent is provided by the Australian government as loans to cover student tuition fees. The Australian government grants include funding for research and for the training of research students. Table 3.2 shows that specific research grants make up less than 10 per cent of the total revenues. However, other estimates for research are much higher than this, at over $8 billion in 2010 – or over 30 per cent of all university revenues (ABS, 2012b). This is because a substantial amount of academic staff time which is funded under the Australian government grants scheme – largely considered funds for teaching – is reported by universities as devoted to research.

Around 80 per cent of funds for VET providers in the public system come as grants from government. Fees from domestic students and overseas students each provide less than 5 per cent of total funds. However, Table 3.2 does not include the fees received by private VET providers. It is estimated that they receive three-quarters of the fees paid by international students in VET (ABS, 2012a). Other fees raise about 6 per cent.

International students in higher education are concentrated in the public universities. They provided 17 per cent of total higher education revenues in 2011, about the same as the revenue from domestic students in fees (which are mainly funded by loans).

Revenue per student or hour

Table 3.3 shows the changes in estimated government recurrent expenditure in constant prices per student or per hour of training from 1999 to 2011 for schools, VET and higher education. VET funding per hour of training delivered fell by about 25 per cent. There was a further decline of 6 per cent in 2012 (Productivity Commission, 2014).

For government schools and higher education, index is for per full-time student. For VET, it is per hour of publicly funded training. Data are in constant prices using the GDP chain price index (Indexes 1999 = 100).

In higher education, on the one hand, government funds per student fluctuated but are a little higher at the end of the period than at the beginning. Schools, on the other hand, have had a notable large increase in real funding per student.

Table 3.3 Indexes of government recurrent expenditure per full-time student (schools and higher education) and per hour of training (VET), Australia 1999 to 2011 (1999 = 100)

	Government secondary schools	VET	Higher education
1999	100	100	100
2005	118	93	101
2011	120	75	103

Source: AWPA (2013).

From 1996 to 2012, the Australian government adjusted its annual funding by much less than the annual increase in costs. The decline in government funds per student for higher education was somewhat reversed and offset by a number of funding adjustments including a real increase in the fees of 25 per cent in 2005 (which could be covered by loans). From 2012, the Australian government has implemented almost full adjustment for cost increases in its annual grants for higher education. However, in 2013 it announced some cuts in funding that will offset much of the indexation for the next 2 years.

The Australian government's funds allocated to VET are still only partially adjusted for cost increases. State governments have not sustained real expenditures for their large share of VET spending (Burke, 2013).

There has been no analysis of the relative needs of VET, schools and higher education. VET does not have the same political clout as schools and higher education. Political promises to non-government schools have led to a continuing increase in real funding for both non-government schools and government schools (Gonski, 2011).

Fees and loans

As background for the consideration of fees in postsecondary education, it can be noted that in Australia all students can attend government schools for which no compulsory tuition fees are charged. About 40 per cent of secondary students attend private schools which charge fees but also receive government subsidies that vary with socio-economic background of the areas from which the students come. The subsidies per student vary from around $3,000 per annum to over $10,000 per student. The private schools charge fees for secondary education that vary from less than $4,000 per annum to over $20,000 per annum. Students attending private schools, especially the high fee schools, tend to be from more advantaged backgrounds and have a much higher rate of entry to higher education (Bradley, 2008; Gonski, 2011).

Fees in postsecondary education were abolished in 1974 with a major reintroduction in higher education in 1989. Initially, the fee in higher education was the same for all fields of tuition, adjusted annually by the consumer price index (CPI). Fees were substantially increased and changed to a three-tier system in 1997. Overall, the fee for the lowest tier of fees increased from 1995 to 2012 by about the same amount as the CPI. In the top tier, the fee paid increased from 1995 by 60 per cent more than CPI and 20 per cent more than Average Weekly Earnings (ABS, 2013a; DAE, 2011).

Table 3.4 Fees and Australian government contribution: higher education 2013

Funding cluster		Government contribution	Maximum student fee	Revenue per student	Government %
1	Law, accounting, administration, economics	$1,900	$9,800	$11,700	16%
2	Humanities	$5,400	$5,900	$11,200	48%
...	...	...	...	...	...
7	Engineering, science	$16,600	$8,400	$25,000	67%
8	Dentistry, medicine agriculture	$21,100	$9,800	$30,900	68%

Source: DE (2013a).

The Bradley (2008) review recommended that maximum fees be retained in higher education for the time being. Bradley considered that with deregulation fees would increase particularly in the well-established institutions, that it could result in an undesirable growth in student debt and that fees were already high by world standards. Bradley noted that New Zealand had reintroduced caps on fees after period of deregulation for reasons of affordability and certainty. An additional point is that access to the more prestigious universities would be more difficult for low income students.

The recent rates of maximum fees and the government subsidy by fields of study are shown in Table 3.4. The average total funding received by a university per student in 2013 was around $16,500 per equivalent full-time student with Commonwealth government grants making up $9,500 and the student fee about $7,000. As shown, there is great variation from the average particularly in the government subsidy which is $21,000 for medicine and related courses but less than $2,000 a year for law and accounting.

Domestic students have the option of paying up front or taking a loan repayable through the national income taxation system. Over 80 per cent of Australian government supported domestic higher education students take an income contingent loan and the others pay upfront (DE, 2013b). No repayment of the loan is required until an annual threshold income, indexed by the CPI, is reached. It was about $51,000 per year in 2013–2014, which is about two-thirds of the average total earnings of an adult employed full time. Repayment starts at 4 per cent and rises to 8 per cent when annual income reached $95,000. The student's debt is also indexed by the CPI. Given the availability of income contingent loans, there is no concession in fees charged to students from less advantaged backgrounds as is still available for most VET courses.

Alongside this system for government-supported places, from 1997 to 2007, universities were allowed to admit extra students at full-cost fees. A variation of the loan scheme called FEE-HELP was introduced for such courses in universities and in private institutions. The Labor government in 2008 abolished full-fee courses for domestic undergraduate courses prior to its extension of subsidised places to all domestic students. Many masters' coursework degrees are full-fee courses. Research degree students are not required to pay fees in the years of the usual duration of their course.

A government review of higher education funding in 2011 argued that 'the current pattern of student fees appears to have developed incrementally without a consistent underlying rationale' (Lomax-Smith et al., 2011). It argued that there was insufficient evidence to support the variation in the proportion funded by the government and recommended it be 60 per cent across all fields of study. This implied an increase in the fees for some of the high subsidy courses and a reduction for ones like law and accounting. The government rejected the recommendation on the grounds that the private benefits from some courses are high enough to justify differential student fees and that a single percentage rate would cause new inequities. A review of public and private benefits by Norton (2012) argued for higher fees on average. He agreed that the existence of public financial and non-financial benefits justifies subsidies but argued that in many courses enrolments to achieve the public benefits could be achieved with much lower levels of government subsidy.

Non-repayment by low income earners is an accepted feature of the scheme. Recent estimates are that about 17 per cent of loans will never be repaid. The average HELP debt was recently around $16,000 and the average time to repay about 8 years (DI, 2013). But the average debt of students at course completion at current fees would be much higher, for example, nearly $30,000 for a 3-year accounting degree.

It was not to be expected that the re-introduction of fees in 1989 even with the provision of loans would improve the position of the less advantaged. However, the political bargain at the time was that the revenues from repayment of loans would allow the government to increase the number of places it supported so that access to higher education would continue to increase. This part of the bargain was well kept in the early years (25% expansion in 3 years after 1988) and the share of low SES rose. The later growth rates in total enrolments were much lower and the proportion of low SES fell though the absolute numbers were a lot higher than before fees and loans were introduced (Coutts, 2010).

VET fees for publicly supported courses are under state policies and they are increasingly divergent. In general, they are well below the level of university fees.

The highest level in NSW in 2013 was around $1,700 compared with the lowest annual charge for university courses of $6,000. However, in contrast to NSW, there is no control of fees in Victoria or in South Australia from 2014.

Students in VET who are receiving some form of government financial living support are usually also allowed a low concession fee. There is variation across states but some exempt Indigenous and persons with a disability from fees and others allow concessional fee rates.

Given the diversity of funding arrangements in VET, the varying length of courses for qualifications at any level and the lack of public information, it is not possible to construct tables for VET similar to that in Table 3.4 for higher education. It also means that it is difficult to substantiate the relative costs across the states and sectors where schools and higher education report on finances per full-time student or equivalent and VET by hour of training. The matter of funding to support quality and equity in VET needs careful and detailed analysis as recommended by AWPA (2013).

International student fees

From 1985, approved VET and higher education institutions were permitted to take full-fee international students and set their own fees above a prescribed minimum. The fees vary widely, partly in line with the prestige of the institution. For example in Management and Commerce, where half of all the international students are enrolled, the annual fee for bachelor degrees at the University of Melbourne was $33,000 per year in 2013, and at University of Central Queensland $18,000. For comparison, as shown in Table 3.4, the annual revenue received by a university for a domestic student for a full-time student in this area was less than $12,000 per student.

Entitlements: demand led provision

The Australian government, following the Bradley review, introduced an entitlement scheme for public universities. Fully introduced in 2012, government funding is provided for every domestic bachelor student and for some postgraduate coursework students a public university enrols. Except in medicine, the universities were free to respond to student choice.

This policy stems from the objectives considered earlier including a commitment to expand the proportion of the working age population holding a qualification and to promote social inclusion. It is also seen to promote competition but limiting it to competition among public universities.

Bradley (2008) assessed the risks of an uncapped entitlement system such as the budgetary consequences, the possibility of poor quality provision and mismatch of student choices with the needs of the economy.

Bradley did not expect the growth in student numbers to be overly large in relation to workforce needs. Reforms were recommended for improved quality assurances but pending their implementation public funding was not to be made available for private providers.

Student choice, along with better information and minor intervention in priority areas, was seen as likely to be as good as or better than the current forms of government determination in meeting the needs of the economy. This recognized that in most jobs there is not a close connection to a particular qualification (Karmel et al., 2008; Skills Australia, 2010).

There was a substantial increase in domestic enrolments averaging nearly 5 per cent per annum from 2009 to 2012 compared with less than 2 per cent per annum in the previous decade (DE, 2013b). Enrolments by students from the lowest SES quartile increased more than the average.

Already, budget concerns have affected funding per student and the new Australian government late in 2013 established a committee to review the system of entitlements. The scheme is likely to be modified.

For the VET sector, as required by the national agreements in 2012, entitlement schemes are being implemented by state governments, but in various ways. The Victorian scheme provides access to a government supported place, generally only to a qualification higher than already held by the student.

For the VET sector, student numbers for Australia as a whole increased nearly 5 per cent per annum 2009 to 2012 with two-thirds of the total increase in Victoria which makes up only a quarter of the national population. In Victoria, the sharp increase in the budget outlay led quickly to several modifications to the scheme. The entitlement was maintained but government funding per hour of training for courses seen to be of lower priority for the economy was cut very substantially. This had the effect of modifying student choices towards areas the government assessed of higher priority for industry, an approach largely abandoned in higher education. Additional funding for public providers for their wider range of costs and community responsibilities was largely removed.

Income support for students and employers

Full-time students in higher education and VET may be eligible for a grant from the Australian government for assistance with living costs, subject to a test of their financial means. For example, a student aged 18 and over independent of parents could receive $10,000 a year or about 20 per cent of average earnings in the community. The student could earn about the same amount without it affecting the benefit.

Bradley (2008) reported that the proportion of students receiving assistance grants in higher education had declined and made a series of recommendations easing the income tests to improve the equity of the distribution and to extend the coverage. In particular, students can now access funds independently of parents' income at age 22 instead of 25. A start-up scholarship (now a loan) providing additional funding equal to about 20 per cent to the grant students living with their parents was introduced. It was for higher education only, not VET.

As a result, the persons receiving grants as a percentage of full-time undergraduates rose from 32 per cent in 2007 to about 36 per cent of a much larger number of full-time students in 2012. In contrast, the number of grants to students in VET – the sector which provides for most of the less advantaged – has not risen (DI, 2013). The ratio of grants to full-time VET students was below 20 per cent in 2012. These data are disturbing and need detailed explanation as this was not to be expected with the liberalization of provision (Dow, 2011).

The Australian government and the states provide considerable financial support to employers who take on apprentices and provide some direct payments to apprentices. In general, these are not targeted on the disadvantaged though apprentices whose employment it subsidises tend to be from lower SES background. Some schemes extend the coverage for equity groups such as Indigenous, persons with disabilities, persons over 45 years and long-term unemployed. There has been little comprehensive evaluation of incentives provided to employers. A recent report suggests that they have not been particularly effective in promoting additional completions of apprenticeships (DAE, 2012).

Funding for higher learning needs

Since the proportion of students from low SES had stagnated, Bradley (2008) advocated funds to support their admission and assist their progress in higher education. Funds are allocated to those universities which lift their enrolments of low SES and for the development of activities in partnership with schools, VET providers and other stakeholders to raise the aspirations and capacities of those from low SES backgrounds (DE, 2014).

In the VET sector, there is funding provision for higher learning needs but it is not as publicly quantified. State funding for VET is generally explicit about additional funding for Indigenous students. Various forms of course funding implicitly provides additional funds for the tuition of less advantaged students.

The Australian government provides a programme outside its VET funding for unemployed persons with low literacy and numeracy skills. It provides support for job seekers. This can include training and job experience. It provides extensive support for recent migrants in English language programmes.

Better use of funds

Competition

It is argued that efficiency in education can be increased if its provision is more influenced by market forces. This should encourage the use of lower cost methods of production and re-orient provision in the direction of the needs of the purchasers. This should benefit all students including the less advantaged.

The effectiveness of a more competitive system may be limited in a number of areas. Where government funds underpin much of student demand and those funds are subject to policy change, suppliers feel safest providing courses where setup costs are limited. This could reduce the suppliers of capital intensive courses. Where a programme for less advantaged involves ongoing mentoring, the supply may be restricted without the promise of longer-term government support. Where there is uncertainty of funding, the development of an ongoing professional teaching workforce may be compromised. Such issues are central to the debate on the role of the public provider of VET for which several states are reducing or eliminating any funding advantage relative to for-profit private providers.

Government policy on competition for international students is largely unrestricted though visa and migration policies have significant effects on the size of the market. Policy on competition for domestic students is more restricted. In higher education, the entitlement scheme with very minor exception is restricted to public universities. The universities have little capacity to compete on price as the maximum fee is prescribed (Table 3.4). In striking contrast, the Australian government has strongly supported competition among public and private providers in VET (COAG, 2012b) and Victoria and South Australia have deregulated fees.

Anderson (2006) evaluated the early development of the market in VET. Both public and private providers agreed that market forces had increased innovation and responsiveness at least to larger clients but that marketing and administrative costs had expanded strongly, and that the effects on balance for quality and equity were negative. The market in VET has been extended greatly since Anderson's study with a recent increase in the access of private providers to public money and, in some states, considerable competition on price which was not permitted in earlier times and still not permitted in higher education.

Other ways to efficiency

New technologies provide opportunities to reduce costs. The major development in online education is Massive Open Online Courses (MOOCS). Some Australian universities have joined international consortia. One of the concerns expressed is how well less advantaged students will fare with MOOCS. Norton (2013) has provided an assessment of the likely importance of online provision and MOOCS and there are almost daily reports of new initiatives.

Governments have been able to stimulate efficiencies by partially funding on outputs. This is embodied in mission-based compacts which have been signed by each university.

Teachers' salaries are the biggest cost and steps to change salary structures and promotion procedures are frequently proposed in the public sector. The move to making public funding available to private providers in the VET sector in part could be seen as a means of cutting the wage bill for training as private providers are much less unionised and have fewer conditions on key matters such as teaching hours. While savings are achieved, the effects on the professionalism of staff and the quality of teaching and learning arguably have been negative.

In the VET sector completion rates of whole qualifications have on average been low, until recently less than 30 per cent, though completion of units or subjects has been around 80 per cent. It is argued that the low qualification rate reflected students completing only units relevant to their work needs though the large majority of commencing students indicate an intention to complete. Recent moves to performance-based funding may be a factor in the recent improvement in qualification completion rates to 35 per cent overall and 45 per cent among young persons without a previous qualification (NCVER, 2013e).

Quality

A major concern in recent years has been the quality of postsecondary education. The constraint on funding for both VET and higher education is seen to be a factor.

Bradley (2008) concluded that there were signs of declining quality in Australian higher education. Data on the student experience and engagement with staff in Australia compared unfavourably with similar surveys in the United Kingdom, the United States and Canada. Bradley saw a need for increased funding and for reform to the mechanisms for quality assurance.

There is a strongly voiced concern in universities that funds available for teaching had declined. Ratios of students to academic staff increased especially in the 1990s. The proportion of teaching taken by sessional staff was estimated to be some 40 to 50 per cent (Bradley, 2008). A notable share of university revenues intended for teaching had been used to subsidise support for externally funded research. An increased share of revenue appears to be used for administration. This is not obvious in data on non-academic staff but this may be because some other services such as maintenance of facilities are being outsourced, reducing staff in those areas.

The TEQSA established in 2011 has responsibility for quality assurance in higher education. A recent review has recommended several simplifications to reduce administrative burden (Dow and Braithwaite, 2013).

Many universities are voluntarily engaging in external moderation of their courses both within Australia and overseas. Australian universities strive to improve their ranking on international quality measures. In general, they rank quite highly (Times Higher Education, 2013). Teaching is considered in these rankings but most of the weight is given to research reputation.

In VET, funding constraints have been one of the factors leading to a reduction in face-to-face teaching and a casualization of the workforce. The Productivity Commission (2011b) estimated that 'about 60 per cent of trainers and assessors in TAFE, and 36 per cent in the non-TAFE sector, were employed on a non-permanent basis, compared to 25 per cent of the wider labour market' in Australia.

The large majority of graduates from VET has expressed satisfaction with courses and the work-related benefits and this has changed little over time (NCVER, 2013d). However, there has been a notable decline in employer satisfaction from 2011 to 2013. Employers agreeing that 'vocational qualifications provide employees with the skills they require for the job' decreased 6 per cent points to 78 per cent (NCVER, 2013c).

Complaints about quality became prominent in the last decade with the rapid increase in numbers of international students in VET very largely enrolled in private for-profit training providers (Knight, 2011). The increased provision of public funds to private providers for domestic students in VET has seen complaints about poor quality provision continue. The Productivity Commission has raised this in a number of reports, for example, on training for aged care:

> Unless existing concerns surrounding poor quality training are addressed, much of any increased investment in vocational education and training could be wasted. (Productivity Commission, 2011a)

In response, the Australian Skills Quality Authority (ASQA) undertook a major review of training providers for aged care. A large majority was found to be initially non-compliant. Many programmes were too short to enable students to become competent. There was a lack of assessment in a workplace and a failure to ensure valid assessment of essential skills and knowledge (ASQA, 2013).

The OECD review of Australian VET in 2008 had argued for standardized assessment to ensure consistency. Skills Australia (2011) recommended that there be independent external validation of assessments and the trialling of this was included in National Partnership Agreement among the national and state governments (COAG, 2012b; AWPA, 2013).

It is arguable that a requirement of students or employers to pay a significant part of the costs of training (with loans as needed) may increase the scrutiny of quality. Students in higher education must pay a minimum approaching $6,000 a year for a full-time course but there is no minimum specified for the VET system in Victoria and some providers charge very low fees. The funds provided by the Australian government to employers for VET training under a scheme called the National Workforce Development Fund require even small employers to contribute at least one-third of the tuition costs rising to two-thirds for large employers.

In VET, as in higher education, it is important that students and employers have good information on which to base choice of type and quality of course in relation to fees charged. In early stages of development are the national websites My Skills and My University.

Discussion and conclusion

Finance that facilitates participation in education

The entitlement scheme in higher education, currently under review, means that the Australian government funds all the domestic undergraduate students that a university enrols. On the one hand, the government loan scheme means no domestic student has to pay fees up-front and repayment is only required once a reasonable income is achieved. The loan scheme is not targeted on the least advantaged but they are the ones whose access is most enhanced (compared with a system with fees but no loans). Much of the evidence is that low SES persons who are eligible for university places are little deterred by the fee and loan scheme. On the other hand, subsidised loans are provided for persons who would have attended in any case. But the current scheme has the virtues of political acceptability and apparent fairness.

In the VET sector, the fee and funding arrangements are largely under state government control. In some states, for some courses students may receive a government subsidy only if their study is for a qualification at a higher level than they already have, affecting retraining. For most courses which attract a government subsidy, the fees remain low relative to those in higher education but this may change with deregulation of fees. So far, the income contingent loan scheme for VET has been confined to the diploma and advanced diploma qualifications. The effects on equity of the rapidly changing VET system are hard to assess.

Grants for living expenses are provided by the Australian government for income support for less advantaged full-time students. Recent adjustments have extended the reach of the schemes though whether the size of the grants or their coverage is really adequate is hard to judge. The low proportion of full-time VET student getting income assistance is a major concern.

Grants and other subsidies are provided to employers of apprentices by both the Australian and state governments. This appears to lift the total numbers in training and may help reduce skill shortages but the efficiency of such schemes has been questioned.

Supplementary funds to support the teaching of less advantaged students are provided in higher education. There are such funds in VET but it is hard to assess the extent. Given that the VET students in general are of lower SES and have a much lower level of achievement in secondary education, their need for support is greater.

Overall participation in postsecondary education is high in Australia. The share of less advantaged groups has risen in years of rapid expansion, not sustained in periods of stability or contraction.

VET is the main provider for low SES students. It is also the main provider for Indigenous and for persons with disabilities who have increased their participation rates considerably in recent years.

So far, the system of funding driven by student choice seems to be yielding a reasonable provision of training to meet labour force needs. There is recognition that much of what is provided in both higher education and VET is suitable for a wide range of occupations. But there will remain the need to monitor the system to help improve the matching of education and training to occupational needs especially for more specialized occupations. There is a need within the workforce to improve the use of skills by better management.

Quality and efficiency

There is considerable concern with quality especially in VET. The reasons for possible deterioration in quality include the substantial decline in funding per hour in VET contributing to employment of marginally qualified and casualized staff and the reduction of face-to-face teaching hours. The extension of funding to private providers ahead of improvements in the quality of assessment has contributed to the problem. The need to target the assessment procedures leading to the award of a qualification has been stressed but is yet to occur.

Poor quality education particularly affects the disadvantaged. They are likely to be provided with less support than needed, be less informed, be more likely to take low cost options and be less able to remedy poor choices with further study. If they receive a qualification without receiving the appropriate skills, it is very unlikely that workforce benefits will be realized.

Efficiency in the use of funds can provide for increased participation and better quality provision. It can be enhanced by changing funding mechanisms. This could include adequate and well-regulated competitive funding and some forms of outcome-based funding.

Improved management and new technology, for example, with MOOCS, can reduce costs of delivery. The effects may well be very large and provide a means of freeing funds that can be directed at the less advantaged.

There are attempts to reduce the costs of higher education regulation and administration but the outcomes are yet to be seen.

An important matter is the need for more comprehensive public information. This includes more detailed information on providers and validated evidence on their performance. It includes the provision of data on staffing which is limited in higher education and virtually non-existent in the VET sector. A reportedly large activity of which very little is known is the provision of training by private VET providers other than their delivery of government-supported training.

Future developments

The current political outlook is for stringency in public funding and a concern to reduce regulation and red tape. In such circumstances, how can we lift funding, quality and participation?

International students particularly in higher education have been a very large source of funds. They provide revenue per student usually more than twice that of Australian students and have helped offset other factors diminishing funds for teaching. In the VET sector, the major provision to international students has been by private providers and it is unlikely that this is used to subsidise domestic students. The future prospects for international students are affected by exchange rates, migration regulations and by the effects of competition from other countries including the MOOCs, whose implications for domestic students are yet to be seen.

That VET funding per hour of training is so low and its regulation poor appears to be in part the outcome of the divided responsibilities of the Australian and state government as well as the greater political clout of the advocates for schools and higher education. A first step would be to provide a common national regulator for VET and higher education and common funding model for the whole of postsecondary education – both recommended in Bradley (2008). These should support better quality in VET, continue the developing collaboration of VET and higher education institutions and facilitate the transition of students across the postsecondary system.

Within this new funding and regulatory structure, there could be scope for a general increase in student fees in VET so long as the loan scheme was provided for certificate courses as well as for diplomas. Some argue that the debt involved in HELP would deter less advantaged students but so long as the current income contingency arrangements are continued this should not be a major issue if sufficient counselling and mentoring from the early years of secondary education were provided. Funding schemes involving greater employer contributions to fees could be developed on the lines of the National Workforce Development Fund.

The full implications of the deregulation of fees as in VET have yet to be assessed. It does seem likely that less advantaged students will be limited in their choice of course and provider even if they can still access a place. Deregulating fees in higher education would increase the revenues of some universities. The range of fees currently charged to international students provides some indication of the size of fee change that could occur. As Bradley argued, the implications need careful review and the caution they recommended still seems apt.

Acknowledgements

The views here are my own but many of the ideas in this chapter have been developed in association with members and secretariat of the Australian Workforce and Productivity Agency. I am grateful for suggestions from Marilyn Hart, Peter Noonan, Michael Long, Robin Shreeve and Ana Porta Cubas. Former colleague Joanna Palser provided valuable advice on the structure.

References

Australian Bureau of Statistics (ABS) (2012a), 'Financing Education', *Year Book Australia 2012* (1301.0). Canberra.

— (2012b), *Research and Experimental Development, Higher Education Organisations* (8111.0). Canberra.

— (2013a), *Average Weekly Earnings* (6302.0). Canberra.

— (2013b), *Education and Work* (6227.0). Canberra.

Australian Education International (AEI) (2013), *International Student Enrolments in Australia 1994–2013*. Canberra.

Australian Qualifications Framework Council (AQFC) (2013), *Australian Qualifications Framework Second Edition 2013*. Adelaide.

Australian Skills Quality Authority (ASQA) (2013), *Training for Aged and Community Care in Australia, A National Strategic Review of Registered Training Organisations Offering Aged and Community Care Sector Training*. Melbourne.

Australian Workforce and Productivity Agency (AWPA) (2013), *Future Focus, 2013 National Workforce Development Strategy*. Canberra.

Bannikoff, K. (2013), 'TAFE: How a Good Idea Got Buggered Up', *The Australian TAFE Teacher* 47 (1), 14–17.

Bradley, D. (2008), *Review of Australian Higher Education, Final Report*. Canberra: Department of Education, Employment and Workplace Relations (DEEWR).

Burke, G. (2000), 'Education and the Economy: A Review of the Main Assertions', in T. Seddon and L. Angus (eds), *Beyond Nostalgias: Reshaping Australian Education*. Melbourne: Australian Council for Educational Research (ACER).

— (2013), 'Skills for Growth and Social Inclusion', in P. Smyth and J. Buchanan (eds), *Inclusive Growth in Australia, Social Policy as Economic Investment*. Melbourne: Allen & Unwin.

Council of Australian Governments (COAG) (2012a), *National Agreement for Skills and Workforce Development*. Canberra.

— (2012b), *National Partnership Agreement on Skills Reform*. Canberra.

Coutts, J. (2010), *Measuring the Socio-Economic Status of Higher Education Students, Equity, Performance and Indigenous Branch Higher Education Group*. Canberra: DEEWR.

Davis, G. (2013), *The Australian Idea of a University*, Newman Lecture at Mannix College. Melbourne: Monash University.

Deloite Access Economics (DAE) (2011), *The Impact of Changes to Student Contribution Levels and Repayment Thresholds on the Demand for Higher Education*. DEEWR: Canberra.

— (2012), *Econometric Analysis of the Australian Apprenticeships Incentives Program*. Canberra: DEEWR.

Department of Education (DE) (2013a), *Finance 2012 and Finance 2011*. Canberra.

— (2013b), *Selected Higher Education Statistics*. Canberra.

— (2014), *Higher Education Participation and Partnerships Program*. Canberra.

Department of Industry, Innovation, Climate Change, Science, Research and Tertiary Education (DI) (2013), *Annual Report for 2012–13*. Canberra.

Dow, L. K. (2011), *Review of Student Income Support Reforms*. Canberra: Department of Education, Employment and Workplace Relations (DEEWR).

Dow, L. K. and Braithwaite, V. (2013), *Review of Higher Education Regulation, Report*. Canberra: Australian Government.

Gonski, D. (2011), *Review of Funding for Schooling – Final Report*. Adelaide: DEEWR.

Goozee, G. (2001), *The Development of TAFE in Australia*. Adelaide: NCVER.

Guthrie, H., Stanwick, J. and Karmel, T. (2011), *Pathways: Developing the Skills of Australia's Workforce*. Adelaide: NCVER.

Karmel, T. (2011), 'As Clear as Mud: Defining Vocational Education and Training', National Centre for Vocational Education Research, Adelaide.

Karmel, T., Mlotkowski, P. and Awodeyi, T. (2008), *Is VET Vocational? The Relevance of Training to the Occupations of Vocational Education and Training Graduates*. Adelaide: NCVER.

Knight, M. (2011), *Strategic Review of the Student Visa Program 2011*. Canberra: DEEWR.

Lee, W. S. and Coelli, M. (2010), *Analysis of Private Returns to Vocational Education and Training*. Adelaide: NCVER.

Lomax-Smith, J., Watson, L. and Webster, B. (Expert Panel) (2011), *Higher Education Base Funding Review*, Final report. Canberra: DEEWR.

Long, M. and Shah, C. (2008), *Private Returns to Vocational Education and Training Qualifications*. NCVER: Adelaide.

National Centre for Vocational Education Research (NCVER) (2012), *Tertiary Education 2010*. Adelaide.

— (2013a), *Financial Information 2012*. Adelaide.

— (2013b), *Students and Courses 2012*. Adelaide.

— (2013c), *Employers' Use and Views of the VET System 2013*. Adelaide.

— (2013d), *Student Outcomes Survey 2013*. Adelaide.

— (2013e), *The Likelihood of Completing a VET Qualification 2008–11.*

National Skills Standards Council (NSSC) (2013), *Improving Vocational Education and Training – The Case for a New System.* Melbourne.

National VET Equity Advisory Council (NVEAC) (2013), *National Report on Social Equity in VET 2013.* Melbourne.

Norton, A. (2012), *Graduate Winners, Assessing the Public and Private, Benefits of Higher Education.* Melbourne: Grattan Institute.

— (2013), *The Online Evolution: When Technology Meets Tradition in Higher Education.* Melbourne: Grattan Institute.

Organisation for Economic Cooperation and Development (OECD) (2013), *Education at a Glance.*

Productivity Commission (2011a), *Caring for Older Australian.* Melbourne.

— (2011b), *Vocational Education and Training Workforce.* Melbourne.

— (2014), *Report on Government Services.* Melbourne.

Skills Australia (2010), *Australia's Workforce Futures, A Workforce Development Strategy.* Canberra.

— (2011), *Skills for Prosperity, A Roadmap for Vocational Education and Training.* Canberra.

Thomson, S., De Bortoli, L. and Buckley, S. (2013), *PISA 2012: How Australia Measures Up, ACER.* Melbourne.

Times Higher Education (2013), *World-University Rankings 2012–13.*

Watson, L., Hagel, P. and Chesters, J. (2013), *A Half-Open Door: Pathways for VET Award Holders into Australian Universities.* NCVER: Adelaide.

4

Australia: Aboriginal Education

Anthony Welch, Patricia Konigsberg, Judith Rochecouste and
Glenys Collard

Introduction: learning in traditional Aboriginal society

Education is mostly thought of in institutional terms as formal schooling and as an artefact of 'advanced' cultures (East or West). Both conceptions are false. Aboriginal education is arguably the oldest form worldwide: perhaps 40,000–60,000 years old.

Learning in traditional Aboriginal society, now largely only seen in remote communities and nowhere practised fully, did not occur in institutions and would today be called informal. Generally, small communities practised forms of education that were shaped by both the local environment (landscape) and deeply held spiritual values that linked people to animals, the land and a continuity of existence. People came from the dreamtime (spirit world), were attached to the land and their totem, and returned to the dreamtime after death:

> No English words are good enough to give a sense of the links between an Aboriginal group and its homeland. Our word 'home', as warm and suggestive though it be, does not match the Aboriginal word that may mean 'camp', 'hearth', 'country', 'everlasting home', 'totem place', 'life source', 'spirit centre' and much else all in one. Our word 'land' is too spare and meagre. (Stanner, 1979: p. 230)

Education was a practical initiation into culture: learning by doing. It was 'not so much a preparation for life, as an experience of life itself' (Hart, 1974 cited in Welch, 1996: p. 27). It was oral (there being no written forms) and was in principle lifelong, as individuals gained deeper and more sophisticated understanding of stories and rituals that were in turn passed on to the rising generation. Elders were respected and seen as repositories of wisdom. Moral and physical sanctions existed for breaking the law, or the core code of values (e.g. disrespecting elders, or eloping with a non-kinship partner), and varied according to the transgression. Spearing, or being banned from the community, was a common form of punishment.

Education began early, largely via imitation and practice. Based on songs, myths and stories, education was oral, experiential, integrated and based on a spiritually informed cosmology. The sexual division of labour within the tribe meant that patterns of education were strongly gendered: girls learned from older women; boys from older men. Kinship was an important component, and so it was often the mother's brother who might have particular responsibility for education of a young boy, for example. Indeed, 'kinship welded Koori life together' (Miller, 1985: p. 2; Berndt and Berndt, 1988). People lived in harmony with their environment and learned appropriate skills: boys would learn hunting and tracking, while girls learned to dig and forage for food and look after younger children.

While no written evidence exists, and clearly no census data, it is estimated that at the time of European colonization in the late eighteenth century there were perhaps 250 languages and 500 community groups, totalling perhaps 300,000 individuals. Aboriginal groups were spread across the country and formed linguistic families, some of which still exist (Horton, 1996). Distinctive economic structures depended on local environments (fishing in coastal locations, hunting in desert locations). Shortage of water in desert settings was often associated with a peripatetic existence. Unlike Western societies, economic activity was not oriented towards material gain, but part of kinship and mutual obligations (Rose, 1987; Butlin, 1993). Education was unitary and unifying: it explained one's role and place in society, one's relationship to the land, to kin and to spirit ancestors. Birth was not the beginning of life, death not the end. Spiritual beliefs were expressed through art, music, dance and stories, each of which was learned and refined over the life course. More sophisticated understandings came with adulthood and later life.

Colonialism: the clash of civilizations

The onset of British colonialism in the late eighteenth century saw this traditional world overturned, notwithstanding vigorous, protracted resistance in the form of guerilla warfare (Willmott, 1987; Reynolds, 1990, 2006). Indeed, according to one of Australia's most senior historians of Aboriginal history,

> Black resistance in its many forms was an inescapable feature of life on the fringes of European settlement from the first months of Sydney Cove to the early years of the 20th century . . . . every acre of land in these districts (Sydney and its surrounds) was won from the Aborigines by bloodshed and warfare. (Reynolds, 2006: p. 67, see also p. 107, 168 et passim)[1]

Colonialism disrupted every aspect of Aboriginal existence, as evident in the following quote:

> . . . the newcomers impinged on accustomed patterns of life, occupying the flat, open land and monopolizing water. Indigenous animals were driven away, plant life eaten or trampled (by introduced animals such as cattle, horse and sheep) and Aboriginals pushed back into marginal country – mountains, swamps, waterless neighbourhoods. Patterns of seasonal migration broke down, areas free of Europeans were over utilized, and eventually depleted of flora and fauna. Food became scarcer, and available in less and less variety, and even access to water was often difficult. (Reynolds, 2006: p. 72)

This destruction included traditional educative practices, which were difficult if not impossible to sustain in the face of such onslaught. The Aboriginal population, estimated to have been around 300,000 in 1788, declined dramatically over the following century, to little more than 50,000 (Reynolds, 2006: p. 127).

The British were not the first outsiders to discover Australia. People from various Melanesian groups of Papua New Guinea and the Torres Strait Islands as well as the Maccassans from Indonesia had ongoing early contact with mainland Australians. The Dutch had landed in the early seventeenth century and it is quite possible that Chinese (Ming dynasty) Vice Admirals (Hong Bao and Zhou Man) contacted northern Australian tribes in the early fifteenth century. African coins found on a remote northern island raise the tantalizing possibility of visits by Arab traders almost 1,000 years ago (The National, 2013).

Referring to the Aboriginal population, the British explorer Captain Cook explained in 1770, 'They live in a tranquility . . . not disturbed by inequality of condition. The Earth and Sea furnish them with all things necessary for life' (cited in Welch, 1996: p. 25). Sadly, however, this view was the exception. The most common view was informed by the doctrine of *Terra Nullius*: of an empty land to which the white man could legitimately lay claim. This was a form of internal colonialism, in some ways analogous to the situation of the Ainu peoples of Hokkaido whereby thousands of years of history, and close relationship to the land, were generally ignored by colonists (Shimomura, 2013). An early English settler's characterization gave voice to a view broadly felt and which situated Aboriginal peoples at the base of a commonly assumed civilizational pyramid:

> If their intellectual functions . . . are thus so far above debasement, how is it that the abject animal state in which the [Aborigines] live . . . should place them at the very zero of civilization, constituting in a measure the connecting link between man and the monkey tribe? (Cunningham, 1827, cited in Welch, 1996: p. 28)

Informed by prevailing theories of Social Darwinism and Laissez-faire economic liberalism, as well as a Lockean interpretation of Christianity which held that only those who tilled the land could lay claim to it, white settlers (with some honourable exceptions) rode roughshod over Aboriginal institutions and ideologies. The common understanding of Darwinism, for example, afforded no comfort to Aboriginal cultures:

> The survival of the fittest means that might – wisely used – is right. And thus we invoke and remorselessly fulfil the inexorable law of natural selection (or of demand and supply) when exterminating the inferior Australian and Maori races, and we appropriate their patrimony as coolly as Ahab did the vineyards of Naboth, though in diametrical opposition to all our favourite theories of right and justice – thus proved to be unnatural and false. (Goodwin, 1964 cited in Welch, 1996: pp. 30–31)

Honourable exceptions notwithstanding, racism was also often present in prevailing forms of Christianity which held that Aboriginal peoples held 'no religious beliefs' lacked 'all moral views', and that it was 'the design of Providence that the inferior races should pass away before the superior races' (Mulvaney, 1967 cited in Welch, 1996: p. 31). Nineteenth-century anthropology too assigned Aboriginal cultures a very low place in the prevailing racial hierarchy. Early journals such as the *Australasian Anthropological Journal* and the *Science of Man* legitimated techniques such as craniometry to lend scientific credence to what was in fact simple cultural difference, but which was presented as scientific evidence of Aboriginal inferiority. Lastly, and paradoxically, Enlightenment ideals of freedom and equality were withheld from Aboriginal society, which was seen as too primitive to fit these ideals:

> the egalitarian and libertarian ideals of the Enlightenment spread by the American and French revolutions, conflicted of course, with racism, but they also paradoxically contributed to its development. Faced with the blatant

contradiction between the treatment of slaves and colonial people, and the official rhetoric of freedom and equality, Europeans and North Americans began to dichotomise humanity into men and sub-men (or the 'civilized' and the 'savages'). (Van den Berghe, 1967 cited in Welch, 1996: p. 32)

Effectively, this constellation of values (a potent, if poisonous, cocktail of Christianity, Science and Capitalism) constituted a form of internal colonialism in which both groups occupy the same territory and which, in effect, can socialize the colonized into an acceptance of their inferior status, power and wealth (e.g. Native Americans, or the various native communities of Africa) (Altbach and Kelly, 1984). If Aboriginal people were afforded schooling at all, it was mostly very rudimentary in form, leading only to the most basic occupations (housework for girls, unskilled farm work for boys). Curriculum was based on the 4 Rs: Reading, Writing, Reckoning (arithmetic) and (the Christian) Religion, paying insufficient attention to Aboriginal values or practices. Over the course of the twentieth century, this gradually evolved into a more assimilationist era in which it was assumed that simply opening up black access to unchanged white educational institutions would guarantee progress/equality. In turn, as this limited conception also proved inadequate leaving too many Aboriginal pupils behind, it was succeeded by a more integrationist era which was accompanied by rising black unrest. The current era of 'self-determination, self-management and reconciliation' is one in which funding is still highly controlled and compliance to multiple and competing state and Commonwealth (federal) agencies and ministries is complex, technical and burdensome. This is especially the case for remote communities where educational levels are the lowest in the country, where the first language is still largely an Aboriginal language and where communities are most dependent on outside support (Hughes, 2007, 2008; Scrymgour, 2008). This is not to diminish the problems experienced by Aboriginal people in urban settings who often feel that they become invisible within a non-Aboriginal town or city environment, that they have no support at all and that agencies lack the necessary understanding to be able to help.

Current context

The 2011 Census data showed that Aboriginal and Torres Strait Islander (ATSI) people comprised 2.5 per cent of the Australian population, but the proportion varied greatly by state and territory (see Table 4.1). For

Table 4.1 Indigenous population status by State and Territory, 2011

State/territory	Number of Aboriginal and Torres Strait Islanders	% of total ATSI population (national)	ATSI % of total population (state)
New South Wales	172,624	31.5	2.5
Victoria	37,991	6.9	0.7
Queensland	155,825	28.4	3.6
South Australia	30,431	5.5	1.9
Western Australia	69,665	12.7	3.1
Tasmania	19,625	3.6	4.0
Northern Territory	56,779	10.4	26.8
Australian Capital Territory	5,184	0.9	1.5
Total	548,370	100.0	2.5

Source: Adapted from ABS (2011a–c), Census Counts – Aboriginal and Torres Straits Islander Peoples. www.abs.gov.au/ausstats/abs@.nsf/Lookup/2075.0main+features32011.

the purposes of this chapter, Australian ATSI peoples (i.e. the Indigenous inhabitants of the islands between Australia and New Guinea) are referred to collectively under the terms Aboriginal or Indigenous. However, due to limitations in length, the very different history of Islander peoples is beyond the scope of this chapter. The analysis here, therefore, focuses on Aboriginal experiences generally.

Currently, across Australia teachers are still often poorly prepared for teaching Aboriginal students, staff turnover is high in regional and remote areas and student attendance and achievement levels remain low, especially in remote communities (Gonski, 2011). Notwithstanding its effectiveness, bilingual education was replaced in the Northern Territory with Two-Way Learning, where English was to be taught exclusively in the morning and, if decided by the community in consultation with the Education Department, the locally endorsed Aboriginal language in the afternoon (Government of Northern Territory, 2008). There is still some debate as to how comprehensively the Territory's *Transforming Indigenous* Education policy of 2008 has been implemented particularly with regard to language provision. Although there are currently no definitive data, it is widely claimed that some 250 Aboriginal languages were spoken at the time of initial European contact (Schmidt, 1990), but no more than 100 had survived by 1971 (many with fewer than 10 speakers) (AIAS, 1971). Other sources, however, claim the existence of 145 Aboriginal languages in 2010, of which 110 were critically endangered (House of Representatives, 2012). In some communities, where the local language is still primary, local teachers (more commonly teacher aides) are employed together with white teachers to teach the language at school. ATSI 'elders' may also be called upon to impart local, cultural knowledge.

In all education sectors, while rates of participation and success have improved, the gap between Aboriginal and non-Aboriginal Australians is still large. For example, in 2011 22 per cent of Aboriginal 4-year-olds lived in remote regions of Australia and of these 82 per cent were attending a preschool programme (COAG, 2013). In later years of schooling however, Aboriginal students are less likely to participate in NAPLAN[2] testing for literacy and numeracy raising some question over these results. Nonetheless, current results show a decrease in the gap between Aboriginal and non-Aboriginal reading scores at the primary school level but an increase for Year 9 (the secondary level) (COAG, 2013). However, the reverse was evident for numeracy scores (COAG, 2013). Nonetheless, remoteness still places Aboriginal students at a disadvantage with achievement in both literacy and numeracy continuing to decrease among these students (COAG, 2013).

More positive outcomes have been recorded for Year 12 completion with attainment rising from 47.4 per cent of Aboriginal students nationally in 2006 to 53.9 per cent in 2011, although this is still markedly less than in some other indigenous contexts (COAG, 2013; Shimomura, 2013). A considerable gap persists between Aboriginal and non-Aboriginal students at university; however in 2010 Aboriginal students formed 1.4 per cent of total university enrolments, despite Aboriginal people comprising 2.5 per cent of the Australian population (DEEWR, 2009; Behrendt et al., 2012). Moreover, 68.6 per cent of non-Aboriginal students commencing a degree in 2005 had completed in 2010, while only 40.8 per cent of ATSI students had done so (Behrendt et al., 2012).

In the vocational sector, Aboriginal 20–64 year olds with, or working towards, a Certificate III qualification or above rose from 30.2 per cent to 35.6 per cent between 2006 and 2011, contributing to an overall increase in postschool qualifications among the Aboriginal population (COAG, 2013).

The most recent Behrendt Report[3] recommended that better pathways between vocational education and training (VET) and higher education be developed, with parity with the non-Aboriginal population set as the benchmark. In addition, better and more extensive use of IT should be undertaken for remote students, and universities should adopt a whole-of-university approach to Aboriginal student success, focusing on boosting retention and completion rates (Behrendt et al., 2012).

Two-Way learning: a case study

What the earlier sketch demonstrates is that, while much has been done, much remains to be done to redress persistent and deep disadvantage. While rates of Aboriginal participation and retention in education have increased markedly in recent years, the gap between Aboriginal and non-Aboriginal achievement remains wide. It is also very important to remind ourselves of at least two further points.

First, Aboriginal Australia is highly diverse geographically, socially and educationally. For example, as shown earlier, rates of educational participation, retention and success in remote communities are often well behind those of urban dwellers and continue to be by far the worst in the country for remote desert communities.

Secondly, the character of Australian federalism means that, constitutionally, education is a state responsibility (for more, see Chapter 1 in this volume), hence there are variations from state to state. Also varying are the proportions that the Aboriginal population occupies compared with the overall population (see Table 4.1), as well as the proportions that live in urban as opposed to rural and remote settings. It is among the latter that Aboriginal languages are often still the primary languages. It is in this spirit that the following case study from the geographically vast state of Western Australia in which Aboriginal people occupy 3.8 per cent of the population (second among all Australian states and territories) is presented (ABS, 2007). It focuses on the complex and contested arena of language and how this affects educational success.

The Western Australian Education Department administers one of the largest jurisdictions in the world, covering an area of 2,645,615 square kilometres. The Department employs 20,560 teachers (of whom 167 are Aboriginal) and in addition 606 Aboriginal and Islander Education Officers. Aboriginal students make up 8.29 per cent of the general student population (7,935 Aboriginal students in remote locations and 14,310 in regional and metropolitan centres) (Western Australian Department of Education, 2012). It is estimated that approximately 85–90 per cent of these students speak Aboriginal English (a dialect of English now recognized by linguists, see later) as either their first or their second language. In view of these statistics and the ongoing low achievement of Aboriginal students, the Western Australian Education Department has supported extensive academic research, staff training and materials development to improve the outcomes of these learners.

In particular, a reciprocal Two-Way bidialectal approach has been strongly promoted through the Department's *ABC of Two-Way Literacy and Learning*

Project. This 'Two-Way' approach calls for educators to critically reflect on the unidirectional method of teaching that is conventionally used to assist Aboriginal learners. The *ABC of Two-Way Literacy and Learning* uses Aboriginal English research data to guide both Aboriginal and non-Aboriginal educators towards exploring language difference including the deeper level of cultural meaning. This includes taking account of the different histories of Aboriginal and non-Aboriginal people in Australia and acknowledging the differing conceptual understandings, in order to construct mutually trustful relationships between Aboriginal and non-Aboriginal educators.

Additionally, the Western Australian Two-Way bidialectal approach advocates programme delivery inclusive of both Aboriginal and non-Aboriginal students and sets in place teaching and learning practices where both Aboriginal and non-Aboriginal learners can learn from each other. From its inception, the *ABC of Two-Way Literacy and Learning Project* has maintained strong ties with the Aboriginal community and emphasizes respect for, and acceptance of, the different ways that Aboriginal students speak English and interpret knowledge and experience (Malcolm, 1997).

English deconstructed: the Australian situation

English established itself in Australia in various ways. First, it was *regionalized* as speakers of different British English dialects settled in Australia. It absorbed local influences and led to a new Australian norm. *Australian English*, as it is known today, has two main socio-lectal varieties (Collins and Blair, 2001). Australian Vernacular English (Pawley, 2008) is a colloquial variety spoken by many working class and country men and women across the nation, while Standard Australian English (SAE) has been heavily influenced by Standard British English and codified in dictionaries and style guides. SAE is used in Australia's educational, political, economic, legal and social institutions.

English in Australia was also *indigenized* by speakers who spoke traditional Aboriginal languages and Aboriginal people continue to maintain this variety. Developing from a contact situation, English was pidginized and used as an auxiliary language alongside traditional languages. Eventually, as Aboriginal people were displaced from their lands and even prohibited from speaking their own languages, the pidgin form was used for communication with other Aboriginal people. In some places, subsequent generations of Aboriginal people adopted this pidginized English as their main language, turning it into a creole.

In the course of time, under the pressure of the majority culture, some of these pidgins and creoles came under renewed English influence, and Aboriginal forms of English emerged. At present, 'we are now in a situation where levelling has taken place across Aboriginal English varieties to the extent that we can say that (despite regional differences), there is one Aboriginal English. However, we cannot say that Aboriginal English is a *form* of Australian English, in that it is fundamentally different in origin, structure and conceptual base' (I. G. Malcolm personal communication, 2 September 2012). Thus Aboriginal English is a separate dialect.

It is uncommon for educators to take account of possible discrepancies in their Aboriginal students' understandings of SAE. In primary schools, when it comes to literacy instruction, the focus is mainly on spelling, reading and writing without taking into account dialectal variation. By the time students reach secondary school, the emphasis generally shifts to the study and production of the various types of texts or genres, ranging from the literary to exposition, and texts needed for study and daily living. Literacy is further emphasized in the face of high-stakes testing. However, the introduction of standardized National Assessment Program Literacy and Numeracy (NAPLAN) tests in Years 3, 5, 7 and 9 in recent years has had the affect of narrowing the range of approaches to literacy and content, and is undermining opportunities to acknowledge the existence of other dialects (e.g. Aboriginal English) in schools. Moreover, it fails to accommodate the different paths to literacy and the acquisition of standard English language experienced by non-native speakers of SAE, notably by Aboriginal Australians (Wigglesworth et al., 2011; House of Representatives, 2012; The Conversation, 2012; ACTA, 2013). The validity of Aboriginal English as the students' home language, as the language they use to describe their experience and worldview and as the language that carries their cultural heritage, is rarely recognized. Too frequently, it has been seen as a non-standard linguistic code with poor pronunciation and incorrect grammar that needs eradication or remediation.

Aboriginal English differs from Australian English in more ways than just sounds, words and syntax, however. The differences lie deeper, in specific text forms, pragmatics and underlying conceptualizations. For most Aboriginal learners, the language they hear at school is not what they are accustomed to at home. This means they are more likely to misunderstand or get confused by SAE (Sharifian et al., 2012). As a result, students become distracted and lose interest: behaviour that is quickly interpreted as a lack of concentration or performance ability. Consequently, Aboriginal learners are often mis-diagnosed with learning difficulties or disabilities. Once this occurs, the students adopt a negative self-belief, doubting their own ability to succeed and resigning themselves to failure. Without awareness that the underlying problem is the difference between Aboriginal English and Standard English, both teachers and students struggle finding ways to improve.

Two-Way bidialectal education recognizes that Aboriginal learners have to work with the two dialects for maximum success. But first they need to recognize the existence of the two dialects and become aware of the differences between the two. This needs to occur at all levels of language – at the level of linguistic structures and features, and at the deeper cultural conceptual level. Within the Two-Way bidialectal approach, Aboriginal English is accepted as an alternative medium of classroom expression for its speakers. This is important in that it provides the learners with a tool for learning as well as a basis for expanding their current repertoire to include SAE (Malcolm et al., 2003).

For Two-Way bidialectal Education to be really effective, both Aboriginal and non-Aboriginal conceptualizations of the world and how we express them need to be exposed. This can only effectively occur when an ongoing genuine exchange of ideas and experiences can take place in which both parties agree to approach collaboration without prejudice and ulterior motives. The flow of knowledge needs to be educative to each party and it needs to go both ways. To date, this has been most effective when Aboriginal and non-Aboriginal educators work as partners in *Two-Way Teams*. In schools, Two-Way Teams can be a non-Aboriginal teacher and an Aboriginal and Islander Education Officer. However, other scenarios include the collaboration between a non-Aboriginal teacher and an Aboriginal Language Teacher or community member, or in the adult education sector between a non-Aboriginal lecturer and an Aboriginal student. Using a framework that includes 'relationship building', 'mutual comprehension building', 'repertoire building' and 'skill building' (Malcolm and Truscott, 2012), Two-Way Teams learn about each other's words and language use. In particular, the importance of the home dialect (in this case, Aboriginal English) to the learner is acknowledged and valued.

The management of Two-Way bidialectal education

The recognition of Aboriginal English

Research into Aboriginal English commenced in Australia in 1960s, first in Queensland, then in the Northern Territory, and since the 1970s in Western

Australia. Other studies in New South Wales, Victoria and South Australia have since confirmed that Aboriginal English exists throughout Australia (Malcolm, 1995).

After two successful joint projects with Edith Cowan University in Western Australia (Malcolm, 1995; Malcolm et al., 1999), the *ABC of Two-Way Literacy and Learning* was conceptualized in 1998. This project instigated a Two-Way approach to both research and education and investigated how issues such as the recognition of culture and home language and the structure of the learning environment influence educational processes, and how Aboriginal English can be effectively utilized by Aboriginal learners in the classroom (Malcolm, 1995). These and subsequent projects have produced numerous research publications and curriculum support materials gradually enhancing the empowerment of Aboriginal and non-Aboriginal educators.

The establishment and maintenance of the *ABC Project*

The establishment and maintenance of the *ABC Project* within a government department did not come without challenges. The project required travel across the vast area of Western Australia (approximately 2.6 million square kilometres) to work with all leading Aboriginal and non-Aboriginal educators and to garner community support. Workshops had to be conducted, first with Aboriginal educators and then with non-Aboriginal cohorts to ensure that each group had the opportunity to bring out the issues important to them without having to compromise their concerns by being sensitive to other points of view. Workshop content concentrated on raising awareness about Aboriginal English by highlighting the need to value and take account of dialect difference by incorporating *English as an Additional Language and Standard English as an Additional Dialect* (EAL/D) strategies in teaching, and by emphasizing Two-Way processes (Department of Education and Department of Education and Training, 2012).

To develop this further, the *ABC of Two-Way Literacy and Learning Capacity Building Project* was established in collaboration with the Department of Training and Workforce Development in 2004. This project used a cascading model of action-learning professional development. Fourteen Two-Way Teams from nine education regions were trained over 12 days during the course of 1 year, and supported by centrally based Aboriginal and non-Aboriginal educators and academics. Each team delivered professional learning to a further 2 Teams in their region, making a total of 42 trained educators. Much progress was made by participating schools and training sites. However, in many cases the ongoing implementation had to rely on the goodwill of those involved to ensure its sustainability. To improve dissemination, the *Tracks to Two-Way Learning Resource* was then developed (Department of Education and Department of Education and Training, 2012).

Influencing system-wide policy

The *ABC of Two-Way Literacy and Learning* project has also implicitly influenced system-wide policy. The grounds for systemic recognition of Aboriginal learners were laid in 1988 with a report led by Dr Paul Hughes, which officially recognized for the first time that educators needed to ensure that the curriculum reinforces rather than suppresses the cultural identity of Aboriginal learners. Some years later, the *National Review of Education for Aboriginal and Torres Strait Islander People* (DEET, 1994, 1995) recognized the need for support of Aboriginal English-speaking students and stressed the need for 'Two-Way education'; however, it failed to recognize the positive effects that a learner's first language or dialect can have on achieving bicultural objectives (Malcolm and Königsberg, 2007).

In 1995, a policy on Aboriginal English was commissioned by the Department of Education, Western Australia. Although the policy was never officially implemented, this impetus had far-reaching effects on the future development of curriculum in the state. For example, the term *Aboriginal English* was embedded in Education Department's major policy document (Curriculum Council of Western Australia, 1998). In 2003, a review of the *Achievements of Aboriginal and Torres Strait Islander Students in English Language Competence Project* (AAAJ Consulting Group, 2003) recognized the need to use Aboriginal English in course design and student assessment. In 2006, the Western Australian *English as an Additional Language or Dialect (EAL/D) Course* recognized the acceptance of Aboriginal English speakers into a course designed specifically for those learning SAE as an additional language or dialect (Curriculum Council, 2006). In the same year, recognition of the critical importance of Aboriginal cultures and languages, including Aboriginal English, as well as the need to explicitly teach SAE was finally adopted nationally with the publication of the *Australian Directions in Indigenous Education 2005–2008 Report* (MCEETYA and Curriculum Council, 2006). This document provided directions in Aboriginal Education at a national level.

The inclusion of the term *Aboriginal English* and the explicit teaching of standard English as an additional dialect in the newly developed *Australian*

Curriculum (ACARA, 2010) is the result of much of the supporting research and advocacy contributed by people involved in the work of the *ABC of Two-Way Literacy and Learning*.

Influencing system-wide implementation

The most recent resource, the *Tracks to Two-Way Learning*, which incorporates past key research findings and related educator training materials, is already guiding ongoing implementation. Two recent Western Australian initiatives show how the materials and guidance provided in the *Tracks to Two-Way Learning* have led to additional effective initiatives. The *Language, Literacy and Learning Two-Way Professional Learning Course* (Department of Education, 2013) uses the *Tracks to Two-Way Learning* as an underpinning to teacher training. The resource is being used within the Department of Education to improve bidialectal approaches to language and literacy learning in early childhood education. Another major resource currently being developed by the Department of Training and Workforce Development is a *Certificate III in Two-Way Aboriginal Liaison*. When accredited, this certificate course will introduce a new approach to teaching adult literacy and numeracy that values and capitalizes on Aboriginal English (or creole) and gives appropriate recognition to the social, cognitive and linguistic practices of Aboriginal people who use Aboriginal English or an Australian creole as their first or 'home' language. The researchers and academics involved in this work continue to support the view that a sustainable, organic and inclusive cultural and linguistic balance can be achieved within *mainstream* education and training. However, since these projects are long-term endeavours, a passion for Two-Way learning and an open-minded appreciation of, and genuine interest in, cultural differences are all essential for its success.

Conclusion

Despite the fact that Aboriginal education is the most ancient form of structured learning (much older than Plato, or Confucius), it was massively disrupted by colonialism from which it has never really recovered. While rates of participation among Aboriginal students in current education systems have improved significantly, their achievement levels still lag well behind the national average especially at upper secondary and higher education levels (Otsuka,

2008; Behrendt et al., 2012). While the Behrendt Report recommendations may show a way forward, at least in higher education, three factors still stand out: more respect by non-Aboriginal Australians; the dependence of success in higher education on achievements in lower levels of education; and the need for considerable improvement in the health, housing and financial hardships faced by Aboriginal families which obstruct educational achievement in the next generation. More than 20 years after the landmark Aboriginal Deaths in Custody report charted the dimensions of disadvantage (Australian Government, 1991), more than 20 years after the Supreme Court's Mabo decision finally granted recognition of Aboriginal land rights and 5 years after the then Prime Minister issued a formal apology to the 'Stolen Generation' in Australia's national parliament,[4] racism and disadvantage still divide the country. It exists in both social and economic terms: ATSI people aged 18 years and over received a median gross weekly equivalized household (GWEH) income of $445 per week, cf. the non-Indigenous median GWEH income of $746 per week (Behrendt et al., 2012). In education, while great strides have been made and substantial sums invested, participation and retention rates still significantly lag national averages, especially at secondary and higher education and in remote communities. In 2010, 45.4 per cent of ATSI pupils remained enrolled from Year 7 to Year 12, compared to 79.4 per cent of non-Indigenous pupils (Behrendt et al., 2012: p. 6).

This pattern of disadvantage is not restricted to schooling outcomes. While ATSI students made up an encouraging 4.6 per cent of all enrolments in vocational education and training (VET) in 2010 (NCVER, 2010), they are eight times more likely to enrol in a VET course than in university study. For non-Aboriginal students, the ratio is 2:1 (Behrendt et al., 2012: p. 7).

Within the higher education sub-sector, in 2010 ATSI students made up 1.4 per cent of all enrolments in university, 1.0 per cent of total full-time equivalent university staff and 0.8 per cent of academic staff. 2010 saw 47.3 per cent of the ATSI enrollees (of whom two-thirds were women) enter university on the basis of their prior education, relative to 83.0 per cent of non-Indigenous student population. In that same year, 40.8 per cent of ATSI students who commenced a bachelor course in 2005 had completed their course, compared to 68.6 per cent of non-Indigenous students (Behrendt et al., 2012: p. 8).

The pattern of difference sketched earlier translates into poorer workplace outcomes. For example, ATSI people made up just 0.8 per cent of the professional workforce in 2006, 0.6 per cent of the managerial workforce and remain less likely to have a degree or higher qualification compared to non-Indigenous professionals (Behrendt et al., 2013: pp. 9–10). Much remains to be done therefore to redress decades of educational disadvantage.

Acknowledgement

The authors would like to acknowledge the valuable comments of Emeritus Professor Ian Malcolm, Margaret McHugh and Cheryl Wiltshire on drafts of this paper.

Notes

1   In his earlier (1990) book, Reynolds acknowledged that resistance was by no means universal; that accommodation was also part of the story.
2   The National Assessment Program – Literacy and Numeracy (NAPLAN).
3   The Behrendt Report or *Review of Higher Education Access and Outcomes for Aboriginal and Torres Strait Islander People* was commissioned by the Australian Government in response to an earlier *Review of Australian Higher Education* (Bradley et al., 2008), called the 'Bradley Review', which recommended commitment to improved higher education access and outcomes for people of Aboriginal and Torres Strait Islander descent.
4   In Australia, the term 'Stolen Generation' refers to Aboriginal people who were forcibly removed from their families, and who often grew up with little or no knowledge of their family's whereabouts, and their own origins.

References

AAAJ Consulting Group (2003), *Achievements of Aboriginal and Torres Strait Islander Students in English Language Competence Project*. Review conducted for the Curriculum Council of Western Australia, the Aboriginal Education and Training Council and the Department of Education and Training. Perth: Department of Education and Training.

Altbach, P. and Kelly, G. (1984), *Education and the Colonial Experience*. New Brunswick: Transaction Books.

Australian Bureau of Statistics (ABS) (2007), *Population Distribution, Aboriginal and Torres Strait Islander Australians, 2006* (Cat. No. 4705.0). Available at: http://www. abs.gov.au/ausstats/abs@.nsf/mf/4705.0 (Accessed: 28 March 2014).

— (2011a), *2011 Census Counts – Aboriginal and Torres Strait Islander People*. Available at: http://www.abs.gov.au/ausstats/abs@.nsf/Latestproducts/2075.0Main%20Features 32011?opendocument&tabname=Summary&prodno=2075.0&issue=2011&num=& view (Accessed: 28 March 2014).

— (2011b), *2011 Census Counts – Torres Strait Islander People*. Available at: http:// www.abs.gov.au/ausstats/abs@.nsf/Latestproducts/2075.0Main%20Features52011? opendocument&tabname=Summary&prodno=2075.0&issue=2011&num=&view (Accessed: 28 March 2014).

— (2011c), *2011 Census Counts – Aboriginal and Torres Strait Islander People in Indigenous Regions*. Available at: http://www.abs.gov.au/ausstats/abs@.nsf/ Latestproducts/2075.0Main%20Features42011?opendocument&tabname=Summary &prodno=2075.0&issue=2011&num=&view (Accessed: 28 March 2014).

Australian Council of TESOL Associations (ACTA) (2013), *Draft ACTA Response to NAPLAN Inquiry* (unpublished MS).

Australian Curriculum, Assessment and Reporting Authority (ACARA) (2010), *The Australian Curriculum*. Available at: http://www.australiancurriculum.edu.au/ (Accessed: 28 March 2014).

Australian Government (1991), *Royal Commission into Aboriginal Deaths in Custody*, Vols 1 and 2. Canberra: Australian Government Publishing Services.

Australian Institute of Aboriginal Studies (AIAS) (1971), *Papers on the Languages of Australian Aboriginals*. Canberra: AIAS.

Behrendt, L., Larkin, S., Griew, R. and Kelly, P. (2012), *Review of Higher Education Access and Outcomes for Aboriginal and Torres Strait Islander People Final Report*. Canberra: Australian Government. Available at: http:// www.innovation.gov.au/HigherEducation/IndigenousHigherEducation/ ReviewOfIndigenousHigherEducation/Pages/default.aspx (Accessed: 28 March 2014).

Berndt, R. M. and Berndt, C. H. (1988), *The World of the First Australians*. Canberra: Aboriginal Studies Press.

Bradley, D., Noonan, P., Nugent, H. and Scales, B. (2008), Review of Australian Higher Education Final Report. Available at: http://www.industry.gov.au/HigherEducation/ Documents/Review/PDF/Higher%20Education%20Review_Title%20page%20 to%20chapter%202.pdf (Accessed: 28 March 2014).

Butlin, N. (1993), *Economics and the Dreamtime*. Cambridge: Cambridge University Press.

Collins, P. and Blair, D. (2001), 'Language and Identity in Australia', in D. Blair and P. Collins (eds), *English in Australia*. Amsterdam: John Benjamins, pp. 1–13.

Conversation (The) (2012), *Anxious Kids Not Learning: The Real Effects of NAPLAN*. 16 September. Available at: http://theconversation.com/anxious-kids-not-learning-the-real-effects-of-naplan-9526/ (Accessed: 28 March 2014).

Council of Australia Governments (COAG) (2013), *Indigenous Reform 2011–12: Comparing performance across Australia*. Available at: http://www.

coagreformcouncil.gov.au/sites/default/files/files/National%20Indigenous%20 Reform%20Agreement%20-%2030%20April%202013(1).pdf (Accessed: 28 March 2014).

Cunningham, P. (1827), *Two Years in New South Wales* (2nd edn). London: Henry Colburn.

Curriculum Council (2006), *English as an Additional Language or Dialect Course of Study* (Accredited 23 November 2005). Perth: Curriculum Council.

Curriculum Council of Western Australia (1998), *Curriculum Framework for Kindergarten to Year 12 Education in Western Australia.* Perth: Curriculum Council of WA.

Department of Education (2013), *Language, Literacy and Learning Two-Way Professional Learning Course.* Perth: WestOne Services.

Department of Education and Department of Education and Training (2012), *Tracks to Two-Way Learning.* Perth: WestOne Services.

Department of Education, Employment and Workplace Relations (DEEWR) (2009), Number of Full-time and Fractional Full-time Indigenous Staff by State, Higher Education Provider, Function and Gender. Available at: www.deewr.gov.au (Accessed: 28 March 2014).

Department of Employment and Training (DEET) (1994), *National Review of Education for Aboriginal and Torres Strait Islander People, Summary and Recommendations.* Available at: http://www.voced.edu.au/node/17318 (Accessed: 28 March 2014).

— (1995), *National Review of Education for Aboriginal and Torres Strait Islander People, Final Report.* Available at: http://www.voced.edu.au/node/3317 (Accessed: 28 March 2014).

Gonski, D. (2011), *Review of Funding for Schooling* (Gonski Report). Available at: http://www.afr.com/rw/2009–2014/AFR/2012/02/20/Photos/c396c252–5b66–11e1–b121–7532de62367a_schooling%20funding.pdf (Accessed: 28 March 2014).

Goodwin, C. D. (1964), 'Evolutionary Theory in Australian Social Thought', *Journal of the History of Ideas* 25 (3), 393–416.

Government of Northern Territory (2008), *Transforming Indigenous Education.* Darwin: Government of Northern Territory.

Hart, M. (1974), *Traditional Aboriginal Education, Kulila.* Sydney: Australian and New Zealand Book Company.

Horton, D. (1996), *Aboriginal Australia* (Map). Canberra: Aboriginal Studies Press, AIATSIS and Auslig/Sinclair, Knight, Merz. Available at: http://www.ourlanguages.net.au/languages/language-maps.html (Accessed: 28 March 2014).

House of Representatives (2012), *Our Land, Our Languages.* Report from Standing Committee on Aboriginal and Torres Strait Islander Affairs. Available at: http://www.aph.gov.au/Parliamentary_Business/Committees/House_of_Representatives_Committees?url=/atsia/languages2/report.htm (Accessed: 28 March 2014).

Hughes, H. (2007), *Lands of Shame. Aboriginal and Torres Straits Islander Homelands in Transition.* Sydney: Centre for Independent Studies.

— (2008), *Indigenous Education in the Northern Territory*. Sydney: Centre for Independent Studies.

Malcolm, I. (1995), *Language and Communication Enhancement for Two-Way Education Report*. Perth: Edith Cowan University.

— (1997), 'Two-Way Bidialectal Education'. Paper presented to the American Association of Applied Linguistics Conference, Orlando, FL, 8–11 March.

Malcolm, I., Haig, Y., Konigsberg, P., Rochecouste, J., Collard, G., Hill, A. and Cahill, R. (1999), *Towards More User-Friendly Education for Speakers of Aboriginal English*. Perth: Education Department of Western Australia.

Malcolm, I., Kessaris, T. and Hunter, J. (2003), 'Contrasting Language in Indigenous and School Context', in Q. Beresford and G. Partington (eds), *Reform and Resistance in Aboriginal Education: The Australian Experience*. Perth: University of Western Australia Press, pp. 92–109.

Malcolm, I. and Königsberg, P. (2007), 'Bridging the Language Gap in Education', in G. Leitner and I. Malcolm (eds), *The Habitat of Australia's Aboriginal Languages; Past, Present and Future*. Berlin: Mouton de Gruyter, pp. 267–297.

Malcolm, I. G. and Truscott, A. (2012), 'English Without Shame: Two-Way Aboriginal Classrooms in Australia', in A. Yiakoumetti (ed.), *Harnessing Linguistic Variation to Improve Education*. Rethinking Education Series No. 8. Oxford: Peter Lang Publishing Group.

Miller, J. (1985), *Koori: A Will to Win*. Sydney: Angus & Robertson.

Ministerial Council on Education, Employment, Training and Youth Affairs (MCEETYA) and Curriculum Council (2006), *Australian Directions in Indigenous Education 2005–2008 Report*. Available at: http://www.mceetya.edu.au/verve/_resources/Australian_Directions_in_Indigenous_Education_2005–2008.pdf (Accessed: 28 March 2014).

Mulvaney, D. J. (1967), 'The Australian Aborigines 1606–1929: Opinion and Fieldwork', in J. Eastwoord and F. Smith (eds), *Historical Studies: Selected Articles* (First Series). Melbourne: Melbourne University Press, pp. 1–56.

National Centre for Vocational Education Research (NCVER) (2010), *VET Participation and Outcomes for Equity Groups*. Available at: http://www.nveac.natese.gov.au/__data/assets/pdf_file/0004/56353/Performance_Measures_2010_-_NCVER.pdf (Accessed: 28 March 2014).

Otsuka, S. (2008), *Culture and Achievement*. Saarbrücken: VDM Publishing Group.

Pawley, A. (2008), 'Australian Vernacular English: Some Grammatical Characteristics', in K. Burridge and B. Kortmann (eds), *Varieties of English: The Pacific and Australasia*. Berlin: Mouton de Gruyter, pp. 362–397.

Reynolds, H. (1990), *With the White People*. Melbourne: Penguin Books.

— (2006), *The Other Side of the Frontier. Aboriginal Resistance to the European Invasion of Australia*. Sydney: UNSW Press.

Rose, F. (1987), *The Traditional Mode of Production of the Australian Aborigine*. Sydney: Angus & Robertson.

Schmidt, A. (1990), *The Loss of Australia's Aboriginal Language Heritage*. Canberra: Aboriginal Studies Press.

Scrymgour, M. (2008), *Transforming Indigenous Education*. Speech to Northern Territory Legislative Assembly. Available at: 300408-Transforming-Indigenous-education-1.pdf (Accessed: 28 March 2014).

Sharifian, F., Truscott, A., Konigsberg, P., Malcolm, I. and Collard, G. (2012), *'Understanding Stories My Way': Aboriginal-English Speaking Students' (Mis)understanding of School Literacy Materials in Australian English*. Perth: Department of Education.

Shimomura, T. (2013), *A Comparative Study of Indigenous Education*. Saarbrücken: Lambert Academic Publishing.

Stanner, W. (1979), 'After the Dreaming', in W. Stanner (ed.), *White Man Got No Dreaming: Essays 1938–1973*. Canberra: Australian National University.

The National (2013), 'Were the African Coins Found in Australia from a Wrecked Arab Dhow?' Available at: http://www.thenational.ae/news/world/were-the-african-coins-found-in-australia-from-a-wrecked-arab-dhow (Accessed: 28 March 2014).

Van den Berghe, P. L. (1967). *Race and Racism: A Comparative Perspective*. New York: Wiley.

Welch, A. (1996), *Australian Education. Reform or Crisis?* Sydney: Allen & Unwin.

Western Australian Department of Education (2012), *Information Services, System Performance, Data: Term 2, 2012* (unpublished manuscript).

Wigglesworth, G., Simpson, J. and Loakes, D. (2011), 'NAPLAN Language Assessments for Indigenous Children in Remote Communities: Issues and Problems', *Australian Review of Applied Linguistics* 34 (3), 320–343.

Willmott, E. (1987), *Pemulwuy. The Rainbow Warrior*. Sydney: Weldon.

5

New Zealand: The Politics of National Standards in Primary Schools

Gregory Lee and Howard Lee

Introduction

As in most Western societies, today education in New Zealand is undergoing profound change, with the government introducing a number of initiatives ostensibly to enhance students' achievements. We know only too well – as education historians – that such interventions invariably have a substantial impact on the nature, shape, content and direction of education policy and practice.

This chapter explores one significant education reform policy being pursued currently by the National Government, deemed necessary to improve the quality of education in the compulsory education sector. While any number of current initiatives could have been selected for analysis – for example, changes to school assessment and the curriculum, increased funding for the independent (i.e. private) school sector, public–private partnerships (PPPs) for the construction and ownership of new schools, reductions to tertiary students' access to loan entitlements and living allowances and the introduction of the highly controversial charter schools – we have chosen to focus on the (re)introduction of National Standards. Our rationale for choosing to examine this initiative is because it serves to underline the need for politicians to proceed with considerable caution whenever they claim to be acting in the best interests of students and their parents. Teachers and teachers' professional associations (unions), as we shall see, are capable of not only mounting highly articulate arguments to garner public (particularly parent) support but also resisting any initiatives they believe would compromise the best learning outcomes for their students.

Throughout this chapter, we have been guided by the often forgotten, fundamental, historical reality that while politicians and administrators have determined educational *policy* in fact it was teachers, parents and pupils who have been largely responsible for shaping educational *practice*. Taking up this point in 1982, Dr Beeby, the Director of Education in New Zealand from 1940 to 1960, offered a timely reminder to those who sought to implement educational reforms without genuine community consultation when he observed perceptively that:

> Whatever purposes politicians and administrators might have had for education, their plans could be deflected when ambitious parents, acting individually but in unspoken accord, decided they wanted the schools to do something different for their children. . . . There is always some tension between the controllers and the consumers of education and, in the long run, the consumers' purposes usually prevail. (1982: pp. v–vi)

This chapter critically analyses the relevance of Beeby's conclusion 30 years later in light of a recent key education event in New Zealand: the (re)introduction of National Standards. In doing so, it brings into sharp focus some fundamental questions concerning the highly politicized nature and direction of contemporary state education in New Zealand.

Aotearoa/New Zealand is a country with a population of 4.3 million people (Laveault et al., 2010: p. 5) and a land area spanning 103,734 square miles (268,671 square kilometres). Sixty-eight per cent of its residents describe themselves as 'New Zealand European', 15 per cent as Maori (the indigenous people), 9 per cent as Asian, while 7 per cent identify themselves as Pacific Island (Pasifika) persons (Laveault et al., 2010: p. 5). Attendance at school is compulsory for boys and girls from 6 years of age to 16 years, although children can remain at secondary school until 19 years and can enter a primary school at 5 years of age (ibid.: p. 5).

The New Zealand schooling system has two broad sectors: primary and secondary. The former is intended for 5- to 13-year-olds (Year 1 to Year 8) – and constitutes some 57 per cent of the total number of pupils – while 13- to 18-year-old (Year 9 to Year 13) boys and girls attend secondary schools (ibid.: p. 5). The primary school sector includes contributing (or decapitated) schools for Year 1 to Year 6 pupils, full primary institutions for Year 1 to Year 8 pupils and intermediate schools for Year 7 and Year 8 boys and girls. The percentage of pupils attending contributing, full primary and intermediate schools is 47.8, 39.3 and 12.9, respectively, although 54.7 per cent of primary schools are full primary and 6 per cent are intermediate schools (ibid.: p. 7). Fewer than 1 per cent (0.09%) of children (6,787 youth) are home-schooled (ibid.: p. 7).

In the secondary school arena, 70 per cent are classified as Year 9 to Year 13 institutions. Seventy-eight per cent of secondary students attend these schools, with Year 7 to Year 13 'extended secondary schools' absorbing the remaining 22 per cent of boys and girls (Laveault et al., 2010: pp. 6–7). New Zealand secondary and primary schools are of three types – state (public); state integrated (special character, independently owned, institutions, based upon a religious denomination in most instances); and private (independent). The state schooling system is secular (i.e. non-denominational). Eighty-five per cent of all students attend state or public schools (these account for 83.5 per cent of the three kinds of institutions) compared with 11 per cent of youth who are enrolled in state integrated and 4 per cent of pupils enrolled in private schools. The latter make up only 3.75 per cent of the total number of schools in New Zealand, whereas state-integrated institutions comprise 12.8 per cent of the total number of schools (p. 7).

The educational context for implementing 'National Standards'

The great enemy of the truth is very often not the lie – deliberate, contrived, and dishonest, but the myth – persistent, pervasive, and unrealistic. (John F. Kennedy, 1962)

The National Standards policy, launched by the National Party on 10 April 2007, identified three core requirements that all New Zealand primary and intermediate school authorities would be expected to provide:

1. Clear National Standards in reading, writing and numeracy, designed to describe all the things that children should be able to do by a particular age or year at school. They will be defined by benchmarks in a range of tests.
2. Effective Assessment that will require primary schools to use assessment programmes that compare the progress of their students with other students across the country. Schools will be able to choose from a range of tests, but there will be no national examinations.

3. Upfront Reporting (in plain language) to give parents the right to see all assessment information, and to get regular reports about their child's progress towards National Standards. Schools will be required to report each year on whole school performance against National Standards (New Zealand National Party, 2007).

The rationale for introducing National Standards, the National Party declared boldly, was for primary school authorities from Kaitaia to Bluff (i.e. across New Zealand) to have a 'set of shared expectations about what students should be achieving' and for teachers to use the standards to 'clearly identify students who are at risk of missing out on basic skills and becoming a permanent part of the "tail" of under-achievement' (New Zealand National Party, 2007).

Following the election of the John Key-led National Party to office in November 2008, the new government wasted no time introducing The Education (National Standards) Amendment Bill into the House on 9 December 2008. In a marked departure from a long-established precedent, this bill was not subjected to the usual parliamentary select committee scrutiny; rather, it was passed under urgency that same day ('School Standards Must Be Raised', 2009: p. B6).

The new legislation authorized the Minister of Education to set national literacy and numeracy standards against which Years 1–8 (i.e. primary and intermediate school age) students would be assessed (The Education (National Standards) Amendment Bill, 2008). In February 2009, Anne Tolley, the newly appointed Minister of Education, informed principals that although National Standards had yet to be set, the Ministry would soon begin consulting on standards throughout 2009 with a view to their implementation in 2010 (Crooks, 2009: p. 6). The need for these standards, she argued, was all the more urgent given the concerns voiced by the Education Review Office (ERO) at the February 2008 Parliamentary Education and Science Select Committee, that 'the schooling system as a whole was not using the huge potential of these assessment tools to support the creation of programs [sic] to improve the education of students'. The overall level of student achievement, Tolley predicted confidently, would rise when all school teachers utilized these 'valuable [National Standards] tools' fully (Crooks, 2009: p. 6; New Zealand Parliamentary Education and Science Select Committee, 2008: p. 14).

The public was informed that Ministry of Education staff would work with small teams of literacy, numeracy and assessment experts to develop draft National Standards and would also consult with schools, parents and the community over a 6-week period (25 May to 3 July 2009) (Tolley, 2009). During this time, a Standards Reference Group met with representatives from the New Zealand Educational Institute (NZEI), the Post-Primary Teachers' Association (PPTA) and the New Zealand School Trustees' Association (NZSTA) (Tolley, 2009a, b).

The National Government's case for 'National Standards'

As Minister of Education, Tolley argued consistently that there was an urgent need to 'raise student achievement' and for parents to be better informed about what their children 'can and can not achieve' in literacy (reading and writing) and numeracy for each year of their primary and intermediate schooling (Todd, 2009). Teachers were expected to use a simple four-point categorical scale – 'above', 'at', 'below' or 'well below' standard – to capture and report students' achievements against what was required for each of level, progression and achievement stage and then to use that information to make overall teacher judgements (OTJs) regarding students' achievements against the National Standards benchmarks (Chamberlain, 2010).

The introduction of National Standards – described as being one of the Government's 'flagship policies in education' ('Tolley Firm on Standards', 2009) – and assessing children against such standards, Tolley asserted, meant that parents would know how well their child was doing against each National Standard, how that child compared with others in the same age group, if their child was experiencing any difficulties and how the teacher and school would address this and the steps that parents could take to support their child's learning at home (Beaumont and Broun, 2009: p. A1). Tolley was adamant that National Standards would not involve a single national test but, instead, would use 'effective assessment tools to provide feedback that supports student learning and teacher effectiveness' along with appropriate consultation to establish 'who needs access to what information' ('Tolley Firm on Standards', 2009).

Having reiterated publicly that National Standards in literacy (reading and writing) and mathematics were designed specifically to 'address the widening gap between the highest and lowest performing children' (Hartevelt, 2009b), Tolley was obliged to explain the process by which this remediation would occur. Since each of the National Standards in literacy (reading and writing) and mathematics had three components – a description of what achievement in the standard should look like; an exemplar of that level of achievement and assessment tasks and tools for measuring that standard (New Zealand Education

Gazette, 2009: p. 3) – Tolley predicted that there would be much greater clarity now in terms of the learning outcomes that could reasonably be expected of most students by the end of each school year (p. 3).

Tolley's rationale for introducing National Standards

The Minister admitted that her championing of National Standards owed much to the survey data contained in two ERO reports, both published in 2007, that documented the extent to which primary (and secondary) schools had used assessment information effectively to improve the quality of teaching and learning. Together these reports – *The Collection and Use of Assessment Information in Schools* (March 2007) and *The Collection and Use of Assessment Information: Good Practice in Primary Schools* (June 2007) – provided Tolley with empirical evidence she needed to justify the introduction of National Standards.

The March 2007 report presented the results of a detailed survey undertaken by the ERO of 314 primary, intermediate and secondary schools during the first half of 2006. Having evaluated the quality of assessment information provided in 118 full primary, 125 contributing and 10 intermediate schools (New Zealand Education Review Office, 2007a: p. 5, 2007b: p. 2), the ERO declared that schools' effectiveness in collecting and using assessment information varied widely, with barely one half of the schools exhibiting effective practice across the whole curriculum (New Zealand Education Review Office, 2007b, p. 3). The survey data revealed, furthermore, that:

- Fifty-eight per cent of schools had developed and implemented an effective, integrated school-wide approach to assessment processes and information.
- Over 80 per cent of primary schools had developed effective assessment processes and tools for literacy and numeracy.
- The achievement information in 57 per cent of schools demonstrated students' achievement and progress.
- The interaction of assessment with teaching and learning was effective in 54 per cent of schools.
- In 42 per cent of schools, students used information about their achievement for further learning.
- Forty-three per cent of schools were establishing and using school-wide information to improve student achievement.

- Fifty-one per cent were effective in reporting information about students' achievements to the community (New Zealand Education Review Office, 2007b: p. 2).

A cursory look at these data appears to indicate few assessment-related issues that warranted urgent attention, particularly in the primary sector where more than 80 per cent of the schools surveyed had developed 'effective assessment processes and tools for literacy and numeracy' (New Zealand Education Review Office, 2007a: p. 27). However, buried deeper in the same report was damning evidence that 'most primary schools did not collect and analyse their students' achievements in curriculum areas other than mathematics and English' (New Zealand Education Review Office, 2007a: p. 21).

If these findings were reliable and were broadly representative of all New Zealand primary schools, then one is left wondering why Tolley should wish to introduce National Standards in literacy and numeracy when the quality and quantity of assessment data being gathered and reported in the *other* curriculum areas was demonstrably deficient. Might this be further evidence of the National Government's obsession with National Standards in literacy and numeracy, to the detriment of those other curriculum areas deemed less important?

The data also suggest the need for improvement in other facets of assessment with barely one-half of the schools having initiated effective school-wide assessment processes and information, demonstrated students' achievements and progress, related assessment to teaching and learning and being able to report information about their students' achievements to their communities effectively (p. 2). The report concluded by noting a statistically significant difference between low- and high-decile schools, with low-decile schools performing poorly in all of the areas investigated (New Zealand Education Review Office, 2007a: p. 18, 29, 33, 44).

Having accepted the ERO's criticism that schools were underperforming on gathering, documenting and disseminating assessment information, Tolley zeroed in selectively on schools' inadequate reporting of achievement information to their communities (Laugesen, 2009). Accordingly, in nearly all of her numerous public pronouncements on National Standards, as reported on the radio (National Radio Morning Report), television and in the national print media, Tolley was unwavering in her insistence that parents needed and wanted clearer information about how their children were achieving at school (Clark, 2010b; Lee and Lee, 2009). Such an observation was hardly surprising, however, given that most parents take an interest in their child's school achievements.

The teacher unions' response

Given the heightened publicity that surrounded the introduction of National Standards, how did the nation's primary school principals, teachers and teachers' unions respond to Tolley's claims?

While principals welcomed the new National Standards as a tool to assist teachers in evaluating what level their students should be achieving at, most voiced deep concern over reporting this data to the Ministry of Education because they believed it was highly likely that such data would be compiled and/or manipulated to create league tables (Todd, 2009). The American and British experience, Philip Harding, Principal of Paparoa Street School in Christchurch, observed, clearly revealed that 'because you get what you measure, you better be sure that what you want to measure matters most' (Todd, 2009). For Denise Torrey, President of the Canterbury Primary Principals' Association, the new National Standards were antithetical to the focus of the recent *The New Zealand Curriculum* (2007) that encouraged teachers to exercise greater autonomy in responding to and planning for the learning needs of their students (Todd, 2009).

Ernie Buutveld – the President of the New Zealand Principals' Federation, an organization representing approximately 2,300 school principals throughout New Zealand – was also concerned that the media would misuse school data. Warning his fellow principals that 'Britain is just realising its mistake in narrowing its curriculum and undermining its curriculum with testing', Buutveld concluded that the speed with which National Standards were being implemented would result in one outcome only, whereby 'the urgent will drive out the important' (New Zealand Principals' Federation, 2009).

The then NZEI President, Frances Nelson, saw the matter very differently initially and was optimistic that the new National Standards would represent a marked improvement on those assessment tools used in schools already. Having been informed by Mary Chamberlain, Group Manager of the Ministry of Education, that about 84 per cent of Year 1 children would be expected to achieve the numeracy standards set for that age group, compared with a figure of 61 per cent for Year 8 boys and girls (Hunt, 2009a: p. 1), Nelson seemed unconcerned because, she reasoned, these were average achievement rates and therefore not every student would be capable of achieving the set standard (p. 2).

However, 2 weeks later Nelson became decidedly more pessimistic about National Standards when she announced that they would be acceptable to the teaching profession only if they put children's learning first and supported high-quality teaching ('Strong NZEI Turnout', 2009: p. 1). Nelson was adamant that any steps taken to make school assessment information available nationally for the purpose of league table comparisons would be 'destructive and [would] defeat the purpose of implementing the standards' because '[league tables] shifted the focus from the learning needs of children across a broad range of areas to ranking schools solely on literacy and numeracy results' (p. 1).

Echoing the NZEI's position, Geoff Lovegrove, the Editor of the New Zealand Principals' Federation monthly magazine – *NZ Principal* – informed his colleagues that in Britain primary school teachers had refused steadfastly to administer high stakes national tests, declaring them to be driven politically rather than educationally ('Strong NZEI Turnout', 2009: p. 2). Lovegrove concluded by acknowledging that while teachers had a duty to assess thoroughly, to interpret and use the results to enhance students' teaching and learning and to report accurately and honestly the actual progress and achievement of students to parents, the real reason for National Standards being introduced was to enable politicians to 'belt [teachers] around the ears with league tables, in the guise of "national standards"' (p. 2).

Defending National Standards as 'the best [educational] disinfectant'

Despite the earlier-mentioned trenchant criticism from the teachers' unions and school principals, Tolley continued to insist that, while individual pupil achievement details probably would not be passed on to the Ministry of Education, information about each school's performance would be sent (Hartevelt, 2009a). Pressed for her views about the merits of comparing individual schools and how this might be prevented and/or managed, Tolley conceded that the Government was powerless to prevent the media from accessing information and from compiling and publishing their own league tables (Todd, 2009). Nevertheless, Tolley was adamant that communities had the right to access all of the achievement information available because 'the more information that's out there the better . . . The best disinfectant is fresh air' (Hartevelt, 2009a).

The media attacks and the principals' reply

In a remarkable show of solidarity for the Government's National Standards policy, the nation's print media launched a stinging attack on the teachers' unions and school principals. The Editor of *The New Zealand Herald* urged the government to 'not give way to the principals' who, it was alleged, had for too long 'treated parents as children incapable of reading a league table or much else' ('Govt Mustn't Give Way', 2009). Parents, the Editor concluded, liked league tables because:

> They are helpful when it comes time to choosing a school. They are also helpful in keeping the pressure on all schools to perform to the best of their ability. If the profession dislikes that pressure, or considers it unhelpful to educational effort, its customers disagree. And ultimately the customer, even of public education, is always right. ('Govt Mustn't Give Way', 2009)

The next day, *The Dominion Post* Editor berated the NZEI for 'rebelling' openly against the Minister's plan to inform parents about how well their children's schools were performing. '[The NZEI] are forgetting that schools are run for the benefit of pupils and parents, not those who work in them' ('Patients Must Come First', 2009: p. B4).

In the midst of this increasingly critical media attention, the New Zealand Principals' Federation held its annual conference in Palmerston North. Having accepted the invitation to address the conference, Tolley dismissed promptly any suggestion of a law change to prevent National Standards data being translated into league tables because parents needed access to all information about their children's progress. Tolley also admonished the Federation for having deliberately spread 'misleading information' about the Government's policy on National Standards – 'National standards do not mean standardised national testing. They are about consistent assessment throughout the country' (Torrie, 2009: p. 3). Having listened to Ernie Buutveld reiterate principals' concerns over National Standards, Tolley warned the 400 delegates that 'the Government will not resile from National Standards. Parents want them, they have a right to them and this government is going to deliver them' ('Tolley Firm on Standards', 2009; Torrie, 2009: p. 3; Wood, 2009: p. A3).

Tolley's resolve contrasts sharply with the key findings of the Principals' Federation Standards Survey summarized by Buutveld at the July conference. Of the 1,000 primary school principals surveyed, 23 per cent were opposed implacably to National Standards with a further 72 per cent expressing serious reservations about their introduction, the potential for the data to be captured in league tables and the very short timeline allowed for their implementation (Buutveld, 2009a). When asked what they would do if instructed to report data that the media could then use to compile league tables, 77 per cent of principals stated they would comply partially by maintaining their current planning and reporting policies, 20 per cent would comply because they were required to legally, while 2 per cent of principals stated they would comply fully (Buutveld, 2009a; Torrie, 2009: p. 3). The survey also asked whether boards of trustees (BOTs) and school communities supported their principals' stance regarding National Standards. Of the 56 per cent of boards who had discussed the principals' stance, 96 per cent expressed their support; and of the 32 per cent of communities who had discussed the issue, 91 per cent indicated they supported their principals (Buutveld, 2009a). Data such as these served only to harden the principals' resolve to boycott the National Standards policy.

Frustrated at Tolley's ongoing refusal to acknowledge that National Standards would lead invariably to high-stakes assessment and league table reporting by the media, Buutveld took the Federation's arguments to the media. In an opinion piece published in *The New Zealand Herald* on 9 July, Buutveld agreed that parents deserved access to all of the assessment information gathered about their children's achievements and progress. He assured readers that the Federation would support fully any process that involved reporting individual student's achievements to parents and the provision of aggregated data to the BOTs (Buutveld, 2009b).

Buutveld's article was criticised sharply by *The Dominion Post* Editor, who urged Tolley to 'stick to her guns' over National Standards because 'parents had every right to march [their children] off to a school that is performing better, taking the state funding attached to him or her with them'. The editorial concluded by asking readers 'What is wrong with sharing with taxpayers – those who pay to keep state schools operating – just which schools do well and which do not?' ('Better to Make It Plain', 2009: p. B4).

Other supporters of National Standards (and league tables) also weighed into the public debate, citing the need for greater monitoring, control and accountability of teachers and schools (Coddington, 2009). Some media commentators argued that league tables would not only help to identify schools experiencing problems and needing additional assistance but also provide an excellent incentive for schools to compare their performance with neighbouring schools of a similar decile and, in so doing, 'to lift their standards' (Stirling, 2009: p. 5). Other writers sought to remind teachers that they were 'paid servants of the education system, not its masters', that league tables enabled parents to make intelligent choices about the best school for their children to attend, and that teachers should not be 'absolved from the performance measurements and competitive pressures that other industries and professional groups are subject to' (Du Fresne, 2009: p. 14).

National and international critiques of National Standards

A number of New Zealand-based assessment specialists did not share Tolley's optimism about the purported benefits of National Standards. Lester Flockton, formerly Co-Director of The University of Otago's NEMP (National Education Monitoring Project) unit, was adamant that Tolley's 'standards raise standards' mantra was motivated politically and that it ignored the wealth of research evidence that socioeconomic factors were the strongest predictor of student achievement (Flockton, 2009: p. 30; Hunt, 2009a: p. 1).

Others were more forthcoming about the potential for National Standards to spawn a system of national (as in Britain) and state-wide (as in the United States) tests. At the international assessment symposium held in Queenstown, New Zealand, on 16–17 March 2009, attended by Tolley, assessment experts urged caution regarding the National Standards strategy (Laugesen, 2009). Emeritus Professor Jim Popham from the University of California, Los Angeles, observed that the No Child Left Behind Act (2002)[1] in the United States had forced school authorities to become fixated on tests scores rather than on providing students with broader curricula and learning experiences (Laugesen, 2009: p. 24). Having listened carefully to Tolley's 'very thoughtful analysis of what was possible [in New Zealand] and what they were going to avoid', Popham was confident that there was now 'a very strong recognition of the perils of ill-conceived national testing' (p. 27).

From policy to practice: the consultation to implementation timeline

Tolley envisaged initially that the draft National Standards would be refined and published in October 2009 in readiness for BOTs to embed them in their charters for 2010. Thereafter school authorities would be required to use the Standards to guide teaching and learning, to report children's progress and achievements against the Standards to parents and to include baseline data and targets in their 2011 Charters (Hunt, 2009b: p. 3).

However the NZEI, both the Canterbury and Otago Principals' Association, and the New Zealand Principals' Federation urged Tolley repeatedly to reconsider introducing National Standards because, they argued, approximately 90 per cent of primary schools used a range of nationally and internationally recognized assessment tools already to monitor their students' achievement (Beaumont, 2009a: p. A17; Lewis, 2009: p. 3; 'National Standards for Schools', 2009: p. 4). Having refused initially to extend the implementation timeline, Tolley relented finally. National Standards would be phased in from 2010; each school would have to include National Standards targets in their annual charters for 2011; schools would continue to embed National Standards throughout 2011 and by May 2012 all school authorities would be required to report achievement data against set National Standards targets (Hunt, 2009a: p. 3; New Zealand Ministry of Education, 2010a, 2010b, 2011a–c; Tolley, 2009b; Wood, 2009: p. A3).

The real reason why Tolley agreed to a longer timeframe, according to Kelvin Smythe – a former school inspector, education commentator and critic – was not to appease educators but because the Ministry of Education had encountered significant problems 'mapping' the standardized tests, the curriculum levels in *The New Zealand Curriculum* (2007) and National Standards with the as TTle (Assessment Tools for Teaching and Learning) assessment tools (Smythe, 2009). Tolley's decision, he concluded, was pragmatic rather than educational.

NZCER: an independent research voice

In endeavouring not only to provide an independent viewpoint on National Standards but also to distance the message from the messenger, the New Zealand Council for Educational Research (NZCER) sent a four-page submission to the Ministry of Education in July 2009 that identified three concerns with National Standards. These concerned their use, the timing of their introduction and the need for ongoing research into how the policy would translate into practice (New Zealand Council for Educational Research, 2009).

The NZCER reported that while National Standards could act possibly as a catalyst for improving learning and teaching, the validity of using these to identify schools that needed to raise their students' levels of achievement ought to be scrutinized owing to the imprecision of the standard and the potential for the standards' results to be reported in simplistic league tables acknowledged as being unreliable and invalid indicators of educational quality (pp. 1–2). The NZCER also warned that literacy and numeracy should not become 'the sole focus of school accountability', and that National Standards 'must not become a straitjacket that prevents schools from providing students with engaging and enriching curricula' (p. 3). Finally, their submission exhorted the Government to 'road test' National Standards for at least 1 year prior to implementation, to gauge their likely impact on the implementation of *The New Zealand Curriculum* (2007: p. 3) and to design a purpose-built independent and secure student data management system, capable of storing any data generated by schools and of being accessible only to schools (pp. 3–4). Neither Tolley nor her Ministry (who had contracted the NZCER to assist in the development of National Standards) responded to the submission.

The following month, the NZCER published its analysis of the Ministry of Education's public consultation exercise regarding the proposed National Standards for literacy and numeracy (Wylie et al., 2009: p. v). Contracted by the Ministry to evaluate the 4,968 submissions received (representing 9,526 individuals), the NZCER identified and reported on four key themes: stakeholder understanding of the purpose of National Standards; areas of concern and/ or areas for improvement; barriers to implementing National Standards; and information which parents needed in order to engage effectively with their children's education (pp. 5–9).

Although space limitations preclude a detailed analysis of responses from each of the different sectors, the general trends are as follows. 'Stakeholders' were not confident that the criteria to evaluate students' achievements in the draft National Standards were set at an appropriate level. Twenty-three per cent were concerned about the potential identification and subsequent labelling of students, particularly those making progress but not at the level required to meet or exceed the expected standard, while 20 per cent believed that National Standards would seriously constrain the nature, scope and autonomy of the recently introduced *The New Zealand Curriculum* (2007; Wylie et al., 2009: pp. viii–viii, 7, 38: table 12).

Notwithstanding assurances by Tolley that the Government wanted to avoid the compilation of comparative league tables of schools' performance in the literacy and numeracy standards, one-third of all respondents remained apprehensive about the potential for the media to compile such tables and for parents and school communities to draw unfair comparisons between schools without acknowledging their different demographic contexts (p. viii, 7 and 36: table 11).

In summary, then, because individual schools were able to choose which assessment tools to use, school authorities might not be measuring the same things, in the same way, for all students. Thus the data produced nationally would be invalid and unreliable, and therefore of little benefit in determining whether or not a child has met the prescribed standard of achievement.

Hattie's National Standards critique

The National Standards debate intensified significantly in the same month when John Hattie – widely regarded as being the architect of National Standards – launched a stinging attack, declaring that National Standards would force teachers to teach students according to their school year rather than their ability level (Laxon, 2009). He also asserted that National Standards were at odds fundamentally with a levels-based curriculum, that they would create a clash between age-based standards and ability-based learning and that this situation would encourage mediocrity because students who met a minimum standard would move mechanically through all subjects at the same pace invariably, as evident in the United States. Hattie predicted that because most teachers would 'teach to the test', education would be 'set back 50 years' (Laxon, 2009). Hattie's views resonated with the views of many educators, school principals, teachers and their unions.

Post-consultation resistance

In a further attempt to undermine National Standards, a group of principals announced publicly that it would deliberately 'fudge' and enhance results by choosing the easiest test available (Beaumont, 2009b: p. A4; Hunt, 2009c: p. 3). This strategy drew a predictable response from the media. The mere suggestion that principals might subvert the Government's 'flagship education policy' infuriated *The Dominion Post* Editor, who threatened to 'unmask' those principals who sought to derail Tolley's plans. Questioning why these 'public servants' should retain their positions, the Editor then asked why 90 per cent of prison inmates were 'functionally illiterate' when most had received at least a primary school education ('Listen and Learn, Teachers', 2009: p. B4). The Editor's explanation was simple – teachers, knowingly, had failed children – as was the suggested remedy: to ensure that all children 'learn the basics at primary school, rather than have the taxpayer pay for remedial education later in life' (p. B4).

What was omitted from this commentary – in fact, from almost all print media accounts to date – has been *robust research-based evidence* to prove that National Standards would lead to improvements in students' literacy and numeracy abilities and would reduce the 'long tail' of student under-achievement.

The prime minister hits the 'panic button'

With a nationwide boycott of National Standards becoming increasingly likely, Prime Minister Key relieved Tolley of her Associate Minister of Education portfolio on 25 January 2010 to enable her to concentrate on the National Standards roll out (Young, 2010a). Aware of the very positive reception to the NZEI's 'Hands Up For Learning: Trial National Standards, Not Our Kids' campaign and the growing public unease with National Standards, Key announced a '$26 million charm offensive' to publicize the purported advantages of National Standards (Hartevelt, 2010a). However, this move did not placate opponents of National Standards who observed that Tolley still 'talked to' rather than 'talked with' people, an observation that was echoed by the PPTA President, Kate Gainsford (Trevett, 2010). At this point, Tolley announced that she would soon tour New Zealand in a bid to 'sell' National Standards to the public. Her timing could not have been worse because the NZEI's own nationwide (anti) National Standards 'bus trip' was well underway already. Beginning in Northland and Bluff, the buses travelled to hundreds of schools, and NZEI staff and invited speakers addressed dozens of public meetings throughout the country. The increasing level of community support for the NZEI's National Standards campaign confirmed the Government's worst fears that it had seriously underestimated the public's opposition to National Standards ('Govt Should Hold Its Nerve', 2010).

An increasingly worried Prime Minister – whose 2008 election manifesto had identified National Standards as a cornerstone policy – now announced a $200,000 mail out to 350,000 households, indicating that all National MPs would begin a 'round of public meetings to explain the policy' (Kay, 2010; Young, 2010b). Key also singled out for criticism the teacher unions, blaming them for 'protecting' 30 per cent of primary school teachers who allegedly were underperforming (Kay, 2010).

The teachers' unions and Principals' Federation were incensed by Key's claims, and castigated him for 'ripping into teachers and [their] unions' and for 'bashing schools and blaming teachers' ('National Standards Tool', 2010). They further observed that, according to the ERO's own estimate, barely 10 per cent of teachers could be labelled as 'poor' – a figure Key had inflated to 30 per cent ('Key's Focus Not on Students', 2010; see also Snook, 2010a, b). By now, some of the traditionally pro-National Standards media commentators began to question the wisdom of Key 'taking on the teacher unions' (Armstrong, 2010), noting that the Government had lost the battle over bulk funding earlier (Espiner, 2010; Watkins, 2010). Nevertheless Key and Tolley refused to backtrack, arguing that the national economy could 'grow by up to $6 billion annually if Kiwi children lifted their academic performance' (Hartevelt, 2010b).

Very soon after, Hattie re-entered the National Standards debate, announcing that while he did not support league tables personally he would begin work on a national league table system because the introduction of National Standards 'made them inevitable' (Laxon, 2010). Hattie also undertook to run workshops for teachers, to allow them to 'better understand' how to implement the standards and to demonstrate how his e-asTTLE (electronic assessment) software could be used alongside National Standards (The University of Auckland, 2010). Within a fortnight, Tolley announced Hattie's appointment to the newly established five-person technical advisory group – the National Standards Independent Advisory Group (NSIAG) (Tolley, 2010a).

Critics of National Standards questioned the 'independence' of this group promptly because its members were known supporters of National Standards (Beaumont, 2010) and because vocal opponents, such as Emeritus Professor Warwick Elley, were notably absent (Clark, 2010a). In September 2010, in an effort to be seen to be consulting with the education sector, Tolley replaced the NSIAG with the National Standards Sector Advisory Group (NSSAG), added more members and sought to 'attract the confidence of the sector both in NSSAG and in the process of change being experienced in the education sector' (NSSAG, 2010). Although the NZEI and the Principals' Federation Executive attended early meetings, they withdrew their support subsequently, frustrated that their concerns were being ignored (NZEI, 2011).

Statutory intervention and the public's right to access information

Tolley now faced the prospect of individual schools' BOTs refusing to include National Standards targets in their charters (Hunt, 2010). A number of these BOTs also urged Tolley to again consider trialling National Standards prior to implementation (Binning, 2010) but Tolley, backed by the School Trustees' Association (STA), steadfastly rejected this suggestion. Although Tolley in December 2009 had warned that she would not hesitate to dismiss errant BOTs and replace them with Limited Statutory Managers (LSMs) (Trevett, 2009), Key now downplayed this threat by stating that he preferred to work with schools in the first instance (Latham, 2010; Law, 2010). Any schools that remained non-complaint, he argued, would 'need to answer to the parents . . . why they are prepared to allow one in five young New Zealanders to leave school without adequate literacy and numeracy skills' (Law, 2010).

With the increasing likelihood of statutory intervention, the Boards Taking Action Coalition (BTAC) recommended that schools now include National Standards targets in their charters in order to satisfy the requirements of the 1989 Education Act but that they also append a 'statement of duress' (Garrett-Walker, 2011). Most schools (93%) complied but no data exist regarding how many schools included a duress statement (New Zealand Parliamentary Debates, 2011).

The general election and National Standards

During the latter half of 2010, debates about National Standards persisted, with ERO and NZCER reports having indicated serious, ongoing, problems with their implementation. Approximately two-thirds of pupils were failing the National Standards (Hartevelt, 2010c). The media gave National Standards a temporary reprieve in 2011 as attention turned to the November 2011 general election. In the lead up to the election the National Government again reiterated its earlier, and by now well-worn, National Standards mantra that because 'one child in five leaves school without the basic skills they need to succeed in a modern economy', there was an urgent need to 'boost literacy and numeracy and [to] lift achievement in our schools. We want every child to have the best possible start to life, to reach their full potential, and have a bright future' (New Zealand National Party, 2010: p. 1). As the election drew closer, the National Government sought to tap into parents' support for National Standards. Its election manifesto opened with the claim that:

> Parents invest heavily in their children's education, both in cost and emotionally. We need to make sure they are getting a return on their investment. National standards will strengthen accountability and performance measurement so that parents and students are getting the most from their schools, and the education system is helping lift student achievement. (New Zealand National Party, 2011: p. 1)

Having won the election Key reshuffled his cabinet immediately and installed Hekia Parata as Minister of Education. Parata had a clear brief – to implement National Standards, to improve the quality of teaching, and generally shake up the education sector – but got into difficulty quickly. Parata's announcement of her intention to 'strengthen the accountability of schools' by publishing their National Standards results on a website similar to the Australian MySchool site (Hartevelt, 2012a) was condemned swiftly by the NZEI President, Ian Leckie, who claimed it would produce government-sanctioned league tables that would not only label children, schools and their communities unfairly and inaccurately but also do nothing to lift achievement (Hartevelt, 2012a). Leckie observed further that because National Standards were not moderated there was huge variation in the way schools were using them. He concluded that 'junk information in [results in] junk information out' (Hartevelt, 2012a).

Media publishes 'very ropey' National Standards data online

On 31 May 2012, media joined in the debate when John Hartevelt of Fairfax Media sent an Official Information Act request to the Ministry of Education asking for National Standards results for all primary and intermediate schools in Wellington (Hartevelt, 2012c). Three weeks later, Fairfax was informed that the Ministry had refused the request. Fairfax complained to the Ombudsman immediately, who agreed that the Ministry had no grounds for withholding the information being sought and who instructed the Ministry to supply the National Standards data (Hartevelt, 2012c). In early August, Parata announced that all schools would soon have their National Standards data published on the Government's Education Counts website (Hartevelt, 2012c). However, the public did not have to wait long for these data to be made available because 6 weeks later Fairfax released its own School Report site listing results from more than 1,000 schools (Edwards, 2012; Hartevelt and Francis, 2012).

At first glance, the (unmoderated) data appeared to paint a grim picture of students' achievement with the percentages of students deemed to be below or well below the standards for reading, writing and mathematics at 23.7, 32.0 and 27.6 per cent, respectively (Hartevelt and Francis, 2012). Interestingly, the proportion of girls achieving at or above the standard in reading (80.5%), writing (75.0%) and mathematics (72.7%) exceeded that for boys – 72.0, 61.2 and 71.9 per cent, respectively (Hartevelt and Francis, 2012).

But just how statistically rigorous were these data? Ten weeks before Fairfax published its report card, the Prime Minister admitted that the raw data would be 'very ropey', although he firmly believed such information was useful for parents to know (Hartevelt, 2012b). Hartevelt also conceded that the compilation and publication of schools' raw data was problematic and that 'anyone who read the National Standards results as a proxy for quality' would be foolish because, without moderation, 'one school's "well below" may be another's "at" or "above". There is just no way of knowing – yet – exactly how the standards have been applied across schools' (Hartevelt, 2012d).

Having acknowledged this limitation, however, Hartevelt then defended the decision to publish the results, at the same time as declaring that 'there is more to [schools] than the numbers you see on this [web]site'. He concluded that:

> If there are problems with the National Standards – and it's pretty clear that there are – the Government, teachers, parents and education leaders are going to have to figure out how to fix them. If they have to be scrapped, then those that would have them scrapped will have to win the argument. In the meantime, the public should expect that the media will work to turn over National Standards information and report on it as best it can. (Hartevelt, 2012d)

What is noteworthy is Hartevelt's expectation that the government, teachers, parents and education leaders would be able to 'fix' the 'problems' so that Fairfax could continue to publish its reports online. This ignores the reality that since early 2009 many parents, teachers, principals, education unions and education academics and leaders had been very critical of National Standards and yet it was these people who now were to be made responsible for solving a problem of the Government's own making.

Confronting the 'long tail' of student underachievement

Notwithstanding the 'ropey' and unmoderated 'league table' data, many commentators still persisted in arguing that National Standards would reduce the 'tail' of student underachievement. Few, it seems, identified the strong correlation between individual schools' raw data and their decile ranking whereby poor student achievement was correlated positively with increasing levels of deprivation, inequality and poverty (Edwards, 2012; McLauchlan, 2012). In other words, family background, resources and socioeconomic status have a very powerful impact upon student achievement (Nash, 1993; Berliner, 2009; Snook and O'Neill, 2010). The National Standards mantra conveniently ignores this overarching reality and, instead, shifts responsibility for student achievement away from the government and politicians and places it squarely upon the shoulders of teachers and schools (Thrupp, 1998, 2009, 2010; Lee and Lee, 2009).

Although the recently released National Standards data for 2012 reveal small achievement gains overall for boys and girls, and for Maori and Pasifika students when compared with the 2011 data, Maori and Pasifika students still continued to achieve on average at a level approximately 10 per cent lower than for non-Maori students (New Zealand Ministry of Education, 2013). Once again, the proportion of girls achieving 'at or above the standard' in reading (81.9%), writing (77.8%) and mathematics (74.1%) exceeded that for boys – 73.2, 62.6 and 73.0 per cent, respectively (New Zealand Ministry of Education, 2013).

Announcing these results in June 2013, Parata concentrated on the 'small but incremental improvement in reading, writing and mathematics' while downplaying the decline in achievement as students moved through the year levels (Francis, 2013). The introduction of National Standards and the publication of data that revealed achievement gains (albeit very small), Parata concluded confidently, meant that the Government had delivered on its election promise to raise student achievement (Courtney, 2013).

But just how meaningful were these raw 'league table' achievement data, given that they did not include achievement in curriculum areas other than reading, writing and mathematics nor did they inform parents about the quality of education delivered, the resources made available in schools, or take into account the extent to which parents were able to provide their children with support, encouragement and educational resources? Thus, far from being a 'level playing field' where quality of inputs are matched against quality of outputs, National Standards simply focuses solely on raw achievement data with no consideration given to the differential 'inputs' available to students. Any results, therefore, are meaningless unless (and until) they factor in the reality that children arrive at different schools with different levels of family resources and with different levels of academic achievement. National Standards, as they are configured currently, are incapable of addressing these underlying inequalities.

'Mapping' National Standards to NCEA Level 2

One of the Government's key justifications for introducing National Standards, according to Minister Tolley, was to reduce the failure rate for Year 12 students – proclaimed widely by Tolley to be one in five students – who needed to gain the National Certificate of Educational Achievement (NCEA) Level 2 qualification for employment or further training purposes (Hartevelt, 2009b; 'Tolley Firm on Standards', 2009; Tolley, 2010b; Young, 2012). While such a goal appears laudable, the process of 'backward mapping' from the secondary school NCEA Level 2 qualification to primary school National Standards was highly problematic, given the absence of research evidence demonstrating any relationship (and/or statistical correlation) between the milestone levels of achievement at primary and secondary schools (Smythe, 2010). By implementing National Standards, Tolley had sought to create the *illusion* of a single seamless progression of learning across two entirely different schooling sectors simply because she *assumed* that such an association existed or ought to exist.

Unfortunately for Tolley, the situation is all the more complex because NCEA is neither a compulsory qualification nor a compulsory programme of study for secondary school students. Rather, NCEA is optional and allows students to choose subjects in addition to literacy (reading and writing) and mathematics. Accordingly, it made little sense to have compulsory National Standards that supposedly would 'scaffold' to the optional NCEA qualification (New Zealand Principals' Federation, 2011).

National Standards – A hidden agenda?

Since the Government's National Standards are neither 'national' in terms of their coverage nor denote a common education 'standard', it is to be wondered whether there is an alternative or hidden agenda behind their introduction. For their part, the teachers' associations and the Principals' Federation have insisted repeatedly that the current government is keen not only to introduce a performance pay system for teachers but also to utilize National Standards as the tool with which to identify and reward teachers whose students achieve highly (Buutveld, 2009b; Thrupp, 2010; Hartevelt, 2012e). The Organisation for Economic Co-operation and Development (OECD) concluded recently, however, that such a strategy is highly problematic because the relationship between student achievement and performance-related pay schemes remains indeterminate owing to difficulties over how performance is defined and measured, what the scale of the rewards is and whether rewards operate at the school or individual level (OECD, 2012). Any attempt by politicians to introduce performance-based remuneration would need to confront the reality therefore that the 'very ropey' National Standards provide no reliable data upon which to make such judgements.

National Standards in retrospect

It is important to acknowledge that the National Standards policy launched in April 2007 was not the first time that national assessment for Year 1–8 students had been proposed. In 1997, 1999 and 2005, the National Party favoured introducing national testing while the opposition Labour Party had also contemplated national testing, albeit briefly, in 1997 (Lee and Lee, 2000a, 2009). The changing emphasis from national testing to National Standards by 2007, as we have argued elsewhere, was designed to minimize the likelihood of resistance from both the public and the education sector (Lee and Lee, 2009).

Testing times? The future of National Standards in New Zealand

In New Zealand, the question that needs to be asked is whether National Standards are capable of delivering meaningful achievement information for teachers and parents. We believe that this question can best be answered by acknowledging that during the past two decades a 'culture of performativity' (Ball, 2000, 2003) has permeated the New Zealand primary and secondary school sectors, driven by the political appetite for ever-increasing monitoring, reporting, accountability and surveillance mechanisms for schools in general and teachers in particular (Lee and Lee, 1992, 2000a, b, 2001, 2009; Lee, 2003). These demands, as Rowe and others have argued, are symptomatic of a market ideology of education where 'winners' and 'losers' emerge (Fiske and Ladd, 2000; Rowe, 2000). Consequently, the 'standards' mantra becomes an indispensable part of any major change initiatives that embrace narrowly defined, 'quick fix', homogenizing models of educational achievement and accountability. Stobart (2008) has analysed this trend and concluded that 'it is hard to find a country that is not using the rhetoric of needing assessment to raise standards in response to the challenges of globalization' (p. 24).

'High stakes' assessment in historical context

As a strategy ostensibly designed to tackle student underachievement in the twenty-first century, the National Standards policy is highly problematic. Far from being visionary it blatantly ignores most, if not all, of the important lessons that have emerged from several decades of experience that New Zealand and other countries have amassed in relation to national curriculum, assessment and testing systems. With nearly six decades experience of national primary school testing (1878–1937) to draw upon, New Zealand politicians and the public need to be reminded that the system was abandoned in 1937 because most, if not all, of what was worthwhile educationally was being driven out by the narrow and relentless focus on 'the standards' (Lee and Lee, 1992, 2000a, 2009; Lee, 1993a, 2003).

With the National Standards genie now well and truly released from its bottle, it is doubtful whether future governments would be able to put it back. The public's insatiable appetite for 'outcomes', coupled with its apparent willingness to accept uncritically pronouncements from politicians who endorse simplistic and unreliable 'league tables', means that in all likelihood National Standards are destined to remain a feature of New Zealand's educational assessment landscape for the foreseeable future.

Note

1   The No Child Left Behind Act (2002) stipulated that existing state-wide accountability systems were to be aligned with specific state education standards, with states being responsible legally for developing content and performance standards, measuring improvement, implementing and administering assessment (including assessing students with limited English proficiency), reporting this assessment data and applying sanctions when performance goals are not met (United States Department of Education, 2002).

References

Armstrong, J. (2010), 'Key Forced Down from Lofty Perch to Take on the Teachers', *The New Zealand Herald*. Available at: http://www.nzherald.co.nz/nz/news/article. cfm?c_id=1&objectid=10623753 (Accessed: 29 March 2014).

Ball, S. (2000), 'Performativities and Fabrications in the Education Economy: Towards the Performative Society', *Australian Educational Researcher* 17 (3), 1–24.

— (2003), 'The Teacher's Soul and the Terrors of Performativity', *Journal of Education Policy* 18 (2), 215–228.

Beaumont, N. (2009a), 'Teachers Balk at League Table Approach to School', *The Dominion Post* A17.

— (2009b), 'Threat to Fudge Exam Results', *The Dominion Post* A4.

— (2010), 'Tolley Calls in Critic for Education Panel', *The Dominion Post*. Available at: http://www.stuff.co.nz/national/education/3342445/Tolley-calls-in-critic-for-education-panel (Accessed: 29 March 2014).

Beaumont, N. and Broun, B. (2009), 'Setting ABC standards', *The Dominion Post* A1.

Beeby, C. E. (1982), 'Introduction', in D. McKenzie (ed.), *Education and Social Structure: Essays in the History of New Zealand Education*. Dunedin: New Zealand College of Education, pp. 15–32.

Berliner, D. C. (2009), *Poverty and Potential: Out-of-School Factors and School Success*. Boulder, CO: Education and the Public Interest Center & Education Policy Research Unit. Available at: http://epicpolicy.org/publication/poverty-and-potential (Accessed: 29 March 2014).

'Better to Make It Plain' (Editorial). (2009), *The Dominion Post* B4.

Binning, E. (2010), 'Trustees in Firing Line if Teachers Snub Standards', *The New Zealand Herald*. Available at: http://www.nzherald.co.nz/nz/news/article.cfm?c_id=1&objectid=10628302 (Accessed: 29 March 2014).

Buutveld, E. (2009a), *Generating Futures: Presidential Address to the Annual Meeting of the New Zealand Principals' Federation*. Palmerston North. Available at: www.nzpf.ac.nz (Accessed: 29 March 2014).

— (2009b), 'Govt Plans for Schools Won't Tell Full Story', *The New Zealand Herald*.

Chamberlain, M. (2010), 'Blueprint for National Standards', *New Zealand Education Gazette* 89 (18). Available at: http://www.edgazette.govt.nz/Articles/Article.aspx?ArticleId=8187 (Accessed: 29 March 2014).

Clark, J. (2010a), 'National Standards: Are They Up To Standard?' *New Zealand Journal of Teachers' Work* 7 (1), 15–28.

— (2010b), 'National Standards: The Public Debate – What Was It All About?', *New Zealand Journal of Teachers' Work* 7 (2), 106–124.

Coddington, D. (2009), 'Teach School Big Shots a Lesson in Parent Power', *New Zealand Herald*. Available at: www.nzherald.co.nz/news/article.cfm?c_id=1objectid=10563885 (Accessed: 29 March 2014).

Courtney, B. (2013), 'Raw Data 'Useless' for Schools', *Stuff Nation*. Available at: www.stuff.co.nz/stuff-nation/9064717/Raw-data-useless-for-schools (Accessed: 29 March 2014).

Crooks, T. (2009), 'Will National Standards Lift Student Achievement?', *NZEI Rourou* 19 (18), 6.

Du Fresne, K. (2009), 'Dirty Words Offend Many Teachers', *Manawatu Standard* 14.

Edwards, B. (2012), 'NZ Politics Daily: National Standards Data upon Us', *The National Business Review*. Available at: http://www.nbr.co.nz/article/nz-politics-daily-national-standards-data-upon-us-ck-129798 (Accessed: 29 March 2014).

Espiner, C. (2010), 'National's Standards – A Fight It Won't Win', *Stuff Nation*. Available at: http://www.stuff.co.nz/national/blogs/on-the-house/3286456/Nationals-standards-a-fight-it-won-t-win (Accessed: 29 March 2014).

Fiske, E. B. and Ladd, H. (2000), *When Schools Compete: A Cautionary Tale.* Washington, DC: Brookings Institution Press.

Flockton, L. (2009), 'School Lines. Who is "Minding" a Good Education for Our Children? Politicians? Policy makers? Principals?' *NZ Principal* 24 (2), 29–30.

Francis, C. (2013), 'Students' Achievement 'Increasing', *Stuff Nation*. Available at: http://www.stuff.co.nz/national/education/8780900/Students-achievement-increasing (Accessed: 29 March 2014).

Garrett-Walker, H. (2011), 'Schools Call Off Standards Protest', *The New Zealand Herald*. Available at: http://www.nzherald.co.nz/nz/news/article.cfm?c_id=1&objectid=10750265 (Accessed: 29 March 2014).

'Govt Mustn't Give Way on League Tables' (Editorial) (2009), *The New Zealand Herald*. Available at: http://www.nzherald.co.nz/news/article.cfm?c_id=1objectid=10581711 (Accessed: 29 March 2014).

'Govt Should Hold Its Nerve on Standards' (Editorial) (2010), *The New Zealand Herald*. Available at: http://www.nzherald.co.nz/opinion/news/article.cfm?c_id=466&objectid=10623467 (Accessed: 29 March 2014).

Hartevelt, J. (2009a), 'Govt to Fast Track School League Tables', *The Press*. Available at: www.stuff.co.nz/national/education/2319002/Govt (Accessed: 29 March 2014).

— (2009b), 'Fear of Marking Children for Life Under New Standards', *Stuff Nation*. Available at: http://www.stuff.co.nz/national/education/3024182/Fear-of-marking-children-for-life-under-new-standards (Accessed: 29 March 2014).

— (2010a), '$26m to Win Over Parents on Tests', *The Dominion Post*. Available at: http://www.stuff.co.nz/national/education/3268678/26m-to-win-over-parents-on-tests (Accessed: 29 March 2014).

— (2010b), 'Test Scores Help Economy', *The Press*. Available at: http://www.stuff.co.nz/national/education/3290903/Test-scores-help-economy (Accessed: 29 March 2014).

— (2010c), 'Two Thirds of Pupils Failing New Standards', *The Press*. Available at: http://www.stuff.co.nz/national/education/4038443/Two-thirds-of-pupils-failing-new-standards (Accessed: 29 March 2014).

— (2012a), 'Primary Results May Go Online', *The Press*. Available at: http://www.stuff.co.nz/national/politics/6351597/Primary-results-may-go-online (Accessed: 29 March 2014).

— (2012b), 'School Standards Report Card 'Ropey', *Stuff Nation*. Available at: http://www.stuff.co.nz/national/education/7208255/School-standards (Accessed: 29 March 2014).

— (2012c), 'Schools' National Standards Results to Go Online', *Stuff Nation*. Available at: http://www.stuff.co.nz/national/education/7433734/Schools-National-Standards-results-to-go-online (Accessed: 29 March 2014).

— (2012d), 'Our Standards for School Report', *Stuff Nation*. Available at: www.stuff.co.nz/national/education/7715002/Our-standards-for-School-Report (Accessed: 29 March 2014).

— (2012e), 'National Standards 'May Aid Rating of Teachers', *Stuff Nation*. Available at: http://www.stuff.co.nz/national/education/7723197/National-Standards-may-aid-rating-of-teachers (Accessed: 29 March 2014).

Hartevelt, J. and Francis, C. (2012), 'How New Zealand Schools Rate', *Stuff Nation*. Available at: http://www.stuff.co.nz/national/education/7715044/How-New-Zealand-schools-rate (Accessed: 29 March 2014).

Hunt, T. (2009a), 'Optimism and "Craziness" – Govt Releases Draft Standards', *New Zealand Education Review* 14 (19), 1–2.

— (2009b), 'National Standards to Begin Next Year', *New Zealand Education Review* 14 (30), 3.

— (2009c), 'Plans to Scuttle National Standards are Mooted', *New Zealand Education Review* 14 (33), 3.

— (2010), 'Boards Get Warning Over Standards', *The Dominion Post*. Available at: http://www.stuff.co.nz/national/politics/3347095/Boards-get-warning-over-standards (Accessed: 29 March 2014).

Kay, M. (2010), 'Key Kicks Off National Standards Campaign', *The Dominion Post*. Available at: http://www.stuff.co.nz/national/education/3283150/Key-kicks-off-education-national-standards-campaign (Accessed: 29 March 2014).

'Key's Focus Not on Students: Principal's Union' (3 February 2010), *Stuff Nation*. Available at: http://www.stuff.co.nz/national/education/3288467/Keys-focus-not-on-students-principals-union (Accessed: 29 March 2014).

Latham, D. (2010), 'Can Tolley Pass the Exam?' (Opinion), *The Otago Daily Times*. Available at: http://www.odt.co.nz/opinion/opinion/91636/can-tolley-pass-exam (Accessed: 29 March 2014).

Laugesen, R. (2009), 'No Child Left Behind?' *New Zealand Listener* 217 (3595), 24–27.

Laveault, D., MacBeath, J., Nusche, D. and Santiago, P. (2010), *OECD Review on Evaluation and Assessment Frameworks for Improving School Outcomes: New Zealand Country Background Report 2010*. Paris: Organisation for Economic Co-operation and Development.

Law, T. (2010), 'Key Prefers to 'Work With' Rebel Schools', *The Press*. Available at: http://www.stuff.co.nz/national/politics/3438282/Key-prefers-to-work-with-rebel-schools (Accessed: 29 March 2014).

Laxon, A. (2009), 'Education 'Set Back 50 Years' by Reforms', *The New Zealand Herald*. Available at: http://www.nzherald.co.nz/nz/news/article.cfm?c_id=1&objectid=10587936 (Accessed: 29 March 2014).

— (2010), 'Expert Plans School Ratings', *The New Zealand Herald*. Available at: http://www.nzherald.co.nz/nz/news/article.cfm?c_id=1&objectid=10624506 (Accessed: 29 March 2014).

Lee, H. (1993a), 'Initiating the Paper Chase: The Proficiency and Junior Civil Service Examinations', in R. Openshaw, G. Lee and H. Lee, *Challenging the Myths:*

Rethinking New Zealand's Educational History. Palmerston North: Dunmore Press, pp. 192–214.

— (2003), 'Outcomes-Based Education and the Cult of Educational Efficiency: Using Curriculum and Assessment Reforms to Drive Educational Policy and Practice', *Education Research and Perspectives* 30 (2), 60–107.

Lee, G. and Lee, H. (1992), *Examinations and the New Zealand School Curriculum: Past and Present* (Delta Research Monograph No. 12). Palmerston North: Massey University Faculty of Education.

— (2001), 'Teacher Education in New Zealand, 1920–1980: Curriculum, Location, and Control', *Education Research and Perspectives* 28 (1), 83–104.

— (2000a), 'Back to the Future? Compulsory National Testing and the Green Paper on Assessment for Success in Primary Schools (1998)', *Waikato Journal of Education* 6 (1), 63–86.

— (2000b), 'The National Certificate of Educational Achievement (NCEA): Fragile– Handle With Care', *New Zealand Annual Review of Education* 10, 5–38.

— (2009), 'Will No Child Be Left Behind? The Politics and History of National Standards and Testing in New Zealand Primary Schools', *Teachers and Curriculum* 11, 35–50.

Lewis, J. (2009), 'Govt Urged to Delay Initiative', *Otago Daily Times*. Available at: http://www.odt.co.nz/on-campus/university-otago/61849/govt-urged-delay-initiative (Accessed: 29 March 2014).

'Listen and Learn, Teachers' (Editorial) (2009), *The Dominion Post*. Available at: http://www.stuff.co.nz/dominion-post/comment/editorials/2823857/Editorial-Listen-and-learn-teachers (Accessed: 29 March 2014).

McLauchlan, D. (2012), 'Chart of the Day, Almost as If There's Some Sort of Relationship Edition', *Dim-Post*. Available at: http://dimpost.wordpress.com/2012/09/22/chart-of-the-day-almost-as-if-theres-some-sort-of-relationship-edition/ (Accessed: 29 March 2014).

Nash, R. (1993), *Succeeding Generations*. Auckland: Oxford University Press.

'National Standards for Schools Deadline Concerns' (2009), *Manawatu Standard* 4.

National Standards Sector Advisory Group (2010), *NSSAG Work Programme*. Available at: http://nssag.minedu.govt.nz/programme-of-work (Accessed: 29 March 2014).

'National Standards 'Tool to Bash Schools' – NZPF' (2010), *The New Zealand Herald*. Available at: http://www.nzherald.co.nz/nz/news/article.cfm?c_id=1&objectid=10623823 (Accessed: 29 March 2014).

New Zealand Council for Educational Research (2009), *Submission on National Standards*. Available at: www.nzcer.org.nz/pdfs/nzcer-submission-national-standards.pdf.

New Zealand Education Gazette (2009), 'Draft National Standards–It's Time to Have Your Say' 88 (9), 3.

New Zealand Educational Institute (NZEI) (2011), *Unacceptable Threats Made to Schools Over "National Standards" Disclaimers* (Media release). Available at: http://www.nzei.org.nz/article/x_category/00546/uid/00693.html.

New Zealand Education Review Office (2007a), *The Collection and Use of Assessment Information in Schools*. Wellington: Author.

— (2007b), *The Collection and Use of Assessment Information: Good Practice in Primary Schools*. Wellington: Author.

New Zealand Ministry of Education (2010a), *Fact Sheet 16: Overview of Monitoring and Evaluation Framework*. Wellington: Author. Available at: http://nzcurriculum.tki.org.nz/National-Standards/Key-information/Fact-sheets/Monitoring.

— (2010b), *Letter to All Schools*. Available at: http://www.minedu.govt.nz/theMinistry/EducationInitiatives/StrengtheningStudentAchievement/LetterToSchools.aspx (Accessed: 29 March 2014).

— (2011a), *Annual Reports: Guidance for Reporting on Student Progress and Achievement*. Wellington: Author.

— (2011b), *National Standards: Questions and Answers*. Available at: http://nzcurriculum.tki.org.nz/National-Standards/Key-information/Questions-and-answers (Accessed: 29 March 2014).

— (2011c), *Strengthening Targets: Resources for Boards*. Wellington: Author.

— (2013), *2012 National Standards Achievement Information*. Wellington: Author. Available at: http://www.educationcounts.govt.nz/topics/121981/122072 (Accessed: 29 March 2014).

New Zealand National Party (2 August 2010), *John Key's Notes. Education – National Standards. Lifting Achievement in Our Schools*. Wellington: Author. Available at: http://www.national.org.nz/web/National_Standards2Aug2010.pdf (Accessed: 29 March 2014).

— (2011), *Policy 2011. Education in Schools: Building Better Public Services*. Wellington: Author. Available at: http://www.national.org.nz/PDF_General/Education_in_Schools_policy.pdf (Accessed: 29 March 2014).

New Zealand Parliamentary Debates (Hansard) (2011), *Questions for Oral Answer – Questions to Ministers, Questions to Members*. Available at: http://www.parliament.nz/enNZ/PB/Debates/Debates/Daily/5/1/d/49HansD_20110927-Volume-676-Week-85-Tuesday-27-September-2011.htm

New Zealand Parliamentary Education and Science Select Committee (2008), *Report of the Education and Science Select Committee: Inquiry into Making the Schooling System Work for Every Child*. Wellington: Author (Chairperson: Brian Donnelly).

New Zealand Principals' Federation (2009), 'Minister of Education Missing in Action, Says NZPF'. Available at: www.nzpf.ac.nz (Accessed: 29 March 2014).

— (2011), 'Contradiction! Standards Compulsory – NCEA Optional'. Available at: http://www.nzpf.ac.nz/list/Releases/2011/CONTRADICTION!%20%20Standards%20compulsory%20–%20NCEA%20Optional.%2020%20January%202011 (Accessed: 29 March 2014).

Organisation for Economic Co-operation and Development (2012, May), *PISA in Focus 16*. Paris: Author.

'Patients Must Come First' (Editorial) (2009), *The Dominion Post*. Available at: http://www.stuff.co.nz/dominion-post/comment/editorials/2557059/Editorial-Patients-must-come-first (Accessed: 29 March 2014).

Rowe, K. J. (2000). 'Assessment, League Tables and School Effectiveness: Consider the Issues and "Let's Get Real!"', *Journal of Educational Enquiry* 1, (1), 73–98.

'School Standards Must Be Raised' (Editorial) (2009), *The Dominion Post* B6.

Smythe, K. (2009), 'The Real Reason Why National Standards Have Been Delayed'. Available at: www.networkonnet.co.nz/index.php?section=latest&id=134 (Accessed: 29 March 2014).

— (2010), 'National Standards: Signposts to a Morass (2)'. Available at: http://www.networkonnet.co.nz/index.php?section=education&id=179 (Accessed: 29 March 2014).

Snook, I. (2010a), 'Letter to the Editor', *New Zealand Listener* 222 (3641), 6–7.

— (2010b), 'Letter to the Editor', *New Zealand Listener* 222 (3642), 6–7.

Snook, I. and O'Neill, J. (2010), 'Social Class and Educational Achievement: Beyond Ideology', *New Zealand Journal of Educational Studies* 45 (2), 3–18.

Stirling, P. (2009), 'Hide and Seek', *New Zealand Listener* 217 (3609), 5.

Stobart, G. (2008), *Testing Times: The Uses and Abuses of Assessment*. London, England: Routledge.

'Strong NZEI Turnout at National Standards Consultations' (2009), *NZEI Rourou* 19 (20), 1.

The Education (National Standards) Amendment Bill (2008). Available at: http://www.legislation.govt.nz/act/public/2008/0108/latest/whole.html (Accessed: 29 March 2014).

The University of Auckland (2010), 'John Hattie to Run Workshops on e-asTTle and National Standards'. Available at: http://www.education.auckland.ac.nz/uoa/home/about/news/template/newsitem.jsp?cid=219183.

Thrupp, M. (1998), 'Exploring the Politics of Blame: School Inspection and Its Contestation in New Zealand and England', *Comparative Education* 34 (2), 195–209.

— (2009), 'Teachers, Social Contexts and the Politics of Blame', *Queensland Teacher's Union Professional Magazine* 6–12.

— (2010), 'Emerging School-Level Education Policy Under National 2008-9', *New Zealand Annual Review of Education* 19, 30–51.

Todd, R. (2009), 'Fear Standards Could Limit Rich Education', *The Press*. Available at: www.stuff.co.nz/national/education/2428248/Fear-standards-could-limit-rich-education (Accessed: 29 March 2014).

Tolley, A. (2009a), 'Consultation Dates on National Standards'. Available at: www.beehive.govt.nz/release/consultation+dates+national+standards (Accessed: 29 March 2014).

— (2009b), *Timeline for Implementation of National Standards*. Available at: http://www.beehive.govt.nz/release/timeline+implementation+national+standards (Accessed: 29 March 2014).

— (2010a), 'Independent Advisory Group for National Standards'. Available at: www. beehive.govt.nz/release/independent-advisory-group-national-standards (Accessed: 29 March 2014).

— (2010b), 'Major New Approach to Lifting Student Achievement'. Available at: http:// www.beehive.govt.nz/release/major-new-approach-lifting-student-achievement (Accessed: 29 March 2014).

'Tolley Firm on Standards' (2009), *New Zealand Herald*. Available at: www.nzherald. co.nz/primary-education/news/article.cfm?c_id=288&objectid=10582439 (Accessed: 29 March 2014).

Torrie, B. (2009), 'Tolley Snaps at Principals', *Manawatu Standard* 3.

Trevett, C. (2010), 'Education Row Gets Personal', *The New Zealand Herald*. Available at: http://www.nzherald.co.nz/nz/news/article.cfm?c_id=1&objectid=10622720 (Accessed: 29 March 2014).

United States Department of Education (2002), *Draft Guidance on the Comprehensive School Reform Program*. Washington, DC: Author.

Watkins, T. (2010), 'Government Offensive Smacks of Desperation', *The Dominion Post*. Available at: http://www.stuff.co.nz/dominion-post/news/politics/3286840/ Government-offensive-smacks-of-desperation (Accessed: 29 March 2014).

Wood, S. (2009), 'Principals in Threat to Boycott Standards', *The Dominion Post* A3.

Wylie, C., Hodgen, E. and Darr, C. (2009), *National Standards Consultation Analysis. Report for the Ministry of Education*. Available at: www.minedu.govt.nz/theMinistry/ Consultation/NationalStandards/SummaryOfResponses/EducationSector.aspx.

Young, A. (2010a), 'Tolley Relieved of Portfolio to Focus on National Standards', *The New Zealand Herald*. Available at: http://www.nzherald.co.nz/politics/news/article. cfm?c_id=280&objectid=10622467 (Accessed: 29 March 2014).

— (2010b), 'Taxpayers Fund PR for School Standards', *The New Zealand Herald*. Available at: http://www.nzherald.co.nz/nz/news/article.cfm?c_ id=1&objectid=10623755 (Accessed: 29 March 2014).

— (2012), 'Straight Talking Education Boss Shuns the Blame Game', *The New Zealand Herald*. Available at: http://www.nzherald.co.nz/nz/news/article.cfm?c_ id=1&objectid=10844483 (Accessed: 29 March 2014).

6

New Zealand: Inclusive Education and Children with Social, Emotional and Behavioural Difficulties

Garry Hornby

Introduction

This chapter considers the important and controversial issue of inclusive education for children special educational needs (SEN), particularly those with social, emotional and behavioural difficulties (SEBD). It provides a critique of policies and practices regarding inclusive education for children with SEN in New Zealand, and discusses the implications for children with SEBD. The findings of two follow-up studies conducted with ex-students of a residential special school (RSS) for children with SEBD in New Zealand are presented in order to illustrate this issue. Conclusions from the studies are that students with significant SEBDs appear to be very positive about the RSS they attended, but when transferred back to mainstream schools this placement subsequently breaks down for the majority of them. The implication is that mainstream schools need to be much better prepared for these students if they are to provide effectively for them. This involves consideration of the following factors: implementation of strategies used in RSS; the professional development of mainstream teachers; transition planning for the return to mainstream schools; support from RSS; ongoing support, from organizations outside the school, for mainstream school teachers as well as for parents and families; and, the development of school organization for meeting the special needs of students with SEBD.

Policy and practice of inclusive education for children with SEN in New Zealand

New Zealand has one of most inclusive education systems in the world with less than 1 per cent of children educated in residential schools, special schools, classes or units in mainstream schools. The 1989 Education Act established a legal right for all children to attend their local mainstream school from age 5 to 19 years. In 1996, the Ministry of Education (MoE) introduced a policy called 'Special Education 2000' which was intended to bring about mainstreaming for all children, that is the inclusion of all children with SEN in mainstream schools.

The 1989 Education Act also set up self-managing schools, so that New Zealand now has one of the most devolved education systems in the world, with individual schools governed by Boards of Trustees made up mainly of parents. The MoE provides policy guidelines but in most cases these are not mandatory, so schools develop their own policies and practices, including those for children with SEN. The only requirement on schools from the MoE regarding children with SEN is a very general one, that schools identify students with special needs and develop and implement teaching and learning strategies to address these needs (MoE, 2009).

When policy and practice regarding inclusive education for children with SEN in New Zealand is compared with that from other countries, such as the United States and England, two differences are clear. First, New Zealand policy for inclusive education has been more radical than that in most countries, with an espoused goal of educating *all* children with SEN in mainstream schools. The impact of this policy is evidenced by the smaller percentage of children with SEN in special schools and classes than is the case in other countries. New Zealand's proportion of just less than 1 per cent compares with England's proportion of around 1.35 per cent, and that in the United States of around 8 per cent. The second difference is that when the actual practice of providing for children with SEN in mainstream schools is compared with that in England and in the United States, glaring deficiencies in the New Zealand system become apparent. These are outlined in Hornby (2012) and discussed later in order to highlight the disparity between the rhetoric and reality of inclusive education in New Zealand.

No specific legislation for children with SEN

There is no specific education legislation in New Zealand regarding children with SEN. The 1989 Education Act that established self-managing schools, as well as the legal right for all children to attend their local mainstream schools from age 5 to 19 years, does provide that a child whose special needs cannot be met in a mainstream school should, with agreement of the parents, be enrolled in a special school, class or clinic. But this is as far as it goes (Varnham, 2002).

This is in stark contrast with the 1996 Education Act in England and the Individuals with Disabilities Education Act (IDEA) (US Department of Education, 1997) in the United States. These are both examples of specific legislation on children with SEN that set out statutory responsibilities for schools regarding provision for children with SEN. For example, the IDEA specifies six principles for the education of children with SEN (Salend, 2011). First, *zero reject*, which requires that the education system cannot exclude students with special needs or disabilities and must provide special education services when needed. Second, *non-discriminatory evaluation*, which requires that children are evaluated fairly and that parents receive guidelines about special education and related services available. Third, *free and appropriate education*, which requires schools to put in place Individualized Education Programs (IEPs) for all children identified as having SEN. Fourth, *least restrictive environment*, which requires schools to educate children with peers of the same age to the maximum extent appropriate. Fifth, *procedural due process*, which includes safeguards for children and their parents including the right to sue if the other principles are not carried out. Sixth, *family and student participation*, which requires that parents and students are fully involved in designing and delivering programmes. These principles provide children with SEN and their families in the United States with a virtual guarantee of an appropriate education. Since legislation for SEN with statutory responsibilities is lacking in New Zealand and schools are self-governing, what schools provide for children with SEN varies widely among schools and ranges from the excellent to the woefully inadequate. However, there is no means of redress for parents who are not satisfied with what a school provides for their child with SEN, except to enrol the child at another school.

No statutory guidelines for schools regarding SEN

In New Zealand, there are no statutory guidelines for schools regarding children with SEN that schools must follow. Guidelines on many SEN issues are provided by the MoE, but schools can choose whether or not to take heed of these. This is in stark contrast with the requirements specified in the IDEA in the United States, outlined earlier, and the detailed statutory guidance for schools provided within the Code of Practice for SEN (DfES, 2001) in England. This Code sets out detailed guidelines for the procedures that must be followed and the resources that must be provided for children with SEN and their families. This includes a three-stage process for assessing and planning interventions for addressing SEN. The third stage of this process requires that a 'statement' of SEN be produced that specifies the programmes and resources that are mandated to be provided for the child. Also mandatory is the need that takes into account the child's views and those of the parents throughout the three-stage process.

In contrast, since statutory guidelines are absent in New Zealand, provision for children with SEN varies widely. In some cases it is excellent but in many cases it is inadequate.

No requirement to have SENCOs or SEN Committees

Establishment of Special Educational Needs Coordinators (SENCOs) in all New Zealand Schools, with a full time equivalent staff time allocation of least 0.2 in primary schools and 0.4 in secondary schools, was recommended in the Wylie Report (2000) on special education, but was never implemented by the MoE. As a result, schools may have staff assigned to this role but typically limited time allocation is made for them to carry out the requirements of this job. Typically, the SENCO role is added to the responsibilities of school principals, deputy principals or other senior staff, with either limited or no time allocation to carry out the necessary tasks. Furthermore, most of these named SENCOs do not have any training in the SEN field.

No requirement for SENCO training

For New Zealand schools that do have SENCOs identified, there is no requirement for them to have qualifications on SEN or to undergo training once they are assigned this role. This is in contrast to England where training is compulsory for SENCOs. Relevant training on SEN is available at most New Zealand universities but this needs to be undertaken at the teachers' own expense and in their own time, so currently few of them take up these opportunities. Therefore, many of the staff named as SENCOs in schools do not have the training or experience with SEN to effectively carry out the SENCO role.

No requirement for Individual Education Plans

While comprehensive guidance on Individual Education Plans (IEPs) is provided to schools (MoE, 2011), individual schools decide which children will have IEPs, the format and content of IEPs and the extent to which parents are involved. Therefore, whether students with SEN have IEPs or not varies widely between schools and IEP procedures are often inadequate, particularly with regard to the effective involvement of parents (Hornby and Witte, 2010).

No statutory training for mainstream teachers on SEN

Until 2011, there was no requirement on institutions offering teacher education to include training on teaching students with SEN. Recently, the Tertiary Education Commission (TEC, 2011) has specified the SEN content of teacher education by providing an appendix to the graduating teacher standards that sets out the knowledge and skills on SEN in which teachers need to become competent. This is a major step forward, but will take several years to implement. A small-scale survey of school principals has found that they are keen to see the new SEN content included in teacher education programmes, but philosophical and implementation issues raised by the academics who are supposed to deliver this content suggest that it will not be a straightforward task (Hornby and Sutherland, 2014). Meanwhile, the vast majority of practising mainstream school teachers have had minimal or no training on teaching students with SEN. Also, there is no requirement for NZ teachers, once qualified, to undertake continuing professional development, like there is in other countries such as England and Australia, so it is only a minority of teachers who take up opportunities for professional development regarding SEN that are available.

No statutory school/educational psychologist involvement

In New Zealand, educational psychologists are based in MoE Special Education Services, with other staff such as speech/language therapists, and typically operate on a case allocation model. That is, they work in mainly a reactive rather than a proactive model of service provision (Hornby, 2010). This means that, rather than helping schools develop effective practices for all children, including those with SEN, they are constrained to work with the 2 per cent of children with the most severe learning and behavioural difficulties. They may be involved in IEPs if invited by schools or parents but have no mandated involvement. In contrast, in England and the United States, psychologist input is mandated in assessment and programme planning for children identified as having moderate to severe levels of SEN.

No school counsellors or social workers in elementary and middle schools

New Zealand schools do not have counsellors in primary or middle schools, but there are guidance counsellors (GCs) in high schools. Social workers are not based in schools, but schools have access to social workers who serve several schools. Thus, although the majority of SEN and mental health issues emerge during the primary and middle school years, children in New Zealand have limited access to professionals who can provide specialist help with these until they reach secondary schools, by which time problems have become entrenched.

No coherent policy about inclusive education

Although 99 per cent of children are educated in mainstream schools, New Zealand still has 7 RSS and 28-day special schools. Many of the special schools have satellite classes in mainstream schools and some have these classes in several mainstream schools. A few mainstream schools still have special units or classes, including around six special units in Auckland and three in Christchurch. However, many special classes have been shut down in the last 20 years, and special schools have also been under threat due to MoE policy on inclusion. Interestingly, in the recent national Review of Special Education (MoE, 2010) consultation was around four options for the future of special schools, one of which was closure of all special schools. Only 1 per cent of submissions agreed with closing special schools. Ninety-nine per cent were in favour of keeping special schools. However, this has not stopped a vocal minority calling for their closure. For example, a group calling themselves the 'Inclusive Education Action Group' has been lobbying the government to further the inclusion agenda and close special schools.

Recent government policy in New Zealand has focused on ensuring that all schools are 'fully inclusive' (MoE, 2010). It also notes that special schools will continue to exist but does not clarify what their role will be. It therefore appears to be supporting a continuum of provision for SEN but exactly what this involves is not made clear. Since New Zealand has no specific legislation on provision for children with SEN and therefore no statutory guidance for schools, the lack of a coherent policy on inclusive education for children with SEN leaves schools to develop practices based on their interpretation of the non-statutory guidance provided by the MoE. Thus, the wide variation in the type and quality of the procedures and practices employed by schools to cater for students with SEN is likely to be the case for some time to come.

Another consequence of the lack of specific legislation on the education of children with SEN is that there is no protection for the special education facilities that have been established. So when new Ministers of Education are looking for areas in which to make cuts in their budgets, such facilities are particularly vulnerable. One area that has come under the spotlight in New Zealand in recent times is provision for children with severe SEBD. This is a very challenging area of special education that has been the subject of two research studies that I have conducted over the past few years (Hornby and Witte, 2008a, b; Hornby and Evans, 2014). But it has recently become very topical with the closure of one of only four residential schools for children with SEBD and the threatened closure of another. In the following section, the findings of the two studies are summarized and the debate about the wraparound service that is to replace them is discussed.

Studies of graduates of a residential school for children with SEBD

Study one

A follow-up study was conducted with ex-students of a RSS for children with SEBD (Hornby and Witte, 2008a). The RSS enrolled children from a wide geographical area within New Zealand and catered for up to 32 children.

Participants

Data were obtained on 29 out of a possible 49 (59.2%) ex-students from a cohort that had attended the RSS approximately 14 years earlier. Of the 29 ex-students, 22 were male and 7 were female and ages ranged from 21 to 27 years with a mean of 24 years. Their ages when they began attending the school ranged from 8.0 to 12.9 years with a mean of 10.6 years. The length of time they attended the RSS ranged from 10 to 30 months with a mean of 18 months.

Procedure

Interviews conducted with ex-students and/or their caregivers focused on quality of life indicators including educational achievement, employment, community adjustment and ex-students' views of their education. A summary of the findings is presented as follows.

Educational achievement

Twenty-seven out of twenty-nine participants (93%) had left school with no qualifications whatsoever. Over half of the sample (17/29) left school before reaching the official school leaving age of 16 years and a further 10 did not complete high school.

Employment

At the time of the survey, 9 out of 29 (31%) of the ex-students were working full-time and 6 (21%) were working part time. Four ex-students (14%) were in prison and the remaining ten were on either unemployment, sickness, disability or other benefits. Since leaving school, only 3 of the 29 ex-students had never had a full-time job. The types of jobs that ex-students had held were ones that required minimal training or qualifications, were low paid and had minimal job security or prospects.

Community adjustment

At the time of the survey, none of the 29 ex-students were married. However, 11 were in de facto marital relationships, 2 were engaged to be married and another 2 had been married but were by then divorced. Fourteen of them were still single. Also, half of them (14/29) already had children. Nineteen of the ex-students (66%) reported that they had a criminal record.

Views of their education

An analysis of comments made by ex-students in the interviews (Hornby and Witte, 2008b) showed that nearly all of the ex-students (18 out of 21) had positive things to say about their time at the RSS. A major finding was that many ex-students commented on how time at the RSS had helped them address their learning difficulties and achieve more academically, as well as helped them to gain better control over their behaviour. Other positive aspects of the special school commented on by ex-students in this study included: smaller class sizes; more one to one attention; a clear disciplinary structure; a safe school environment; the high quality of relationships between students, teachers and residential staff; and, the wide range of activities available in which to participate. In contrast, all of the ex-students had negative things to say about the mainstream schools they attended after they left the RSS. Examples of this were the labelling and stereotyping they had experienced from mainstream teachers.

Conclusions from study one

Despite their positive views about the help they had received at the RSS, the majority of ex-students had been unable to complete high school and had gained no educational qualifications. The majority had poor employment prospects and had a high level of involvement with the criminal justice system.

Study two

The aim of the second study was to further investigate the main findings of the previous study of a RSS cohort. It aimed to address concerns about why, for the majority of ex-students, the advances made at the RSS had not been maintained sufficiently to sustain them through their time at mainstream secondary schools.

The goal of the second study was to identify key factors in ensuring educational success for ex-students from the RSS. A cohort of children who attended the special school 5 to 7 years earlier and who should have been attending mainstream secondary schools at the time of this study were identified by the RSS principal. Mainstream schools were surveyed by questionnaires and follow-up telephone calls to enable the identification of ex-students who were being successfully maintained at the schools.

Nineteen students were located who were under 16 years of age and therefore should still have been at school. Of these 19, 8 had already left school, 2 were being home-schooled, and 1 had moved to tertiary education. Of the remaining eight still attending secondary schools, one refused to be interviewed, one was experiencing severe family issues and another lived too far away to be included. So the remaining five students were the study participants.

Ages of the five students ranged from 14.7 years to 15.1 years. All were in mainstream classes at state secondary schools, two at boys high schools, three at co-educational schools. One boy lived with his grandparents, two with their mothers and two with their mother and a step-father.

Each of the students, plus a parent or guardian, as well as a key person from the school staff was interviewed using face-to-face interviews. Examples of questions were, 'What individual coping behaviours have hindered or helped success in mainstream schools', 'While at mainstream school what agencies have been helpful or a hindrance?' Completed interview pro-formas from the five groups of participants were analyzed to identify themes that emerged from responses to the questions addressed in the interviews. The four themes that emerged focused on: schools, parents and families, outside agencies and personal factors.

Schools

The schools that the five students attended varied from doing nothing special to assist the student, to being extremely flexible in order to maintain them at school. For example, one school allowed a student to spend most of a school year with the school caretaker while gradually being integrated into lessons with specially selected teachers. Whereas, another school did not even realize that the student had previously been at a RSS, so did nothing special at all.

Most schools did little to investigate students' abilities and special needs. Regular behaviour management procedures such as daily report forms and time-out rooms were widely used as part of schools' general procedures for behaviour management, but individualized educational programmes (IEPs) and individualized behaviour plans (IBPs) were rarely used. All schools had GCs, form teachers and deans for each year group who were involved with the ex-students, but none of these had made home-visits. However, GCs were pivotal for four out of the five students. Home–school links were generally tenuous with most contacts made when prompted by students' behavioural difficulties.

Parents and families

Families with whom the five participants were living varied from being disengaged from them, to being totally committed to ensuring they finish school. None of the five students came from homes with two natural parents living with them. Grandparents were carers for one child and were involved with two others. It was notable that each student had one person who took a personal interest in or had a close relationship with him. For two it was their mothers, for one a stepfather, for another it was a grandparent and for another it was the school caretaker, who was also a family friend.

Outside agencies

Involvement varied from no agencies outside school being involved with the student, to multi-agency involvement with staff from seven different agencies involved with one student. None of the participants reported positive involvement of educational professionals from outside the school such as educational psychologists or SEN resource teachers. In most cases, the children's carers reported that support from outside agencies was inadequate to meet their needs.

Personal factors

One student reported that he was going to school because he wanted to do better than his siblings, who he saw as 'losers'; one wanted to 'better himself'; one had a goal of becoming a pilot; and the other two reported going to school because their carers said they had to. All five said friends were an important reason for them wanting to be at school. Three of the students were affected by bullying at school and one of these had been in hospital twice after being beaten-up at school.

Conclusions from study two

All five participants were facing challenging issues and were considered to be at risk of not completing high school. The main factor keeping them on track was support from the mentors that each child had. Four out of five schools lacked coherent plans to cater for these students' needs and seemed unable or unwilling to make adaptations to their standard procedures to do this. The guidance and support that the RSS had provided on transition to the mainstream schools appeared long forgotten.

Findings from this study support the view that, in order for students with significant SEBD to successfully complete their schooling, procedures need to be put in place for ongoing assistance and support throughout their time in secondary schools, both at school and in their homes.

Conclusions on finding from both studies

Conclusions are that students with significant SEBDs appear to be very positive about the RSS they attended, but when transferred back to mainstream schools this placement subsequently breaks down for the majority of them. The implication is that mainstream schools need to be much better prepared for these students if they are to provide effectively for them. This involves consideration of the following factors: implementation of strategies used in RSS; the professional development of mainstream teachers; transition planning for the return to mainstream schools; support from RSS; ongoing support from organizations outside the school for mainstream school teachers as well as for parents and families, and, the development of school organization for meeting the special needs of students with SEBD.

Closure of SEBD residential schools

Given the positive feedback on RSS reported earlier and the resulting concerns about the ability of mainstream schools to provide effectively for students with SEBD, it was surprising that rather than working to strengthen mainstream school provision for addressing SEBD, the New Zealand MoE has moved to close two of the four RSS for children with SEBD. At the end of 2012, one school was closed and another is under threat of closure during 2014.

The alternative provision suggested by the MoE is an expansion of the wraparound service for children with severe behavioural difficulties, which has been developed in the United States. However, research carried out to date on wraparound in the United States has reported limited evidence of its effectiveness. Studies have found high drop-out rates, and for the children who remain in wraparound, its impact on outcomes has typically been small. The only meta-analysis of research on wraparound published to date could find only seven studies considered rigorous enough to be included (Suter and Bruns, 2009). Of these seven, four studies used non-equivalent comparison groups and three used randomized control groups, which are considered to be more rigorous. For the four comparison group studies, the drop-out rate ranged from 15 to 35 percent and the effect sizes ranged from 0.5 to 0.67. For the three randomized control studies, only one reported a drop-out rate and this was 35 percent, while effect sizes ranged from 0.11 to 0.22. These are not very convincing findings, particularly when compared with the much larger effect sizes found for other educational interventions for children with behavioural difficulties (Hattie, 2009; Cooper and Jacobs, 2011). Hence, the authors of the meta-analysis concluded that wraparound cannot, at this time, be considered to be a practice with a sound base of research evidence (Suter and Bruns, 2009).

This conclusion is supported by the findings of a recent survey in New Zealand conducted by the Principals' Federation. This found that, of the schools which had accessed the MoE intensive wraparound service, 53 per cent reported that it did not bring about sustainable positive behavioural change, compared with 19 per cent which considered that it had, and 26 per cent which considered that it was too early to tell.

The earlier findings are not surprising because the wraparound approach depends on support services such as itinerant teachers, educational psychologists, social workers and health service personnel working in effective partnerships with schools and families. International research conducted over many years on multi-agency working such as this has found that, despite good intentions, it is in practice very difficult to carry out effectively (Atkinson et al., 2002).

In addition, the research studies reported earlier have shown that it is sometime after children return to mainstream schools following intensive intervention that things go badly wrong, resulting in most cases of these children leaving the school system before they are 16 years. The MoE has specified that wraparound funding will be available for children only for 2 years, which for most will not see them to age of 16 years. As stated earlier, the finding from our two studies suggests that ongoing support is needed throughout all their years of schooling in order for these children to successfully complete secondary school.

So it is clear that the effectiveness of any service for children with severe behavioural difficulties is dependent on the ability of mainstream schools to cater effectively for them when they complete intensive intervention. This needs to be the major focus of attention if the education of these children is to be improved and needs to be addressed before any consideration of reducing current provision by closing residential schools.

This will require the training of all mainstream school teachers and the development of school organization so that they all have clear structures for identifying and providing appropriate programmes for pupils with SEN, including those with behavioural difficulties. For example, it is essential to have trained SENCOs in all mainstream schools, as was recommended in the Wylie Review (2000), but has not yet been implemented.

Until these changes are brought about in mainstream schools, it is essential to have the residential schools available to cater for children with severe behavioural difficulties. When children are enrolled in one of the residential schools, it is because their families, local schools and support services have been unable to provide adequately for their educational and social needs. For these children being taken out of their local environment into a residential school is what saves them from a complete meltdown. Not having these schools as a last resort option for these very vulnerable children will put enormous stresses on the mainstream schools they will attend, and on their families in trying to cope with them at home. So closing these schools, which appears to be de facto MoE policy, despite this not being its espoused policy, is damaging to the New Zealand education system.

Despite lack of convincing international research evidence for the effectiveness of wraparound and considering the negative reports from principals on its implementation in New Zealand schools, as well as the findings of follow-up research on young people who attended the RSS, the move to close residential schools in favour of wraparound provision cannot be justified on educational grounds and appears to be motivated by financial concerns.

Conclusion

The main issue is that without specific legislation and detailed policy on children with SEN, including those with SEBD, provision for these children is always vulnerable to financial cuts or closure. New Zealand has legislation to protect the rights of people with disabilities but no legislation to protect the rights of children with special needs, including those with SEBD. New Zealand has a code of practice for international students studying here to ensure that effective procedures are in place in schools to provide for their needs. But it does not have a code of practice for SEN to make sure that children with special needs are supported and effectively educated in New Zealand schools. Without specific legislation on SEN and statutory guidance for schools, children with special needs, including those with SEBD, will continue to be at risk of not gaining the education that they need to become happy and productive citizens.

References

Atkinson, M., Wilkin, A., Stott, A., Doherty, P. and Kinder, K. (2002), *Multi-Agency Working: A Detailed Study*. Slough, England: National Foundation for Educational Research.

Cooper, P. and Jacobs, B. (2011), *Evidence of Best Practice Models and Outcomes in the Education of Children with Emotional Disturbance/Behavioural Difficulties: An International Review*. Trim, Ireland: National Council for Special Education.

DfES (2001), *Special Educational Needs: Code of Practice*. Annesley, England: Department for Education and Skills.

Hattie, J. (2009), *Visible Learning: A Synthesis of Over 800 Meta-Analyses Relating to Achievement*. London: Routledge.

Hornby, G. (2010), 'The Demise of Educational Psychology in New Zealand: A Personal View', *Psychology Aotearoa* 2 (1), 26–30.

— (2012), 'Inclusive Education for Children with Special Educational Needs: A Critique of Policy and Practice in New Zealand', *Journal of International and Comparative Education* 1 (1), 52–60.

Hornby, G. and Evans, W. H. (2014), 'Including Students with Significant Social, Emotional and Behavioural Difficulties in Mainstream School Settings', in P. Garner, J. Kauffman and J. Elliott (eds), *The SAGE Handbook of Emotional & Behavioral Difficulties* (2nd edn). London: Sage, pp. 335–347.

Hornby, G. and Sutherland, D. (2014), 'School Principals' Views of Teaching Standards for Inclusive Education in New Zealand', in P. Jones (ed.), *Infusing Insider Perspectives into Inclusive Teacher Learning: Potentials and Challenges*. London: Routledge, pp. 47–56.

Hornby, G. and Witte, C. (2008a), 'Follow-Up Study of Ex-Students of a Residential School for Children with Emotional and Behavioral Difficulties in New Zealand', *Emotional and Behavioral Difficulties* 13 (2), 79–93.

— (2008b), '*Looking Back on School* – Views of Their Education of Adult Graduates of a Residential Special School for Children with Emotional and Behavioral Difficulties', *British Journal of Special Education* 35 (2), 102–107.

— (2010), 'Parent Involvement in Rural Elementary Schools in New Zealand: A Survey', *Journal of Child and Family Studies* 19 (6), 771–777.

Ministry of Education (MoE) (2009), *National Administration Guidelines*. Available at: http://www.minedu.govt.nz/NZEducation/EducationPolicies/Schools/ (Accessed: 28 March 2014).

— (2010), *Success for All: Every School, Every Child*. Wellington: Ministry of Education.

— (2011), *Collaboration for Success: Individual Education Plans*. Wellington: Learning Media.

Salend, S. J. (2011), *Creating Inclusive Classrooms: Effective and Reflective Practices* (7th edn). Boston, MA: Pearson.

Suter, J. C. and Bruns, E. J. (2009), 'Effectiveness of the Wraparound Process for Children with Emotional and Behavioral Disorders: A Meta-Analysis', *Clinical Child and Family Psychology Review* 12, 336–351.

TEC (2011), *Graduating Teacher Standards: Aotearoa New Zealand: Appendix 2.2 Special (Inclusive) Education*. Wellington: Tertiary Education Commission.

US Department of Education (1997), *Individuals with Disabilities Education Act*. Washington, DC: Author.

Varnham, S. (2002), 'Current Developments in New Zealand: Special Education 2000 and Daniels v. the Attorney General: Equality of Access to Education for Children with Special Needs in New Zealand', *Education and the Law* 14(4), 283–300.

Wylie, C. (2000), *Picking Up the Pieces: Review of Special Education*. Wellington: NZCER.

7

New Zealand: Māori Education in Aotearoa

Te Kawehau Hoskins and Elizabeth McKinley

Introduction

Māori education in Aotearoa New Zealand today is shaped by a number of socio-historical forces. The gaping disparity in outcomes between indigenous Māori students and Pākehā (New Zealand Europeans) has its genesis in the colonial provision of education for Māori driven by a social policy of cultural assimilation and social stratification for over 100 years. From the 1970s, Māori activism across the social field has led to significant recognition of Te Tiriti o Waitangi/Treaty of Waitangi as the country's founding constitutional document, a formal social policy of biculturalism and iwi (tribes) positioned as partners with the state. In a 50-year period, the Aotearoa New Zealand educational landscape has transformed from one focused on Māori assimilation to a set of policy goals emphasizing the importance of 'Māori enjoying education success as Māori'. Despite such a remarkable and progressive shift, inequalities are not easily undone. The state admits 'system failure' in Māori achievement (Ministry of Education, 2012b), and is being challenged to develop and implement integrated and multilevel approaches to address Māori educational outcomes.

In this chapter, we outline the key features of the Aotearoa New Zealand compulsory education system as it relates to Māori education. Two strong characteristics of the system are the role of the Treaty of Waitangi in the development of a Māori language medium education pathway, and the bicultural partnership goals influencing the 'mainstream' education system. We provide a brief overview of educational achievement for Māori and comment on some of the effects the country's decentralized, self-managing schooling structure has had on Māori educational goals. We then foreground a number of current educational issues and challenges that are identified in national research and policy as a focus for development. These issues concern quality leadership, teaching and learning – including the role of whānau (extended families), community and iwi in school and educational leadership. We conclude this chapter by suggesting a number of schooling priorities: the need to work towards informed educational decision making based on the careful collection and analysis of individual and school performance data; improving school leadership to facilitate quality teaching and learning for Māori learners in particular and encouraging greater parental/whānau participation and engagement with schools and their students' learning.

Key contexts

The education of Māori students is located within three main broad contexts. First, the signing of the Treaty of Waitangi between the British Crown and Māori leaders in 1840 underpins the contemporary recognition of a bicultural and bilingual education system in Aotearoa New Zealand. Second is the persistence of ethnically stratified disparities in student outcomes. National and international comparisons continue to identify a profile of inequitable student outcomes for Māori students (Nusche et al., 2012). Third, the schooling sector is administered and governed by stand-alone, self-managing schools. This system creates challenges for the consistent take-up and implementation of Māori educational policy and for the sharing of successful practices between schools for Māori education. The implications of the earlier three contexts for Māori will be discussed in turn.

The Treaty of Waitangi

Article two of the Treaty affirmed the '*tino rangatiratanga*' (self-determination) of *Māori hapū* (sub-tribes), and article three guaranteed Māori hapū equality with British subjects (Orange, 1987). Together these articles guarantee Māori a determining role in their own education, and the right of Māori students to their Māori identity, language and culture (Durie, 2001). Māori language and educational activism from the 1970s led to the development of a discrete education pathway delivered in *te reo Māori* (the Māori language) from early childhood to university. *Kōhanga reo* (early childhood), *kura kaupapa Māori* (5–12 years old, primary school), *wharekura* (13–18 years old, secondary school) and *whare wānanga* (tertiary) represent responses to both language loss and system failure (Smith, 1997). The development of this parallel *'kaupapa Māori'* (Māori philosophy) educational pathway, as well as the emergence of national educational goals privileging biculturalism and Māori success 'as Māori', constitute a significant transformation of the Aotearoa New Zealand educational landscape.

Driving these educational developments has been a range of research initiatives. Research activities have included theorizing the development of kaupapa Māori praxis (Jones et al., 1992; Jenkins, 1994; Hohepa et al., 1996; McKinley, 1996; Smith, 1997; Barton et al., 1998; Smith, 1999; Lee, 2005). Curricula have also been produced for Māori-medium schooling settings (Ministry of Education, 1993, 2007, 2008a). In addition, researchers have mounted a fierce challenge to English-medium education generating indigenous, kaupapa Māori and leftist critiques of state education drawn from the work of Paulo Freire (1972), Critical Theory (Gibson, 1986), Bourdieu's theory of cultural reproduction (Harker, 1985; Jones, 1989) and structural racism in schools (Simon, 1993).

The increasing influence of the Treaty of Waitangi and consideration of its implications for education has led to a national Māori education strategy *Ka Hikitia: Managing for Success 2008–2012* (Ministry of Education, 2008b). Based on goals proposed by the Māori education community (Durie, 2001), *Ka Hikitia* (meaning 'to step up') applies to all schools and sets the outcome of 'Māori achieving education success as Māori'. Schooling must not continue as an assimilating force but prepare Māori to actively participate as members of Māori society and contribute meaningfully to its development. Schooling must also provide Māori access to full range of contemporary global knowledges, such that Māori can participate fully as citizens of the world (Durie, 2001, Ministry of Education, 2008b).

To strengthen *Ka Hikitia* as a school system strategy, the Ministry of Education has renewed its commitment (begun in 1998) to work in formal and informal partnership relationships with iwi in order to realize the shared goal of Māori educational success – both academic and cultural (Ministry of Education, 2011). Iwi are understood as connecting with and enhancing the contribution of whānau in raising the achievement of Māori learners. Further, it is whānau and iwi who are the prime sources of Māori and iwi identity, language and culture, and are thus best placed to determine and measure what success 'as Māori' might be. The hope is that a collaborative and cohesive strategy involving the Ministry of Education, schools, iwi, whānau, the wider Māori community – and Māori students themselves – will deliver outcomes recognized as valuable by all.

Educational achievement

The second key context for Māori education is a focus on academic achievement. This is a particularly urgent issue facing the education sector as international comparisons of student achievement in the compulsory school sector have, over a 15-year period, revealed an unchanging and concerning picture. In literacy, Aotearoa New Zealand students typically perform very well in international comparative studies, but have one of the largest 'spreads' of any OECD country, representing ethnically stratified disparities. This is also backed up by recent National Standards data[1] where Māori students, as a group, achieve below their Pākehā counterparts. At the secondary school level, the percentage of Māori students leaving school with the National Certificate of Educational Achievement (NCEA) Level 2 in 2012 is 51.3 per cent compared with 63.1 per cent for Pasifika (co-grouped students from Pacific Islands), and 77.0 per cent for Pākehā. Retention figures, which reflect issues of engagement in learning, follow similar patterns with 64.7 per cent Māori staying at school until their seventeenth birthday, compared to 78.9 per cent for Pasifika and 82.8 per cent for Pākehā.

Current literature indicates that prior achievement is a major barrier to entering university for many Māori school leavers. Māori are less likely to transition into degree-level study than other ethnic groups. Of all 2004 school leavers, 33 per cent of Pākehā students began a bachelor's degree, compared with 13 per cent of Pasifika and 11 per cent of Māori students (Ussher, 2007). However, the disparity in transition rates between ethnic groups is greatly reduced when only students eligible to enter university are compared, although Māori are still less likely to enrol in a bachelor's degree (Ussher, 2007; Loader and Dalgety, 2008). Of students who left school with University Entrance in 2004, 82 per cent of Pākehā students moved on to degree-level study, compared with 77 per cent of Pasifika and 70 per cent of Māori students (Ussher, 2007). The major constraint on the number of Māori attaining degrees is the number of Māori secondary school students achieving University Entrance or better (Earle, 2007).

Self-managing schools

Far-reaching reforms of educational administration known as *Tomorrow's Schools* occurred in 1989 under the fourth New Zealand Labour government. These reforms, including the 1989 Education Act, have been widely criticized as conforming to a 'new right' agenda of state minimization, consumer choice and school competition (Grace, 1990; Lauder, 1990; Lauder and Wylie, 1990; Middleton et al., 1990). Yet the reforms were also, paradoxically, premised on Labour's commitment to equity for various social groups – including for Māori – as part of a commitment to biculturalism, and to meeting the particular needs of Māori education (Department of Education, 1988; Middleton, 1992). The reformed administration of the sector made primary schools self-managing, stand-alone units individually accountable to boards of trustees (secondary schools already had elected boards), and to new state agencies formed by splitting up the then Department of Education. The resulting new Ministry of Education has responsibility for overall educational policy, and the various agencies for implementation.[2] The reforms sought to make individual schools more accountable for achievement through separating evaluation and review of schools from support and advice.

The New Zealand Council of Educational Research (NZCER) has undertaken regular national surveys of *Tomorrow's Schools* since 1989. The most recent is the 2013 book by chief NZCER researcher Cathy Wylie, *Vital Connections*, which argues that the reforms fragmented the sector by disconnecting relationships between schools and the Ministry of Education, among schools themselves, and schools from central and local support. The system, therefore, 'lacks the kind of knowledge-sharing and connection-building features that fuel deep and wide development' (Wylie, 2013: p. 46). Primary schools had previously been nested within district education boards, and sharing knowledge around teaching and learning had been a key feature of their interactions (Wylie, 2013). The competitive nature of the reforms de-incentivize collaboration (particularly in the urban centres), thereby limiting schools' ability to improve outcomes for priority learners like Māori.

Recent strategies to reconnect schools and the Ministry of Education remain individualized and local Ministry of Education offices lack the authority to take an area-wide approach that could support schools to achieve more than they can on their own (Wylie, 2012, 2013). Although Māori educational networks have often cut across such barriers, significantly greater collaboration and resource sharing (including human) is possible in the Māori-medium sector. For the mainstream sector, where the majority of Māori students are located, there are examples of successful practice that could be shared, were collaboration and re-connection to become a supported feature of the system.

The disconnection between schools and the Ministry of Education can mean that national Māori education policies and initiatives may fail to garner school commitment. Further, the relative autonomy of schools means that the Ministry of Education's ability to compel schools only extends so far (McKinley and Hoskins, 2011). The significant variability of school action on Māori student achievement and the slow development of school–community/iwi relationships is arguably evidence of this. The Ministry must therefore take a greater professional learning and development approach to the implementation of Māori education strategy. The recent performance audit on the implementation of *Ka Hikita* by the Office of the Auditor-General (2013) recommends better co-ordination of educational agencies to support schools to understand, action and commit to *Ka Hikitia*, and promotes the sharing between schools of teaching practice effective for Māori educational success.

Challenges

Māori student achievement has been a key government priority in education over the last decade. However, government agencies recognize that there are significant challenges facing them and educational institutions, if Māori potential is to be realized (Education Review Office, 2010; Ministry of Education, 2010a). In *Ngā Haeata Mātauranga 2008/09*, the annual report on Māori education (Ministry of Education, 2010a), the Minister of Māori Affairs and the Associate Minister of Education, the Hon. Dr Pita Sharples writes, 'the challenge is to create an education system that supports the right of Māori students to live and learn as Māori, to reach their potential, and go on to contribute to their whānau, iwi and our nation' (Ministry of Education, 2010a: p. 4). There are two explicit goals in his statement. The first is to create an environment that allows Māori students to succeed as Māori. This is seen as an inherent right of all Māori students to be able to access and have the opportunity to engage with and learn about *te ao Māori* (the Māori world) in order to prepare them to live in Māori society. The second goal is for Māori students to succeed on the same terms as their peers, to have access to global knowledge and achieve in the environment of the knowledge economy. The real challenge for the education system is to deliver equally on both these goals.

The most significant challenge for Māori educational advancement is the experiences and outcomes of the majority of Māori students who are in predominantly English-medium schools. Viability of this schooling form is crucial. English-medium schools are where Māori dimensions are inserted into an existing framework, what Durie (2001) calls 'the Māori added pathway' (p. 8). While adding Māori components to existing curriculum alone has not shown promise for shifting achievement patterns (May and Sleeter, 2010), attitudes towards Māori agendas and programmes have made considerable positive shifts within this framework over the last 40 years. In the context of self-managing schools, however, such developments have occurred in ad hoc ways. The focus of current research and policy indicates that school level developments for Māori student success include quality teaching, learning and leadership with the latter dimension incorporating the leadership of, and effective engagement with, whānau, community and iwi.

Quality teaching and learning

Many theories of school-based achievement attribute causal significance to what teachers and their students do on a day-to-day, moment-by-moment basis in their teaching and learning. The constant within school variance in achievement is usually interpreted as being a result of variation in quality teaching (Alton-Lee, 2003, 2004; Hattie, 2009). Teacher quality in our schools presents a major challenge according to the literature (Timperley et al., 2007; Bishop et al., 2010). Researching the effectiveness of teaching necessarily involves pedagogical practices in classrooms, that is, knowing about how teachers present and respond to students, as well as something about how teachers' actions are perceived and responded to by students. In addition, research suggests that there is a need for intensive and knowledgeable instruction on literacy and numeracy/mathematics at high quality levels in content areas.

The promotion of professional learning and development in schools has an impact on outcomes for students (Timperley et al., 2007). The building of greater knowledge and expertise for the whole staff in the effective teaching of Māori students has been targeted in Aotearoa New Zealand. For example, *Te Kotahitanga*, a professional development programme for secondary schools, focuses on a culturally responsive pedagogy of relations. The aims include creating classroom relations where the cultural experiences of all students have validity, the pedagogy is interactive and dialogic and participants are connected through the establishment of a common vision of what constitutes educational excellence (Bishop et al., 2010).

Another challenge for our schools, particularly at the high school level, is the access and opportunity Māori students have to learn in specific curriculum areas. The *Starpath* Project for Tertiary Participation and Success is a research and development project aimed at identifying obstacles to achievement in secondary schools that serve our low socio-economic communities, especially among Māori and Pacific students. *Starpath* research (Madjar et al., 2009) has shown that Māori students in English-medium schools are often guided into pathways that are not aimed at higher education, and hence do not always have the opportunity and access to learning needed to meet their tertiary aspirations. Academic preparation is central to students wanting to undertake tertiary education, and the key is that students are *appropriately* prepared. This involves raising expectations of Māori students, improved information and communication with students and their whānau regarding subject pathways and their relationship to career choices, and enabling curriculum transitions according to achievement and aspiration changes.

The access and participation challenges in Māori-medium education differ from those in English-medium schools. The central challenge here, because the schools are deliberately kept small, is the breadth of curriculum that can be successfully offered. Often, there are not enough students and/or teaching expertise on staff to form classes in some subject areas (e.g. science related subjects, senior mathematics). While these schools try to increase the curriculum range through video conferencing, correspondence and other means, there is no research on the academic achievement success of students using these forms of pedagogy. Some parents are unconcerned by a narrower curriculum, while others are prepared to shift their children to larger English-medium schools for their child's senior study years. Gaining a clear picture of the achievement of students in Māori-medium compulsory schooling sector is extremely difficult because the numbers are very small. However, Māori parents who engage in this form of education strongly value other forms of achievement in addition to qualifications. Parents sending their children to kaupapa Māori schooling do so explicitly for their child to achieve proficiency in te reo Māori (Māori language) and cultural competencies, and achievement in these areas is very strong.

School leadership

Leadership in New Zealand schools has been a state focus for nearly 10 years (Ministry of Education, 2003). Both a diminishing supply of school leaders and the need to re-focus school leadership to *educational* concerns (in the context of self-managing schools where leaders face significant administrative and financial management responsibilities) have underpinned the development of a national leadership strategy. The following documents represent research and policy statements informing a range of strategies, professional development programmes and standards: *Kiwi Leadership for Principals* (Ministry of

Education, 2008c); *School Leadership and Student Outcomes: Identifying What Works and Why* (Robinson et al., 2009); *Tū Rangatira: Māori-medium Leadership* (Ministry of Education, 2010b) and *Leading from the Middle: Education Leadership for Middle and Senior Leaders* (Ministry of Education, 2012a). The Māori education strategy *Ka Hikita* (Ministry of Education, 2008b) also foregrounds the role of professional leadership as one of the most effective levers in improving educational provision for, and realizing the potential of, Māori students.

Despite the acknowledgement in research literature that school leadership may be broadly located and distributed, principals and school leaders are the clear targets of the strategy. It is their *pedagogical* leadership that is evidenced as having the most direct and substantial impact on student outcomes (Robinson et al., 2009). However, what much of the leadership literature fails to suggest – in a context of significant social inequity – is that schools require leaders with a sophisticated understanding around questions of social justice and equity in education. Leaders who can embed such understandings into a range of leadership dimensions, and gain an unreserved commitment from their institutions as a whole, are better placed to accelerate positive educational outcomes for Māori students in particular (Johnson, 2002; Ministry of Education, 2008c).

The policy strategy of 'Māori achieving educational success as Māori' cannot be achieved without Māori community and iwi leadership in education and schooling. A leadership strategy that sees school leaders alone deciding when and how consultation with Māori will occur and concerning what, or that sees whānau as resourcing school-determined priorities and programmes (Robinson et al., 2009) is unlikely to make gains in Māori students' success. Research suggests that effective school-whānau engagement is important for developing continuities between community and school – particularly where the gap between school and home culture is wide (Biddulph et al., 2003; Robinson et al., 2009). As the performance audit of *Ka Hikitia* (Office of the Auditor-General, 2013) points out: Māori success as Māori is crucial, but many schools struggle to measure it. Many school leaders also lack the capability and/or commitment to provide leadership for Māori priorities, or to support Māori leadership values in schools. Nor is this a task for school leaders alone. As the audit suggests 'more direct engagement and communication with, and stronger input from, whānau and iwi' is required (Office of Auditor-General, 2013: p. 8). Schools need to be supported to develop meaningful and sustainable relationships with whānau, community and iwi in order to create educational environments where Māori students can succeed as Māori.

The Treaty of Waitangi points to a partnership approach in education and schooling in Aotearoa New Zealand that extends beyond whānau as active supporters of their students. Recognition of the Treaty involves Māori participation in governance and decision making at all levels. There are a small number of compelling examples of successful joint leadership that give effect to the Treaty in school governance. One central Auckland school has been operating a successful Treaty based co-governance structure for over 10 years. Using the school's policy-making capacity, the board of trustees and a co-opted representative Māori governance group (including iwi representation) work together to govern the school (Hoskins, 2010; Office of the Auditor-General, 2013). While schools are encouraged to gain better representation of Māori interests through board structures and better targeting of whānau and community members, their self-managing setup means schools can, and do, ignore such encouragements. Examples of partnership commitment at the level of school governance are therefore ad-hoc, and where they do exist, have relied heavily on the persistence of Māori school communities and the commitment of individual school leaders.

Crown–Iwi educational partnerships are one mechanism by which the state is pursuing greater Māori influence in education. Such partnerships are consistent with the Treaty settlement process that involves both historical redress and the establishment of ongoing relationships between individual iwi and the crown. These partnerships provide an opportunity for the state to support iwi to prepare educational plans that reflect iwi educational goals and aspirations. The Ministry of Education (2011) has recently introduced guidelines for conducting educational relationships with iwi to promote a more productive engagement with iwi, schools and educational agencies. Together, Māori school communities and hapū/iwi level engagement may achieve educational partnerships that can deliver on the promises of the Treaty, and ensure greater Māori determination of how educational success as Māori is understood and enacted in schools.

Priorities

Although international indicators show that the Aotearoa New Zealand education system is working for the majority of our students (Alton-Lee, 2003, 2004), within these indicators there are inequitable numbers of Māori students who face educational disparities among themselves and their non-Māori peers. This trend is historical and deeply entrenched. Therefore, to grow an education system that performs strongly for all students requires change from the individual school to system level. Urgent collective school and sector action is required to ensure priority students can achieve education success, and that Māori students in particular can enjoy and achieve success as Māori (Ministry of Education, 2008b).

The government has a number of priorities for Māori education in the compulsory school sector formed around addressing the achievement disparity between Māori students and other groups. The government's target of 85 per cent of 18 year olds achieving the NCEA Level 2 or equivalent for every group of students in 2017 (Ministry of Education, 2012b) provides the education system, and secondary schools in particular, with both the challenge and the impetus for change. In order to achieve the target, there are a number of strategies the government believe are key levers for change in schools. These include the use of data as a tool in educational decision making; increasing Māori student achievement in literacy and numeracy; improving instructional leadership in schools and greater involvement of whānau in their child's education.

Māori educational achievement will not begin to be addressed without schools engaging in more comprehensive self-examination procedures. This means informed educational decision making being based on the careful analysis of data that describe how opportunities to learn are allocated to students (Madjar and McKinley, 2011). It is critical that schools develop the knowledge and skills to organize and use quality data for this process. Currently, data, and its effective use, are very uneven across educational sectors and individual schools. Better and more extensive use of databases in schools to allow the tracking of individual students and school performance are urgently needed, if evidence-based decisions about student educational progress are to be made. Performance data should be able to be linked from primary to secondary schools, and across schools for individual transient students. While policymakers are requiring schools to focus on achieving high standards for all students, few schools presently have the knowledge and skills to set up reliable databases and effectively use the data they currently collect in support of this focus (Irving and Gan, 2012).

The use of data to help mobilize efforts in schools and to increase achievement in numeracy and literacy may seem obvious. Evidence from the *Secondary Literacy Project*[3] and from ongoing *Starpath* project analyses is that a major barrier to success for Māori students at NCEA Level 2 and Level 3 (and University Entrance) is the literacy requirements in specific subject areas. There is a focus on English, mathematics and science as these provide: the core teaching and achievement areas for passing NCEA levels; the basis for engaging effectively in the New Zealand curriculum and they are identified as critical to the national need for an excellent system (Gluckman, 2011 – a report from the Prime Minister's chief science advisor). The national and research-based evidence shows that patterns of success, especially for Māori students, have not changed markedly in the upper levels where there are major barriers for these groups in gaining the literacy and numeracy requirements for University Entrance. The demands for increased high school graduation rates and for more highly skilled graduates require increased effectiveness in these later NCEA years. Properly managed databases and data use in schools can be used to personalize learning, identify problems, formulate responses and interventions, improve school policy and practice, evaluate effectiveness and distribute resources more effectively.

School improvement research has repeatedly shown that improvement in teaching and learning is not sustained unless the school's leadership can create the conditions under which teachers inquire into and continually improve the effectiveness of their practice. Students learn more in schools where teachers report that school leadership is more effective in, or more focused on, setting goals and expectations, resourcing those goals strategically, ensuring quality teaching, leading teacher learning and ensuring a safe and orderly environment (Robinson et al., 2009). The comprehensive nature of most New Zealand schools means that much of the variation in student achievement lies within schools rather than between them (OECD, 2012). The government priority is in part, as previously indicated, to build a meaningful relationship with iwi and to improve school governance structures to be more inclusive of Māori aspirations. In addition, there is a need to address school leadership as well. Priorities include the improvement of principal training options, improved principal selection processes and to interrogate and establish what appropriate resourcing is for what has become a very complex role in the school.

Last but not least is the goal to improve the involvement of parents/whānau in their child's education. Parental engagement is seen as essential in raising Māori student achievement. Research suggests that: parental engagement has more effect at early childhood and decreases as the age of the child increases; parental influences are multiple; parental expectations and their discussions about learning are the most critical success influences and parental participation in the discussion about schooling and learning is positively related to achievement (Clinton and Hattie, in press). Work on gaining more Māori parental engagement with the school is a challenge for both schools and parents/whānau. Further research needs to be carried out investigating Māori parental engagement and its effects on Māori student achievement.

Conclusion

The New Zealand state has incorporated Māori-identified educational goals into national educational policy in response to persistent Māori demands for an education system that delivers both cultural and academic outcomes. If integrated into a whole of government framework, the education system can make a significant contribution to achieving these goals where the roll-out of strategy includes a vigorous, consistent and coherent approach to the leadership of the strategy and its planning, implementation, resourcing and communication across all educational agencies and schools. In the context of self-managing schools, this means support and resourcing for professional learning; school collaboration and the sharing of successful practice and greater whānau, Māori community and iwi engagement, leadership and decision making at all levels of the education sector. These elements combined are essential foci for change. In schools themselves, a continued emphasis on improving school leadership to facilitate quality, culturally responsive teaching and learning is required to raise Māori achievement. Better collection, analysis and sharing of school and individual performance, participation and completion data – used regularly to fine-tune teaching and school practices – represent immediate priorities for Māori education.

Notes

1   For statistics see www.educationcounts.govt.nz, unless otherwise stated.
2   Education Review Office (ERO) – independent school evaluator; New Zealand Qualifications Authority (NZQA) – qualifications development and Ministry of Education – curriculum development.
3   http://www.educationcounts.govt.nz/publications/series/Secondary_Literacy.

References

Alton-Lee, A. (2003), *Quality Teaching for Diverse Students in Schooling: Best Evidence Synthesis Iteration*. Wellington, New Zealand: Ministry of Education.

— (2004), *Using Best Evidence Syntheses to Assist in Making a Bigger Difference for Diverse Learners*. Wellington, New Zealand: Ministry of Education.

Barton, B., Fairhall, U. and Trinick, T. (1998), 'Tikanga reo tātai: Issues in the Development of a Māori Mathematics Register', *For the Learning of Mathematics: An International Journal of Mathematics Education* 18 (1), 3–9.

Biddulph, F., Biddulph, J. and Biddulph, C. (2003), *The Complexity of Community and Family Influences on Children's Achievement in New Zealand: Best Evidence Synthesis Iteration*. Wellington, New Zealand: Ministry of education.

Bishop, R., O'Sullivan, D. and Berryman, M. (2010), *Scaling Up Education Reform: Addressing the Politics of Disparity*. Wellington, New Zealand: NZCER Press.

Clinton, J. and Hattie, J. (2013), New Zealand Students' Perceptions of Parental Involvement in Learning and Schooling. *Asia Pacific Journal of Education* 33(3), 324–337.

Department of Education (1988), *Tomorrow's Schools: The Reform of Education Administration in New Zealand*. Wellington, New Zealand: Government Printer.

Durie, M. (2001), *A Framework for Considering Māori Educational Advancement*. Opening address to the Hui Taumata Mātauranga Tuarua, Taupo, New Zealand.

Earle, D. (2007), *Te whai i ngā taumata atakura: Supporting Māori Achievement in Bachelors Degrees*. Wellington, New Zealand: Ministry of Education.

Education Review Office (2010), *Promoting Success for Māori Students: Schools' Progress*. Wellington, New Zealand: Education Review Office.

Friere, P. (1972), *Pedagogy of the Oppressed*. Middlesex, England: Penguin.

Gibson, R. (1986), *Critical Theory and Education*. London, England: Hodder & Stoughton.

Gluckman, P. (2011), *Looking Ahead: Science Education for the Twenty-First Century. A Report from the Prime Minister's Chief Science Advisor*. Auckland, New Zealand: Office of the Prime Minister's Chief Science Advisor.

Grace, G. (1990), 'The New Zealand Treasury and the Commodification of Education', in S. Middleton, J. Codd and A. Jones (eds), *New Zealand Education Policy Today: Critical Perspectives*. Wellington, New Zealand: Allen & Unwin/Port Nicholson, pp. 27–39.

Harker, R. (1985), 'Schooling and Cultural Reproduction', in J. Codd, R. Harker and R. Nash (eds), *Political Issues in New Zealand Education*. Palmerston North, New Zealand: Dunmore Press, pp. 57–72.

Hattie, J. (2009), *Visible Learning*. New York: Routledge.

Hohepa, M., McNaughton, S. and Jenkins, K. (1996), 'Māori Pedagogies and the Roles of the Individual', *New Zealand Journal of Educational Studies* 31 (1), 29–40.

Hoskins, T. K. (2010), *Māori and Levinas: Kanohi ki te kanohi for an Ethical Politics* (unpublished doctoral thesis). The University of Auckland, Auckland, New Zealand.

Irving, S. E. and Gan, M. (2012), 'Data systems in secondary schools: The state of play', *Computers in New Zealand Schools* 24 (2), 108–136.

Jenkins, K. (1994), 'Māori Education: A Cultural Experience and Dilemma for the State – A New Direction for Māori Society', in E. Coxon, K. Jenkins, J. Marshall and L. Massey (eds), *The Politics of Learning and Teaching in Aotearoa – New Zealand*. Palmerston North, New Zealand: Dunmore Press, pp. 148–179.

Johnson, R. (2002), *Using Data to Close the Achievement Gap*. Thousand Oaks, CA: Corwin Press.

Jones, A. (1989), 'The Cultural Production of Classroom Practice', *British Journal of Sociology of Education* 10 (1), 19–31.

Jones, A., McCulloch, G., Marshall, J., Smith, L. and Smith, G (1992), *Myths and Realities: Schooling in New Zealand*. Palmerston North, New Zealand: Dunmore Press.

Lauder, H. (1990), 'The New Right Revolution and Education in New Zealand', in S. Middleton, J. Codd and A. Jones (eds), *New Zealand Education Policy Today: Critical Perspectives*. Wellington, New Zealand: Allen & Unwin/Port Nicholson, pp. 1–26.

Lauder, H. and Wylie, C. (1990), *Towards Successful Schooling*. London, England: Falmer Press.

Lee, J. B. J. (2005), 'Articulating ako: Māori pedagogy in New Zealand Education', Proceedings of the Diversity Conference 2004, *International Journal of Diversity*, UCLA, LA, 6–9 July 2004, pp. 563–571.

Loader, M. and Dalgety, J. (2008), *Students' Transition Between School And Tertiary Education* (2nd edn). Wellington, New Zealand: Ministry of Education.

Madjar, I. and McKinley, E. (2011), *Understanding NCEA*. Wellington, New Zealand: New Zealand Council for Educational Research.

Madjar, I., McKinley, E., Jensen, S. and van der Merwe A. (2009), *Towards University: Navigating NCEA Course Choices in Low-Mid Decile Schools*. Auckland, New Zealand: Starpath Project, The University of Auckland.

May, S. and Sleeter, C. E. (2010), 'Introduction. Critical Multiculturalism: Theory and Praxis', in S. May and C. E. Sleeter (eds), *Critical Multiculturalism: Theory and Praxis*. New York: Routledge, pp. 1–16.

McKinley, E. (1996), 'Towards An Indigenous Science Curriculum', *Research in Science Education* 26 (2), 155–167.

McKinley, E. and Hoskins, T. K. (2011), 'Māori Education and Achievement', in T. McIntosh and M. Mulholland (eds), *Māori and Social Issues*. Wellintgton, New Zealand: Huia, pp. 49–65.

Middleton, S. (1992), 'Equity, Equality and Biculturalism in the Restructuring of New Zealand Schools: A Life-History Approach', *Harvard Education Review* 62 (3), 301–322.

Middleton, S., Codd, J. and Jones, A. (1990), *New Zealand Education Policy Today: Critical Perspectives*. Wellington, New Zealand: Allen & Unwin/Port Nicholson.

Ministry of Education (1993), *Te anga marautanga o Aotearoa*. Wellington, New Zealand: Ministry of Education.

— (2003), *Report of the Ministerial Taskforce into Secondary Teacher Remuneration.* Wellington, New Zealand: Ministry of Education.

— (2007), *The New Zealand Curriculum.* Wellington, New Zealand: Learning Media.

— (2008a), *Te marautanga o Aotearoa.* Wellington, New Zealand: Learning Media.

— (2008b), *Ka hikitia: Managing for Success/Māori Education Strategy 2008–2012.* Wellington, New Zealand: Ministry of Education.

— (2008c), *Kiwi Leadership for Principals: Principals as Educational Leaders.* Wellington, New Zealand: Ministry of Education.

— (2010a), *Ngā haeata mātauranga: The Annual Report on Māori Education, 2008/09.* Wellington, New Zealand: Ministry of Education.

— (2010b), *Tū rangatira: Māori-Medium Educational Leadership.* Wellington, New Zealand: Ministry of Education.

— (2011), *Whakapūmautia, papakowhaita, tau ana – Grasp, Embrace and Realise: Conducting Excellent Education Relationships between Iwi and the Ministry of Education.* Wellington, New Zealand: Ministry of Education.

— (2012a), *Leading from the Middle: Educational Leadership for Middle and Senior Leaders.* Wellington, New Zealand: Learning Media.

— (2012b), *Statement of Intent 2012–2017.* Wellington, New Zealand: Ministry of Education.

Nusche, D., Laveault, D., MacBeath, J. and Santiago, P. (2012), *OECD Reviews of Evaluation and Assessment in Education: New Zealand 2011* [OECD Publishing]. Available at: http://dx.doi.org/10.1787/9789264116917-en (Accessed: 1 April 2014).

OECD (2012), *Equity and Quality in Education: Supporting Disadvantaged Students and Schools* [OECD iLibrary]. Available at: http://dx.doi.org/10.1787/9789264130852-en (Accessed: 1 April 2014).

Orange, C. (1987), *The Treaty of Waitangi.* Wellington, New Zealand: Bridget Williams Books Ltd.

Office of the Auditor-General (2013), *Education for Māori: Implementing Ka Hikitia – Managing for Success* (Parliamentary paper). Wellington, New Zealand: Office of the Auditor-General. Available at: http://www.oag.govt.nz/2013/education-for-maori/docs/education-for-maori.pdf (Accessed: 1 April 2014).

Robinson, V., Hohepa, M. and Lloyd, C. (2009), *School Leadership and Student Outcomes: Identifying What Works and Why. Best Evidence Synthesis Iteration.* Wellington, New Zealand: Ministry of Education.

Simon, J. (1993), Streaming, Broadbanding and Pepper-Potting: Managing Māori Students in Secondary Schools. *Access: Critical Perspectives on Cultural and Policy Studies in Education* 12 (1–2), 30–42.

Smith, G. H. (1997), *The Development of kaupapa Māori Theory and Praxis* (unpublished doctoral thesis). The University of Auckland, Auckland, New Zealand.

Smith, L. T. (1999), *Decolonising Methodologies: Research and Indigenous Peoples.* Dunedin, New Zealand: Otago University Press/Zed Books.

Timperley, H., Wilson, A., Barrar, H. and Fung, I. (2007), *Teacher Professional Learning and Development. Best Evidence Synthesis Iteration.* Wellington, New Zealand: Ministry of Education.

Ussher, S. (2007), *Tertiary Education Choices of School Leavers.* Wellington, New Zealand: Ministry of Education.

Wylie, C. (2012), 'Improving Learning Opportunities: Why Schools Can't Do It on Their Own', *In Set: Research Information for Teachers* 1, 44–48.

— (2013), *Vital Connections: Why We Need More Than Self-Managing Schools.* Wellington, New Zealand: NZCER Press.

8

Aid to Pacific Education: From Projects to SWAps

Hilary Tolley and Eve Coxon

Introduction

This chapter builds on an earlier review by the same authors, Aid to Pacific Education: An Overview (Coxon and Tolley, 2005). That publication arose from a background paper developed in 2003 at the request of the convenors of the 'Reclaiming Aid to Pacific Education' conference. Its purpose was to provide conference participants with some of the information they needed to inform their scrutinizing of educational aid to the Pacific region. In the words of the convenors, 'while educational aid has been an integral part of education development for all Pacific countries, it has not received adequate scrutiny by Pacific people' (cited in Coxon and Tolley, 2005: p. 28). Particular focuses of the background paper included: an exploration of aid to education in the 'development' context over time, and how this was reflected in aid to Pacific education; a discussion of predominant international aid delivery trends in the 1990s and into the twenty-first century and developments during that same time period in the aid policies and practices of the two major bilateral donors – Australia and New Zealand – to Pacific education.

The 2005 chapter indicated that official development agencies active in the Pacific region were reflecting the increasingly evident process of 'global convergence' in development objectives and delivery models (Coxon and Tolley, 2005: p. 48). With reference to turn of the century global declarations, it discussed how these were shaped by the 1990s debates and contestations around aid's (in)effectiveness which gave rise to global shifts in perceptions about how 'development' is defined, about the relationship between education and development and the relationship between aid and development. A series of international conferences and meetings, organized by various UN organizations and other key development agencies, led to what Glennie describes as the globally agreed 'Better Aid Agenda' of 'the New Aid Era' (2008: pp. 14, 21). The latter term was coined to describe the period beginning in 2000 with the UN Millennium Summit which produced a set of globally agreed 'millennium development goals' (MDGs) – including universal primary education and gender equity in primary and secondary education – to be achieved by 2015.

This chapter continues that discussion. It pays particular attention to the notion of 'partnership' that has since become central to the aid and development discourses upheld at global, regional and national levels. It then draws on recent research findings to explore the development of the sector-wide approach (SWAp) as the aid delivery mechanism seen as enabling 'partnership' in aid relationships, and how this has been actioned in the delivery of educational aid in two Pacific countries. This chapter highlights the extent to which global and regional agenda drive the so-called partnerships that set out to shape education development in the Pacific. In exploring the complex realities of national educational contexts, however, it demonstrates how national social and cultural agency mediates the effects of global/regional agenda.

Thus, this chapter – in making apparent how contemporary trends in educational aid delivery at global, regional and national levels work out on the ground – fits in well with the objectives of the 'Education Around the World' series. Also, with its focus on Australia and New Zealand as the major external influences on educational development in Pacific islands countries, it encompasses the three main sections of this volume. Despite the growing number of 'new' international development actors providing significant amounts of financial support to education in the Pacific, and the ongoing education development assistance provided by other donors, Australia and New Zealand continue their historically established role as the dominant shapers of education in the Pacific region. The 'region' as defined here is that within the Pacific Forum, the key political organization in the region to which Australia, New Zealand and 14 Pacific islands countries belong.

'Partnership' in educational aid: the aid effectiveness agenda

Given the extent to which education development in Pacific islands countries is externally financed and influenced, exploring how 'partnership' is enacted and worked out at regional and national levels requires that it be located within the globally agreed 'aid effectiveness' agenda.

Although the word 'partnership' in development parlance is not new, in the past decade it has become so prevalent in development discourse that 'partnerships' are now seen as being central to all development practice (Cassity, 2010; Barrett et al., 2011; Tolley, 2011). At the level of rhetoric, 'partnership', as the coordinated participation of development partners (DPs) is perceived as the means of creating a more equal relationship between aid donors and recipients. For partners to work effectively towards the same goal, their relationship must be equal, transparent and open. Furthermore, a partner-driven development programme requires that the recipient should take the lead in defining its development needs. Translating the rhetoric of partnership into practical reality remains a key problematic, however.

In the twenty-first century development context, 'partnership' is advocated as a means to achieving social change and economic growth (Tomlinson, 2005) and ensuring 'better aid effectiveness'. Within these global partnership discourses, the importance of building 'ownership' is identified as a key to achieving development goals and expectations; often described as putting the 'partner' in the driving seat. While this description presumes that the drivers know how to drive and where they are going, who is actually holding the map or pays for the petrol is rarely made explicit (Tolley, 2011: p. 39). Some commentators argue that the actual workings of the 'partnerships' indicates they are more to do with establishing what the donors agree as more efficient management structures and processes than addressing historically formed power differentials between aid donor and aid recipient (Baaz, 2005).

How the Australia and New Zealand governments have sought to influence Pacific education through their official aid programmes over the past decade has undoubtedly been shaped by this approach to aid delivery and the aid effectiveness agenda's focus on 'partnerships' (Coxon and Cassity, 2011) between aid donors (now known as DPs) and recipient governments (now known as partner governments). The 2005 Paris Declaration identified five fundamental principles – ownership, alignment, harmonization, results and mutual accountability – as the basis of its 'practical action-orientated roadmap to improve the quality of aid and its impact on development' (OECD, 2005/2008). This was deepened by the 2008 Accra Agenda for Action (AAA), which focused particularly on ownership, inclusive partnerships and delivering results. Many Pacific governments are signatories to the Paris Declaration and the AAA.

Also, in 2007 regional leaders endorsed a set of Pacific Aid Effectiveness Principles, developed by the Pacific Forum Secretariat in close alignment with the Paris Principles. Following on from this, the Pacific Education Development Framework (PEDF), released in March 2009 by the Pacific Forum Leaders, now identifies harmonization as one of its guiding principles. Harmonization is defined as:

> . . . a shared commitment between countries and development partners to align development activities with partner countries' national priorities; and giving importance to the national leadership role in coordinating development assistance with a focus on managing for results. (Pacific Islands Forum Secretariat, 2009a: p. 5)

Noted too is the extent to which Australia and New Zealand have worked to strengthen their partnership in the Pacific. This was demonstrated by the signing of the *Australia–New Zealand Partnership for Development Cooperation in the Pacific* on 9 August 2009. The Partnership focuses on the language of 'shared vision', 'common strategic direction' and 'complementary approaches to development in the Pacific' (Government of Australia and Government of New Zealand, 2009: p. 1). The partnership was endorsed as a first step in implementing the *Cairns Compact on Strengthening Development Coordination* signed by all members of the Pacific Islands Forum in August 2009 (Pacific Islands Forum Secretariat, 2009b; Coxon and Cassity, 2011).

In summary, over the past decade, in conjunction with the various global declarations entered into by national governments and the official multilateral and bilateral development agencies active in the region, there has been convergence both in development objectives and delivery models in the Pacific. Global agreements increasingly have determined *what* educational aid should be allocated to in all development contexts including those of the Pacific. The mechanisms for *how* educational aid should be delivered have also been structured within the aid effectiveness agenda, most significantly by the 2005 Paris Declaration for which 'partnership' and the associated notions of 'local ownership' and 'harmonization' are central (Coxon, 2010).

Described as 'a new paradigm of effective aid' (Menocal and Mulley, 2006: p. vii), the Paris Declaration represents an unprecedented level of global consensus and resolve to reform the delivery of aid. Underlying it is the view that all parties should utilize aid more effectively, giving greater support to partner country efforts to strengthen governance and improve development outcomes. It strongly promotes the SWAp as the aid modality most likely to strengthen partnerships between the donors involved in delivering aid to a particular sector in a particular country context, and between donors and recipients.

The SWAp

The process of shifting from project to sector aid (Cassels, 1997) led to the development of the SWAp concept: the means of consolidating the support, review, monitoring and evaluation of different development agencies for the good of the sector-wide development plan of a country (UNESCO, 2007). In other words, long-term partnerships to utilize development assistance to support nationally defined policies and strategies in the sector concerned. SWAps, therefore, have become the embodiment of the 'new aid architecture' and its embrace of the MDGs (2000), the Paris Declaration (2005) and the AAA (2008). The adoption of SWAps in education and health, in particular, has become synonymous with partnership and ownership agenda (Tolley, 2011: p. 39).

While there is no single definition of a SWAp, it is generally accepted that, in their ideal form, SWAps can be described as,

> . . . long term partnerships, involving government, civil society and donor agencies. Under the leadership of the national authorities, partners commit their resources to a collaborative program of work that includes the development of sectoral policies and strategies, institutional reform and capacity building. [In the case of education, t]he aim of these reforms is improvement in the quality and accessibility [of education]. . . . Implicit in the collaboration is the development of processes for partners to negotiate strategic and management issues, and monitoring and evaluation of progress against agreed criteria. (Hill, 2002: p. 1728; cited in Tolley, 2011: p. 40)

The Overseas Development Institute (ODI, 2008: p. 5) upholds the widely held view that '. . . a SWAp should not be seen as a blueprint, but rather as a framework setting a direction of change – towards better coordinated and more effective aid management'.

SWAps in the Pacific

Soon after the signing of the Paris Declaration, the SWAp approach was being engaged across the region by Australia's and New Zealand's international aid agencies, AusAID and NZAID (now known as the New Zealand Aid Programme), respectively, and three major multilaterals: the Asian Development Bank (ADB), the European Union (EU) and the World Bank (WB). At the second Pacific Forum Education Ministers' Meeting (PFEMM) in 2002, NZAID precipitated the Paris Declaration by spearheading suggestions that the region moves away from the project approach and adopts the SWAp as the primary mechanism for educational support and donor collaboration. New Zealand's championing of the SWAp led to this becoming an increasingly dominant approach across the region, particularly in education. Several Pacific states are in various stages of education SWAps including Solomon Islands, Tonga, Samoa, Vanuatu, Cook Islands and Papua New Guinea. Although at the start of each education SWAp donor partners varied from case to case, NZAID and AusAID have been involved in each and one or another is the dominant donor partner in most.

The remainder of this chapter explores the workings of education SWAps in Solomon Islands and Tonga, two small multi-island developing states in the south-west Pacific.

Tonga and Solomon Islands as SWAp case studies

The independent research study that informs this chapter (Coxon et al., 2011) drew on qualitative and comparative case study methodologies to examine the broad SWAp experiences of key education ministry and donor stakeholders in both contexts. An extensive literature review and interviews with key informants from the Ministries and education community members, as well as DP officials, were undertaken in both study countries over a 2-year period.

Apart from being the two earliest examples of Pacific SWAps, these countries present a conspicuous contextual contrast that illustrates the extent of variance in development and educational contexts that occurs across the region. While both countries are archipelagos comprising very small areas of land in vast areas of ocean, Solomon Islands has five times the population of Tonga. Although 90 per cent of Solomon Islanders are described as Melanesian, there is great cultural and linguistic diversity between communities with 87 listed language groups. Britain, the country's colonial administrator until 1978, had done little to develop the country and infrastructure, and provincial services to this day remain poor. Over 80 per cent of the population live rurally, often in communities of less than 200 people. The spread of Christianity from the mid-nineteenth century was so extensive that nearly all Solomon Island communities are represented by at least one branch of Christian faith. Nowadays, the church plays a vital role in the provision of education, particularly at primary level (Tolley, 2011).

The Kingdom of Tonga is politically rare having been under continuous monarchical rule for over 1,000 years and being the only Pacific islands state to have avoided direct colonization. Polynesian by ethnicity, the majority of the population is Tongan and complex traditional, social stratifications, in which status and rank play powerful roles in formal and personal relationships, are still adhered to. The Christian faith also features strongly in everyday life and Tongan is the official language of the country, along with English. This cultural and linguistic homogeneity, plus the long-standing existence of a 'strong' centralized state has had significant educational effects (Coxon, 1988). Tonga has for many decades provided virtually universal access to 6 years of compulsory, free primary education, with very high rates (over 90%) of transition to secondary education and reported adult literacy rates of close to 100 per cent. The missionary legacy has remained an important influence in the country's education system and for over a hundred years education in Tonga has been operated by two separate systems – government-operated schools and the non-government church-operated schools. Broadly, although the Government of Tonga (GOT) through its Ministry of Education retains close control over national education policy, it focuses on the provision of primary education, with a general understanding that church schools take the majority responsibility for provision at secondary school level. Despite this tacit but generally workable agreement, there has long been a 'distant relationship' between government and the other educational providers (Coxon et al., 2011). More about the Tongan education system can be found in the contribution by Johansson-Fua on Education in Polynesia in this volume.

In comparison, Solomon Islands' education indicators are considerably lower: adult literacy levels are 69 per cent for men and 56 per cent for women. Primary school access is estimated at 80 per cent and primary completion (up to Year 6) is 60 per cent of initial enrolment; transition to junior secondary schooling is 31 per cent and enrolment in senior secondary, just 15 per cent. The most recent Human Development Index (UNDP, 2013) rates Solomon Islands 143rd of 186 countries, second to lowest in the Pacific islands region. Tonga ranks 95th (having dropped from 54/177 in 2005) and ranks highest for the Pacific region.

A crucial factor in Solomon Islands' low human development indicators was the destabilizing conflict suffered between 1998 and 2003 which left an essentially bankrupt government and the central state on the point of near-collapse. Following extensive regional consultation, the Australian-led regional intervention force, the Regional Assistance Mission to Solomon Islands (RAMSI), was deployed in July 2003 to restore law and order and re-establish other essential systems. Education development was seen as a key component of Solomon Islands' broader economic recovery, social restoration and development strategy, and in urgent need of assistance. As part of the reconstruction process, the first Education Strategic Plan (ESP) 2004–2006 was developed with three long-term strategic goals: (i) to provide equitable access to quality basic education for all children; (ii) to provide access to community, technical, vocational and tertiary education that will meet individual, regional and national needs for a knowledgeable, skilled, competent and complete people and (iii) to manage resources in an efficient, effective and transparent manner (Tolley, 2011). Solomon Islands was the first Pacific state to undertake a SWAp in education with the development of the Education Sector Investment and Reform Plan (ESIRP) in 2004, which was originally intended to encompass all forms of formal and informal educational activity. The fact that ESIRP began with only two donors, NZAID and the EU, was a deliberate decision by the Solomon Islands authorities who saw it as an advantage in terms of building relationships and making initial progress under the SWAp. To quote the then Permanent Secretary (PS) for Education:

> Our experience encouraged us to identify which donors were more likely to work in ways that suit us through a SWAp arrangement . . . they agreed to our request that they guide and lead [the ministry] to an extent but not overpower; let them learn from their mistakes . . . and provided really good technical advisors – a key ingredient of the SWAp success; we know who we want and they work for us. (Pedersen and Coxon, 2009: p. 8)

The partnership was formalized in a Memorandum of Understanding (MoU) signed in June 2004 which effectively operationalized the SWAp model as a mechanism to support the implementation of the ESP 2004–2006, and cemented the shared understandings, commitments, terms and conditions agreed by the partners. The ESP has since moved through its second phase guided by the *National Education Action Plan 2007–2009* (NEAP) and is now in its third phase. The number of donors (including AusAID) involved in the sector has grown gradually and, in order to engage all active DPs within the sector-wide programme, an education sector donor coordination group has been established.

For Tonga, despite its strong and early investment in education and health, economic development was unable to keep pace with the needs of an increasing population. This resulted in considerable migration levels, an increasing dependency on aid, declines in public services and growing youth unemployment. On entering its seventh strategic development plan (SDP7, 2001–2003), the GOT recognized considerable inequalities within its social fabric, and the overarching focus of the SDP7 became improving the quality and standard of living for all Tongans. In 2002, Tonga's Ministry of Education engaged in a consultative process to align the education sector with the demands of the twenty-first century and to meet the equality demands of the SDP7. In 2004, the Cabinet approved the Education Policy Framework (EPF) 2004–2019 with its three specific goals: (i) to improve equitable access and quality of universal basic education up to Year 8; (ii) to improve access and quality of post-basic education; and (iii) to improve the administration of education and training (Tolley, 2011). Around the same time, the GOT also indicated its willingness to move towards a SWAp in education, with two key features in mind. One was the intention to coordinate and align all official aid to education within the EPF. The other key feature was based on an understanding that a SWAp would involve the government working with non-government stakeholders across the education sector. With the launch of Tonga's Education Sector Programme (TESP) in 2005, Tonga became the second Pacific state to introduce a SWAp to education aid delivery. The two key DPs at the outset of TESP were the WB and NZAID.

Analysing SWAp progress in each case study

Figure 8.1 is a visual reflection of how the researchers viewed the progression of the key SWAp components within each country. It is based on the 'breadth-depth' model developed by ODI (2008: p. 5) as a means of characterizing and tracking the evolution of a SWAp in different contexts. The findings for each country covers the period from the beginning of the SWAp until the end of the field research period in 2010 (as reported in Coxon et al., 2011) and elaborated under SWAp component sub-headings (Figure 8.1).

Ownership/leadership by host country

Few formal policy and planning processes existed at the time the Solomon Islands SWAp was introduced; the 1998–2003 Tensions had all but destroyed governmental infrastructure and service delivery systems. However, national political will and donor commitment were strong at the inception of the SWAp and have been maintained throughout. The Education Sector Advisor (an international consultant funded through the SWAp) played a central role in the re-establishment of Ministry systems and processes. The inclusive nature of this assistance led to the generation of a strong sense of local ownership, especially

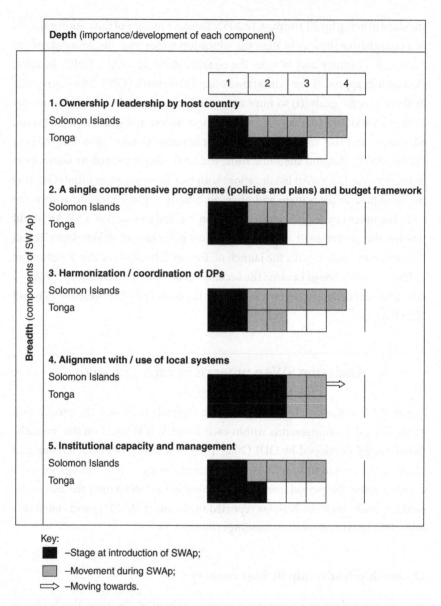

Key:

■ –Stage at introduction of SWAp;

▢ –Movement during SWAp;

⇒ –Moving towards.

Figure 8.1 Progress of case study countries in key SWAp components.

evident in the then PS and her senior management team. Significant progress was made in delegation and communication within the Ministry:

> Before . . . there was a Project Management Team [PMT] which looked after all the work of the SWAp. That has now changed . . . to a Coordination Team as it was not clear what the roles and responsibilities were between Heads of Department

[HOD] and the PMT. Now we have a set hierarchy. The collective management team has the Minister, the PS, the Under Secretaries and the Sector Advisor who are responsible for all the planning in the sector development. Under that, there is the Coordination Team made up of the Sector Secretary, the Under Secretaries of Planning, Accounts and Administration, and the Sector Advisor. Under that, we have a HOD group who meet every month. The Coordination Team meets fortnightly and its major role is to advise the PS; it takes the job of doing the work of the PS collectively to advise her. (field notes, anon)

The twice yearly Education Sector Coordinating Committee Meeting (ESCC) provided a valuable opportunity for a wide group of stakeholders – including other ministry, provincial government and church representatives, donors, trade unions and teachers – to come together and learn about and discuss new policies, proposals and activity implementation. One interviewee noted that 'Most of us are starting to drive in the second phase'.

In Tonga, by contrast, the education ministry has been long characterized by a historically developed system of top-down management through which Tonga has achieved the strongest educational outcomes in the Pacific. Therefore, at the start of its SWAp the institutional climate in Tonga's education ministry was far beyond what existed in Solomon Islands. Despite strong leadership in the past, however, educational leadership during the first decade of the millennium was not particularly robust. Amidst a relatively turbulent political environment, the uncertain leadership, combined with what one key participant described as 'the cumbersome TESP funding arrangements proposed by the Development Partners', clumsy implementation (which led to the 'project mentality' prevailing) and perceived micromanagement by NZAID as lead DP, all contributed to a sense of 'imposition' rather than a locally led and driven partnership arrangement. As one participant mentioned:

. . . sometimes we need to remind the donors that we should be driving the project. There's been a lot of things that we have had to negotiate and discuss with the donors. It's not been easy and even under the current arrangement I don't think it's a full SWAp with Tonga because we still have to go through a lot of difficulties in financial management, reporting and requirements from the donors.

[W]hen the SWAp started we felt we were always being dictated to – do this, do that! But then we said 'no' and whatever we suggested from then on worked.

Overall, the research findings indicated that the SWAp experience had not allowed the already existing strong sense of educational ownership to grow in

Tonga, while in Solomon Islands there was considerable growth from a very low base.

A single comprehensive programme (policies and plans) and budget framework

As previously noted, few formal policy and planning processes existed in post-conflict Solomon Islands at the outset of the SWAp and the first 5 years responded to an ambitious and fairly unrealistic sector plan. This then developed into the NEAP which formed the central planning document. Although considerable policy development proceeded once the SWAp began, including the establishment of planning and budgeting processes, the 2009 Public Expenditure Review, initiated under the SWAp arrangement, identified several funding gaps which later informed current prioritization.

The final stages of the research indicated that the clear value of the SWAp, in terms of planning, was being recognized:

> By having a SWAp, by having a NEAP, by having a budget in place to support the NEAP, we are able to negotiate with DPs like UNICEF and say, sorry your interests are part of a wider context. You need to adapt to us and also your reporting and budgeting. We do the same with the World Bank. Even with AusAID. It helped us very much. . . . [We can] also relate to our human resources and budgeting. It has helped us to focus and come to ideas that we need more qualitative support for early grades, more support for TVET, specialised leadership training. TVET was never part of a wider context – now they are a sub-sector. We now know what human resources are needed . . . because we have been talking about it since 2004. (field notes)

While policy production was prolific during the life of the Solomon Islands SWAp and clear progress had been made in prioritizing activities under the NEAP, accurate costing procedures were still requiring development.

As previously explained, Tonga was relatively mature in its educational processes at the start of the SWAp. Following a donor-led review of the education sector in 2003, the Tonga EPF 2004–2019 was prepared on behalf of the GOT by two international consultants. This Policy Framework provided a comprehensive statement of long-term sectoral goals and highlighted the policy areas that needed to be developed. The early years of the SWAp, however, were marked by a lack of careful planning of the reform process, by both the Ministry and the DPs, and the articulation of policies and the development of strategies for their implementation remained outstanding. This stagnation was seen by some informants as due to the EPF being perceived as donor-driven and deficient in some areas. As such, it had never been totally accepted by key players within Ministry.

Moreover, in Tonga there was less acceptance of the need to raise capacity within the Ministry from the beginning; as one interviewee explained, 'Tonga has sufficient expertise and doesn't need expats'. This belief could have been based on local knowledge of how strong the education ministry had been in the past, or it could be the result of working alongside a number of expensive and largely ineffective international consultants contracted through the DPs (the WB in particular) to enhance the Ministry's management capacity. Whichever, at the time the study was underway it was clear that management skills across the Ministry were in need of strengthening, especially in areas of programme planning, forecasting, costing, budget control, monitoring and reporting. Despite the considerable capability that existed, the structures and procedures that would enhance the capacity required for achieving a fully prioritized and costed sector plan, supported by clearly articulated policies, were yet to be established. It was noted, however, that the drafting of a new Education Act was an ongoing TESP activity throughout the research period. This was seen as an important step in providing the necessary mandate for the development of policies and strategies arising from the EPF.

Harmonization/coordination of DPs

A key focus of investigation in this component was the level of common understanding of the concept of a SWAp among the stakeholders. Early in the research, the authors asked participants from each case study country to explain their understanding of the concept of a SWAp. Not surprisingly, responses were varied and wide ranging as demonstrated by the following small participant sample:

> A SWAp is aligning planning, budgets, reporting and management with what's going on in the sector. It is aligning donor support in a seamless manner to avoid multiple reporting.

> SWAps are a way of working, a dynamic continuum. Sector wide has to be across ministries but it also has to be sector deep involving all the institutions (churches, etc.). Ideally it should be locally led.

> SWAps are an approach for donors to come together and put funding into one basket. The ministry develops its own programme and it allocates funding from the basket.

Ideally it is trying to achieve a partnership – should be a harmonising process. We draw up the plans and priorities; donor role is to assist with support – financial and TA. But the reality is different . . .

A SWAp is when all stakeholders work together – different development partners contribute to the whole sector based on the sector programme. The whole sector includes ECE, Basic Education, TVET, Higher Education and ideally non-formal and adult education.

The key theme emerging from these responses was the need for some level of harmonization among the various stakeholders. Although this is not confined to relationships between donors, or between governments and donors, this section focuses mainly on aspects of the government partner–DP relationship and levels of coordination among the donor community.

With regard to the Solomon Islands Ministry of Education and Human Resource Development (MEHRD) and DP relationship, the deliberate choice of donor involvement at the outset of the SWAp did much to establish local ownership and trust in the DPs. The strong professional and collegial relationships between the Ministry and NZAID as lead DP, which were well-established at the outset, have remained positive and respectful, with both sides willing to listen.

NZAID had also worked closely with the Ministry in developing more harmony and coordination across a range of DPs. In collaboration with MEHRD, NZAID drew up a 'Statement of Partnership Principles between Solomon Islands Government and Development Partners'. This Statement reaffirms the DPs' commitments to the Paris Declaration and the Accra communique, as well as the Pacific Principles on Aid Effectiveness (Coxon et al., 2011). Any DP working in the education sector in Solomon Islands was encouraged to sign the Statement to demonstrate support for shared working principles and objectives even if not involved directly in the SWAp. By the end of the study, another seven bilateral and multilateral agencies had signed up: Australia, Japan, Taiwan, UNESCO, UNICEF, the WB and the ADB.

There was also acute awareness among the Ministry staff and New Zealand's Solomon Islands office of the importance of personal relationships in maintaining positive donor–government relationships, as the following comment indicates, '. . . it is important to have the right people in place and [to know] how we fit in and how we can make the whole thing move'. As another interviewee put it, 'In talking about cohesion and coordination in a SWAP, we talk about people; the outcomes are so closely related to people'.

This need is starkly underscored when considering the aforementioned turbulent relationships between Tonga's Ministry of Education and the DP's involved in TESP (NZAID and WB) for much of the initial SWAp phase in Tonga. However, with a change in key DP staff, relations were restored to a more even keel. As one interviewee commented '. . . [now] we have a say with the SWAp, but it all depends on personalities'. Also, as reflected by a New Zealand official, they had become more aware of the need to understand 'when to drive or not to drive'.

The Tonga Government demonstrated an awareness of the need for more coordination and harmonization with other intergovernmental agencies, and with donors beyond NZAID and WB. But as one ministry officially pointed out, 'we are following the donors' requirements and the financial requirement of the Ministry of Finance and a number of times they draw conflict and so the partnership becomes a myth because we know for sure who's driving it . . .' As a donor representative pointed out, however, '[i]t's a long term iterative process that relies on building trust'.

In spite of efforts to overcome Tonga's early problems with its DPs in the SWAp, there was little movement towards the development and acceptance of a set of partnership principles to guide donor practice within and beyond the SWAp. Thus, harmonization and coordination progress was slow.

Alignment with/use of local funding systems

In Solomon Islands, financial support was clearly tagged towards primary education, and therefore not towards technically sector budget support. As Ministry processes have improved, however, New Zealand's support has become less earmarked with a clear indication that full sector support could be on the cards:

> Our principle is strong. We send in our budget firstly to the government and we only negotiate with the donors when we have the SIG approval. Then we go to the DPs with the gaps. The only thing we pre plan – because it is part of the recurring budget – is all the TA from New Zealand, which is linked to specific areas. We will do the same with AusAID when they sign with the bilateral agreement – it's all approved – we are just waiting for that final signature . . . maybe February.

Although all the donors contribute to the ESF/NEAP in various ways, NZAID was the only donor that worked through SIG processes and provided funding through sector budget support mechanisms – it was reported, however, that the ADB and AusAID were close to doing so. This highlights an important point raised by Cassity (2010) that whereas there appeared to be an increasing trend among donors to support SWAps in education, actual practice indicated that many were, in fact, a long way from aligning with country systems. Despite their having signed the Partnership statement, most DPs indicated an intention to maintain their own ways of doing things. UNICEF and UNESCO activities, for example, remain largely unaligned to the Ministry's work schedule, being instead tied to their own timelines and technical assistance. It was noted that UNICEF, in particular, '... needs to learn to attend our meetings and align with ministry of education and fit into our schedule'. Similarly, Japan's development agency, JICA, and the Republic of China (ROC Taiwan) generally tend to maintain their traditional project approach, 'But we are trying to get them on board'.

Funding in Tonga had always been via the Ministry of Finance – albeit through a convoluted route. TESP's poor financial design was a concern that arose early. Originally, the WB agreed to provide a US$5–6 million loan to Tonga for educational reform with New Zealand providing grant funding. Subsequently, however, New Zealand indicated that it could make an additional grant fund available which meant that the IDA credit could be significantly reduced. Rather than lose the WB loan facility entirely, and access to the technical expertise seen as necessary for successful implementation of the education programme, an 'innovative' two-pronged financial agreement was finally reached between the GOT, the WB and NZAID. First, the WB loan amount was reduced to US$1m and second, NZAID's additional funds (approximately NZ$3m) would be made available to the GOT through a WB managed Trust Fund. The remaining NZAID funds (approximately NZ$11m) were given directly by NZAID as grant funding to the education sector, via the Ministry of Finance. With Tonga not drawing on the loan until the very final stages of the first phase of TESP, all donor funding was effectively supplied by New Zealand.

This '*cumbersome*' funding arrangement led to activities under the SWAp being separated into two funding clusters: Cluster 1, being activities funded by NZAID's additional grant funding provided through the WB and Cluster 2, the activities that would be funded by direct sector budget support to the GOT provided from NZAID's original grant. Thus, rather than these activity clusters being driven by the ESP, they were determined by the complicated funding arrangement designed under the SWAp, administered either through a

WB trust fund – using WB procedures – or as direct budget support. The effect of this initial arrangement undermined the acceptance of the TESP as a locally led sector-wide programme, and resulted instead with it being regarded more as a standalone 'project' imposed from outside. It should also be noted that the WB trust fund was expensive – not only since it involved four currencies and transfers between five bank accounts, but also funds from the grant were also paid to the WB to manage the Trust Fund. Also, although strengthening of GOT financing processes and accountability mechanisms had been taking place since 2007, to the point where the systems were considered robust enough to ensure transparent processes and strong accountability measures (Coxon et al., 2011), it was NZAID's intention to continue funding through the Ministry of Finance but specifically earmarked as educational funding and tagged to particular areas; as commented by an NZAID official, 'I don't think we are at the stage yet where we would feel comfortable with sector budget support in terms of untagged or un-earmarked'.

Institutional capacity and management

Despite the Solomon Islands Ministry having undergone obvious strengthening of capacities in its system-wide planning, a clear desire to build further capacity was expressed and considerable effort and progress were made. Gaps prevailed in some areas, however, most notably in teacher management within the central ministry, most provincial and some church education authorities. Furthermore, the bottom-up planning required for the whole school development plans, which had recently become mandatory, had exposed the urgent need for building management capacity at school level. The growing awareness of the need for greater capacity in data collection, monitoring and evaluation, along with the need for analytical capacity to support government, was also recognized.

In Tonga, the lack of emphasis on the need to raise capacity within the Ministry had led to a neglect in some vital areas, most notably the need for budgetary planning, policy development and data collection and analyses. Where local capacity has been built up, it was clear that this has 'improved the working relationships between us and the church . . . and within the Ministry itself – we are better co-ordinated . . . more communication . . . more harmony'. Overall capacity at an institutional level had been stymied by the lack of a whole-sector vision, but there were some impressive achievements with potential impact at school level, including the recruitment of high-performing national consultants who played a significant role in improving relations between the Ministry and schools:

> [The national consultants] have been good ambassadors for the ministry in schools. It has really helped. It has even helped within the ministry and helped the divisions talk to each other. We have come a long way with working on our partnership issues. Everyone has a better idea of what the whole big picture is. They now see things more strategically. Rather than just working for CDU [curriculum development unit] or Schools or something.

Concluding comments

There can be no doubt that solid, respectful and context-aware inter-personal and 'partnership' relations are critical to the success of any development initiative in small Pacific island nations. Strong, confident national leadership and a receptive, informed donor body working according to a common agenda promotes trust in local ownership and provides an environment conducive for change to occur.

A broad conclusion in terms of our findings pertaining to the different SWAp experiences between the two case study countries is that, despite starting from a significantly 'lower' base in terms of education management and service delivery, Solomon Islands progress towards meeting key SWAp components is stronger than Tonga's. This finding, which goes against the grain of initial expectations regarding SWAp effectiveness, has been reinforced by recent literature. Although earlier writings emphasized the need for certain preconditions, including political stability and a high level of local capacity before entering a SWAp, as Negin (2010: p. 7) remarks, '... some commentators have recently noted the value of whole-of-sector approaches in fragile states lacking strong institutional capacity in order to develop harmonised approaches to strengthening governance'. We are in agreement that the fragility of Solomon Islands state structures including the Ministry of Education at the outset, combined with strong political will to develop the institutional capacity for the improvement of education governance and delivery of basic education services, rendered it fertile ground for a SWAp. Our research suggests that, rather than the previous assumption that very low sectoral capacity and weak delivery of services are serious impediments to SWAp implementation, such weaknesses, if addressed through appropriate partnership relationships with understandings that a lengthy time may be required before results become clear, can lead to an effective SWAp.

Tonga has long proved itself a regional leader in its ability and willingness to provide basic services, including education, to the majority of its citizens. Although Tonga is in a period of political transition, its state structures and overall institutional capacity are relatively strong. Tonga's education SWap might have been more effective had Tonga's historically developed education leadership in the region been recognized by the DPs at the outset. However, although the Tonga SWAp had not been particularly strong in terms of a partnership relationship, or in progress towards meeting key SWAp components, this did not prevent its Ministry of Education employing TESP resources to deliver a relatively high level of service to its education system, which is likely to lead to improved educational outcomes. It must also be concluded that the eventual recognition by the DPs of existing education capacity within Tonga facilitated this.

Finally, although concentrating on a macro-economic and political framework enhances decision making, policy development and human resource development at the top, as encouraged by the SWAp, it is easy to lose sight of the real point of the education aid relationship, which is to improve learning outcomes. Attention, therefore, should be on enhancing existing teaching and learning processes through strengthening and resourcing the key structures of schooling – school and classroom management, curriculum, pedagogy and assessment. Furthermore, given their embeddedness within each country's cultural and historical context, how these processes and structures are to be strengthened must be determined only at national level.

References

Baaz, M. E. (2005). *The Paternalism of Partnership*. London & New York: Zed Books.

Barrett, A. M., Crossley, M. and Dachi, H. A. (2011), 'International Collaboration and Research Capacity Building: Learning from the EdQual Experience', *Comparative Education* 11 (1), 25–43.

Cassels, A. (1997), *A Guide to Sector-Wide Approaches for Health Development: Concepts, Issues and Working Arrangements*. World Health Organisation. Available at: http://whqlibdoc.who.int/hq/1997/who_ara_97.12.pdf (Accessed: 4 April 2014).

Cassity, E. A. (2010), 'New Partnerships and Education Policy in Asia and the Pacific', *International Journal of Educational Development* 30 (5), 508–517.

Coxon, E. (1988), *A Critical Education: The 'Atenisi Alternative'*. University of Auckland, Auckland (unpublished MA thesis).

— (2010), 'Achieving Education for All in the Pacific?' in M. Thrupp and R. Irwin (eds), *Another Decade of New Zealand Education Policy: Where to Now?* Hamilton: WMIR, pp. 185–200.

Coxon, E. and Cassity, E. (2011), 'Education in the Pacific: Rethinking Partnerships', *International Education Journal: Comparative Perspectives 2011* 10 (2), 1–6.

Coxon, E. and Tolley, H. (2005), 'Aid to Pacific Education: An Overview', in K. Sanga, C. Chu, C. Hall and L. Crowl (eds), *Rethinking Aid Relationships in Pacific Education*. Victoria University & University of the South Pacific: Wellington & Suva.

Coxon, E., Tolley, H., Fua, S. J. and Nabobo-Baba, U. (2011), *Researching SWAps in Pacific Education. A Study of Experiences in Solomon Islands and Tonga*. University of Auckland, Auckland.

Glennie, J. (2008), *The Trouble with Aid: Why Less Could Mean More for Africa*. London & New York: Zed Books.

Government of Australia and Government of New Zealand (2009), *Australia–New Zealand Partnership for Development Cooperation in the Pacific*. Cairns, Australia.

Hill, P. S. (2002), 'The Rhetoric of Sector-Wide Approaches for Health Development', *Social Science and Medicine* 54 (11), 1725–1737.

Menocal, A. and Mulley, S. (2006) *Learning from Experience? A Review of Recipient-Government Efforts to Manage Donor Relations and Improve the Quality of Aid. What Factors Enable Countries to Pursue Their Own Development Agendas?* London: Overseas Development Institute. Available at: http://www.odi.org.uk/resources/download/1372.pdf (Accessed: 4 April 2014).

Negin, J. (2010), 'Sector-Wide Approaches for Health: A Comparative Study of Experience in Samoa and the Solomon Islands', *Health Policy and Health Finance Knowledge Hub* 3.

ODI (2008), *Evaluation of Sector-Wide Approach in Environment. Colombia Case Study Report. Characteristics, Opportunities, Risks and Recommendations for Taking the Experience Forward*. London: Overseas Development Institute.

OECD (2005/2008). *The Paris Declaration on Aid Effectiveness (2005) and the Accra Agenda for Action (2008)*. Paris: OECD. Available at: http://www.oecd.org/dac/effectiveness/parisdeclarationandaccraagendaforaction.htm (Accessed: 4 April 2014).

Pacific Islands Forum Secretariat (2009a), *Pacific Education Development Framework (PEDF) 2009–2015*: Pacific Forum Secretariat.

— (2009b), *Cairns Compact on Strengthening Development Cooperation in the Pacific*, *Forum Communique*. Cairns, Australia.

Pedersen, J. and Coxon, E. (2009), *Review of the Solomon Islands Education Sector-Wide Approach. Report to Government of Solomon Islands, NZAID & European Union*. Wellington: Ministry of Foreign Affairs and Trade.

Tolley, H. (2011), 'Partnership in Sector Wide Approaches', *International Education Journal: Comparative Perspectives 2011* 10 (2), 38–54.

Tomlinson, F. (2005), 'Idealistic and Pragmatic Versions of the Discourse of Partnership', *Organization Studies* 26, 1169–1188.

UNDP (2013), *Human Development Report 2013: The Rise of the South: Human Progress in a Diverse World*. New York: UNDP. Available at: http://hdr.undp.org/en/reports/global/hdr2013/ (Accessed: 4 April 2014).

UNESCO (2007), *Education Sector Wide Approaches (SWAps). Background, Guide and Lessons*. Available at: http://unesdoc.unesco.org/images/0015/001509/150965e.pdf (Accessed: 4 April 2014).

Pacific Island Countries: An Overview

Konai Helu Thaman

This chapter contains three parts: (i) an update of my earlier description of the state of (formal) Education in Oceania (Thaman, 2008), from Early Childhood to Tertiary; (ii) a review of progress towards realizing the goals of the Pacific Education Development Framework (PEDF) 2009–2015 and (iii) an evaluative section that problematizes educational development in the Pacific Island region with some suggestions about ways of moving forward.

Often touted as the most culturally diverse and aid dependent region on earth, the Pacific island region is home to some 4 million inhabitants who live in remote and not-so-remote island environments, now called nation states and territories, and sharing a common colonized past as well as the largest ocean on earth. These two things have impacted every island nation and its people in one way or another, including education. In 2009, Pacific Forum Island Countries Ministers of Education endorsed the PEDF as a 'living document' that was to guide educational reforms and development in the region. Linked to various global educational instruments such as the Millennium Development Goals (MDGs), Education for All (EFA), United National Decade for Literacy (UNDL) and the UN Decade of Education for Sustainable Development (DESD), the PEDF is said to be a regional, collective vision of Quality Education for All in Pacific Island Countries (PICs) and Territories. Its implementation strategy is structured at national as well as at regional levels, where a range of activities are pursued, aimed at realizing the goals and priorities of PEDF such as baseline surveys of educational needs; the integration of PEDF priorities into National Strategic and Development plans and the identification of country level support. Details pertaining to sub-regional and national progress towards realizing the goals of PEDF may be found in other parts of this publication. Another important reference is the 2010 Commonwealth Secretariat publication, *Education in Small States: Policies and Priorities* (Crossley et al., 2011). One of the more useful aspects of this book is its focus on the impact of changing global agendas on small islands' policies and priorities, some of which may be more in line with global demands rather than local needs.

The following account is based on my personal analysis of what has occurred in PICs since 2008.

Early Childhood Education

The development of Early Childhood Education (ECE) is one of the main goals of EFA. However, ECE had not always been a priority of most PICs until the early 1990s. Today however, all PICs acknowledge the importance of ECE in their formal education plans although there is great county variation in its delivery. Many do not have a clear policy on ECE which until recently has been the responsibility of non-government and community organizations, especially faith-based ones. Many ECE teachers are primary school trained but there is an increasing number of ECE trained teachers as national as well as regional teacher education institutions had recently included ECE in their training programmes. The impetus for training ECE teachers started with The University of the South Pacific (USP) which offered a Certificate programme in the mid-1980s, and later Diploma and Degree programmes in the 1990s both of which are currently available in distance and flexible modes. The main challenges in ECE include curriculum development and teacher education (especially in relation to mother tongue and culturally inclusive teaching and learning), and the development of clear policies on ECE because of its importance as a foundation for later school learning and language development (Thaman, 2013).

Primary/elementary education

Another goal of EFA is the provision of free and compulsory primary education. With few exceptions (such as Papua New Guinea, Solomon Islands and Vanuatu), most PICs have achieved close to 100 per cent universal primary education. Access to basic education in a region characterized by geographical isolation, absence of policies to enforce school attendance as well as high costs of education, remains a challenge. However, global educational instruments such as MDGs, EFA and DESD together with recent strong advocacy for education as a human right have contributed to an improvement in access to education in many PICs. Many now have legislation ensuring compulsory education and in some places, such as Fiji for example, there are measures in place to ensure that disadvantaged children are able to attend school.

Although approximately 14 per cent of primary age children are not in school yet, a major concern in all PICs is not so much access as the quality and relevance of school education. There tends to be a range of teacher–pupil ratio, from approximately 1–20 in Tuvalu and Tonga to 1–35 in Fiji and Vanuatu. Many PICs train their primary school teachers in their own teachers' colleges which provide both pre-service as well as in-service programmes, while the regional USP provides an in-service BEd (primary) programme, totally via distance and flexible modes. While some PICs such as Fiji, Samoa and Tonga have close to 100 per cent of their primary teachers 'trained' locally, in some countries there continues to be a large percentage of untrained teachers (30%–45% of all teachers) serving in schools, most notably Solomon Islands, Kiribati and Vanuatu. Challenges facing most PICs in relation to primary education include: provision of training opportunities for untrained teachers (a regional project to address this issue is about to be started at USP with funding from the Australian Agency for International Development (AusAID); updating the teacher education curriculum to include ICT competencies, Pacific cultures and pedagogies; quality assurance and developing outcome-based teaching and assessment. There is also a need to upgrade and update physical infrastructure and resources of primary schools particularly in rural and remote areas. External donors (now referred to as development partners) have been assisting many PICs to upgrade basic education either through bilateral agreements (Kiribati, Fiji and Tonga) or regionally through multilateral arrangements such as the recently completed Pacific Regional Educational Development Initiative (PRIDE), a project funded by the European Union (EU) and the New Zealand Agency for International Development (NZAID), and aimed at strengthening the planning capabilities of PICs as well as assistance towards implementation of national strategic plans.

Secondary education

Secondary education continues to be an important priority for all PICs with access still a problem in places such as Vanuatu and Solomon Islands.

Competitive external assessment usually at the end of Year 6 and Year 8 have been the normal entry route for most students although many countries such as those in Micronesia and increasingly in others such as Fiji are using internal assessment methods to determine entry into high schools. A feature of secondary education in the Pacific is the role of non-government organizations (especially faith-based ones), in the provision of secondary education such as in Tonga, Fiji, and Samoa where they are responsible for more high schools than the state. Increasingly now, secondary teachers have formal training (over 50% in some countries) but there continues to be a substantial proportion of untrained teachers serving in Pacific secondary schools, either as university graduates with no formal training, as primary trained teachers or as high school leavers with no training at all. The proportion of untrained teachers varies with each PIC from as high as 65 per cent in Solomon Islands, 34 per cent in Vanuatu, 20 per cent in Tonga and 2 per cent in Cook Islands (SOE/USP, 2012). Teacher education offerings also vary by country with most PICs offering training for teachers of ECE, primary and junior secondary while others depend on USP especially for teacher supply for senior high schools. Some countries such as Vanuatu and Kiribati offer Certificate and Diploma level teacher education programmes for primary and junior high school teachers, while others such as Fiji, Marshall Islands and Samoa offer training for teachers at all levels. The USP offers both a concurrent teacher education programme (BA/BSc GCEd) as well as an end-on programme (GCEd) for university students wishing to serve in Pacific senior high schools and has recently embarked on a special AusAID-funded project to train untrained teachers in Kiribati, Solomon Islands and Vanuatu. Teacher–pupil ratio varies depending on subjects from 1–40 in junior high school English and mathematics to 1–20 in many Years 12 and 13 classes. The high school curriculum had traditionally been tied to university curricula thus making it 'too academic' for many students as well as critics. Previous attempts in the 1970s and 1980s to make the school curriculum more vocationally oriented have failed, although more recent interest in TVET is gaining momentum in some countries. External examinations, usually at the end of Year 12 and/or 13, continue to preoccupy the minds of students, teachers as well as parents as the results are the major determinants of opportunities for tertiary level studies as well as some jobs. An issue related to this has been the regional administration of Form 6 and 7 examinations, with some countries (e.g. Fiji and Tonga) opting to do their own or regional entities (e.g. SnPBEA and USP) offering to do this for selected PICs.

Other challenges facing many PICs insofar as secondary education is concerned include: students'(and teachers') competence (or lack thereof) in English, the medium of instruction in most Pacific classrooms; relevance and quality of subject teaching; inclusion of cross-cutting issues of the Pacific Education and Research Framework (PERF) such as the use of ICT, the place of Traditional Knowledge (TK) in the curriculum; Inclusive Education, HIV/AIDS, gender equality, curriculum relevance as well as training and retaining quality teachers. More recently, quality assurance has emerged as an important issue but a recently endorsed Regional Qualification Framework as well as other regional efforts to address technical and vocational teacher training along with the financing education would help to address this.

Higher education

Although there are increasing aspirations among Pacific peoples to prioritize higher education, the fact is that fewer than 5 per cent of the region's population are able to access higher education institutions and opportunities for those who qualify to enter remain limited due to financial and other reasons. Before the establishment of USP in 1968, most Pacific students had to leave their home countries in order to attend colleges and universities mainly in Australia, New Zealand and to a limited extent, the United States. Today, there are higher education institutions in the region to which many can go including USP, University of Guam, University of Papua New Guinea, Samoa National University, Fiji National University, University of Fiji and Atenisi University (the last two being privately owned universities) and various Community Colleges. There are also the French Universities in Tahiti and New Caledonia. USP is a regional university established to meet the education and training needs of PICs and pioneered the development of distance education in the 1970s, using satellite communication technology to reach its remote and far flung clientele. Today, the university continues to provide lower-cost education to groups of students who cannot or do not wish to participate in conventional education either because of an accident of geography or birth, because of the cost of attending schools or university or simply failure to reach the cut-off points for admission. Today, close to 50 per cent of USP students study via distance and over 20,000 students have received formal qualifications from USP while thousands more have been able to access the university's credit as well as non-credit programmes. With its plan to offer the majority of its programmes online by 2018 Pacific students stand to gain better access to university level courses and programmes at lower costs compared to universities in neighbouring Australia and New Zealand. As well as the main campuses in Fiji and the rest of its 12 member states, there are also sub-centres in the larger countries such as Fiji, Vanuatu and Solomon islands.

Pacific students also take advantage of higher education offered by universities and colleges in Pacific rim countries such as Australia, New Zealand and the United States. These universities offer distance education programmes as well as on-site programmes supported by resident tutors in some countries. Some programmes such as those in vocational education are offered through existing national postsecondary institutions although a new institution was recently established by Australia in Fiji to offer technical and vocational education (TVET)-type programmes and qualifications. Many of these externally owned university programmes are for-profit, targeting a small but influential and affluent clientele in areas such as business and commerce, using curriculum imported from neighbouring countries, with little effort to adapt to local contexts (which is often preferred by those who plan to leave their island homes for those overseas), bringing with it concerns about cross-cultural transfers, globalized curricula and appropriate learning strategies. Other challenges to higher education in PICs include bridging the gap between readily available curriculum resources from foreign universities and less readily available but more relevant and better contextualized materials produced in the region; implications for some groups of students of differential fees introduced by USP in high demand areas; admission policies especially of students with school-based qualifications; students' continuing learning difficulties (associated with the use of English as a medium of instruction); quality assurance issues and accreditation and ensuring a fit between regional and national development needs and what higher education institutions offer students.

Stock-take of educational development: PEDF progress review, 2012

As mentioned earlier, the PEDF 2009–2015 that offers a regional educational vision and development guidelines is aligned to international global instruments such as the MDGs, EFA, UNDL and DESD, and contains the educational hopes and aspirations of the majority of the English-speaking PICs for Quality Education for All. Six priority areas are identified, namely: Early Childhood Care and Education (ECCE); Formal School Education (primary and secondary); TVET; Non-Formal Education; Teacher Development and Systems Governance and Development. Seven cross-cutting themes are included because of their significance to educational reform in the region. These are: Language and Culture, Special and Inclusive Education, Gender and Equity, Information and Communication Technologies (ICTs), Education for Sustainable Development (ESD), HIV/AIDS and Youth and Poverty. As well as PEDF, there exist other regional frameworks which are of a supportive nature. These include the Pacific ESD Framework (endorsed in 2006) and Action Plan (endorsed in 2008), and the Pacific Strategy for Culture and Education (endorsed in 2010), both of which would ensure culturally inclusive EFA in PICs.

The following section summarizes where many PICs stand in relation to PERF. Information was obtained from a Pacific Islands Forum Secretariat (PIFS) 2012 update for the Forum Education Ministers meeting held in Vanuatu in 2012 (PIFS, 2012). Results of a baseline survey conducted in 14 PICs (including Tokelau) showed that while priority areas for each country differed some general observations from survey results could be made.

Access and equity

All PICs face continuing challenges to access and equity with Kiribati, Republic of Marshall Island, Papua New Guinea and Vanuatu having a net enrolment of 90 per cent in primary schools. Others with higher primary enrolment face increasing drop out (push out) rates such as Cook Islands, Federated States of Micronesia and Samoa. Although a newcomer to the education equation, ECCE is now a becoming a fast growth area in terms of both number of children attending ECEs as well as new facilities being established. In relation to primary education, access as measured by enrolment rates (PIFS, 2011) are at satisfactory levels with most countries moving towards achieving universal primary education UPE (MDG 2). However, there are continuing challenges for primary provision, especially in Papua New Guinea, Vanuatu and Solomon Islands. A major constraint for secondary education access continues to be the absence of secondary schools and lack of spaces within existing schools, especially in rural and remote areas. While it can be said that a gender balance in terms of school enrolment has been achieved in many countries, especially in Polynesia and Micronesia, there is growing concern about boys' enrolment and performance, with an apparent increase in the proportion of boys who drop out of school resulting in their lower representation in high school. There are various reasons advanced for this situation but one of the more common explanations relate to the lack of schools in the home villages of students; tuition costs of attending high school and the narrowness of the school curriculum, limiting opportunities for students to develop their potential in areas that do not relate to academic subjects, commonly offered in the curriculum. It may be interesting to note here that Fiji has recently (2013) abolished the payment of school fees for all students thus enabling all students to have free education in 2014. Another issue facing many PICs is the lack of opportunities in the non-formal sector for young people to develop technical and other life skills. A recent re-visiting of TVET through a regional conference held in Fiji in 2011 is again putting TVET on top of some countries' educational agenda as well as issues relating to curriculum relevance, programme quality, accreditation and the quality of teachers/instructors (PIFS 2008: p. 10). Unfortunately, many TVET-related initiatives require extra funding which is not always available at the national level. Finally, most PICs continue to have gaps in the provision of access for children with disabilities although many have embraced the importance of inclusive education for all which prompted the USP to offer a special BEd qualification in Inclusive Education in 2012.

Quality issues

Since political independence, many PICs have been busy pursuing curriculum and other education reforms, aimed at improving education quality. Although there are many perspectives on what quality education is, many agree that without quality teachers there is no quality education. Teacher training therefore is a major component of many countries' quality efforts. As mentioned in earlier sections, some countries still face a shortage of qualified teachers and efforts are being made to address this. An interesting project is being implemented at the regional level with the USP partnering with AusAID to deliver certificate level qualifications for some countries have a large proportion of untrained teachers.

The use of ICTs to improve education delivery at both school as well as tertiary levels has been recognized by many PICs but costs and lack of connectivity remain problematic despite some improvements brought about through financing from external sources. A project, One Laptop per Child, may go some ways to help improve the quality of teaching and learning, especially in rural and remote schools. See Chapter 15 in this volume for more on this initiative. Some countries have moved to improve quality by developing minimum standards including improving facilities and resources, teaching and learning, teacher effectiveness, as well as harnessing leadership and community support. Benchmarking mechanisms such as Quality Assurance Systems and National Qualifications Authorities have also been instituted in some countries to ensure and maintain quality. Improving the professionalism of teachers through policy development has been advocated by international bodies such as the Joint Committee of ILO and UNESCO on the UN Recommendation concerning Teachers and Higher Education Personnel (CEART) which called for teacher policies, as well as systematic professional development of teachers. Pacific researchers and scholars such as Manu et al. (2008) also called attention to important teacher quality issues including: identifying best practice for improving teacher performance; research-based approach to developing evidence-based teacher policies; in-service and pre-service training for untrained teachers; inadequate teacher supply and high teacher–pupil ratios; lack of timely data for forecasting teacher demand and supply; inappropriate or lack of language policies especially those that value Pacific languages as media of instruction; shortage of teaching materials and resources; need to strengthen stakeholder approaches to solicit community support at the school level; need to recruit high quality teacher trainees; improved teacher salary and working conditions and the gradual feminization of the teaching profession especially at the Early Childhood and primary school levels.

Efficiency and effectiveness

A major challenge in most PICs, identified by the Pacific Island Forum Secretariat, is the apparent lack of coordination within and between various sectors that impact education. For example, TVET and non-formal education have traditionally been outside the mandate of Ministries of Education (MOEs) although there is now a Regional TVET Framework setup to provide guidance to countries that wish to embark on developing this sector. Also associated with improving efficiency and effectiveness is the need for strategic policies on continuing capacity building and ongoing professional training, establishing and maintaining Education Management Information Systems (EMIS) to improve decision making; policy development and review of education legislation; partnerships among communities, schools, NGOs and governments; as well as partnerships between various ministries such as Health and Education and, Environment and Education. Insofar as the requirement to integrate elements of the PEDF to national education plans, PIFS reports that there seems to be good coverage within national plans although financial support is needed to further develop new national plans as this task is the responsibility of national governments to fund. Regional initiatives are also expected to assist national governments in this area.

Regional initiatives

For almost four decades now, it has become a necessity as well as a tradition of many PICs to partner with donors and international agencies in almost all levels of educational development through bilateral as well as multilateral agreements. Multilateral or regional initiatives are meant to support national educational development efforts and are commonly expected to be integrated into national plans for the sake of sustainability. An example of this is the Monitoring and Evaluation Framework for PERF developed at the regional level by a taskforce consisting of regional organizations and development partners (USP), the United Nations Educational Scientific and Cultural Organisation (UNESCO), Secretariat of Pacific Community (SPC), the United Nations Children's Fund (UNICEF), AusAID, NZAID and the Oceania National Olympic Committee (ONOC) with the Pacific Island Forum Secretariat as chair. The Monitoring and Evaluation Framework is to be used to track progress at country levels of the PEDF and ensure alignment between PEDF and national education plans. In March 2012 a support tool, the EMIS was agreed upon by FEDM to be developed jointly by UNESCO, the South Pacific Board for Educational Assessment (SPBEA), USP, PIFS with assistance from AusAID.

The Pacific Education Paradox: an analysis of issues and challenges

Materials available on Pacific educational issues and challenges normally consist of a long list of problems many of which relate to the region's geography, climate, cultural diversity and economic standing. Others relate to the education system itself: its structure, policies and processes. These include high population growth rates and rural to urban drift, often challenging the education systems of some countries while depopulation, mainly as a result of outward migration, is the challenge in others. Geographic isolation and susceptibility to natural disasters also cause a number of problems to education systems in terms of access, equity as well as quality. Very large classes are being experienced by many urban schools where the teacher–pupil ratio is often more than 1–40, unfairly straining the resources of the school as well as teachers. Add to this the apparent deterioration of teachers' salaries and working conditions, often resulting in low morale and poor student outputs. Some countries are trying to address this by resorting to building more classrooms, school zoning and/or hiring more teachers but all these require additional funds that many schools do not have. While the need to address all of these issues, and more, cannot be over-emphasized, the final part of this chapter tries to look behind the issues and trends and explore possibilities that may be useful for those who are trying to make a difference in Pacific education.

It is common knowledge among most Pacific educators that despite heavy financial and manpower investment by Pacific governments and external donor agencies, there have been disappointing records in aspects of educational reform, as in other developing regions in the world. Areas of concern continue to include: improved access at all levels of formal education, better contextualization of curricula, as well as improvement in training of teachers and other educational personnel. The quality of education as measured by UN indicators remains low and the effectiveness of most education systems is deemed to be poor (Asian Development Bank, 1996; Pene et al., 2002).

The task of Pacific educators would be to identify the main issues and challenges facing Pacific education, to assess the degree to which current education systems are addressing these and to suggest possible future activities that may lead to the development of more appropriate and meaningful alternative education and development paradigms for future educational improvement in our region. Based on my experiences working in the Pacific as a teacher, teacher educator and curriculum advisor for more than 30 years, I would have to conclude that formal education in most PICs has largely failed in its mandate to provide the quality human resources needed to achieve Pacific development goals. Furthermore, the recent emphasis in and priority for educational reforms in the region, focusing heavily on access and equity, quality, effectiveness and efficiency, have often failed to ask the basic question about the purposes of education and what it is supposed to do for Pacific peoples, their cultures and livelihoods. There is a need to ask this question again and again because the goals of formal education continue to be too broad and abstract, reflecting mainly Western European values, realities, historical referents and philosophical orientations rather than Pacific worldviews, knowledge and value systems. The goals of PEDF reflect concerns of the global community and what it wants developing countries to achieve, often following the footsteps of richer, more developed countries with little or no real input from Pacific peoples and communities. Just as in the nineteenth century schools were established because this was what the missionaries thought was good for Pacific islanders, modern Pacific educational issues and their solutions are often identified by foreign consultants who are employed by Pacific states and paid by external donors as part of various education and other aid packages. Even if we agree on the three main goals of schooling being: (i) promotion of economic progress; (ii) transmission of culture and (iii) cultivation of children's moral and intellectual development – we would have to conclude that in most PICs, schools have failed most Pacific peoples and communities. Theoretically a country's education system addresses all three goals earlier, at the same time: teachers would help children to grow intellectually and morally by expanding their knowledge and understanding of their cultural heritages. This personal growth would empower them to build on that heritage, discover better ways of managing their environments and generate wealth for their societies (Serpell, 1993). Most Pacific educators know that in practice, Pacific education systems have fallen far short of this ideal synthesis mainly because the economic and cultural agendas of formal education have been and continue to be in conflict as schools do not consciously transmit Pacific cultural heritages – the foundation upon which (Pacific) people develop their identities, discover ways of managing their environments and generate wealth for themselves and their communities.

If we look at the pedagogic agenda of Pacific schools, for example, we find assumptions about how to prepare children for adult roles based on the findings of Western psychology (of learners and the learning process) that are often different from those assumptions of Pacific indigenous societies in which many Pacific children live and are socialized. In their home cultures, children learn how to communicate with other people; how their society is organized and what type of technologies are available to them. They learn about the world first from their families and later from other institutions such as the wider community, religious and other kin-based groupings. These institutions often share both a physical as well as a cultural system of meanings and practices, sometimes referred to as an eco-cultural niche (Gallimore et al., 1993). This niche sets the standards by which people's learning is judged, usually through their performance and behaviour. Quality is context-specific and linked to culturally appropriate behaviour and performance. When most Pacific children go to school, the relationship between it and those contexts in which they are socialized becomes a huge issue, but one which is not often acknowledged and/or problematized by those who control what schools do to children and/or provide in the school curriculum.

During the past three decades, some educators have argued that in order to allow for continuity in children's socialization there needs to be some sort of organized caregiving before children start school, hence we have the increased concern for ECE in the region, as mentioned earlier. This expansion, however, is not because of a need to ensure continuity between the child's home and the school environment, rather it is for the most part an attempt to transform children's behaviour so that they are able to fit better into the requirements of primary/elementary schooling, preparing them to learn the specialized (foreign) knowledge that the schools continue to transmit. For how can a Fijian or Tongan child reconcile the values cultivated by her urban schooling with the demands of allegiance to the values of her home culture/village which the schools often implicitly marginalize, even suppress? Clearly for most Pacific Island learners, there continues to be a discrepancy between the goals of schooling and that of their (informal) education in their home cultures and communities.

Such a discrepancy is only part of the educational paradox, however. Another is related to the apparent devaluing of children's home cultures by teachers and educational authorities. Since economic power is usually associated with social prestige, the less powerful in society often aspire to emulate the cultural practices of the economically powerful groups However, in places where economic power is controlled by a group that is culturally different from that to which the child belongs, the need to acquire economically empowering knowledge and understanding at school often lead to a devaluing and de-emphasizing of the culture of the child's community and family (Ogbu, 1978; Scott, 1981). Such a conflict, in my view, may be contributing to school underachievement of many Pacific students today. Two opposing views on this phenomenon currently exist: the first is the so-called blame the victim syndrome where many teachers and even educational authorities blame students' cultures for their learning problems and ultimately failure. Furthermore, we often hear and/or read that Pacific families are giving too much emphasis to collective and cooperative behaviour and cultural conformity rather than autonomy and competitiveness – traits that the school values and requires for success. Supporters of this view believe that most indigenous Pacific cultures are incapable of providing the ingredients required for economic progress in a modern society. A second view is one that sees schooling as a way for the more powerful to dominate the less powerful – popularized by writers such as Freire (1972), Bowles and Gintis (1976) and Bourdieu (1993). These writers and others believe that the power of formal education is a fiction of our imagination, deliberately designed to mystify, domesticate and co-opt students to be participants in a culture that legitimates and reproduces the dominance of those already in power.

A middle of the road position may be to view schooling as more than a mere instrument of political repression and allow the possibility of resistance to schooling as more than mere ignorance of those that oppose it. Perhaps, a more direct focus on the pedagogic agenda of schooling is in order if it is to become a source of empowerment rather than just an instrument of indoctrination and repression. We may need to look at the intellectual content of schooling and use learners' creative imagination to help make school learning culturally inclusive and enriching for learners as well as to the communities that send them there. This needs dialogue among different stakeholders, to work out what kinds of students' learning outcomes schools should foster. This means that schools must shift the focus from subjects and curriculum outcomes to students' learning outcomes. A few PICs are beginning to make such a shift but this path is fraught with challenges.

Focusing on outcomes would make schooling more accountable to Pacific communities because it will provide a picture of the type of student behaviour that can occur as a result of schooling; describe long-term learning; reflect discipline standards beyond the school setting; acknowledge different teaching and learning styles and forms of intelligences; be understandable to students, parents, and communities; address higher order thinking skills and be accessible directly or indirectly to those who wish to access them.

There is more to be said about the outcomes-based approach to learning and its implications for the curriculum, for teachers and for education systems but that is outside the remit of this chapter. Suffice to say that students' learning outcomes would be the foundation for decisions about curriculum, teaching, assessment, professional development, and so on rather than a collection of policies and regulations about how schools (or universities for that matter) should function.

Another issue related to the apparent culturally undemocratic nature of formal education relates to the definition of 'success' in education. Is it achieving 6 years of schooling? Or 12 years of schooling? Most PICs have defined for themselves what educational success might be. For some, it's completion of 6 years of schooling; for others, 12 years of schooling. Many PICs particularly those in Polynesia and Micronesia have achieved almost 100 per cent UPE. However if the results of high school leaving exams (at the end of Year 11 or Year 12) are to be an indicator of success, then most children who start school emerge as failures because of high push-outs and relatively low high school completion rates. The fact is that many schools have failed children rather than the other way around. It cannot be said that Pacific schools are producing more successes than failures and many schools fail to ensure important learning outcomes for thousands of Pacific children.

Some reasons have been advanced for the failure of schools in most PICs. They include: ill resourced and incompetent teachers; ill equipped and badly managed schools and ignorant or delinquent parents. While some educationists blame parents for not prioritizing education, many parents and employers blame the school for being irrelevant to the job market and economic success. One may ask why has there not been a major shift in the education package offered to Pacific learners in PICs? Perhaps, the reason is because so many Pacific leaders and educationists have been greatly influenced by and actually believe in modernization and human capital theories which claim that formal education will produce the type of individuals who will have the necessary knowledge, skills and attitudes for building, expanding and maintaining a modern Pacific society.

Two manifestations are associated with the earlier perspective: the first is a rather elitist one which assumes that public resources are better invested in the few who will succeed and do a good job rather than investing in everyone who may end up doing poorly. This view has necessitated standardized, intelligence and scholastic tests because of their alleged power to predict performance in higher education or the formal sector. Employment therefore would only come to those who are 'selected' because of their superior intelligence. A fundamental question arises here as to why an education system would be designed so that only a minority of the population could succeed. A second and less elitist perspective claims that even in small doses schooling has a variety of beneficial socio-economic consequences somewhat independent of access to employment in the formal sector of the economy, such as, for example, improved agricultural productivity, and better health and nutrition. This view appears to occur independently of either curriculum focus or quality of schooling.

The earlier perspectives assume that formal education is an economic investment, one that seems to be flawed. In many PICs today most primary leavers, if they are lucky, would find jobs in quasi subsistence economic activities while those who migrated to towns or overseas end up in economic and socially peripheral activities such as domestic workers. Research also showed that primary schooling was exclusively perceived as a staircase which leads to secondary schooling and later to higher education and formal sector employment, a view shared by many Pacific people who see schooling as the wisdom of the nation as opposed to traditional wisdom gained outside of school (Thaman, 1988). Others see schools as technologically powerful but culturally alien, often 'extracting' children from their families and cultures and many parents see this 'extractive' nature of schooling as a necessary 'sacrifice' and want schooling to do better at 'extracting' their children, and teachers to help in this work. But essentially most people see education as about schooling, and schooling as about getting to the next level through passing examinations – hence the need to improve teacher effectiveness in the classroom and improve students' performance in external examinations. This view needs to be seriously questioned in order to find out if there are other knowledge, skills and understandings that young people need to learn in order to live worthwhile and sustainable lives in their various Pacific communities (Johansson-Fua, 2006).

A framework for shifting educational focus

The Delors Report on Education for the twenty-first century (1996) made two recommendations that are pertinent to an attempt to find alternatives to the current conceptual framework of Pacific education. The first is a renewed emphasis on the moral and cultural dimension of education, and the second has to do with considerations of life-long learning. Since the received epistemology that guided the work of the Commission was largely Western, it viewed the moral and the cultural aspects of education as separate spheres. However, most Pacific indigenous epistemologies consider that what is moral is what is right by the norms and values of the culture concerned for to assume that something is universally 'moral' is to say that there exists a universal culture, an assertion that begs the question of what actually constitutes such a culture and who defines what is 'moral'.

The emphasis of the Commission on moral and cultural dimension of education is interesting given the overemphasis on the economic dimension of much of the development agenda of most PICs. The Commission suggests that if we focus on the moral and cultural dimensions of education everything else will fall into place whether we are dealing with IT, the environment, basic education, higher education, economic development and so on. This suggestion of the Delores Report is pertinent to the current issue of the mismatch between the output of schooling and the development needs of most PICs due mainly to the narrowness of curriculum offerings in schools. There is a need for a more flexible system that allows for a diversity of curriculum offerings as bridges between different levels and types of education in order to reduce school failure and wastage and broaden the notion of life-long learning to include sustainable living and good citizenship.

Although the Delors Report emphasized the important role of schools for the achievement of Pacific life goals, it is important for all Pacific peoples to acknowledge and value informal as well as non-formal education as these are normally the more relevant and meaningful aspects of education compared to school education and the Report's reference to life-long learning is interesting given that this was/is a major feature of indigenous education in which young people learned traditional patterns of life and their roles in that life, guided by the values of their cultures.

The suggested framework for Education in the twenty-first century consisted on Four Pillars: Learning to know; Learning to do; Learning to live together and Learning to be. These four pillars have a lot to offer modern curriculum reformers in the Pacific. In Learning to Know, it is important to pay attention to the scientific and technological changes as well as social and economic activities and to combine broad education with in-depth understanding of selected subjects that would help lay the foundation for life-long learning. In Learning to do, the school ought to help students develop their abilities and acquire competencies that would enable them to do a job well, deal with unforeseen circumstances and work together as members of a group or a team. The ability to understand other people, their history, traditions and values is important for the third pillar, Learning to live together, which also emphasizes the need for people to create new ways of managing conflicts and developing peaceful solutions to problems. Finally, Learning to be is a pillar that emphasizes independence and a strong sense of personal responsibility for the achievement of common goals. In this, young people may be helped to develop their potential and improve their talents, imagination, physical abilities, aesthetic sense and ways of communicating with others. These pillars need to be contextualized and conceptualized from the perspectives of Pacific peoples and communities if there is to be a shift of curriculum focus from subjects to students (Thaman, 1998).

Conclusion

Whether one is talking about ECE, primary, secondary or tertiary education in PICs, it is important that education does not set up young people for failure.

Sadly this is what is happening. The implication of using the Four pillars of the Delors Report would be a diversified curriculum, reduced academic focus and a concerted effort to prevent children from failure. There will be a need for a synthesis between conventional approaches that focus on abstraction and conceptualization, and approaches that combine work practical, hands on experiences so the young people can develop their capabilities and talents rather than focus on their weaknesses. Children need to be assured that failing exams does not make them failures in life; that schools can be a place for learning for all people, including the elderly as well as those with disabilities.

Some examples of how learning institutions can respond to the challenges mentioned earlier include: working towards helping PICs diversify the school curriculum; establishing research centres where students and teachers can work on applied research on topics that are important for their country; offering occupational qualifications specifically tailored to the needs of Pacific economies; encouraging life-long learning of adults through subsidized programmes that would engender a thirst for knowledge in different aspects of life, including cultural life and finally facilitating teacher and student exchanges among PICs and ensuring that the best students choose teaching as a career by offering incentives to high-performing high school leavers and university graduates.

These are suggestions for action rather than 'business' as usual. There are too many problems facing PICs and the time to act is now. All must work together – students, teachers, parents, government officials, politicians, businesses, church and religious leaders – and commit themselves to partnerships and social dialogue in order to ensure that the different parts of the education equation are working together towards one goal – appropriate behaviour and performance of Pacific young people and sustainable livelihoods for all.

References

Asian Development Bank (1996), *Report on Socio-Cultural Issues and Economic Development in the Pacific Islands*. Manila, Philippines: Asian Development Bank.
Bourdieu, P. (1993), *Field of Cultural Production*. UK: Polity Press.
Bowles, S. and Gintis, H. (1976), *Schooling in Capitalist America*. London: Routledge & Kegan Paul.
Crossley, M., Bray, M. and Packer, S. (2011), *Education in Small States: Policies and Priorities*. London: Commonwealth Secretariat.
Delors, J. (1996), *Learning: The Treasure Within*. Report to UNESCO of the International Commission on Education for the Twenty-first century. Paris: UNESCO.

Freire, P. (1972), *Pedagogy of the Oppressed*. Harmondsworth: Penquin.

Gallimore, R., Goldenberg, C. and Weisner, T. (1993), 'The Social Construction and Subjective Reality of Activity Settings: Implications for Community Psychology', *American Journal of Community Psychology* 21 (4), 537–560.

Johansson-Fua, S. (2006), *The Sustainable Livelihood and Education Project (SLEP): A Research Report*, Presented to the USP Institute of Education. Suva, Fiji.

Manu, S., Johansson-Fua, S. and Tagivakatini, S. (2008), 'Cooperation for Teachers and Education in the Pacific', *NUE Journal of International Educational Cooperation* 3, 81–87.

Ogbu, J. U. (1978), *Minority Education and Caste: The American System in Cross-Cultural Perspectives*. San Diego, CA: Academic Press.

Pacific Islands Forum Secretariat (PIFS) (2008), *The Pacific Education & Development Framework (PEDF) 2009–2015*. Suva, Fiji.

— (2011), *Pacific Regional MDGs Tracking Report*. Suva, Fiji.

— (2012), *Briefing Report to Forum Education Ministers Meeting, on the Progress of PEDF*. Port Villa, Vanuatu.

Pene, F., Taufe'ulungaki, A. M. and Benson, C. (2002), *Tree of Opportunity*. Suva, Fiji: IOE/USP.

Scott, W. R. (1981), *Organisations: Rational, Natural and Open Systems*. Englewood Cliffs, NJ: Prentice Hall.

School of Education, University of the South Pacific (SOE/USP) (2012), *Fast-Tracking Programmes for Untrained Teachers in Pacific Island Countries* (unpublished paper prepared for the Forum Education Ministers Meeting). Port Villa, Vanuatu.

Serpell, R. (1993), *The Significance of Schooling*. Cambridge: Cambridge University Press.

Thaman, K. H. (1988), *Cultural Values, Educational Ideas and Teachers' Role Perceptions in Tonga* (unpublished PhD thesis). Suva, Fiji: USP.

— (1998), *Learning to Be*. Keynote paper, UNESCO Conference on Education for the 21st Century. Melbourne.

— (2008), 'Education in Pacific Island Countries', in G. McCulloch and D. Crook (eds), *The Routledge International Encyclopedia of Education*. London: Routledge, pp. 413–416.

— (2013), *Early Childhood Education: A Foundation for Reclaiming Sustainable Pacific Futures*. Keynote paper, International ECE Conference. New Zealand: University of Auckland.

10

Papua New Guinea: Inclusive Education

Guy Le Fanu and Kapa Kelep-Malpo

Introduction

Inclusive education – broadly defined as the provision of 'Education for All' of good quality in mainstream settings – has acquired increasing prominence in global development discourse in recent years. It has become a justification for, or even *the* justification for, many development initiatives in the field of education. It has become a cause around which coalitions of individuals and organizations have formed – so much so that reference is often made to 'the global movement' for inclusive education. Inclusive education has also become the subject of extensive and energetic academic discussion – a process which has generated a vast and growing literature on the subject. Sometimes, this discussion has focused on the feasibility and appropriateness of inclusive education in low income countries and indeed the so-called developed world. On such occasions, passionate debate has often ensued (especially when educational provision for students with disabilities is being considered) – debate which at times has shed more heat than light on the pertinent issues.

In this chapter, we draw upon a wide range of documentary sources in order to investigate the inclusiveness of educational provision in Papua New Guinea at all levels of the school system, and the factors shaping this provision. We evaluate the inclusiveness of the provision from quantitative and qualitative perspectives. We then discuss the extent to which the inclusiveness/non-inclusiveness of this provision can be explained in terms of 'supply factors', that is in terms of the strengths and weaknesses of the education system itself, and the extent to which it can be explained in terms of 'demand factors', that is in terms of the orientations of local stakeholders to the education system. A recurring theme in the earlier discussion is the extent to which the new national curriculum in Papua New Guinea has promoted inclusive education in terms of both improving educational provision and stimulating educational demand. In the light of our findings, we conclude by discussing the prospects for inclusive education in the country.

However, we will begin by providing a brief history of education in Papua New Guinea, a description of the present education system and an analysis of the contexts and processes shaping this system. This information provides a frame of reference for the rest of this chapter.

Short history of education in Papua New Guinea

Papua New Guinea is located in the South West Pacific and constitutes the eastern half of New Guinea, the world's second largest island and a number of smaller offshore islands. It forms part of Melanesia, a group of countries connected by proximity and linguistic, cultural and geographical similarities (Sillitoe, 1998, see also Chapter 12 in this volume). The land area of Papua New Guinea is 464,000 square kilometres (United Nations Children's Fund [UNICEF], 2004) and consists of coastal areas, river-plains with 'large, meandering rivers' (Sillitoe, 1998: p. 3) and rugged mountain-ranges. Large areas of the country remain densely forested despite the depredations of trans-national timber companies (Adam, 2008).

UNDP estimated that the population of Papua New Guinea was 6.4 million in 2007, of whom 40.6 per cent was under 15 years of age and 86.6 per cent lived in rural areas (United Nations Development Programme [UNDP], 2009). The country is characterized by great linguistic, cultural and ethnic diversity with over 700 languages in regular daily use, although English, *Tok Pisin* and Motu are the three main languages, with English the primary language of classroom communication in primary and secondary schools. According to UNICEF, 'tribal linkages and traditional clan structures remain very strong and fragmented' (2004: p. 16).

Western-style education was introduced in Papua New Guinea by missionaries in the 1870s and 1880s (Crossley, 1998). Before then, there existed what McLaughlin has termed a 'a forty thousand year education tradition' (1994: p. 63) in which children were taught 'technical' and 'revealed knowledge' (p. 65) in village settings by parents and selected elders, a process which involved 'learning by observation and imitation' (p. 70), 'learning by personal trial and error' (p. 70) and 'learning in real life activities' (p. 71).

For most of the colonial period, there was minimal investment in the Papua New Guinea education system, and education was predominantly provided in mission schools run by church organizations (Weeden et al., 1969; Smith, 1987). These schools traditionally tended to focus on vernacular literacy and on providing students with the social and practical orientations and skills that it was believed would enable them to be productive members of their communities (Crossley, 1998). However, prompted by international criticism and the realization that Papua New Guinea would have to be granted full independence sooner rather than later, the colonial administration significantly increased educational expenditure in the 1960s which meant 'primary education was brought within the reach of a large proportion of the population for the first time' (Smith, 1987: p. 233). These years also saw a dramatic expansion in secondary education provision (Smith, 1985) and the introduction of tertiary education, with the University of Papua New Guinea being formally established in 1965 (Murphy, 1985).

During the colonial era, concern was expressed about the relevance and utility of the Western-style education offered to students who would return to their villages after graduation. Post-independence, similar criticism of the inappropriateness of the national curriculum was strongly expressed by national and overseas educationalists who gathered at the Eighth Waigani Seminar in 1974 (Brammall and May, 1975). For instance, Nelson Giraure, District Education Officer for Rabaul, commenting on his school experiences, remarked, 'Most of the content that was being taught to us was as foreign as the English language being taught' (Giraure, 1975: p. 102). Several of the contributors to Barrington Thomas's collection of essays on the Papua New Guinea education system also chose to highlight the irrelevance of the school curriculum (Matane, 1976; McNamara, 1976; Tololo, 1976).

In response to these concerns, the National Department of Education [NDOE] supported a number of innovative curriculum initiatives. These included the Secondary Schools Community Extension Project (SSCEP) from 1978 to 1983, which provided opportunities for 'the integration and application of intellectual skills in practical projects' (Crossley, 1983: p. 174), and the introduction of the *Viles Tok Ples Skul* scheme in North Solomons Province in 1980, which enabled students to acquire early literacy in vernacular and also gave them the chance to learn more about their indigenous customs and culture (Delpit and Kemelfield, 1985).

In 1986, *A Philosophy of Education* was published, a report commissioned by the government to consider the future of the education system in Papua

New Guinea. This drew upon the critiques noted earlier and expounded the value of traditional, village-based education, arguing that education should promote 'Integral Human Development' involving 'socialization', 'participation', 'liberation' and 'equality' (NDOE, 1986: p. 7). The publication of the *Education Sector Review* by the NDOE in 1991 was also important as the document not only drew attention to the failings of the education system, but also identified some specific remedies (NDOE, 2001; Kolant and Pettit, 2003).

The education system in present-day Papua New Guinea

The education system in present-day Papua New Guinea reflects the influence of a comprehensive programme of reform carried out in the last two decades by the national government in partnership with AusAID, the development arm of the Australian government, with some additional assistance being provided by other international development agencies (Packer et al., 2009). This programme of reform has sought to make teaching and learning more relevant and meaningful in schools, and thus reflects the influence of The Eighth Waigani Seminar (1974), *A Philosophy of Education* (1986) and *Education Sector Review* (1991) (see previous section) on contemporary educational thinking within the country, at least at senior government level (Kolant and Pettit, 2003).

The reform programme began with a period of structural reform which involved the replacement of a 6–4-2 school structure – a 6-year community school education followed by a 4-year high school education followed by a 2-year secondary education – with a 3–6-4 structure –a 3-year elementary school education followed by a 6-year primary school education followed by a 4-year education in high schools and secondary schools or alternative provision (NDOE, 2001). The structural changes to the education system commenced in 1993 (Guy, 2010). Vocational training, a skills-oriented education offered as an alternative to secondary education, is provided by vocational training centres (NDOE, 2004).

Structural reform was combined with curriculum reform, and accordingly a new outcomes-based curriculum was introduced nationally in primary schools from 2004 (NDOE, 2003) and in secondary schools from 2008 (NDOE, 2006).[1] The curriculum is intended to be inclusive as it has been 'designed to meet the needs of all students irrespective of their abilities, gender, geographic locations, cultural and language backgrounds, or their socio-economic backgrounds' (NDOE, 2002: p. 25).

Accordingly, the curriculum requires teaching and learning to be more closely related to local contexts and cultures than previously, particularly in the early years of schooling. For instance, it specifies that indigenous languages (of which there are over 700 in daily use and 800 in total Papua New Guinea) should be the basis for classroom communication in elementary schools and that instruction should be bilingual in primary schools, involving the use of both English and vernacular. In addition, teachers should strive to make classroom activities as experiential and participatory as possible, with students being given meaningful opportunities to take control of their own learning. Teachers also need to be responsive to the various types of diversity within the classroom, particularly the educational requirements of girl students and students with special needs. In order to increase the likelihood that all students will achieve all the outcomes within the five learning areas of the curriculum, teachers, working collaboratively with one another and community members should develop intricate schemes of work which take account of the needs of their students, the resources at their disposal, the requirements of the various syllabuses and any external factors likely to impact on teaching and learning. The new curriculum, while seeking to indigenise teaching and learning in schools to some extent, reflects the influence of Western educational thought, particularly in terms of its assumptions that children – interacting creatively with one another – should construct their own learning, that various types of difference and diversity should be validated in the classroom situation and that teaching and learning should be self-conscious, carefully planned and closely monitored processes (Le Fanu, 2011, 2013).

In terms of the organization and management of the education system, the national government has significant responsibilities. These include responsibilities for: planning and policy making; the preparation, delivery and marking of national examinations; the inspection of schools; the training, registration and regulation of teachers and the payment of school fee subsidies to provincial administrations (which then distribute these sums to schools) (Packer et al., 2009). However, significant responsibilities have been delegated to provincial, district and local-level government, as a result of the passage of the 1996 Organic Law on Provincial and Local Level Government (National Executive Council [NEC], 2009). For instance, provincial governments are responsible for managing and maintaining provincial high schools and managing primary and elementary schools, while local governments (in association with local communities) are responsible for maintaining the infrastructure of primary and elementary schools (Packer et al., 2009). Local communities (wards) are also responsible for appointing Boards of Management for primary schools

(United Nations Educational, Scientific and Cultural Organization [UNESCO]/ International Bureau of Education [IBE], 2011).

The government at all levels works in close association with church agencies, as these remain significant providers of basic, secondary and tertiary education – a reflection of the historical involvement of churches in the education system (Weeden et al., 1969; Smith, 1987). For instance, almost 50 per cent of elementary and primary students were enrolled in church agency schools in 2006 (NDOE, 2009). Church agency schools follow the national curriculum and are staffed by government employees. However, church agencies are involved in the management of these schools and financially contribute to their maintenance and resourcing (Tweedie, 2002; Asian Development Bank, Australian Agency for International Development, and the World Bank, 2007). As a result of these inputs, church agency schools tend to have a better reputation than government agency schools. Outside the state system, the International Education Agency (IEA) runs a network of 19 fee-paying schools which follow an international curriculum.

In the field of teacher education, the University of Goroka in the Eastern Highlands is the primary provider of secondary teachers and offers a 4-year course leading to the Bachelor of Education degree. It has also introduced a Postgraduate Diploma of Education Programme for students without an initial teaching qualification (NDOE, 2004). Currently, there are nine primary teacher training colleges offering a 2-year diploma course for grade 12 graduates (Nongkas, 2007; UNESCO/IBE, 2011). A mixed-mode certificate course for elementary teachers is offered by the Papua New Guinea Education Institute (NDOE, 2004). Provincial, district and school authorities are responsible for organizing in-service training for schools, with some funding being provided by the NDOE (2009).

The education system receives significant support from the international development community. The major donors in the field of education have been the governments of Australia, New Zealand, Japan and Austria, and the European Commission, the Asian Development Bank and various UN agencies (Packer et al., 2009). However, the Australian government –working through AusAID – has been the 'major player', contributing between $AUS300 million and $AUS400 million to education since 1995, excluding the large numbers of scholarships it provides for Papua New Guinean students at Australian universities (ibid.). The significant financial contribution of the Australian government is understandable given the proximity of the two countries, the former colonial relationship between them (with Papua New Guinea only achieving full independence in 1975) and the economic, social, political and cultural links between the two countries which collectively constitute their (often uneasy, sometimes antagonistic) post-colonial relationship. It should be stressed that Australia has not been a 'sleeping partner' in the field of education, but has sought to influence educational policy and practice in Papua New Guinea – for instance, by funding the Curriculum Reform Implementation Project (CRIP) which ran from 2000 to 2006, had a total budget of $AUS44 million and employed a number of expatriate advisers (as well as national staff) who worked alongside their Papua New Guinean counterparts in the Curriculum Development Division of the Department of Education (Ryan, 2008). The impact of international development on the education system of Papua New Guinea – particularly on its capacity to provide inclusive education – is a subject which will be addressed later in this chapter.

The inclusiveness of the Papua New Guinean education system

The inclusiveness of an education system can be assessed in terms of access and in terms of quality. Access refers to the physical presence of school-aged children in their local community schools, and is thus measured by indicators such as admission and enrolment. Quality refers to the provision of education that meets the diverse, complex and fluctuating educational needs of all students, including (frequently overlapping) groups of students often marginalized within mainstream education systems: for instance, girls, children with disabilities, members of ethnic minorities and the economically disadvantaged. Quality can be 'inwardly' measured in terms of stakeholder perceptions of educational provision and 'outwardly' measured in terms of student attainment or observed student participation in a range of curricular and extra-curricular activities. Indicators such as transition and retention to some extent measure both the quantitative and qualitative dimensions of educational inclusion.

The relationship between educational access and educational quality is close and complex. For instance, rising levels of access to education systems can not only reflect improved quality of educational provision, but also contribute to these improvements, as schools become more diverse, creative and interesting places in which teachers transform their practice in order to respond to growing student diversity (UNESCO, 2005). However, high levels of access can lessen the quality of education – particularly for students with special educational needs – when there are insufficient teachers, classrooms and resources for rising numbers of students: a phenomenon observed in sub-Saharan Africa since the introduction of Education For All (Mundy, 2002; Arbeiter and Hartley, 2007; Urwick and Elliott, 2010).

In terms of access, the education system in Papua New Guinea has dramatically expanded in the last two decades, largely as a result of the development of the elementary education system. Specifically, the number of schools has nearly tripled, enrolments have doubled and the number of teachers has increased by 75 per cent (Packer et al., 2009). However, the same authors note that 680,000 children aged 6–14 are out of school. Furthermore, in 2003 the gross enrolment rate was 72 per cent, the seventh lowest in the world. The evidence also indicates that net and gross enrolment ratios are much lower in certain provinces than others (NDOE, 2009) and that levels of educational access vary not only between provinces but also within provinces (Rogers et al., 2010). In addition, government statistics show that girls are significantly less likely to be in school than boys in almost all provinces (NDOE, 2009). Although the Department of Education has reported that it does not collect data on the educational enrolment of children and young people with disabilities (NDOE, 2008), reports indicate that these individuals are often routinely excluded from schools, particularly if they are perceived as having educationally complex impairments (Pool, 2009; Banasi, 2010).

In terms of quality, the evidence is scanty, but similarly worrying. When it examined the performance of students in the 2006 grade 8 Certificate of Base Examination, the NDOE found that the results for Literacy, Numeracy and General Skills were well below 40 per cent (NDOE, 2009). NDOE also found retention rates in schools, another proxy indicator of quality of teaching and learning, were similarly disappointing and not significantly different from previous years, with only 67.9 per cent of boy students and 62.1 per cent of girl students progressing from grade 1 to 6 between 2001 and 2006. The Accelerated Girls' Education project, initiated in Papua New Guinea by UNICEF, sponsored some valuable research into the poor quality of educational provision for girls which is discussed in the textbox, *Exclusion of girls from schools in the Highlands.*

When Le Fanu (2011, 2013) observed teaching and learning in two remote rural primary schools in the Eastern Highlands in 2008 and 2009, he found that teachers often struggled to teach in the inclusive manner prescribed by the new national curriculum (described earlier in this chapter). For instance, he noted that classroom activities (particularly in Language and Mathematics) tended to be repetitious, undifferentiated, divorced from the lives of students and so tightly structured that they provided little scope for freedom of thought and expression. Although students were seated in groups, activities generally did not require the collaborative development of ideas, and therefore tended to be carried out by students individually and in silence. Teacher dominance of the interactional space of the classroom meant that there was little room for teacher–student dialogue, and assessment and reporting were narrowly quantitative and norm-referenced. The lack of subject knowledge of some of the teachers was an additional concern. The findings of his study are consonant with the findings of earlier case studies of teaching and learning in schools in Papua New Guinea (Pearse et al., 1989; Pickford, 1998; Zeegers, 2000; Fife, 2005).

However, he also noted that teachers, while not following the prescriptions of the curriculum, often practised 'unorthodox inclusiveness' (Le Fanu, 2011: p. 149). In other words, they had developed their own approaches which demonstrated contextualized awareness of both the requirements of their students and the classroom realities they had to negotiate. In the field of classroom communication, this took a variety of forms including: speaking in short, simple sentences; providing concise definitions; providing specific examples to illustrate concepts and scrutinizing the expressions on their students' faces in order to assess students' levels of comprehension. When their students were on task, they also patrolled the classroom providing support for individuals and small groups. When interacting with their students, they tended to display great sensitivity to the feelings of their students, an essential characteristic in 'shame-based' societies such as Papua New Guinea's (Lindstrom, 1990; Lea, 2001).

In summary, the research evidence broadly indicates that teaching and learning in schools in Papua New Guinea lacks inclusiveness, both in terms of access and quality. However, Le Fanu's research also suggests that pedagogical practices in low income countries should not be judged as 'inclusive' or 'non-inclusive' solely in terms of their conformity to Western norms, but should also be placed in their particular contexts – an approach previously adopted by other researchers in Papua New Guinea (McLaughlin, 1994; Guthrie, 2003; Monemone, 2003; Wallangas, 2003).

Inclusive education: the supply and demand perspectives

When investigating the various factors shaping the inclusiveness of educational provision in particular countries, two inter-related perspectives can be adopted:

a 'supply' perspective and a 'demand' perspective. From the supply perspective, inclusiveness is primarily a consequence of the ability of 'providers' (education systems) to meet the needs of their 'clients' (children and young people, and their families and communities). From the demand perspective, inclusiveness is primarily a consequence of the orientations of these clients to, and their ensuing engagement (or lack of engagement) with, education systems.

As already mentioned, educational demand and supply are inter-related processes. First, they are interactive. For instance, if local people energetically and skilfully advance their educational rights, then educational services will accordingly improve: in this case, demand impacts positively upon supply. Alternatively, if governments provide good quality opportunities for civil society organizations to participate in educational decision making at various levels, then stakeholder commitment to these services may increase: in this case, supply impacts positively upon demand. Second, the two processes are over-lapping, as local stakeholders are rarely passive 'consumers' of educational services, but participate in various ways in the running of schools. Indeed, 'demand' can metamorphose into 'supply'. For instance, in Zambia local people, outraged that they were denied access to the government education system due to its limited geographical coverage, set up their own community schools across the country with minimal assistance from the national government, although with significant support from the international development sector (De Kemp et al., 2008).

The supply perspective

The supply perspective was largely adopted by the World Bank when it carried out a *Public Expenditure and Service Delivery Survey* between 2002 and 2003. This consisted of a quantitative service-delivery survey covering 214 schools in 19 districts across 9 provinces combined with a qualitative study of 12 schools (World Bank, 2004b). The survey drew attention to various problems facing schools across Papua New Guinea, including: poor quality and disintegrating school infrastructure; a shortage of teaching and learning resources; high rates of absenteeism among teachers and recurrent financial crises in schools, due to poor management, delayed payment of school subsidies by education authorities and widespread tolerance of non-payment of school fees (World Bank, 2004a).

World Bank studies are sometimes considered unreliable because they polemically promote the free-market ideology of the organization – for instance, by advocating that the government should play a much-reduced role in the field of education (Bayliss, 2001; Goldman, 2005). However, this study confounds this expectation as it recommends that, in order to preserve equity, the private sector should play a limited role in educational provision in Papua New Guinea (World Bank, 2004a). The findings of the study are also confirmed by other sources. For instance, in his survey of community schools (now renamed primary schools) in two districts of Eastern Highlands Province, Layton (2003) discovered that only 19 of the 37 schools had access to clean drinking water, and that 53.6 per cent of the students had to sit on the floor due to lack of classroom furniture.

The World Bank report believes many of the problems facing schools can be attributed to broader structural failings in the Papua New Guinean education system, particularly criticizing the inspection system and provincial and district administrations for failing to adequately supervise and support schools (World Bank, 2004a). Similar concerns about the capacity of sub-national government have been expressed in a recent AusAID-funded study (Packer et al., 2009).

There is also evidence that the NDOE lacks the capacity to fulfil its responsibilities. For instance, in 2009 the European Union demanded the return of 170 million kina (approximately £42.5 million) which NDOE had been required (but failed) to spend on teacher training and the purchase of textbooks and library books for schools ('EU to seek return of funds', 2009); and the Ombudsman Commission simultaneously discovered that 37 million kina (approximately £9 million) had been withdrawn from the education section infrastructure trust accounts, but none of the money spent on improvements to schools and colleges (Arek, 2009). NDOE suffers not only from poor financial management, but also lack of communication and collaboration between its constituent parts. For instance, Le Fanu (2011) observed disparities between the content of primary syllabuses (the overall responsibility of the Curriculum Development Division) and the requirements of the Certificate of Basic Education sat by primary students at the end of grade 8 (the responsibility of the Measurement Services Unit). Shortages of adequately trained staff further hinder the work of the organization. For instance, in the field of special education, the Special Education Unit has only three employees, but is responsible for co-ordinating special education throughout the country (NDOE, 2009).

Finally, concerns have been expressed about the quality of leadership within primary teachers' colleges (PTCs) in Papua New Guinea and the negativity of their staffroom cultures (Zeegers, 2000; Nongkas, 2007) – failings which reflect the dysfunctionality of much of the higher education sector as a whole (Papoutsaki and Rooney, 2006; Garnaut and Namaliu, 2010).

The earlier educational problems can be placed in the broader context of the challenges faced by the post-colonial government in providing its citizens, particularly those living in rural areas, with government services of good quality, and sometimes any services at all ('The PNG Time Warp', 2007; Kolo, 2008; Paul, 2009). This inability has in turn been attributed to the discrepancy between the bureaucratic demands of state institutions, bequeathed to Papua New Guinea at independence by the colonial administration and the capacity of state employees to meet these demands (Dinnen, 1998; Payani, 2003; May, 2010). Institutional incapacity is not only a product of the kin-based loyalties of state employees, which are antithetical to the exercise of impersonal Weberian rationality (May, 1998), but also the geographical exceptionality of Papua New Guinea, which makes service delivery particularly troublesome. For instance, the main land-mass is bifurcated by mountain ranges, and contains extensive forests and marshland, while the rest of the country consists of far-flung archipelagos (UNICEF, 2004; Borden and Ward, 2006). The ethno-linguistic diversity of the country further impedes service delivery when it results in political fissiparousness (Reilly and Phillpot, 2002).

Problematic contexts of service delivery have hindered the work of international development agencies as well as the national and sub-national government. However, these agencies – in particular AusAID – have sometimes been authors of their own misfortune. Specifically, it has been alleged that AusAID's policies and programmes have often been shaped by the assumption that Papua New Guineans are incapable of running their own affairs (Hughes, 2003; Temby, 2007). Consequently, expatriate consultants have often been employed to closely monitor the work of their civil service counterparts, necessitating abnormally high levels of expenditure on 'technical assistance'. In addition, it has been alleged that AusAID programmes have often assumed that 'the governance of state institutions (is best strengthened) through the transfer of Western values, institutions and practices' (Temby, 2007: p. 20) – an approach which fails to recognize the efficacy and significance of indigenous values and practices. Finally, there is a danger that the AusAID's programmes have been undermined by their own systems and processes. For instance, it has been argued the project cycle has encouraged AusAID to focus on the pursuit of short-term, easily quantifiable outcomes rather than sustained engagement with communities, and also encouraged the adoption of a piecemeal approach which has failed to address the intertwined, multi-layered challenges faced by the education system (Packer et al., 2009).

The AusAID-funded CRIP has been the target of particular criticism in the national press, although it has been defended by CRIP and NDOE. An independent evaluation, commissioned by the National Research Institute, noted the significant impact of CRIP on educational practice in the country, but expressed concerns about the project's internal operations and external impact (Agigo, 2010). Specifically, it was found that the framework for the new national curriculum had been developed by CRIP consultants, in the absence of leadership from the Department of Education. Furthermore, procedures developed by the NDOE were either partially followed or never followed by CRIP: for instance, the curriculum was not properly trialled for quality assurance purposes, and initial training was provided before the relevant teachers' guides and syllabuses had been developed. Based on responses from 159 teachers from four provinces (one from each region), the study also concluded that schools across the country were struggling to implement the new curriculum. This was attributed to various factors including: lack of in-service training of good quality; shortages and absences of teaching and learning materials and the excessive demands placed on teachers by the new curriculum in terms of planning, resource development and assessment and reporting.

The demand perspective

The inclusiveness, or non-inclusiveness, of an educational system can be viewed from a demand perspective as well as a supply perspective – in other words, can be seen as a 'client-driven', not just a 'provider-driven', phenomenon.

A recurring theme in the educational literature on modern Papua New Guinea has been the alienation of local people from the formal education system – a sense of alienation which has often been attributed to the fact that this system is based on inappropriate Western models (NDOE, 1986, 1991, 2002). As a result, local communities have been reluctant to participate in school-related activities, further alienating schools from the communities they are supposed to serve. It has also meant that local stakeholders have failed to invest in and adequately support their children's schooling, and thus negatively impacted on enrolment and retention rates.

This claim was to some extent corroborated by the World Bank's *Public Expenditure and Service Delivery Survey* (2004a) (see previous section) which found that parents in a number of schools investigated were reluctant to become involved in school administration, abandoning this responsibility entirely to local Boards of Management. The survey also found a significant correlation in these schools between low levels of stakeholder participation and low levels of teacher attendance (ibid.). However, the survey also found that other communities were highly involved in schools in certain parts of the school, and that this had beneficial effects. Similar levels of commitment have been described in articles published in *The National*, Papua New Guinea's highest-circulation newspaper, which have recounted how communities have banded together to construct classrooms, refurbish school infrastructure and pay school fees and teachers' salaries (Map, 2006; Alphonse, 2008b; Kiala, 2009). Unfortunately, high levels of stakeholder involvement in the affairs of schools have proved destabilizing, even destructive, when driven by political and financial self-interest (Anis, 2007, 2008; Alphonse, 2008a; 'Principle [*sic*] Transferred', 2008).

The new curriculum has endeavoured to increase stakeholder participation in schools by making the curriculum more relevant to local cultures and contexts, although the extent to which the curriculum has bridged this gap has been exaggerated (Ryan, 2008). However, there is evidence that these reforms have displeased rather than gratified those stakeholders who want schools to provide a Western-style education, believing (rightly or wrongly) that this type of education promotes social mobility, freeing individuals from a life of subsistence labour in impoverished rural communities. This disaffection with the new curriculum was revealed in a survey commissioned by Voluntary Service Overseas in Madang Province which found, for instance, that stakeholders were opposed to the use of vernacular in elementary and primary schools as they felt this would diminish the life chances of students (Epstein, 2007). As one grade 8 student observed, 'They don't speak *Tok Ples* and *Tok Pisin*[2] in the offices and big schools' (Epstein, 2007: p. 17).[3] Furthermore, in her case study of a village in East Sepik, Dobrin (2008) concluded that education authorities, having given communities additional responsibilities under the new curriculum, are using this as a rationale for withdrawing services, further alienating stakeholders from the educational reforms.

An additional factor greatly limiting the participation of local stakeholders in the education system has been poverty, which is particularly prevalent in isolated rural communities (Rogers et al., 2010). From 2003 to 2004, a pilot Curriculum Standards Monitoring Test study was carried out in schools across Papua New Guinea (Freeman et al., 2005). As part of the exercise, questionnaires were distributed to students in grades 3, 5 and 8, the results of which indicated that socio-economic factors had significantly contributed to the inability of the students to fully engage with their education. For instance, the responses showed that the frequent absences of the students from school were often due to factors such as lack of clean clothes, lack of food, the need to help their parents and illness. The responses also showed that students were at a continual risk of dropping out of school, either temporarily or permanently, due to school-fee difficulties. For instance, 69.1 per cent of children in grade 3, 58.6 per cent in grade 5 and 63.3 per cent of students in grade 8 reported that their parents found it hard to pay their fees.

Finally, opposition among stakeholders to the education of certain social groups has negatively impacted on their participation in schools. In particular, there is evidence that the parents of children with disabilities are reluctant to send them to school, especially if these children have mobility difficulties or if it is perceived that these children have educationally complex impairments (Le Fanu, 2011). This has been attributed to over-protective attitudes among family members and parental concerns (which may often be justified) about the capacity of schools to meet the needs of these children. It has also been attributed to the belief that formal education will be 'wasted' on these children, as they will not be able to secure full employment after graduation due to discrimination, however impressive their educational qualifications. Negative social attitudes to the education of girls are also prevalent in the Highlands of Papua New Guinea, and have significantly contributed to their exclusion from schools (see textbox).

Exclusion of girls from schools in the Highlands

In a series of articles published in 2004, Thomas Webster, Director of the National Research Institute, outlined the reasons for the low participation of girls in schools in the Highlands of Papua New Guinea. The articles were based on analysis of research carried out by 'Accelerating Girls Education' teams which visited selected schools in three provinces in 2003.

Webster found that low attendance and participation rates for girls were related to unsatisfactory educational provision – in other words, were significantly supply-driven. For instance, he found a statistical correlation between low attendance and participation rates and lack of female teachers in schools, and reasoned this was because girls required female teachers who could act as their confidantes and role models (Webster, 2004a). He also noted that shortage of resources and facilities particularly impacted on girl students as boy students tended to monopolize these resources and facilities (Webster, 2004b). Lack of toilets in schools had a particularly negative effect on the morale of girl students, especially adolescent girls (ibid.). Concern was also expressed by the high incidence of sexual assaults on girl students by both boy students and male teachers (Webster, 2004c).

However, Webster also found that the low enrolment and participation rates of girls were related to demand factors. He noted that parents were often reluctant to send their daughters to schools, as they believed that it was important that girls should marry early and once married stay at home – a reflection of the resilience of traditional cultural beliefs and practices (Webster, 2004b). Furthermore, parents wanted their daughters to receive a high bride price when they married (a traditional custom in the Highlands), and parents believed that schooling did not increase bride price (ibid.). Parents were also concerned about the safety of their daughters – not only when they were in school, but also when they travelled to and from school, as they often had to walk along rough tracks for long distances (Webster, 2004c).

Webster unfavourably contrasted the Highlands region with the Papua and Island regions where there is greater respect for the rights of women and girls and greater levels of safety and security, and consequently greater participation of girls in schools (2004a).

Conclusion

In this chapter, we have shown that educational provision in Papua New Guinea lacks inclusiveness in terms of both access and quality. This is partly due to the limitations of the education system – limitations which are the consequence of the inter-play of social, cultural, political, economic, historical and geographical factors. However, it is also a result of the alienation of stakeholders from the education system, the impact of poverty on participation in education and stakeholder resistance to the enrolment of certain social groups in schools. The non-inclusiveness of educational provision is therefore a consequence of both supply and demand factors, and the interaction of those factors.

We have also shown the limitations of curriculum reform as an instrument for promoting inclusive education, especially when curricular initiatives are poorly disseminated, do not command widespread stakeholder assent and place excessive demands on an under-resourced and poorly performing education system. Given time and enhanced levels of support, it is conceivable that the curriculum in Papua New Guinea would have 'bedded down' and – adapted by teachers in the light of local realities – have had a widespread positive impact on the quality of teaching and learning in schools. However, this will not now be allowed to happen. In 2012, the incoming Prime Minister, Peter O'Neill, expressed concern about the new curriculum, claiming it placed insufficient emphasis on the teaching of English and was failing to provide students with the skills that would enable them to compete in the global market-place, views which were echoed by his Minister of Education a few days later ('Education to

Review Curriculum', 2012). The prime minister further observed, 'The teaching of traditional languages is the responsibility of parents in the home and in the villages' (ibid.). Accordingly, a task force was established in early 2013 which published a final report with '48 recommendations for a complete overhaul of the system, including a new standards-based curriculum focused on increasing the teaching of English and Mathematics at elementary and primary school levels' (Nalu, 2013). These recommendations were accepted by the prime minister and his cabinet.

The rejection of the reform curriculum signifies a sea-change in educational policy in Papua New Guinea. Accordingly, government-sponsored educational initiatives in the future are likely to place much less emphasis on providing students with the capacities to contribute to village life, and much more emphasis on providing them with the capacities to participate in the global economy. Such initiatives may be inappropriate, given the complex make-up of the country and its position in the world, and further alienate stakeholders from the education system, leading to further policy reversals.

The limited success of the curriculum reform indicates the need for policy-makers and implementers in Papua New Guinea to adopt more effective approaches to promote inclusive education. A promotional document produced by the Australian government describes how the NDOE, working alongside AusAID, will adopt a co-ordinated, cross-sectoral, multi-level approach (Commonwealth of Australia, 2010) – an approach also recommended by Packer, Emmott and Hinchliffe in their 2009 evaluation of AusAID-supported education programmes. For instance, the document describes how NDOE and AusAID will be developing structures and processes which will enable the education system at national, sub-national and school levels to plan educational activities, and ensure these activities are fully financed and all expenditure monitored and recorded. In order to raise awareness of the educational rights of girls, women leaders will be provided with training and appointed as 'district women facilitators' and 'school community facilitators'. AusAID has also decided that all its programmes, including its education programmes, will address disability issues (Commonwealth of Australia, 2008). In education, AusAID will therefore both seek to ensure school buildings are universally accessible and that students with disabilities have access to impairment-specific types of support and resource, for example, access to Braille and sign language tuition and to assistive devices and mobility aids.

The cross-sectoral, multi-level approach adopted by AusAID is impressively wide-ranging, although there are some significant omissions – for instance, there is no mention of capacity building in teacher-training institutions. However, as the programme is so multi-faceted, its success is largely dependent on the harmonious functioning of the various components of the educational system – a highly unlikely state-of-affairs given the present deficiencies of the system. It is also not clear if this programme will be disrupted by the recently announced changes in government education policy discussed earlier in this section. In terms of AusAID's focus on disability, the authors of this chapter have not found any evidence that this focus has yet significantly impacted on educational provision in PNG – although we are aware that AusAID has recently formed a research partnership with the University of Goroka and Leonard Cheshire Disability (a UK-based international development agency) to identify inclusive approaches to the teaching of children with disabilities in schools in PNG.[4]

Another potentially significant recent government initiative has been the introduction of free education. According to the government, education will now be free from elementary class to grade 10, with a 75 per cent subsidy being provided in grades 11 and 12 ('PNG PM O'Neill Highlights Free Education', 2011). If implemented effectively, this policy should significantly increase educational enrolment, except among isolated rural communities who are physically unable to access education. Teachers' unions have expressed concern about the long-term capacity of the government to fund free education and about the impact of increased class sizes on educational quality (Graue, 2011; 'Teacher Union Warns', 2012), although these concerns are partly allayed by the high levels of economic growth witnessed in PNG in recent years – the result of surging international demand for PNG's natural resources (Apina, 2013). However, concerns about the capacity of education authorities to ensure the necessary funds are managed effectively raise concerns about the government's capacity to implement the free education policy effectively. For this, and other reasons discussed in this chapter, the prospects for inclusive education in Papua New Guinea remain shrouded in doubt.

Notes

1   The structural reform was integrated with the curriculum reform because it was intended elementary students would receive a community-oriented, vernacular-based education which would prepare them for primary schooling (NDOE, 2002).
2   *Tok Ples*: the indigenous languages of Papua New Guinea. *Tol Pisin*: 'An English-based pidgin which is the product of nineteenth century colonialism in the Pacific' (Romaine, 1992: p. 1).

3 Popular opposition to attempts to localize the curriculum have been a recurring phenomenon in post-independence Papua New Guinea (Smith and Guthrie, 1980; Swatridge, 1985; Crossley and Vulliamy, 1986; Crossley, 1998).

4 The recent incorporation of AusAID within the Department of Foreign Affairs and Trade (DFAT) of the Government of Australia has further increased uncertainty about the future of AusAID's work in education, especially as this change has seen AusAID lose its status as an independent statutory agency (Betteridge and Howes, 2013).

References

Adam, D. (2008), 'Third Largest Tropical Forest Could Be Halved by 2021, Study Warns', *The Guardian*, 3 June.

Agigo, J. O. (2010), *Curriculum and Learning in Papua New Guinea Schools: A Study of the Curriculum Reform Implementation Project.* Port Moresby: National Research Institute.

Alphonse, A. (2008a), 'School Office Ransacked, 500 Students Sent Home', *The National*, 21 February, p. 6.

— (2008b), 'Landowners Invest in Human Resource', *The National*, 15 September, p. 6.

Anis, A. (2007), 'Passam to reopen in two weeks', *The National*, 19 January, p. 5.

— (2008), 'Parents Disgruntled Over Alleged Misuse of Funds in Primary School', *The National*, 14 February, p. 6.

Apina, A. (2013), 'Bakani: PNG Economy Growing', *The National*, 15 August.

Arbeiter, S. and Hartley, S. (2007), 'Teachers' and Pupils' Experiences of Integrated Education in Uganda', *International Journal of Disability, Development and Education* 49 (1), 61–78.

Arek, M. (2009), 'Where is the Money?' *The National*, 27–29 March, pp. 1–2.

Asian Development Bank, Australian Agency for International Development, and the World Bank (2007), *Strategic Directions for Human Development in Papua New Guinea.* Washington, DC: World Bank Publications.

Banasi, R. (2010), 'Personal Profile', *The Network*, 21, 10.

Bayliss, K. (2001), *The World Bank and Privatisation: A Flawed Development Tool.* London: University of Greenwich.

Betteridge, A. and Howes, S. (2013), 'Principles Released for AusAID's (Deep) Reintegration into DFAT', *Devpolicyblog*. Available at: http://devpolicy.org/in-brief/principles-released-for-ausaids-deep-reintegration-into-dfat-20131008–3/ (Accessed: 1 April 2014).

Borden, W. and Ward, G. (2006), *Country Environmental Profile: Papua New Guinea.* Brussels: European Union.

Brammall, J. and May, R. J. (1975), *Education in Melanesia.* Port Moresby: The University of Papua New Guinea.

Commonwealth of Australia (2008), *Development for All: Towards a Disability-Inclusive Australian Aid Program 2009-2014*. Canberra, ACT: Australian Agency for International Development (AusAID).

— (2010), *Meeting the Challenge: Education in Papua New Guinea*. Port Moresby: Birdwing Press.

Crossley, M. (1983), *Strategies for Curriculum Change with Special Reference to the Secondary Schools Extension Project in Papua New Guinea*, PhD. University of La Trobe, Melbourne, Australia.

— (1998), 'Ideology, Curriculum and Community: Policy and Practice in Education', in L. Zimmer-Tamakoshi (ed.), *Modern Papua New Guinea*. Missouri: Thomas Jefferson University Press, pp. 297–313.

Crossley, M. and Vulliamy, G. (1986), *The Policy of SSCEP: Context and Development*. Port Moresby: University of Papua New Guinea.

De Kemp, A., Elbers, C. and Gunning, J. W. (2008), *Primary Education in Zambia*. The Hague: Policy and Operations Evaluation Department.

Delpit, L. and Kemelfield, G. (1985), *An Evaluation of the Viles Tok Ples Skul Scheme in the North Solomons Province*. Port Moresby and Arawa: University of Papua New Guinea and North Solomons University Centre.

Dinnen, S. (1998), 'Law, Order, and State', in L. Zimmer-Tamakoshi (ed.), *Modern Papua New Guinea*. Missouri: Thomas Jefferson University Press, pp. 333–350.

Dobrin, L. M., 2008. 'From Linguistic Elicitation to Eliciting the Linguist: Lessons in Community Empowerment from Melanesia', *Language* 84 (2), 300–324.

Education to Review the Curriculum (2012), *The National*, 16 October.

Epstein, S. (2007), *Education for Life: A Baseline Study of How the Different Types of Stakeholders in the Madang Educational System Perceive the New Reforms*. Madang: Voluntary Service Overseas and Madang Education Authority.

Fife, W. (2005), *Doing Fieldwork: Ethnographic Methods for Research in Developing Countries and Beyond*. New York: Palgrave Macmillan.

Freeman, C., Anderson, P. and Morgan, G. (2005), *PNG Curriculum Implementation Project: Report on the Pilot Curriculum Standards Monitoring Test*. Port Moresby: Australian Government and AusAID.

Garnaut, R. and Namaliu, R. (2010), *PNG Universities Review: Report to Prime Ministers Somare and Rudd*. Port Moresby: Government of Papua New Guinea.

Giraure, N. (1975), 'The Need for a Cultural Programme: Personal Reflections', in J. Brammall and R. J. May (eds), *Education in Melanesia*. Port Moresby: The University of Papua New Guinea, pp. 101–104.

Goldman, M. (2005), *The World Bank and Struggles for Social Justice in the Age of Globalization*. New Haven: Yale University Press.

Graue, C. (2011), 'Free Education Will Not Work: Union', *Australia Network News*.

Guthrie, G. (2003), 'Cultural Continuities in Teaching Styles', *Papua New Guinea Journal of Education* 39 (2), 57–78.

Guy, R. (2010), 'Formulating and Implementing Education Policy', in R. J. May (ed.), *Policy-Making and Implementation: Studies from Papua New Guinea. State, Society and Governance in Melanesia*. Canberra: Australian National University, pp. 131–154.

Hughes, H. (2003), *Aid has Failed the Pacific. Issue Analysis No. 31*. Sydney: The Centre for Independent Studies.

Kiala, W. (2009), 'Parents assist unpaid teachers', *The National*, 1 May, p. 8.

Kolant, P. and Pettit, J. (2003), *Study Guide, Unit One – Effective School Management*. Port Moresby: Department of Education.

Kolo, P. (2008), 'Forgotten Bird Sanctuary', *Papua New Guinea Post-Courier*, 25 January, p. 27.

Layton, S. (2003), 'Don't Forget the Desks: "Basic Infrastructure in the Community Schools of Eastern Highlands Province"', in A. Maha and T. Flaherty (eds), *Education for 21st Century in Papua New Guinea and the South Pacific*. Goroka: University of Goroka, pp. 66–70.

Lea, D. (2001), 'Melanesia, Philosophy in', in O. Leaman (ed.), *Encyclopedia of Asian Philosophy*. London: Routledge, pp. 351–356.

Le Fanu, G. (2011), *The Transposition of Inclusion: An Analysis of the Relationship Between Curriculum Prescription and Practice in Papua New Guinea*, EdD. University of Bristol.

— (2013), The Inclusion of Inclusive Education in International Development: Lessons from Papua New Guinea. *International Journal of Educational Development* 33 (2), 139–148.

Lindstrom, L. (1990), 'Local Knowledge Systems and the Pacific Classroom', *Papua New Guinea Journal of Education* 26 (1), 5–16.

Map, W. (2006), 'Tambul People Contribute K40,000 for School Fees', *The National*, 3 July, pp. 1–2.

Matane, P. (1976), 'Education for What?' in E. Barrington Thomas (ed.), *Papua New Guinea Education*. Oxford: Oxford University Press, pp. 57–60.

May, R. J. (1998), 'From Promise to Crisis: A Political Economy of Papua New Guinea', in P. Larmour (ed.), *Governance and Reform in South Pacific: State and Society in Papua New Guinea*. Canberra: National Centre for Development Studies, Australian National University, pp. 302–323.

— (2010), 'Public Sector Reform Since 2001', in R. J. May (ed.), *Policy Making and Implementation: Studies from Papua New Guinea*. Canberra: Australian National University, pp. 27–38.

McLaughlin, D. (1994), 'Through Whose Eyes Do Our Children See the World Now? Traditional Education in Papua New Guinea', *Papua New Guinea Journal of Education* 30 (2), 63–79.

McNamara, V. (1976), 'High School Selection and the Breakdown of Village Society', in E. Barrington Thoma (ed.), *Papua New Guinea Education*. Oxford: Oxford University Press, pp. 67–76.

Monemone, T. (2003), 'Formalistic Teaching is Not Imposed: It is Indigenous to Papua New Guinea', *Papua New Guinea Journal of Education* 39(2), 85–90.

Mundy, K. (2002), 'Malawi: Externally Driven Reforms and Their Adoption During Democratic Transition', in J. Moulton, K. Mundy, M. Walmond and J. Williams (eds), *Education Reforms in Sub-Saharan Africa: Paradigm Lost?* Westport, CA: Greenwood Press, pp. 13–51.

Murphy, P. (1985), 'UPNG as an Agent of Social Stratification: An Analysis of Output by Sex', in E. Barrington Thomas (ed.), *Papua New Guinea Education*. Oxford: Oxford University Press, pp. 146–143.

Nalu, M. (2013), 'Education in Crisis: Report', *The National*, 9 August.

National Department of Education (NDOE) (1986), *A Philosophy of Education for Papua New Guinea: Ministerial Committee Report*. Port Moresby: NDOE.

— (1991), *Education Sector Review, Volume 1: Executive Summary and Principal Recommendations*. Port Moresby: NDOE.

— (2001), *The State of Education in Papua New Guinea*. Port Moresby: NDOE.

— (2002), *National Curriculum Statement for Papua New Guinea*. Port Moresby: NDOE.

— (2003), *Implementation Support Booklet for Head Teachers of Primary and Community Schools: Supporting the Implementation of Upper Primary Curriculum*. Port Moresby: NDOE.

— (2004), *Achieving a Better Future: A National Plan for Education 2005 to 2012*. Port Moresby: NDOE.

— (2006), *Lower Secondary Education Reform: Lower Secondary Implementation Handbook*. Port Moresby: NDOE.

— (2008), *Papua New Guinea Country Report. Inclusive Education: The Way Forward*. Port Moresby: NDOE.

— (2009), *Achieving Universal Education for a Better Future: Universal Basic Education Plan 2010–2019*. Port Moresby: NDOE.

National Executive Council (NEC) (2009), *Achieving Universal Education for a Better Future: Universal Basic Education Plan 2010–2019*. Port Moresby: Government of Papua New Guinea.

Nongkas, C. M. (2007), *Leading Educational Change in Primary Teacher Education: A Papua New Guinea Study*, PhD. Australian Catholic University, Brisbane.

Packer, S., Emmott, S. and Hinchliffe, K. (2009), *Improving the Provision of Basic Education Services to the Poor in Papua New Guinea. A Case Study*. Canberra: Australian Government/AusAID Office of Development Effectiveness.

Papoutsaki, E. and Rooney, D. (2006), 'Colonial Legacies and Neo-Colonial Practices in Papua New Guinean Higher Education', *Higher Education Research & Development* 25 (4), 421–433.

Paul, M. (2009), 'Services Less Effective After Independence', *The National*, 4 August, p. 9.

Payani, H. (2003), 'Bureaucratic Corruption in Papua New Guinea: Causes, Consequences and Remedies', in D. Kavanamur, C. Yala and Q. Clements (eds),

Building a Nation in Papua New Guinea: Views of the Post-Independence Generation. Canberra: Pandanus Books, Australian National University, pp. 91–106.

Pearse, R., Sengi, S. and Kiruhia, J. (1989), 'Community School Teaching in the Central Province: An Observational Study', *Papua New Guinea Journal of Education* 26 (1), 69–84.

Pickford, S. (1998), 'Post-Colonial Learning: Classroom Rituals as Social and Cultural Practice', *Papua New Guinea Journal of Teacher Education*, 5, 6–14.

PNG PM O'Neill Highlights Free Education (2011), *Radio Australia*, 30 August.

Pool, M. (2009), 'Personal Profile', *The Network*, 18, 10.

Principle Transferred, Locals Want Him Back (2008), *The National*, 22 January, p. 5.

Reilly, B. and Phillpot, R. (2002), '"Making Democracy Work" in Papua New Guinea: Social Capital and Provincial Development in an Ethnically Fragmented Society', *Asian Survey* 42 (6), 906–927.

Rogers, C., Bleakley, R., Ola, W. and CARE Integrated Community Development Project Team (2010), *Rural Poverty in Remote Papua New Guinea. Case Study of Obura-Wonenara District.* Canberra: Australian National University/CARE.

Romaine, S. (1992), *Language, Education and Development: Urban and Rural Tok Pisin in Papua New Guinea.* Oxford: Oxford University Press.

Ryan, A. (2008), 'Indigenous Knowledge in the Science Curriculum: Avoiding Neo-Colonialism', *Cultural Studies of Science Education* 3 (3), 663–683.

Sillitoe, P. (1998), *An Introduction to the Anthropology of Melanesia.* Cambridge: Cambridge University Press.

Smith, P. (1985), 'Colonial Policy, Education and Social Stratification, 1945–1975', in E. Barrington Thomas (ed.), *Papua New Guinea Education.* Oxford: Oxford University Press, pp. 49–66.

— (1987), *Education and Colonial Control in Papua New Guinea: A Documentary History.* Melbourne: Longman Cheshire Pty Limited.

Smith, P. and Guthrie, G. (1980), 'Children, Education and Society', in G. Guthrie and P. Smith (eds), *The Education of the Papua New Guinea Child: Proceedings of the 1979 Extraordinary Meeting of the Faculty of Education.* Port Moresby: University of Papua New Guinea, pp. 5–21.

Swatridge, C. (1985), *Delivering the Goods: Education as Cargo in Papua New Guinea.* Manchester: Manchester University Press.

Teacher Union Warns Governmental Free Education Plan will Fail (2012), *Education International*, 5 January.

Temby, S. (2007), *Good Governance in Papua New Guinea: An Australian Agenda.* Melbourne: School of Social and Environmental Enquiry, The University of Melbourne.

The PNG Time Warp (2007), *The National*, 28 June, p. 22.

Tololo, A. (1976), 'A Consideration of Some Likely Future Trends in Education in Papua New Guinea', in E. Barrington Thomas (ed.), *Papua New Guinea Education.* Oxford: Oxford University Press, pp. 209–225.

Tweedie, L. (2002), *Listen and Learn: A Policy Research Report on Papua New Guinean Teachers' Attitudes to Their Own Profession.* London: Voluntary Service Overseas.

United Nations Children's Fund (UNICEF) (2004), *UNICEF in Papua New Guinea.* Port Moresby: UNICEF.

United Nations Development Programme (UNDP) (2009), *Human Development Report 2009/10. Overcoming Barriers: Human Mobility and Development.* New York: UNDP.

United Nations Educational, Scientific and Cultural Organization (UNESCO) (2005), *Guidelines for Inclusion: Ensuring Access to Education for All.* Paris: UNESCO.

United Nations Educational, Scientific and Cultural Organization–International Bureau of Education (UNESCO/IBE) (2011), *World Data on Education: Papua New Guinea* (7th edn). Paris: UNESCO/IBE.

Urwick, J. and Elliott, J. (2010), 'International Orthodoxy versus National Realities: Inclusive Schooling and the Education of Children with Disabilities in Lesotho', *Comparative Education* 46 (2), 137–150.

Wallangas, G. (2003), 'Formalism is Both Indigenous and Imposed', *Papua New Guinea Journal of Education* 39 (2), 96–100.

Webster, T. (2004a), 'Advantages of Female Teachers', *Papua New Guinea Post-Courier* 18 June, p. 11.

— (2004b), 'Reasons Why Students Drop Out', *Papua New Guinea Post-Courier* 30 July, pp. 11–12.

— (2004c), 'Girls Likely to Lose Out in Plan', *Papua New Guinea Post-Courier* 22 October, p. 11.

Weeden, W. J., Beeby, C. E. and Gris, G. B. (1969), *Report of the Advisory Committee on Education in Papua and New Guinea, 1969.* Canberra: Ministry for External Territories.

World Bank (2004a), *Papua New Guinea Poverty Assessment.* Washington: World Bank.

— (2004b), *Papua New Guinea: Public Expenditure and Service Delivery.* Washington: World Bank.

Zeegers, M. (2000), 'Rhetoric, Reality and the Practicum: Reconstructionism, Behaviourism and Primary Teacher Education in Papua New Guinea', *Asia-Pacific Journal of Education* 28 (2), 149–163.

11

Fiji: Evolution of Education from Colonial to Modern Times

Akhila Nand Sharma, Steven J. Coombs, Subhas Chandra
and Manueli Sagaitu

Introducing Fiji and its education system

Fiji is a small island state located in the South Pacific some 1,500 miles off the east coast of Australia and roughly 1,300 miles north of New Zealand. As a country, Fiji is an archipelago of several hundred islands with four main large islands: Viti Levu, Vanua Levu, Kadavu and Taveuni. Technically, the country's name is Fiji Islands. The population of Fiji Islands in 2013 was just under 0.9 million people, with most people living in the main island of Viti Levu and the capital city Suva. Fiji's islands have a rich and long history and culture and were originally an ancient kingdom that under duress from Tonga in the 1870s voluntarily offered cession to Britain in 1874. It was not until independence in 1970 that Fiji became an independent country in the modern world. It was during Colonial times that Fiji's main industry of sugar was developed and this led to many indentured people from India working on the plantations. This shifted the cultural and population axis such that by independence in 1970 the 'Indo-Fijian' population threatened to democratically outnumber native Fijians setting up future tensions. According to the Constitution of the Republic of Fiji (2013), all Fiji citizens are now called 'Fijians' and the indigenous Fijians 'iTaukei'.

This chapter explores the educational consequences of Britain's colonial impact on Fiji and the influx of the Indo-Fijian populace. It goes on to chart the evolution of the education system through Colonial times to the present and also the development of higher education in the last 50 years. The various ethnic divisions in the schooling system are explored with the consequent educational gaps and challenges still being felt to this day. Since independence the Government of Fiji has been destabilized by a number of military coups from 1987 with the last one in 2006, resulting in Fiji being withdrawn from the Commonwealth. On a more positive note 2013 saw the publication of the new Fiji constitution and a timetable to have new elections in September 2014. If all goes well, Fiji will rejoin the Commonwealth and be open to more economic investment with hopefully a positive impact on educational challenges and opportunities. While the political and cultural challenges in Fiji are unique, there is no doubt that many of the educational issues are shared widely across the many small island nation states of the South Pacific.

The origins and development of the Fijian education system

When formal education was introduced in Fiji about two centuries ago, it was highly academic, examination-driven and foreign-oriented. It appeared to work well then because it was teacher-centred and examination-led, much in line with the rest of the world. The students succeeded in external examinations through employing mostly surface learning approaches. Initially, most students were enrolled from middle and upper social classes. Most educational establishments at that time encouraged teachers to employ the 'rote-learning' mode of pedagogy and instruction. Despite this limited education approach, many students did succeed and managed to go through both primary and secondary education and in some cases onto tertiary education. Others left school to go on and enter a few of the waged employment opportunities available at that time. Since the establishment of The University of the South Pacific (USP) in 1968, there have been drastic changes in the nature of education in Fiji. At least two more universities have been recently established to meet the growing demand for higher education as is the case globally. In the past, universities in and beyond Fiji had only enrolled an elite-selected student body, usually funded by public sources. These earlier graduates were mostly prepared for the few white-collar professional employment opportunities available in the Government and commercial sectors. However, as the school system unfolded, social trends led to more people staying on in education and training with greater numbers progressing to higher education. While actual numbers are not available, the 2012 Annual Report of the Ministry of Education (MoE), National Heritage, Culture and Arts indicates that access and retention to education and training had improved (Fiji, 2012). The Report also shows that Government funding to the three universities – Fiji National University, the USP and the University of Fiji – had not increased significantly. Therefore, the expansion of numbers impacted upon the funding model for tertiary education, with a shifting of the cost burden from public to private hands, in particular to students and parents.

In more recent times following the launch of the 2013 Fiji Constitution, the 2014 National Budget has lightened the cost burden upon parents by making primary and secondary education free. For tertiary education, however, the budget has made provision for low interest student loans to cater for greater access and progression onto higher education and training (Fiji, 2013). Therefore, at the compulsory primary and secondary school levels government funding from public sources has increased significantly. Consequently, the Fijian Government has taken greater control of school management, curriculum development, assessment and staffing. Another major change that has transpired over recent years is the diversification of the student and staff population. In the case of primary and secondary schools, pupils and their teachers have become much more multi-racial. They were largely divided upon ethnic lines when Fiji's schooling system began in the nineteenth century under the British. The recent changes have also transformed the mode of teaching and learning, focusing much more on integrating vocational education with academic subjects, and adopting pedagogical strategies to make learning more of a pleasure. Using deep learning approaches, students not only become active learners, but also develop positive feelings and a sense of ownership. However, a lot of work in this direction still needs to be done as the culture of a more transmission-focused pedagogy is hard to change. This is the case in many other similar countries that are attempting to bring in a more inclusive system of pedagogy linked to developing critical and creative skills suited to the skill set required of the knowledge economy. Crossley et al. (2011) reported similar attempts in other Small Island States, such as the radical programme being implemented in Mauritius that appears to replicate contemporary Fijian education policy and practice towards a more student-centred learning practice supported by ICT as learning technologies.

This chapter focuses upon the changing nature of Fijian education and schooling; the management of its schools; the adopted assessment system and vocational education opportunities.

The changing nature of education and schooling: Fiji's ethnic divide and social inequality

When Fiji became a British Colony on the 10 October 1874, there was already a well-established network of small iTaukei village schools. These were established by the Methodist Church missionaries who had arrived in 1835 (Coxon, 2000; Qovu, 2013). These schools employed locally identified iTaukei teachers who taught basic numeracy and literacy using materials printed in the local dominant Bauan dialect (Tavola, 1991; Qovu, 2013). The programme entitled 'Vuli Wilivola' was geared towards providing an in-depth understanding of the iTaukei-translated version of the Holy Bible (Qovu, 2013). At the same time, there were a few centrally located Roman Catholic schools which were managed by the Marist missionaries who had arrived 6 years earlier in 1829 (Coxon, 2000). The subjects offered at these schools were more academic in nature, and usually taught by European teachers. 'English language' gradually became the medium of instruction.

This educational approach employed by the Roman Catholic missionaries was favoured by the British administrators during the first decade of colonial rule. They had assisted in establishing and supporting similar schools for European children in Suva and Levuka. However, the approach to the education of iTaukei children was one of non-intervention, respecting cultural and traditional differences at the time. This parallel system of educational opportunity did not distract or deter the aspirations of the iTaukei in their educational policy and approach (Tavola, 1991). Qovu (2013) confirms the views of Coxon (2000) and Tavola (1991) pointing out that by 1900 there was a Methodist supervised school in almost every native Fijian iTaukei village, whereupon the children's full attendance at such community centres was viewed as a norm of their childhood.

Historically, the iTaukei people lived in close knit communities along the coastal fringes and the river valleys. They were largely involved in small-scale subsistence agriculture and provided labour for government administration. The Government's effort to engage them in the sugarcane plantations, which became the dominant crop, did not succeed because of the nature of the work. The labourers employed from the iTaukei community returned to a life of affluent subsistence in their villages (Tavola, 1991). Reinforced by the colonial policy of 'protecting' indigenous peoples, this prohibited the commercial exploitation and employment of iTaukei people in this industry. Thus the sugar cane planters faced an immediate and severe labour shortage. This prompted the Government to import labour from India as had been done in Africa, the Caribbean and Mauritius (Tavola, 1991; Qovu, 2013). Between 1879 and 1916, 62,837 Indian indentured labourers were brought to work on the sugarcane plantations. This action of the colonial administrators was necessitated by a common understanding that as the sugar industry had become the backbone of Fiji's colonial economy it needed many more low-cost manual workers than were available locally.

During the early years of their arrival, the Indo-Fijian request for the provision of academic education for their children was not accommodated by the Colonial administrators (Gounder, 1999; Qovu, 2013). However, by 1890 the Methodist mission as well as some Indo-Fijian religious organizations had established schools for their children. This evolution laid the foundation of strong Indo-Fijian community provision and involvement in the education of their young people. At this early stage, iTaukei children and adults were generally more advanced in terms of educational access, attendance and literacy levels than their Indo-Fijian counterparts (Coxon, 2000).

After the enactment of the 1916 Fiji Education Ordinance which had introduced the grant-in-aid scheme for all schools, the Colonial Government became much more involved in formal education and operated within a structure of state–community partnerships (Coxon, 2000). The Colonial Government effectively continued to support the development of racially divided schooling with now three parallel systems operating that were to create Fiji's future inequalities. Several education commentators such as Coxon (2000) and Qovu (2013) point out that although many more iTaukei compared to Indo-Fijian children had attended primary schools, the quality of education in their schools that were remotely located in rural and outlying islands was generally much lower, disqualifying them from the grant-in-aid educational funding. At the same time, many Indo-Fijian schools, especially those in urban areas, had met the prescribed grant-in-aid standards and were therefore able to qualify for the available financial educational grants. This scheme served to further widen the disparity levels in both the physical structures and the academic standards between the two ethnically divided Fijian school systems. To reduce this ever widening gap and improve the quality of Fijian education, it became necessary in later years to introduce affirmative action (AA) policies in favour of iTaukei and Rotuman people.

This unfortunate situation of the lack of funding support towards improving academic education outcomes for the iTaukei people had been allowed to gather momentum over many decades. By the mid-1940s, the enrolment figures had radically changed, with the consequence of more Indo-Fijian children attending school. The Indo-Fijian communities, as Sharma (1997), Coxon (2000) and Qovu (2013) point out, had preferred that their children had access to the more academic curriculum that was also available only to European children. Thus, the tri-partite educational system favoured two racial groups over the native Fijian creating an unlevel playing field *via* the embedding of systematic inequality. The academic curriculum for these two racial groups was generally the more favoured choice, rather than the agricultural and other vocational educational foci the Colonial government promoted for non-European schools. Ravuvu (2003) points out that the strong urge by the Indo-Fijian communities for academic education had been influenced through their early childhood experiences encountered back in India before they had embarked on their indentured trips to Fiji. For instance, there were already numerous and well-established universities and colleges in India well before 1879. Consequently, there was an established system of primary and secondary schools providing academic education for those Indian parents who were able to financially afford to send their children for further education. Hence, academic education pathways and their potential opportunities for social advancement was already a part of the indo-Fijian culture and expectation for their children.

Town and country: Fiji's urban and rural divide

Unfortunately, inequality has been structurally embedded within the Fijian education system ever since the Colonial period and remained as a legacy well into modern and recent times. As we have seen, inequality was reinforced by the Colonial grant-in-aid funding policy that was further exasperated by major differences of culture and resources between folk living in urban and rural contexts. Coxon (2000) argued that social inequality originating from those early years had indeed resulted from disparities in the quality of provision between rural and urban schools. Coxon (2000), White (2001) and Puamau (2001) also report that by 1916 the system of state–community partnerships had been firmly established across Fiji. This meant that schools that had already been advantaged through their geographic and socio-economic locations were further encouraged to maintain their status quo and improve their advantages overtime, thereby widening the educational 'gap'. Conversely, rural schools that mainly served the iTaukei people were strongly disadvantaged by the education system that they had to operate within. This politically sponsored systemic inequality was the major cause underpinning the continuing disparity in the academic outcomes between iTaukei students and the children of other ethnic groups (Puamau, 2001; Uluivuda, 2001; White, 2001; Nabobo-Baba, 2006; Sharma, 2000; Qovu, 2013).

The overwhelming argument that we and many others make (Coxon, 2000) is that the combined effect of the above educational policies from 1800 up to early

1900 had favoured and thereby reinforced ethnically divided education. Key factors had included the Colonial education policy; geographical location; socio-economic advantages; cultural, linguistic and religious differences. In summary, ethnically divided schooling has been embedded within Fiji's education system for well over a century and created a legacy felt to this day.

Education policy in post-colonial Fiji

Both the 1969 and the 2000 Fiji Education Commission Reports highlighted the issue of divergent community ownership of schools. This is the connection between a particular school's resources and the degree of wealth they have access to *via* their local community. Disparities in wealth across divided communities had significantly contributed to Fiji's present binary education system. First, they have perpetuated the differences in the quality of schooling and life chances available for children from the different communities. Secondly, they have also effectively maintained sectarian separation by ethnicity since early 1800 (Coxon, 2000).

The earlier views clearly indicate that for well over a century the present education gap has been created largely through misguided education policies. This has led to an inequality of the academic achievements between Fiji's two main ethnic groups, the Indo-Fijians and those of the iTaukei people. Whitehead (1986) also supports this argument when she reported that the iTaukei people have been historically educationally disadvantaged. She cites the following factors: first was the lack of assistance and direction from the former Colonial Government. Second was the continuing adherence to the century-old ethnically divided system of schooling. She further confirmed that this was the historical root cause of the lower educational attainment of the iTaukei population and that this had also laid the foundation of the inherited education system in Fiji.

However, the earlier education gap has slowly but positively been addressed since 2002 with the introduction of the legally framed AA policy initiatives within the 2001 Social Justice Act. According to Qovu (2013), the Ministry of Fijian Affairs Scholarship Scheme and the investment in selected Government Secondary Schools, called Centres of Excellence, have yielded positive outcomes in terms of academic achievement and learning environment including: learning resources, classrooms and other facilities (Qovu, 2013). Qovu's (2013) research study revealed that '. . . for the Fiji Seventh Form Examination [Year 13] alone, Indigenous Fijian students had improved their pass rate from 63.5 percent for 2005 to 73.5 percent in 2006' (p. 236). He said, however, that a lot more could still be achieved if the implementers of the AA policy had encouraged inclusiveness in their approach and had placed emphasis on the transparency of their actions.

Fiji's interpretation of the UN's 'education for all'

The present Military Government decided to discontinue any racial discrimination policies. Consequently, 'education for all Fijians' replaced the AA policy that was exclusively targeted for 'iTaukei' and 'Rotuman' people. In doing so, this policy now provides educational assistance to all needy Fijians. Echoing the provisions of the 2013 Constitution of the Republic of Fiji, the 2014 National Budget articulates that the Government would provide 'free education for primary and secondary students and loan schemes for tertiary students at extremely low interest rates' (Fiji, 2013: p. 3). The current education policy initiatives now cater for the following:

- The removal of all forms of discrimination in respect of access and selection in schools, ensuring every child a free education with equal opportunity in the school system.
- The racial names of schools were changed so that they now reflect more inclusive learning spaces for all Fijians.
- The abolishment of three external examinations in primary and lower secondary schools, so as to reduce drop-out rates.
- The provision of free transport to all students that meet the access and entry criteria at the primary and secondary school levels.
- The zoning of schools to bring education closer to all children.
- The completion of the provision of free textbooks to all primary schools and the commencement of the same provision for secondary schools.
- The continuing Government's initiative to work closely with non-government school authorities to provide education facilities for the inflow of all children into the school system.
- The expansion and upgrading of rural high schools up to form seven levels, and to provide easier access for rural students to go straight to university and advanced technical education.

The earlier education policies run parallel to the Fijian version of Education for All (EFA) initiatives which were introduced in 2010 to replace the AA policies in education. The increase in the amount of funding for the EFA programmes during 2010 and 2011 financial years clearly indicate the confidence of the present Government of the continuing success of the initiatives for the development of Fiji's education system that provide education for all Fijians. The Fijian EFA initiative has continued to increase annual financial allocations towards development of education for rural, remote and outer island schools, but also includes support for urban and semi-urban schools. However, Sowell (2004) confirms that the permanent presence of socio-economic inequalities is fairly universal and therefore remains as a long-standing challenge to all educational policy-makers including those in Fiji. His extensive research study of AA Policies in 16 countries affirms that no permanent or successful solution has been designed in any national setting and is a testament to the consistent lack of creative workable solutions on the ground. Perhaps, the recent UN's renewal of the 2000 Millennium Development Goals (MDGs) to a proposed new agenda of Sustainable Development Goals may go some way towards resolving this thorny problem. To expect temporary programmes such as Fiji's AA Policy or EFA to adequately address such deeply entrenched issues is somewhat optimistic. The success of such initiatives rests largely on the competence and commitment of the national and local leaders, teachers and other members of the stakeholder community on the ground. Top-down government policies clearly need to be able to hand-shake with grassroots practice. The standard paradigm of educational policy and planning needs to fundamentally shift towards systems that systematically and sustainably enable educational policy, planning and practice. Such a grounded approach towards educational development and greater likelihood of social impact is also argued by Crossley et al. (2011) who powerfully maintain:

> Given the magnitude and unpredictability of the global environmental, economic and political challenges faced by small states in today's rapidly changing world, the importance of well-grounded, cross-sectoral and multi-disciplinary initiatives . . . . (are required). . . ., if contextually appropriate and sustainable development is to be achieved. (p. 57)

School community partnerships in Fiji

Community participation in schooling has always been celebrated in Fiji. While it makes useful contributions to local teaching and learning, many school communities do not have the capacity or expertise to adequately meet the changing demands of education systems required for the twenty-first century. Therefore, the nature of this partnership and collaboration needs to be revitalized by a new relationship between central government and local communities and reshaped to fit the demands of a quality education system. For this to happen, the initial stage ought to involve the preparation of teachers for this new style of community partnership and engagement. The present model of local community participation in Fiji's schools has evolved over many years. With the diversification of student and staff population, there is an opportunity to reconsider the model of community participation and the previous ownership of the schools. Improvements could be made with community participation in classroom programmes and homework supervision, for example, more parent teaching assistants. Parental representation from different ethnic backgrounds on School Boards and committees also needs to be instituted.

In Fiji many early childhood centres, primary and secondary schools are owned and managed by local school committees. Similarly, many religious and cultural organizations have built and managed their own schools. However, the nature of partnership between the Fijian Government and the school management committees that include private and religious organizations has been drastically changed over the last few years. The Government has now standardized school management procedures. It has also taken control of curriculum development and the appointment of staff, including school head teachers/principals. The majority of funds for teachers' salaries, students' school fees and capital development are now provided by the Government from which it can leverage central control of the educational system. Therefore, the school's local managerial role in the community has been reduced to merely the maintenance of buildings, equipment and facilities. Local schools in Fiji now have hardly any input in the implementation of staff appointments and curriculum development.

There is still a marked variation in the standard of basic school facilities and resources. Schools serving remote and poor urban communities are often in an appalling state of repair. As previously discussed, this arose from the time of the 1916 Education Ordinance, which introduced the Grant-in Aid Scheme for schools. Disparities between the Indo-Fijian community schools and their iTaukai counterparts were reinforced through this policy. However, problems such as an over-emphasis upon rote-learning linked to perceived success in external examinations continue to remain in predominately Indo-Fijian schools. This pedagogical approach is re-enforced in these schools by the local community with other consequences such as sports remaining a low priority.

One consequence of the military coup in 1987 and thereafter was that many Indo-Fijian people left the country leaving a lot of free space in their community schools. The good quality academic reputation of these schools created a new opportunity and attracted many iTaukei students to enrol in the free spaces left behind. Many predominately Indo-Fijian-managed schools now have more iTaukei students than those drawn from the Indo-Fijian community, bringing much greater diversity in the student population and thereby altering the main mission of the school and the modes of teaching and learning. The management committees of these schools, however, remained in the hands of the same people. The iTaukei parents therefore do not have a proper voice in the management of Indo-Fijian owned and managed schools and vice versa. However, in the last few years and up to the launch of the new Fijian constitution in 2013, the racial names of these schools have now been changed to more neutral 'labels'. This multi-racial education policy now enables Fijian students of any racial background to potentially enrol in schools that have available places. The Fijian government also intends that Fijian parents drawn from all communities will in future be involved in the management of their local community schools.

The demands on Fiji's teacher education system

The dramatic increase in student population of the urban schools has not only yielded student and staff diversity, but also increased the demand for appropriately qualified teachers. This problem is more pronounced in primary schools. Until recently, most teachers in Fiji have entered the teaching profession without first obtaining a degree qualification. With the establishment of the USP, Fiji National University and the University of Fiji, this situation is slowly changing. Most teachers now complete their first degrees and teacher education qualifications as pre-service and in-service professional learning 'employee' students. Rural primary schools have the most teachers who are still not sufficiently qualified and experienced. Providing appropriate in-service teacher education programmes linked to university qualifications still remains a challenge in Fiji. However, as discussed in the contribution to this volume by Lingam, Raturi and Finau, new modes of delivery and access through distance and flexible learning courses combined with emerging online and mobile learning training opportunities by Fiji's main universities seek to resolve this situation. It should also be noted that large numbers of teachers were trained many years ago and have since not attended any form of professional development programme. This situation has become more acute owing to the recent reduction of the teacher retirement age in Fiji to 55 years. The retirement age policy leaves many schools with less experienced head teachers/principals incapable of developing successive school-based leaders.

The increase in the student participation rate and enrolments in general has increased the student/teacher ratio. In urban schools, the larger classes are now up to 50 students. However, there is much variation in the student–teacher ratio between rural and urban schools. While there are many consequences for overcrowded classrooms, the authors note from their empirical local knowledge in Fiji that teachers are generally not prepared to manage large classes on the one hand and small composite classes on the other. Successfully managing both large and small classes requires different pedagogical strategies and approaches for which many teachers in Fiji are ill-equipped. Resolving this issue requires in-service input in the form of high-quality teacher education combined with ongoing teacher continuing professional development (CPD) as a new life-long learning policy for the profession. With appropriate CPD, it will become possible for teachers to manage these classes of varying sizes. Rural schools tend to have problems associated with composite classes, but usually with lower student–teacher ratios and the quality of teaching could improve if teachers learn new forms of pedagogy supported by high quality and relevant on-the-job CPD as a form of professional learning (Sorensen and Coombs, 2009).

Embedding Fiji's culture within the curriculum

The academic nature of the Fijian National Curriculum does not provide sufficient space to include the study of the socio-cultural groups that make up the Fijian people. Focus on high external examination results and the overcrowding of the curriculum with academic subjects did not allow for the inclusion of non-formal education as well as the study of diverse cultures that Fiji is fortunate to have. Furthermore, a few TVET and vernacular subjects that are in the school curriculum are optional and students tend to prefer academic subjects instead. Recognizing the significance of uniting all Fijians by common and equal citizenry and by respecting each other's cultures, customs, traditions and languages, the 2013 Constitution of the Republic of Fiji chapter 2, section 31 (p. 34) notes, 'Conversational and contemporary iTaukei and Fiji Hindi languages shall be taught as compulsory subjects in all primary schools'. While this initiative of the Government is welcomed, there is clearly a need for more suitably qualified language teachers to implement this policy successfully. At the same time, the socio-cultural issues and community tensions of Fiji need to be accommodated in some form of citizenship education, perhaps through formal, non-formal and informal educational approaches. The authors feel that the local teacher training institutions including Fiji's universities should review these areas of culture, languages and citizenship within their teacher education curriculum for both pre-service and in-service groups.

Assessment and examinations

External examinations were significant features of Fiji's education system since the introduction of formal education by Christian churches, Indian migrants and the British Colonial Government. Initially, these examinations operated at five levels of schooling. They had serious consequences on classroom practice; how the stakeholders evaluated schools and what the students did after leaving school. External examinations were also employed as 'gatekeepers' to control admission to more advanced levels of schooling and higher education. In recent years, significant changes have happened with the localization of external examinations and the discontinuation of two primary and one secondary school external examinations from 2011 onwards. This reduction of examination hurdles was intended to improve the retention rate of students in Fiji's schools and also improve access to higher levels of education. Fiji now has only two external examinations – the Fiji School Leaving Certificate (FSLC) examination taken after 12 years of education, and Form 7 exams set the year after the FSLC for university entrance. The latter is equivalent to the Foundation Examination pathway at the USP. Despite the disappearance of three external examinations, the education system in Fiji is still overly academic, driven by the remaining external examinations. The pre-occupation of schools now is to prepare students for the two remaining examinations, especially the FSLC where the participation rate has increased owing to the discontinuation of the other former 'gate-keeping' examinations. The transmission pedagogical mode of teaching and learning still continues as this is seen by teachers and other members of the local community as a successful short-term preparation strategy for external assessment tests. The current school system does not provide sufficient 'life-skills' for students to obtain blue-collar jobs or get involved in self-employment opportunities. Schools do offer vocational subjects, but those that are available are optional and perceived of as low status. The justification for this significant reform to reduce the number of external examinations in the national education agenda incorporates social aspects that are directly intended to promote engagement within primary and secondary education for all Fijian children. The intention is that the educational development of the students is free from any anxiety that is claimed to be induced by the external examinations and the possible trauma that could accompany failure of these regular tests and examinations.

An even more compelling rationale focuses on the equal opportunities that the reformed education system now offers to segments of the population that are economically disadvantaged or impoverished. Hence, students from poor families and those from remote and isolated rural areas would be able to continue their education unhindered up to the Form 6 level. This social reform at the national level can be acknowledged as a motivating element that is likely to rekindle the expectations and aspirations of even the most unfortunate Fijians.

Another significant development that dates back to independence in 1970 and is still continuing is the Psychological Assessment Unit. It was established at USP's School of Education in conjunction with the Fiji Government. The terms of reference for this Unit were to 'carry out research, and give advice on, matters relating to educational and vocational guidance to both the public and private sectors' (Bennett, 1971: p. 2). Within this brief the Unit developed or adapted a battery of six psychological tests – two tests for non-verbal reasoning ability, two speed and accuracy tests, a vocabulary test and a test of mechanical comprehension conducted with the Pacific Vocational Interest Analysis. These tests were administered to all Form 5 students in Fiji and the results were used for career guidance and selection within the end-of-school or post-school continuum. The tests were an adjunct to the formal school and national assessment practices. In 1975, the use of these and any other aptitude tests for educational and vocational guidance and selection became the responsibility of the newly established Fiji National Training Council. The academic staff associated with this Unit continued to offer professional advice on test technicalities as well as teach educational measurement and evaluation for the education degree programmes for staff located at the University Assessment and Examinations Unit. This role of this Unit could be revisited to assist it to enhance and support the provision of better pathways into employment, higher education and life-long learning.

With the disappearance of many external examinations, internal assessment systems were introduced at the school level. As part of their Masters of Education research projects, some of USP's School of Education students are currently studying the quality of the implementation process of the school-based internal assessment. Preliminary findings indicate that teachers and their principals/ head teachers are not well-prepared to execute this mode of assessment with the implication that specialist CPD in educational assessment needs to be provided. The external examinations are now mostly replaced by several internally set tests. Many teachers now complain that they are burdened by completing a lot of internal assessment-related documents for the MoE. This administration impacts upon their valuable teaching time. The authors recommend an MoE-led inquiry into the nature of how internal educational assessment is being delivered in Fiji's schools. Better pedagogical integration with formative assessment linked more fully into the curriculum may be one-way forward. One option could be to link on-the-job CPD curriculum development projects as part of school improvement programmes.

Teaching for quality learning: the teacher-centred to student-centred paradigm shift

The authors believe that teaching for quality learning should be stressed at all levels of the schooling system – early childhood, primary, secondary and tertiary. The lecture and teacher-dominated approach to teaching has continued to prevail at all levels of the education system. This didactic and behaviourist mode of teaching and learning concentrates on surface learning approaches such as memorizing or rote-learning. However, there is a gradual shift from surface to deep learning where the focus is on student-centeredness and authentic student engagement in the learning process. At the tertiary level, in particular, students are encouraged to move from declarative to functioning knowledge. There is no doubt that this is a significant cultural step change in the teacher's perception of what constitutes as the role of teaching for improving the quality of a learner's learning.

There is insufficient space in this chapter to fully address this issue; however, it is recommended by the authors that teachers adapt the principles of constructive alignment (Biggs and Tang, 2011). Constructive alignment emerges from the constructivist school of educational psychology which defines quality teaching and learning by situating students in the centre of the learning framework. It is anchored on the theory of constructivism in learning, and alignment of the learning components. The former drives the students into the world of knowledge construction or creation, engagement in learning, creativity, application of learning, deep learning and life-long learning. The latter is for teachers to align both teaching learning activities (TLAs) and assessment tasks (ATs) with the intended learning outcomes (ILOs). Briefly, the ILOs contain verbs that indicate the level of achievement and the content to be learnt. The TLAs address the verbs and the ATs with rubrics that enable the learner and the teacher to judge how well the content has been learnt. In essence, this system of pedagogy recognizes the benefits of ongoing formative ATs as a means of delivering a high-quality curriculum learning experience. As the local and longest established university,

USP has begun to conduct workshops on this concept for its teachers/lecturers and it is expected that it will slowly permeate throughout education system in Fiji and the South Pacific.

Throughout this chapter, the issues surrounding the quality of teaching and learning in Fiji's schools have been explored. There is generally an excessive amount of rote-learning and teacher-directed pedagogy. Students are continuously prepared for the two external examinations that still exist. Employers have complained about the lack of initiative shown by school leavers and the inability for them to think critically and apply learning to life-long learning needs (Sharma, 2000). It is observed that many graduates are not sufficiently prepared for reflective learning and working and getting involved in problem-based learning. The principles of constructive alignment and reflective learning have not yet adequately entered into Fiji's classrooms as well as its tertiary institution's lecture rooms. It is suggested by the authors that schools and tertiary institutions in Fiji consider the pedagogical benefits of student-centred learning and refection as espoused by critical theorists such as David Boud (Boud et al., 1985), whereupon greater learner empowerment enhances curriculum ownership, transfer of skills and deeper learning in general.

Future challenges: the case of technical, vocational education and training

Fiji's social, political and economic contexts have changed enormously since independence and the four military coups. The Fijian economy has become more diversified but is still vulnerable, like many small island states, to external and internal shocks (Crossley et al., 2011). Fiji is part of a fast changing world and needs an education system (Fiji Islands Education Commission/Panel, 2000) to cater for the emerging context of globalization and the knowledge economy. This has been underpinned by the Fijian government (Fiji, 2014) setting up a new Tertiary Scholarship and Loans Decree to allow greater access to Higher Education and Vocational Training. Some initiatives in vocational education and vocationalization of the school curriculum have taken place guided by regional initiatives such as the Pacific Education Development Framework (PIFS, 2009). From all these government and regional initiatives, it emerged that Fiji required increased capacity of TVET so as to provide new education and life-skills opportunities for future students to obtain waged and self-employment, thus developing the full potential of students to progress into an uncertain world of the future.

The technical vocational education and training (TVET) section in Fiji comes under the MoE. It is, therefore, reasonable to chart the progress of TVET reforms in Fiji from 1995 to 2013 that also builds upon a regional framework for developing TVET capacity (PIFS, 2012).

In 1995, the use of a vision and mission statement was not in practice, but a notable shift in the MoE's vision is apparent over the years. In 2000, the vision was 'education and training for changing needs'; in 2005, the theme was 'holistic education for peace, prosperity' and finally in 2013: 'quality education for change, peace and progress'. Prevalent in the statements are the reference and use of such words as holistic, empowering, full potential, inheritance, national and cultural identity, peace, progress and sustainable development. While TVET is typically driven by international economic trends with local emphasis according to regional and national labour markets, the aspirations noted from the MoE mission statements closely reflected the UN's World Declaration on Education for All (EFA). Fiji has been under a military run government since its last coup of 2006, however, the desire for peace and progress has continued to exist and is amply reflected in the 2013 Constitution of the Republic of Fiji and the 2014 National Budget. Consequently, the Government has emphasized and prioritized a number of initiatives in TVET at the school, higher education and community levels and supported externally by initiatives such as Australian Aid's: *The Pacific Education and Skills Development Agenda* (AusAID, 2011).

As part of TVET integration into the mainstream school curriculum, the Fijian MoE introduced its first four Basic Technology subjects in primary schools in 1995. This was also combined with three first Technology subjects for Form 7 in secondary schools, together with the supply of computers to selected schools. The efforts and intention at that time was: 'to take modern technology into the school system and to prepare TVET students for the world of work' (Fiji's MoE Annual Report, 1995–2013: p. 20).

The 1997 Compulsory Education Act required children aged 6–15 years to remain in school until after completing Class 8 or Form 2 level education. The role of TVET increased accordingly, being the major provider for essential skills for students' future employment. In 2000, while 95 per cent of all secondary schools offered various TVET subjects such as agriculture, computer studies, Home Economics, Industrial Arts and vocational trades, a large number of these TVET teachers are employed without a teaching qualification. Both the USP and the National University of Fiji have now begun preparing TVET teachers at the undergraduate Certificate and Diploma degree levels, not only for schools, but also for the industrial and community training sectors. Through its 2013 and 2014 National Budgets, the Government has funded the National University of Fiji to prepare TVET graduates for self-employed and managed agricultural projects. Several students are taking advantage of this agricultural scholarship scheme. For many, this Government initiative is seen to be moving in the correct direction for upgrading the TVET curriculum, which to-date has been considered as the second-class educational option for the majority of the students who do not succeed in academic education (Sharma, 2000, 2001).

Funding from outside the Government falls under the Fiji Education Sector Programme (FESP) that includes funding from the Australian Government aid programme (AusAID, 2011) as well as from the European Union. The proposed inter-governmental bilateral total aid investment from Australia's Department for Foreign Affairs and Trade (DFAT) for Fiji is estimated at Aus$54.6 (Australian DFAT, 2014) and covers projects in education, health and so on. The relative value of this external funding input is estimated[1] around 10 to 20 per cent of the annual TVET MoE budget. This financial assistance has greatly impacted on the delivery of TVET including: the 'basic employment skills training' (BEST) programme; the enterprise education; franchising and accreditation of the Fiji National University courses in high schools and vocational centres and the general improvement of infrastructure in schools and teacher training institutions.

The Fiji Institute of Technology that traditionally catered for TVET in Fiji was amalgamated with four other national tertiary institutions in 2010, including nursing, medicine, agriculture and teacher training. It now forms the new Fiji National University. This amalgamation allowed the TVET sector to better access specific training needs for the local labour market, particularly vocational courses offered at the graduate level. In the past, Fiji depended heavily on the regional USP and other overseas universities for graduate level TVET. Another flexible response to improve access and mobility of vocational education has been through the Government slowly implementing a new modular approach of delivering TVET throughout the education system, as recommended in the report of the Fiji Islands Education Commission/Panel (Fiji Islands Education Commission/Panel, 2000). Accordingly, TVET was also to be introduced as a broad base in primary schools. It was to support the development of basic life skills and provide an introduction to the nature of vocational studies. At the secondary school level, the Commission suggested several TVET modules including: Art and Crafts; Music and Sports. The modules were expected to familiarize students with TVET and develop skills that they could pursue in their future career. In other words, students were given the opportunity to discover their vocational potential or talents.

There is a general need for increasing the capacity of further educational research into Small Island States (Crossley, 2011). Expanding educational research capacity could then look into the possibility of how Small Island States could adopt a more inclusive educational approach for TVET within the mainstream educational systems. A new system of education where vocational education can be integrated within the academic courses offered in secondary schools. In brief, TVET has now begun to receive prominence in Fiji and is becoming a key part of the MoE's as well as the Region's educational policy (Fiji, 1995–2013; Fiji Islands Education Commission/Panel, 2000; PIFS, 2009, 2012). It is highly likely that Fiji and the Pacific Island Forum Regional body will carefully review, adapt and contextualize the most appropriate international educational models that help to integrate TVET into its formal education systems. However, the authors would suggest caution with such practice so as to avoid the trap of policy borrowing as highlighted by Crossley et al. (2011).

Conclusion

Since the colonization of Fiji in 1874, there has been a remarkable transformation in the nature of education and schooling. This became necessary to address the dynamic, complex, social, economic and political demands. A characteristic of Fiji's education system is its highly academic and Western orientation. To improve the quality of education, the Government of Fiji has taken a number of innovative educational reforms including abolishing three external examinations so as to reduce drop-out rates. Another major contemporary reform is the provision of free education for primary and secondary students and the introduction of low interest loan schemes for tertiary students. Further significant initiatives involve efforts to remove all forms of discrimination in respect of access and selection in schools, the introduction of the zoning of schools to bring education closer to all children and the provision of inclusive TVET curriculum initiatives for potential access by all children.

These reforms are not without problems. Their impact so far has greatly increased participation rates and enhanced the racial diversity of schools' student and staff populations. The student diversity not only is ethnic in nature but also includes those with learning disabilities. The overall aim is to widen participation throughout the education system through enabling greater access and retention opportunities. However, to provide accessible learning for all students there is still a need to offer a much wider range of programmes, and to bring in a greater range of pedagogical approaches and strategies catering for the diverse needs of individual learners as well as retaining them within the system. Fiji has made a positive start towards this educational journey, but there is still much work to be done.

Note

1   Estimated from past budget allocations sourced from Fijian government reports (Fiji, 1995–2013).

References

AusAID (2011), *The Pacific Education and Skills Development Agenda*. Available at: http://aid.dfat.gov.au/Publications/Pages/2651_8620_8141_6991_5567.aspx (Accessed: 7 April 2014).

Australian Department for Foreign Affairs and Trade (DFAT) (2014), *Australian Aid Budgets*. Available at: http://aid.dfat.gov.au/countries/pacific/fiji/Pages/default.aspx (Accessed: 7 April 2014).

Biggs, J. and Tang, C. (2011), *Teaching for Quality Learning at University* (4th edn). England: Society for Research into Higher Education and the Open University Press.

Bennett, M. J. (1971), 'Organisation and Functions of the Psychological Unit', in *Mimeograph*. USP: School of Education.

Boud, D., Keogh, R. and Walker, D. (1985), *Reflection: Turning Experience into Learning*. Abingdon: Routledge.

Coxon, E. (2000), 'Primary Education in Fiji', in Fiji Islands Education Commission/Panel (ed.), *Learning Together: Direction for Education in the Fiji Islands*. Suva, Fiji: Government Printer, pp. 69–89.

Crossley, M. (2011), 'Strengthening the Development of Educational Research Capacity in Small States', in M. Martin and M. Bray (eds), *Tertiary Education in Small States: Planning in the Context of Globalisation*. Paris: UNESCO/IIEP.

Crossley, M., Bray, M. and Packer, S. (2011), *Education in Small States: Policies and Priorities*. London: Commonwealth Secretariat.

Fiji (1969), *Education for Modern Fiji. The Report of The Fiji Education Commission*. Suva: Government Printers.

— (1995–2013), *Annual Reports*. Suva, Fiji: Ministry of Education, National Heritage, Culture and Arts.

— (2012), *Annual Report*. Suva, Fiji: Ministry of Education, National heritage, Culture and Arts.

— (2013), *Constitution of the Republic of Fiji*. Fiji: Quality Print.

— (2014), Government of Fiji: Tertiary Scholarship and Loans Decree 2014 (DECREE NO. 2 OF 2014). Available at: http://www.fiji.gov.fj/getattachment/f6d9bcc8–6220–491a-a47c-8a7a293037a9/Decree-No-2---Tertiary-Scholarship-and-Loans-Decre. aspx (Accessed: 7 April 2014).

Fiji Islands Education Commission/Panel (2000), *Learning Together: Direction for Education in the Fiji Islands*. Suva, Fiji: Government Printer.

Gounder, P. (1999), *Education and Race Relations in Fiji 1835–1998*. Lautoka: Universal Printing Press.

Nabobo-Baba, U. (2006), *Knowing and Learning: An Indigenous Approach*. Institute of Pacific Studies, USP: Suva, Fiji.

PIFS (2009), *Pacific Islands Forum Secretariat: Pacific Education Development Framework*. Available at: http://www.paddle.usp.ac.fj/collect/paddle/index/assoc/ pifs046.dir/doc.pdf (Accessed: 7 April 2014).

— (2012), *Pacific Islands Forum Secretariat: A Regional Framework for Technical and Vocational Education and Training (TVET) Development in Pacific Island Countries: 2012–2015*. Available at: http://www.forumsec.org/resources/uploads/attachments/ documents/2012FEdMM.08_Paper.pdf (Accessed: 7 April 2014).

Puamau, P. (2001), 'A Post-Colonial Reading of Affirmative Action in Education in Fiji', *Race, Ethnicity and Education* 4 (2), 109–123.

Qovu, E. (2013), *A Critical Review of the Affirmative Action Policy in Education of the Indigenous Fijians 1987–2006: Policy, Rational and Implications* (unpublished PhD thesis). Fiji: The University of the South Pacific.

Ravuvu, S. (2003), 'Re-Inventing the Cultural Wheel: Re-Conceptualizing Restorative Justice and Peace Building in Ethnically Divided Fiji', in S. Dinner, A. Jowitt and T. N. Cain (eds), *A Kind of Mending: Restorative Justice in the Pacific Islands*. Canberra: Pendants Books.

Sharma, A. (1997), 'Positive Discrimination Policy in Education. A Critical Review', in G. Chand and V. Naidu (eds), *FIJI: Coups, Crises and Reconciliation, 1987–1997*. Fiji Institute of Applied Studies: Suva, Fiji, pp. 101–115.

— (2000), *Vocational Education & Training in Fiji: Management at the Secondary School Level*. New Delhi: Anamika Publishers & Distributors.

— (2001), 'Technical Studies in Secondary Schools in Fiji: A Modular Approach', *Directions* 23 (2), 25.

Sorensen, N. and Coombs, S. (2009), 'Creating a Culture of Professional Learning: The Role of Metaphor, Teacher Narrative and Improvisation in School-Based CPD', In *BERA International Conference*. Manchester: Manchester University, pp. 2–5.

Sowell, T. (2004), *Affirmative Action around the World. An Empirical Study*. New Haven: Yale University Press.

Tavola, H. (1991), *Secondary Education in Fiji: A Key to the Future*. Suva, Fiji: USP.

White, C. (2001), '"Affirmative Action and Education in Fiji: Legitimation", Contestation and Colonial Discourse', *Harvard Educational Review* 71 (2), 240–268.

Whitehead, C. (1986), *Education in Fiji Since Independence. A Study of Government Policy*. Wellington: New Zealand Council for Educational Research.

Uluivuda, R. (2001), *Blueprint for Affirmative Action on Fiji Education*. Matavatucou, Tailevu, Fiji: Queen Victoria School.

12

Melanesia: An Overview

Salanieta Bakalevu, Jeremy Dorovolomo and Alfred Liligeto

Introduction

The developing countries of Melanesia, like the rest of the Pacific region, are changing rapidly as they experience the characteristic changes and developments of the global community. The new economic order is global, production has become global and education is considered in its relation to global economic and social development. As the conditions of globalization have shifted the goals of the education systems of the east/west and north/south (Luke, 2007), Melanesian nations have to deal with the conflicts between the old and the new, the traditional and the modern, indigenous and Western. They have to decide on the societies and economies they want to build as well as the priorities and best purposes for the future. Luke proposed that they take up the challenges of new economies and blend cultures, global and regional networks and engagements (Luke, 2007).

To prioritize is not always easy. Sir Peter Kenilorea, Solomon Islands' first prime minister, wrote in the 1970s that the term 'priority' is an alien word to Melanesia, not because of limitations in the local languages but because the term is in the language of the modern, economic planners (Kenilorea, 1973). He saw the term as strongly related to modernization and progress and would need to be a part of the Melanesian value system in order to make forms of judgement on various developmental issues that affect Melanesia. The issues included education, health, industrialization and rural–urban development conflict, political development and national identity. In a discussion of Pacific pasts and futures, Luke (2007: p. 14) proposed that countries do not simply modernize but that there must be 'critical understanding of and engagement with their present circumstances and conditions'. He suggests that educational institutions become sites of this cultural contact and change. This chapter looks at some of the overarching issues, trends and challenges in education in Melanesia, and attempts to propose a possible agenda for moving forward.

The Melanesian landscape

Melanesia is one of the three sub-regions of Oceania and denotes both an ethnic and a geographical grouping of islands and peoples who belong to an ethno-cultural family. Ali and Crocombe (1982) see this as a 'geopolitical' context. Melanesia shares the Pacific region with Micronesia to the north and Polynesia to the east. It extends from Papua New Guinea (PNG) in the north-western end of the Pacific Ocean to FLNKS New Caledonia in the south-west and Fiji in the south-east. FLNKS stands for *Front de Libération Nationale Kanak et Socialiste*, a socialist pro-independence alliance of political parties in New Caledonia whose supporters are mostly from the indigenous populations.

Melanesia occupies 95 per cent of the Pacific region's landmass and consists of 8.1 million people (Laban, 2008 in Mwaraksurmes, 2011). This population represents the largest group and 85 per cent of the total Pacific population. PNG's population alone of about 7.3 million people represents 75 per cent of the Pacific region's population and over 85 per cent of the population of Melanesia. The Melanesians group of countries speak over 900 languages (Crowley, 1995) and more than 800 of these are spoken in PNG alone (PNG Strategic Plan, 2010–2030). The statistics suggest that the overall progress for the region is dependent on PNG's progress and the characteristic diversity of Melanesia and the Pacific region.

For the purpose of this chapter, the Melanesian areas to be discussed are Papua New Guinea, Solomon Islands, Vanuatu and Fiji. The four countries have had a close historical association. They are all members of the Pacific Islands Forum Secretariat (PIFS) until recently when Fiji was suspended following the country's 2006 coup d'état. Three of the countries: Fiji, Solomon Islands and Vanuatu are members of The University of the South Pacific (USP) region. There are common characteristics, practices and challenges that define Melanesia generally as well as parts of Melanesia. Among Pacific islanders, two features that distinguish most Melanesians are their brown skin and frizzy hair. The indigenous people of Vanuatu, PNG and Solomon Islands share common cultural practices. They have their own versions of Pidgin English – *Bislama* in Vanuatu,

Tok Pisin and *Hiri Motu* in PNG, *Pidgin Inglis* in Solomon Islands – but there are many common elements that make it possible for the three groups to converse together fluently. There is also the traditional way of preserving breadfruit over the fireplace that is a common practice in the southern parts of Solomon Islands and the eastern part of PNG (Mwaraksurmes, 2011). Writing about education in Vanuatu, Niroa et al. (2010) highlighted the challenge of 'smallness, scattered islands, remoteness, isolation, linguistic and cultural diversity, relative paucity of resources and a degree of underdevelopment, and a feeling of dismay in the face of Westernisation, modernisation and globalisation pressures' (p. 228) that is common across the region. All states are highly rural in character and between 70 and 80 per cent of the population live in rural areas. While rurality poses immense challenges of access and equity, its advantage is in the way the rural communities maintain cultural and traditional solidarity and ties to the land and community, characteristics that are sacred to the people. Maintaining an identity and integrity for plural societies is an ongoing pre-occupation for Melanesian states.

Challenges for education in Melanesia

Education in Melanesia is at the crossroads. On the one hand, the traditional education systems are primarily concerned about cultural training and transmission, and preparing the young for life in society. Education is embedded in the socialization processes, practices and activities in society (Bakalevu, 2003). On the other hand, the formal education systems of the schools were introduced during the 100 years of European and colonial experience. Melanesia's educational experience with the colonizers is represented by the dichotomy of development and exploitation. Faracias (1997) labelled Western education in PNG, Solomon Islands and Vanuatu an unmitigated failure that has been successful mainly in 'transforming powerful sovereign peoples into slaves' (p. 23). According to Faracias, many people still have the 'cargo mentality' to serve the 'master' and in the process increasingly reject their identity, culture and lifestyle. The positive influence of colonial experience is the Christian heritage of the missionaries that was significant in the establishment of many schools. Today the churches continue to have significant influence in education. They administer the largest numbers of schools, which are by comparison better resourced and more competitive in terms of school administration and the kinds of programmes offered.

The pull between the traditional and the formal education systems and finding a good balance is an ongoing challenge. While all countries have made considerable progress in achieving access to formal education in recent years, there is less apparent progress in improving its quality. For example, the tracking assessment of Millennium Development Goals (MDG) by the Australian Government Overseas Aid Program (AusAID, 2009) showed that more children are entering school but many do not remain to complete primary education. In particular, low completion rates were recorded for Solomon Islands and Vanuatu. The same report from AusAID (2009) quoted the example of a 2007 survey of literacy levels in Vanuatu, which found that 27 per cent of children who had completed 6 years or more of schooling could not write three simple dictated sentences. In addition, standardized tests in Solomon Islands show that a large proportion of children do not achieve expected learning outcomes in literacy and numeracy (ibid.). However, the same report also highlighted that Vanuatu was the only country in the Pacific region that was showing progress in reducing poverty (ibid.).

Geographical issues – rural communities, small populations, rugged terrains and natural disasters

The geography of the Melanesian islands includes an extensive sea area that surrounds the scattered islands; the sea area is many times their land spaces. Inland, the main islands consist of rugged terrain and many parts still densely forested. In this region, development in education is often threatened by natural disasters – earthquake and tsunami in PNG, Solomon Islands and Vanuatu and hurricanes, cyclones and flooding in Fiji. An implication of this scattered and rugged geographical context is the high cost and immense difficulty in the delivery of education. Achieving efficiency and effectiveness in these areas is an ongoing challenge. All countries have complex geography. Fiji, Solomon Islands and Vanuatu are small and part of the 37 countries in the world with a population of less than 1.5 million. Fiji's population (2009 estimate) is 845,602 and its 300 islands cover a land space of 18,333 square kilometres; Solomon Islands has a population of about 518,338 (2010 Census) and the archipelago of almost 1,000 small islands and coral atolls cover a land area of 28,379 square kilometres; Vanuatu has a population of 234,023 (2009 Census) and the volcanic islands cover a land area of 12,189 square kilometres.

PNG is not small. Its story is complex. The 2012 Pacific Regional MDGs Tracking Report by the PIFS (2012) reported that PNG was 'off track on all the goals' (p. 3). It noted that around 2 million people remain poor and/or face hardship. The reasons for this are complex and mainly 'rooted in the geography of the country, its political economy and its social and political processes' (Camack, 2009: p. 8). PNG is a nation of over 7 million people and a land area of about 464,000 square kilometres. It is made up of 600 volcanic islands and coral atolls and is subject to volcanic eruptions and earthquakes. About 90 per cent of the PNG population people are rural dwellers. The National Census (2000) recorded a population growth rate of about 3 per cent per annum and predicted to reach 7.5 million by 2020, a prediction that is already achieved. It is important to note that the PNG government had expressed reservations about the global MDGs, considering them as over-ambitious, unrealistic and out of reach. It therefore developed its own set of national targets and indicators for each MDG. There is indication that against these localized targets, the country is recording slight progress (PIFS, 2012).

The majority of the rural population in Melanesia are farmers who have a livelihood of subsistence agriculture and small-scale income-generating activities. In recent years, migration into urban areas has increased rapidly as parents desire postsecondary education opportunities for their children and jobs with a higher level of income. The MDG 1 indicators (AusAID, 2009) highlighted concerns about one-third of Pacific peoples living below the poverty line, especially those living in urban areas. Vanuatu's large rural population where subsistence economy and food security remain strong has worked in its favour. It is the only country in the Pacific region that is likely to reduce poverty by half by 2015. The development of rural areas has been high on the agenda of national development schemes. In Fiji for example, increased budgetary allocation for rural development has focused on improving infrastructure that includes roads and highways, high-rise bridges to guard against constant flooding, better means of telecommunication, more postprimary school and health facilities and accessible markets. These are aimed at increasing interconnectedness between the urban and rural. Growth in the agriculture sector and market accessibility and engagement are positive developments.

Education for what?

There is strong perception among education stakeholders in the region that the current education and training systems are not addressing the needs of the local and regional markets. The academic and exam-oriented curriculum is pushing out many students and producing others who are not equipped for the employment market. The lack of coherence in secondary education is a concern. Severely limited secondary school places, outdated assessment systems, limited postsecondary opportunities and increasing numbers of untrained teachers are worrying trends that have contributed to high numbers of school drop-outs. High drop-out rate is of great concern because they add to the large numbers of out-of-school youths and the unemployed. Such groups could add to social and health problems. The combined effects of these factors have caused confusion and anxiety among the elders and community leaders and unsettled traditional structures and systems. There are grave concerns about changing forms of identity, values and beliefs that are pulling young people away from their communities. As they are influenced by consumer culture, mass media and new technologies, they are finding the traditional structures and systems archaic and out of touch (Table 12.1).

Language dilemmas

As mentioned earlier, Melanesia has more than 900 local languages. The languages of instruction (LoIs) in formal schooling, however, are the foreign languages of the colonizers – English and French. In PNG, Solomon Islands and Fiji, the language of classroom instruction is English. Vanuatu has more than 105 different vernacular languages but the national language is *Bislama*. The official languages are *Bislama*, English and French, but French and English are LoIs. Many of the early schools used the local languages as the medium of instruction but gradually changed to English in the Anglophone schools and French in the Francophone schools. Maintaining this dual system is very costly and is one of the constraints to progress in Vanuatu.

In Fiji, English is the official language while Fijian and Hindi are taught in school as part of the curriculum. In Solomon Islands, English is the official language and the LoI, but there are some 70 native languages and many dialects. Pidgin is the Lingua Franca and the preferred medium for most of the population. PNG has over 800 vernacular languages. However, *Tok Pidgin* and *Motu* are the main languages of communication. An Education Review in 1991 allowed the local vernaculars to be the language of instruction in the elementary and primary schools, while English remained the LoI at higher levels of education and in administration and commerce. So language issues continue to pose huge learning challenges for students for whom English and French are their third or fourth language, at the very least. For many students, English is the main barrier to understanding because for them a lesson in any subject is first and foremost a lesson in the English language. Writing in 1998, Bakalevu noted that speaking

Table 12.1 Progress towards the MDGs

	MDG 1 Eliminate extreme poverty and hunger	MDG 2 Achieve universal primary education	MDG 3 Promote gender equality and empower women	MDG 4 Reduce child mortality	MDG 5 Improve maternal health	MDG 6 Combat HIV/ AIDS and other diseases	MDG 7 Ensure environment stability
MELANESIA	□	□	□	□	□	□	□
MELANESIA (EXCL PNG)	○	○	○↑	○	○	○	○
FIJI	○↑	△	○	△	△	○	△
PNG	□	□	□	□	□	□	□
SOLOMONS	○	○	□	□	□	○	□
VANUATU	○	○	○↑	△	○	△	□

Note: The arrows denote improvement (↑) or regression (↓) from the assessment in the 2011 Pacific Regional MDGs Tracking Report

On Track △   Off Track □   Mixed ○

Source: Pacific Islands Forum Secretariat (2012) Pacific Regional MDGs Tracking Report, p. 6.

in Fijian was forbidden and punishable at the boarding school that she attended in the 1960s. Fifty years on, similar rules remain in most schools, only now they are justified as necessary for the common good and nation building. English and French are seen as international languages and therefore necessary for survival in the global community. In Solomon Islands and PNG, the core challenge is in finding a common language among the several spoken vernacular languages.

Teacher quality

Teachers are the corner-stone of educational development (Maclean, 2009b: p. 37) and good schools require good teachers (Delors et al., 1996). The large numbers of untrained teachers in Melanesia is affecting the quality of education. This is particularly concerning for Vanuatu and Solomon Islands where remote and rural schools employ untrained teachers, some of whom have worked in this capacity for many years. The Vanuatu Education Sector Strategy (VESS, 2007–2016) for the period 2007–2016 noted that untrained primary teachers account for over half of the total teacher population and that teacher productivity is exacerbated by the high pupil–teacher ratio. For the Solomon Islands, about one-third of primary teachers are unqualified, meaning they do not meet the minimum qualification requirement for primary education, which is completion of Form 5. Teacher training and improving teacher qualification is the top priority for the primary education system. The Vanuatu Institute of Teacher Education (VITE) and the Solomon Islands National University (previously Solomon Islands College of Higher Education) are not able to meet the needs of teacher education in their countries.

Fiji and PNG have more teacher education institutions. PNG has 13 teacher education institutions. Two of them, PNG Education Institute and University of Goroka, are government owned while the other 11 are operated by the churches. Three universities – University of Goroka, Pacific Adventist University and Divine Word University – offer degree and postgraduate programmes while the other ten institutions offer various types of diplomas. PNG's challenge is its fast growing population. The 2006 statistics record 45,000 teachers, 1.2 million students in 4,000 elementary, 3,300 primary, 170 secondary and 140 vocational schools (PNG Education Corporate Data, 2006). Low salaries and high staff turnover also affect teacher quality. In Vanuatu and Solomon Islands, teachers do not see the need for (further) training since it does not bring any benefits or improve their status. It is reported that teacher salaries have not received a rise in a long time. So the primary focus must be on raising the professional competence of teachers and improving their knowledge and skills.

The status of teachers and teacher education in Fiji is probably the best developed in the region. In fact, it has been reported and discussed openly in the media for some time that there is an oversupply of trained teachers in Fiji. Fiji hosts three universities: the Suva campus of the regional USP, the Fiji National University and the University of Fiji. The three institutions have strong and vibrant teacher education programmes that train teachers for all levels: early childhood education, special education, primary education, secondary education and tertiary teaching. The country has gained immensely from hosting the USP's biggest campus and its headquarters in Suva, which has enabled many teachers to have a degree qualification as well as postgraduate qualifications. In a report about teachers and teacher education in Fiji, Tagivakatini (2007) reported an 'almost 100% teacher-trained teaching force'. She noted that of the total 9,337 teachers in 2005, only 53 (0.6%) teachers were untrained. The highest number of untrained teachers was among secondary teachers (35 out of 4,141), while there were 17 untrained primary teachers out of a total of 5,006, and 1 untrained tertiary teacher out of 87.

Tagivakatini also highlighted the number of teachers pursuing higher qualifications and noted that tertiary teachers account for 85 per cent of teachers with degree qualifications, followed by secondary teachers at 51 per cent, special education at 6 per cent and primary teachers at 2.5 per cent. Over the last few years, teachers with bachelor's degree increased by 25 per cent for primary teachers and 15 per cent for secondary teachers. The increase by primary teachers corresponded to the offer of the Bachelor of Education for primary teachers at the USP. This programme became totally externalized in 2007 making accessible to every primary teacher in the Pacific region.

Political issues

Writing about indigenous governance in Melanesia, White (2006) described a region of weak or failing states. He identified competing forms of instability. On the one hand, external observers lay blame on inter-ethnic animosities that need stronger central institutions and management. On the other hand, the growth of nationalistic ideals among the people is focused on empowerment of local governance. In a world that is in constant turmoil, the countries of the Pacific including those of Melanesia are experiencing similar divisive posturing and political violence over issues of land claims, political representations and affirmative action as other countries across the globe. All these have implications for education.

PNG has a troubled past due to ethnic, economic and political contentions. Camack (2009) described a weak sense of nation, chaotic politics at all levels and lack of political will. These and the country's geographic exceptionality make service delivery highly problematic:

> PNG is an exemplar of the thesis that environment is destiny, for its extreme landscape has left its mark on the nation in numerous ways. It consists of more than 600 islands . . . The nation hosts nearly 6 million people divided into more than 850 language groups (clans or *wontoks*), with strong cultural identities and traditions. (Camack, 2009: p. 6)

In Fiji, race remains the most significant factor in politics. The political unrest and coup culture that began in 1987 has origins that stem from complex issues about land and constitutional reform. Fiji's multiracial and multi-cultural population has experienced diversity as a challenge. Politics along communal and ethnic lines has strengthened racial stereotypes. The interim government has advanced the ideology of a united Fiji for all – one nation and one people in the People's Charter. Only time will tell what the future holds.

Social unrest in Solomon Islands has severely affected development and progress. Since independence in 1978, this Melanesian nation has struggled to unite the country and develop a sense of national identity. Disputes that related mainly to land ownership erupted into spates of violence from 1999 to 2003. Regional assistance and cooperation came to the rescue in the form of the Regional Assistance Mission for the Solomon Islands (RAMSI) in 2003. RAMSI has helped to stabilize the situation and rebuild the country's institutions and continues to retain a presence in that country today.

Social and political tensions, natural disasters, unemployment, poverty and disease are continuing challenges in Melanesian countries. Schooling and education have not delivered the required results as evidenced by a large number of students that drop-out of school every year and at all levels. School drop-outs in turn add to the numbers of unemployed and at-risk groups in society. With urban migration, the rise in unemployment, congested facilities and the levels of poverty also increase. Poverty and unemployment mean that parents and guardians are not able to pay for their children's schooling needs.

Educational aid

All Melanesian countries have received substantial aid and support from development partners since the 1990s. The format of aid provisions has undergone many changes. Australia is the leading donor across the Pacific region with the latest estimated funding of AUD1104 million in 2012–2013 and increasing to AUD1125.9 for 2013–2014. In recent years, the majority of Australian aid is delivered through bilateral programmes and the priority areas for assistance are agreed to with each government under a Partnership for Development developed in 2008. It is noted that education and health remain development priorities in 2013–2014. Other major donor agencies for the region have been the New Zealand Agency for International Development (NZAID), The World Bank (2003), Asia Development Bank (ADB), European Union (EU) and the Japan International Cooperation Agency (JICA).

We classify aid as an educational challenge. While aid is highly valued and has benefited Melanesia and the greater Pacific, there have been concerns about its intent, nature and usage. Tavola (2005) and Taufe'ulungaki (2002) have questioned why the quality of lives of Pacific Islanders has not tangibly improved after decades of so much aid expenditure. The donors themselves have been disappointed that funding put into education and training has not materialized into anticipated employment benefits (AusAID, 2006). The importance of relationships within aid contexts is critical (Sanga, 2005) and both donors and recipients need to work at improving their relationships towards greater mutuality, openness and trust (Sanga and Taufe'ulungaki, 2003). An analysis of aid projects in Fiji (Ruru, 2010) and PNG (Maha, 2009) highlighted lack of ownership, alignment and harmonization as the barriers to effective aid delivery and sustainability of projects. Many countries have experienced aid delivery where aid donors have assumed a superior position and made unilateral decisions about what is good for the country. When donors have brought in expatriate consultants with little knowledge of the country to monitor the work of highly qualified and experienced locals, relationships are affected leading to a great deal of mistrust of the donor. Tavola (2005) also warned that failures will continue to abound and sustainability will not be achieved if decisions that inform aid continue to be made without reflecting on Pacific experiences and views of the world.

The sector-wide approach (SWAp) to aid delivery, examined in Chapter 8 in this volume, is the currently dominant mechanism developed for encouraging coordination and harmonization between donors and recipients. It is an integrated programme for a particular sector with the major aim of creating a single pool of funding into which are placed all donor funds in support of a particular national policy programme (Coxon and Tolley, 2005). Under the SWAp, project funds contribute directly to a sector-specific umbrella and are tied to a defined sector policy under a government authority. All countries have embarked on donor-funded SWAp development projects.

Social, economic and educational reforms

A new economic order has brought about changes. The global economy is transforming the labour market throughout the world and placing new demands on education and the quality of graduates. The reliance of the knowledge-based economy upon ideas and know-how as sources of economic growth and development, along with the application of new technologies, have important implications for the educational priorities and on how people learn and use knowledge in their lives and communities. The Pacific region faces employment challenges which have serious implications for its economic development and social stability. The demographic profile of Pacific youths indicate that around a high percentage of 15–29 year olds has little chance of gaining formal sector employment so there is a need to acquire greater skills and knowledge that would provide for effective livelihoods. The Pacific 2020 background paper on Employment and Labour Markets (AusAID, 2006) points to a skills deficit in the region, which can be traced back to 'a mismatch between the skills derived through the region's education and vocational training systems and the needs of regional labour markets' (p. 9). The report proposes a re-orientation of the aims of schooling to 'produce people with skills relevant to the specific markets and approaches focused on initiative and creativity as well as managerial and supervisory skills' (p. 10). A fundamental rethinking of the role and place of secondary education requires that technical and vocational education (TVET) becomes an integral part of that reform (Maclean, 2009a). This will be discussed further at the end of this chapter.

Educational reforms

Vanuatu

The VESS for 2007–2016 proposed four major goals for education: (i) improve access, (ii) raise the quality and relevance of education, (iii) improve planning and management and (iv) develop a 'distinctively Vanuatu education system'. In 2009, the Vanuatu Education Roadmap (VERM) defined a medium-term framework and a set of priorities for achieving the goals of VESS. VESS and VERM now drive change in the Vanuatu education system. Perhaps, the biggest undertaking for the government and people of Vanuatu in this decade is the harmonization programme of the Francophone and Anglophone systems that have been running in parallel and separately for many years. Under VESS, the 'unification of curriculum content' under the Vanuatu National Curriculum Statement (VNCS, 2010: p. iii) is the major priority. The country is looking to the VNCS to begin what was perceived almost impossible. The VNCS is home-grown and will guide the development of National Curriculum Standards Frameworks for Kindergarten to Year 13 (VNCS, 2010: p. iii). This harmonization is a huge educational and political development that has immense implications for equitable and relevant education for the population of Vanuatu.

Fiji

The development of education in Fiji has been the subject of six successive education commissions since 1909. In terms of economic growth since independence, the country has made much progress but suffered setbacks following four coup d'états. The 2000 Education Commission undertook a very comprehensive review of the country's education system and made several recommendations that were to make up the basis of reforms. As a result, the Ministry of Education made several important policy decisions that prescribed initiatives promoting equitable opportunities. Since 2000, the government has implemented measures to ensure more effective and accelerated implementation of policies that promote quality education and the achievement of the Education for All (EFA) goals. These included expansion of the compulsory years of education to Year 10, the maintenance of fee-free education in the first 8 years of schooling, development of a National Curriculum Framework, abolishment of national examinations in primary and lower secondary levels to ensure that all students receive at least an education up to Year 10 and the development of an Early Childhood and Education (ECED) policy. The most recent initiative is the introduction of bus fare/transportation assistance for school children from disadvantaged families who qualify under a means test, and the provision of free tuition and textbooks. These initiatives are expected to make significant improvement, narrow the access gap and generally improve quality.

In the last decade, Fiji's Ministry of Education has received an average 20.41 per cent of the national budget, which is the highest portion. The highest portion of this allocation goes to primary education programme increasing from over FJD110m in 2003 to over FJD120m in 2006. This is an indication of the country's commitment to supporting basic education and achieving the UNESCO goal of universal primary education (Fiji EFA Report, 2007).

Papua New Guinea

PNG's education system began major structural and curriculum reform programmes in 1992 to address persistent issues of access, retention, curriculum relevance, quality and standards (Maha, 2009). A combination of structural and curriculum reforms resulted. Structurally, the school system changed from a 6-4-2 structure (6-year community school education followed by a 4-year provincial high school education followed by a 2-year national high school education) to a 3-6-4 structure (3-year elementary and community education followed by 6 years of primary education followed by 4 years of provincial high school and national secondary school). The language of instruction is the vernacular at elementary school, bilingual at lower primary and progressively moving to English only at the higher levels. The Curriculum Review and Implementation Project (CRIP) was a 5-year project (2000–2005) that was funded by AusAID and aimed to reform the primary school curriculum. After going through a series of development stages, the new curriculum was implemented in 2004 (Maha, 2009). The selected curriculum change was the Outcomes-Based Education (OBE), which called for the development of outcomes that students must achieve for each stage of their schooling. Poor implementation and monitoring of the reforms have not helped reform processes, as noted in Chapter 10 in this volume. Although individual provinces have reported some improvement, there is insufficient empirical evidence to reach specific conclusions about the success of these reforms.

In 2010, the government decided to introduce fee-free education for the first 3 years of basic education (extended to grade 10 in 2011) and better coordination among the major development partners in the education sector with the Government of PNG. A recent announcement by Prime Minister O'Neill is that OBE would be replaced by an objectives-based curriculum. He also said that English would replace *Tok Pisin* as the language of instruction from elementary level.

Solomon Islands

Political unrest and tensions, natural disasters, low literacy rates, a high population growth rate and poverty are key challenges that face the Solomon Islands government today. The literacy rate in Solomon Islands is the lowest in Melanesia and the Pacific while its population growth rate is one of the highest in the region. The high rural population with limited access to education is a big factor in its development. Improving the quality of basic education is a major priority for the Ministry of Education and Human Resources Development as stated in the following vision of its National Education Action Plan (NEAP) 2007–2009:

> Our vision is that all Solomon Islands will develop as individuals and possess knowledge, skills and attitudes needed to earn a living and to live in harmony with others and their environment. We envisage a united and progressive society in which all can live in peace and harmony with fair and equitable opportunities for a better life. We envision an education system responsive to its clients and efficiently managed by its stakeholders and clients. (NEAP, 2007–2009: p. 12)

What is the way forward for education in Melanesia?

Educational policies and reform plans are not by themselves sufficient to effect change (Pauly, 1991 cited in Bacchus, 2000). While policies attempt to inform us what to do, it is the professionally prepared individuals who have to translate the policies into effective practice (Bacchus, 2000). What the countries need are systematic approaches for a continuing learning and changing process. This emphasizes better use of resources and empowerment of individuals and organizations. It requires that systematic approaches be considered in devising capacity development strategies and programmes (UNDP, 1997 cited in Thomas and Peng, 2009). There are unique commonalities among the states of Melanesia that also justify a regional approach to development. There is a general awareness that education particularly at the higher level is an important engine for sustainable development to meet the countries' social and economic needs. The educational challenge for them is determining the best form of education and schooling that serves their interests and that improves the quality of education. This is seen as important for better economic growth and sustainable development.

A regional approach for development

The Pacific has a long history of regional cooperation and integration that has benefited all countries in many different ways. At a Pacific Islands Forum meeting in 2005, the leaders endorsed the 10-year Pacific Plan to 'provide a framework for effective and enhanced engagement between Forum countries and Pacific territories and with their non-state actors and development partners' (p. 2). The plan is based on the concept of regionalism – countries working together for their joint and individual benefit. The Pacific Plan's strategic objectives are:

economic growth, sustainable development, good governance and security. The Pacific Education Development Framework (PEDF) was formulated in 2009 as the coordinating agency for regional activities in education and in providing an advocacy and a leadership role in policy dialogue at the regional level.

The University of the South Pacific remains one of the most successful initiatives of Pacific regionalism. It was established as a 'regional solution' with an applied role, 'to be an agent of development, to meet the manpower needs of the newly emerging countries, to assist governments in planning and implementing their development programmes, and to research and publish' (Chandra et al., 2011: p. 216). The university's aim for tertiary education is 'to ensure that the Pacific Islands safeguard their future in a world increasingly dominated by competitiveness derived from knowledge' (Chandra, 2011: p. 133). The Secretariat of the South Pacific Community (SPC) is another successful regional institution. The SPC works in a wide range of sectors with the aim of achieving three development outcomes – sustainable economic development, sustainable natural resource management and development and sustainable human and social development.

An emerging powerhouse in Pacific politics is the Melanesia Spearhead Group (MSG), which is a sub-regional organization comprising four Melanesian states of Fiji, PNG, SI, Vanuatu as well as the FLNKS of New Caledonia. Its purpose is:

> to promote and strengthen inter-membership trade, exchange of Melanesian cultures, traditions and values, sovereign equality, economic and technical cooperation between states and the alignment of policies in order to further MSG members' shared goals of economic growth, sustainable development, good governance and security.

A key feature of the Group is the MSG Trade Agreement, which is a preferential trade agreement that fosters and accelerates economic development and provides a framework for regular consultations on matters of trade and development between the member countries. The MSG is expected to become a critical element of growth and development and propel the MSG states to be 'makers' rather than 'takers' in world economic policies. In 2013, the countries of Melanesia will mark 25 years of Melanesian solidarity and growth.

Higher education capacity building

Tertiary education remains one of the most important factors of human capital development, which is a key contributor to economic growth and economic recovery (Tewarie, 2011: p. 233). Pacific island leaders were conscious of this when they gave priority to tertiary education at USP 'to be an agent of development, to meet the manpower needs of the newly emerging countries, to assist governments in planning and implementing their developments programmes' (Chandra, 2011: p. 216). In the last 10 years, more tertiary institutions have developed in the region. The USP and the national universities will need to continually improve the quality of their provisions requiring 'significant injection of resources as well as fundamentally changes in mindsets' and move into a client-oriented environment (ibid.: pp. 146–147). The Certificate and Diploma qualifications that have been the norm for a long time are now insufficient as countries look to a degree as the basic qualification for the skilled jobs. At the same time, the nature of the qualifications must meet the knowledge and skills demands of the nations' economies.

The demands of modern organizations and the world of work have redefined the qualities of the effective school and university graduate. Considering that a strong emphasis on capacity building is central to achieving economic growth and reducing poverty (Moock, 2001 cited in Thomas and Peng, 2009), a concerted effort aimed towards education for employment, leadership and social and economic advancement, and knowledge for national growth and competitiveness (Thomas and Peng, 2009; Chandra, 2011: p. 133) must be pursued vigorously. Vocational training needs to be aligned with private sector labour market opportunities and skill requirements in the formal and informal sectors (AUSAID, 2006). The ADB Report on TVET (ADB, 2008) expressed concern at the large numbers of school-leavers who lack the practical skills that are useful in the labour market. The report classified PNG, Vanuatu and Solomon Islands as 'land-rich, low-income countries' that have a positive agricultural potential. The prospects for these countries mainly lie in the rejuvenation of the rural economy through increased agricultural productivity. This would demand institutional changes and improved training systems. In particular, a diverse range of specialist agricultural skills in both the subsistence and commercial sectors will be highly desirable. The report puts Fiji with the 'advanced' islands states that have relatively good prospects from tourism, remittances and emigration (ibid.: p. 9).

It is ironic that while there are limited jobs in the formal sector, much of the current school curriculum is still preparing students for white-collar employments. The Melanesian countries have limited jobs in their formal economy for their expanding populations. This makes the informal sector the best and most realistic site for expansion. Thus, for many, the challenge is for the education system to put more resources in relevant TVET training that would help to fill the identified skills gaps in that sector. The traditional perception that TVET is second-rate choices for learners must change and communities, parents and learners must be assisted to understand that TVET is important as a provider of life skills for employment and citizenship, initiative and self-sufficiency and self-employment. While some form of TVET is already part of secondary curriculum, a more concerted at mainstreaming TVET or vocationalizing the secondary school curriculum could do much to support the new agenda. The idea is that skills development for the world of work permeates the entire curriculum (Maclean, 2009b: p. 39). In this type of reform it is important that the local knowledge, skills and wisdom, as well as relevant insights and practices from the global world be woven together.

Blending of the old with the new

Indigenous educators have long been critical of the perpetuation of colonial and Western ways at the expense of local knowledge, languages and methods. This chapter has highlighted the challenge faced by students, teachers and communities in adapting to new ways, which are antithetical to what they know. Allan Luke (2007) proposed a blending of the old with the new and finding a model that would suit our people:

> ... the challenges of blending, adopting, choosing how these education systems can and should be shaped lie with you. In one of those ironies of globalisation, you now have the technological tools, the local expertise and the scope and purview of international developments, and the emergent sense of shared problems, approaches and community to set a firm ground for local and regional answers. These answers will be found in careful and unique blends of old and new, of Indigenous, colonial and 'globalised' knowledge and approaches. (Luke, 2007: p. 34)

The central educational issue, according to Luke, is not about *either* Westernization *or* saving the essential indigenous ways of knowing – but about deliberately orchestrating a site for blending and to bringing together of both traditions and practices. He challenged teacher education and teacher educators to consider uniquely the Pacific models of teacher education. One such group under the Re-Thinking Pacific Education Initiative (RPEI) first met at USP in 2001 in an attempt to address what they saw as a Pacific education crisis (Sanga and Thaman, 2009). Since then, the Re-Thinking Pacific Education Initiative by and for Pacific Peoples (RPEIPP) has taken on a variety of tasks at national and regional levels to create awareness and encourage dialogue about the type of education to prepare citizens for a truly international community that does not neglect the richness and the value of cultural variation.

References

Ali, A. and Crocombe, R. (1982), *Politics in Melanesia*. Suva, Fiji: Institute of Pacific Studies, The University of the South Pacific, pp. xii.

Asian Development Bank (ADB) (2008), *Skilling the Pacific: Technical and Vocational Education and Training in the Pacific*. Manila: Asian Development Bank.

AUSAID (2006), *Pacific 2020: Background Paper: Employment and Labour Markets*.

— (2009), *Tracking Development and Governance in the Pacific August*.

Bacchus, K. (2000), 'Challenges Facing Fiji in Its Efforts to Improve the Educational Services', in Report of the Fiji Islands Education Commission/Panel (ed.), *Learning Together: Directions for Education in the Fiji Islands*. Suva, Fiji: Government Printer, pp. 59–68.

Bakalevu, S. L. (2003), 'Ways of Mathematising in Fijian Society', in K. H. Thaman (ed.), *Educational Ideas from Oceania*. Suva, Fiji: Institute of Education, The University of the South Pacific, pp. 56–67.

Camack, D. (2009), 'Chronic Poverty in Papua New Guinea', *Background Paper for the Chronic Poverty Report 2008–09*. Chronic Poverty Research Centre. Available at: http://www.chronicpoverty.org/uploads/publication_files/CPR2%20Background%20 Papers%20Cammack%20New.pdf (Accessed: 7 April 2014).

Chandra, R. (2011). 'Tertiary Education in Fiji: Between Globalization, Regional Imperatives, and National Aspirations', in M. Martin and M. Bray (eds), *Tertiary Education in Small States*. IIEP Policy Forum: UNESCO Publishing, pp. 133–148.

Chandra, R., Koroivulaono, T. and Hazelman, V. (2011), 'Leveraging Technology for Tertiary Education in the South Pacific', in M. Martin and M. Bray (eds), *Tertiary Education in Small States*. IIEP Policy Forum: UNESCO Publishing, pp. 215–232.

Coxon, E. and Tolley, H. (2005), 'Aid to Pacific Education: An Overview', in K. Sanga, C. Chu, C. Hall and L. Crowl (eds), *Re-Thinking Aid Relationships in Pacific Education*. Wellington: Victoria University of Wellington, pp. 28–82.

Crowley, T. (1995), 'Melanesian Languages. Do They Have a Future?' *Oceanic Linguistics* 34 (2), 327–344.

Delors, J. et al. (1996), *Learning: The Treasure Within*. Paris: UNESCO.

Faracias, N. (1997), 'The Turtle's Cargo: Western Education in Melanesia, Papua New Guinea, the Solomon Islands and Vanuatu', *New Internationalist* 291, 23–30.

Fiji Education For All Mid-Decade Report (2007), Fiji: Ministry of Education.

Kenilorea, P. (1973), 'Priorities in Melanesian Development', in R. J. May, S. V. Nuffle and D. Maynard (eds), *Priorities in Melanesia*. Canberra: Research School of Pacific Studies, Australian National University, pp. 23–26.

Luke, A. (2007), 'Teacher Education and Globalisation: Blending Pacific Pasts and Futures', in P. Puamau (ed.), *Pacific Voices: Teacher Education on the Move*. Pacific Education Series No. 3. Suva, Fiji: Pride Project, The University of the South Pacific, pp. 13–36.

Maclean, R. (2009a), 'TVET Issues, Concerns and Prospects', in E. Tokai and J. Teasdale (eds), *The Role of TVET in Pacific Secondary Schools*. Suva, Fiji: Pride Project, University of the South pacific. Pacific Education Series No. 7, pp. 13–30.

— (2009b), 'The Importance of Secondary Education and TVET', in E. Tokai and J. Teasdale (eds), *The Role of TVET in Pacific Secondary Schools*. Pacific Education Series No. 7. Suva, Fiji: Pride Project, University of the South pacific, pp. 31–40.

Maha, A. (2009), 'A Reflection on the Reform and Implementation of the Primary Curriculum in Papua New Guinea', in K. Sanga and K. Thaman (eds), *Re-Thinking Education Curricula in the Pacific: Challenges and Prospects*. Wellington: Victoria University of Wellington, pp. 83–95.

Mwaraksurmes, A. S. (2011), *Stance Marking Tools in Vanuatu Mathematics Education: Towards a Gelagel Framework* (unpublished PhD thesis). New Zealand: Victoria University of Wellington.

Niroa, J., Tamata, E. and Patrick, G. (2010), 'A Comprehensive Pilot Project for Teacher Capacity Building', in P. Puamau and B. Hau'ofa (eds), *Best Practice in Pacific Education*. Suva, Fiji: Pride Project, The University of the South Pacific, pp. 227–241.

Pacific Islands Forum Secretariat (PIFS) (2012), *Pacific Regional MDGs Tracking Report*. Suva, Fiji: Pacific Islands Forum Secretariat.

Papua New Guinea (PNG) Development Strategic Plan 2010–2030 (2010). Port Moresby, Papua New Guinea: Department of National Planning and Monitoring.

PNG Education Cooperate Data (2006).

Ruru, D. (2010), *Strengthening the Effectiveness of Aid Delivery in Teacher Education: A Fiji Case Study* (unpublished PhD thesis). Wellington, New Zealand: Victoria University of Wellington.

Sanga, K. (2005), 'A Strategy for Rethinking Aid Relationships', in K. Sanga, C. Chu, C. Hall and L. Crowl (eds), *Re-Thinking Aid Relationships in Pacific Education*. Wellington: Victoria University of Wellington, pp. 11–27.

Sanga, K. and Taufe'ulungaki, A. (2003), *Re-Thinking Educational Aid in the Pacific*. Report on the Pacific Regional Conference on Educational Aid. Wellington: Victoria University of Wellington.

Sanga, K. and Thaman, K. H. (2009), *Re-Thinking Education Curricula in the Pacific: Challenges and Prospects*. Wellington: Victoria University of Wellington.

Solomon Islands National Education Action Plan (NEAP) (2007–2009).

Tagivakatini, S. (2007), 'Teachers and Teacher Education in Fiji', in S. J. Fua and K. Sanga (eds), *Teachers and Education in the Pacific: A Desk Study Report*. Suva, Fiji: Institute of Education, The University of the South Pacific, pp. 34–52.

Taufe'ulungaki, A. M. (2002), 'Introduction', in F. Pene, A. M. Taufe'ulungaki and C. Benson (eds), *Tree of Opportunity: Rethinking Pacific Education*. Suva, Fiji: Institute of Education, The University of the South Pacific, pp. 1–4.

Tavola, H. (2005), 'Foreword', in K. Sanga, C. Chu, C. Hall and L. Crowl (eds), *Re-Thinking Aid Relationships in Pacific Education*. Wellington: Victoria University of Wellington.

Tewarie, B. (2011), 'The University of the West Indies: Regional Tertiary Education in the English-Speaking Caribbean', in M. Martin and M. Bray (eds), *Tertiary Education in Small States*. IIEP Policy Forum, Paris: UNESCO Publishing, pp. 121–132.

The World Bank (2003), *Lifelong Learning in the Global Knowledge Economy*. Washington, DC: World Bank.

Thomas, S. M. and Peng, W. (2009), 'Enhancing Quality and Capacity for Educational Research', in D. Stephens (ed.), *Higher Education and International Capacity Building*. Oxford: Symposium Books Ltd., pp. 51–78.

Vanuatu Education Sector Strategy (VESS) (2007–2016).

Vanuatu National Curriculum Statement (VNCS) (2010), *Alternative Indicators of Well-Being for Melanesia: Changing the Way Progress is Measured in the South Pacific*. Noumea, New Caledonia: Secretariat of the Pacific Community (SPC).

White, G. (2006), 'Indigenous Governance in Melanesia', in *State, Society and Governance in Melanesia* project. ANU. Available at: http://scholar.google.com/scholar_url?hl=en&q=http://ips.cap.anu.edu.au/sites/default/files/SSGM_IndigenousCustomaryGovernance_ResearchPaper_06.pdf&sa=X&scisig=AAGBfm3qfN9AqusZ5MtA7NP-ic3LTNidqg&oi=scholarr

13

Polynesia: In Search of Quality Education

Seu`ula Johansson-Fua

Introduction

The search for 'quality education' in Pacific Island countries is becoming more and more elusive. We do not quite know what it looks like, but we have been told many times of its existence and that it is somewhere out there. We have also been told by various agencies, development partners and consultants of the many roads towards this elusive 'thing'. We have also been given significant funding over the last 40 years to aid in the search for 'quality education' in our region.

This chapter presents a picture of the current status of selected Polynesian education systems, including their strengths and challenges. It then focuses on the priority issues and concerns of each of these education systems and puts forward suggestions designed to help in attaining quality education for our region.

While it is not possible to cover all of the Polynesian countries in this chapter, I have selected three countries that collectively demonstrate the range of challenges that Polynesian states face in their search for quality education. This chapter therefore focuses on the following countries: Cook Islands, Tonga and Tuvalu. These countries are member states of The University of the South Pacific (USP) and of the Pacific Island Forum Secretariat (PIFS).[1] The USP and PIFS member countries are either independent (Tonga and Tuvalu) or in free association with New Zealand (Cook Islands) and have authority over their education systems. Polynesian countries, such as Samoa (www.mesc.gov.ws), Niue (www.minedu.govt.nz), Tokelau (www.tokelau.org.nz) and others are not included in this discussion. However, all of these Polynesian states share similar challenges due mainly to their size, political history and economies of scale.

I have used the term 'Polynesia' here, in reference to a number of Pacific Island countries that share similarities in culture, language and development. These countries also share a rich history of trade, migration, warfare and alliances. These countries have also shared history in the spread of Christianity, formal education and colonialism, and in more recent history of political independence, regionalism, migration and struggle for self-sufficiency in a global climate.

These Polynesian countries also share a similarity in the history of formal education. For all of the Polynesian countries, formal education arrived with the missionaries, either with the Catholic missionary or with the Methodist missionaries in the early 1800s. With the departure of the missionaries in the early 1900s, the roles of educational providers were slowly replaced by New Zealanders and Australians serving as school principals, educational administrators and teachers. With the move for independence in the 1960s, more Polynesians took over positions in each country's education system. However, the influence of New Zealand and Australia in the education system of these countries has continued to today in the form of donor assistance and employment of consultants in aid of educational development in each of these countries (Sanga and Taufe`ulunga, 2005; Sanga et al., 2005). The influence of New Zealand and Australia in the development of the education system of these Polynesian countries is evident in the curriculum, assessment, teacher education, financing and administration of these systems.

I have used the Pacific Education Development Framework (PEDF) 2009–2015 as a guide to assess the current context of the selected Polynesian educational systems. The PEDF was approved by the Forum Education Ministers' Meeting (FEdMM) in March 2009 to be the guiding framework for educational development in the region. All of the selected Polynesian countries in this study are members of the FEdMM. The PEDF framework is grounded on two key ideas: a commitment made by Pacific countries to global instruments on educational development, the Education for All (EFA) agenda and goals, the Millennium Development Goals (MDGs) that are related to education, the United Nations Literacy Decade and the UN Decade of Education for Sustainable Development (DESD). The second key idea is the national and regional response to the specific needs and challenges in education of the Pacific region. The PEDF is also in alignment with the Pacific Plan, the region's master development plan for all sectors. The PEDF is based on a regional vision for 'quality education for all in Pacific Island countries'.

The subsequent sections of this chapter examine the current context of each education system of the Polynesian countries previously identified. This includes, in each instance, background information, current status of the education system and the challenges and priority for each country. For each country,

I illustrate their efforts to attain 'quality education' and why the search for quality education, in Polynesia at least, is really a search for relevancy in education.

Cook Islands

Background

Geographical location

The Cook Islands is located to the north west of New Zealand and to the west of French Polynesia. The Cook Islands is a group of 15 small islands spread across an exclusive economic zone of 200 nautical miles. It has a total landmass of 236.7 square kilometres. Like most Pacific islands, it is vulnerable to cyclones and hurricanes. The main island Rarotonga, of 67 square kilometres, in the southern Cook Islands, hosts the country's capital Avarua.

Political status

The Cook Islands became a British protectorate in 1888, was later transferred to New Zealand in 1900. The Cook Islands has been a self-governing parliamentary democracy in free association with New Zealand since 1965. People of the Cook Islands have automatic right to New Zealand citizenship and move freely between the two countries. The close association between the two countries has influenced development in the Cook Islands in many ways.

Economic status

The Cook Islands economy is based on tourism, pearl industry and fish exports. With limited arable land, most of the agriculture production is in the southern group. The northern islands of Manihiki and Penrhyn are the centres of the pearl production, while the southern islands of Rarotonga and Aitutaki are the centres for tourism.

Social status

The Cook Islands have an estimated population of 10,777 (July 2012). Cook Islands Maori accounts for 87 per cent of the population (2001 Census) with remaining population either part Cook Islands Maori or other. English is the official language and Maori is widely spoken. Cook Islands have a young population, with a total median age of 32.9 years and with 24 per cent of the population between 0 and 14 years old. The country has a growth rate of −3.1 and a birth rate of 15.22 births/1,000 population (est. 2012), and a total infant mortality rate of 15.3 deaths/1,000 live births. Cook Islands population have a total life expectancy at birth of 74.9 with females expected to live longer at 77 years old (est. 2012). The country spends 4.4 per cent of its GDP on health (est. 2009) and there are 1.7 physicians/1,000 population (2004). The Cook Islands has one of the highest HDI in the region (CIA, 2013).

Educational system

Overview

Education in the Cook Islands is mainly provided by the government. There are a total of 31 educational providers, with 24 Early Childhood Education (ECE) centres, 11 primary schools and 4 secondary schools. There are also 15 area schools which provide services from ECE to secondary school under one school and one management. All schools, private and government alike, receive 100 per cent funding from the government. This also means that all schools are open to the government's review system and processes including financial audit. Although governance of public schools is under the Ministry of Education, each public school has its own stakeholder committee that oversees their strategic plans, policy and goals. Private schools are usually associated and operated by a religious organization, with religious instructions and are governed by School boards.

In 2012, the total school population was at 4,152 with a total of 270 teachers. The total budget for the education sector in 2011/2012 was $NZD13,856,984, of which $NZD10,091,905 was government's appropriation to the Ministry of Education, $NZD2,090,000 was from donor funding. From this budget $NZD1,675,079 was the total grant given to Private schools for the 2011/2012 year (Cook Islands Ministry of Education, 2012).

Early childhood education (ECE)

In 2012, there was a total enrolment of 482 students, which was a slight decrease from an enrolment of 512 in 2011 (Cook Islands Ministry of Education, 2012). However, when seen over the last 5 years, there has been a steady increase in enrolment of children at ECE level. Refer to Figure 13.1. The largest number of enrolment at ECE, as reflected in the figure, is with schools in Rarotonga, the island having the largest concentration of population.

The steady increase in enrolment at ECE has been the result of significant effort put in by the Cook Islands Ministry of Education to improve services

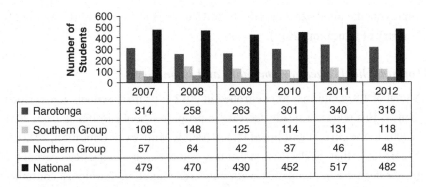

	2007	2008	2009	2010	2011	2012
■ Rarotonga	314	258	263	301	340	316
▨ Southern Group	108	148	125	114	131	118
■ Northern Group	57	64	42	37	46	48
■ National	479	470	430	452	517	482

Figure 13.1 ECE enrolment 2007–2012
Source: Cook Islands Ministry of Education (2012).

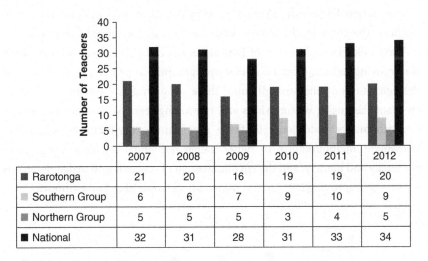

	2007	2008	2009	2010	2011	2012
■ Rarotonga	21	20	16	19	19	20
▨ Southern Group	6	6	7	9	10	9
■ Northern Group	5	5	5	3	4	5
■ National	32	31	28	31	33	34

Figure13.2 ECE teachers 2007–2012
Source: Cook Islands Ministry of Education (2012).

for ECE. This has included programmes in raising awareness and encouraging parents to take leadership in the education of their children. Additional efforts have also included improvement in resourcing ECE centres and developing policy to ensure quality programmes are delivered.

The Cook Islands Ministry has recently rolled out a new curriculum for ECE with a programme to ensure that teachers at ECE level are well versed with the new curriculum and gain specific qualification in ECE. In 2012, there was total of 34 ECE teachers, again reflecting a steady increase in the Ministry's investment in ECE. Refer to Figure 13.2. In the last 5 years, the Ministry has been steadily improving the pupil–teacher ratio, from 15 in 2008 to 14 in 2012 (Cook Islands Ministry of Education, 2012).

Formal school education (primary and secondary)

A total of 1,874 children were enrolled in 2012 at primary schools across Cook Islands. This reflects a steady decrease in primary school enrolment, from 2031 in 2007 to the current enrolment (Cook Islands Ministry of Education, 2012). It is more likely that the decrease in primary school enrolment has been part of the greater decrease in population, with outwards migration. Rarotonga continues to enrol more students at 1,233 for 2012, followed by 445 enrolment for the southern group and 197 for the northern group. Refer to Figure 13.3.

Similarly there has also been a steady decrease in the number of teachers at primary school level, with 125 in 2007 and by 2012 there were 111 primary school teachers. The pupil–teacher ratio over the last 5 years has ranged from 14 to 16.

The Cook Islands Ministry of Education, since 2002, has been working hard at improving its literacy and numeracy programmes at primary school. Current strategies to continue strengthening these programmes have included focus on Maori language, writing skills and improving teachers' content knowledge of Mathematics. Additional to these programmes are focus on improving assessment methodologies to better gauge individual students' progress in numeracy and literacy; and the encouragement of research into pedagogy that is relevant to improving literacy and numeracy in Cook Islands classrooms.

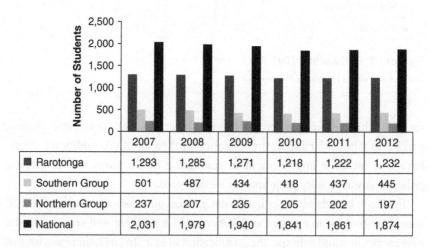

	2007	2008	2009	2010	2011	2012
■ Rarotonga	1,293	1,285	1,271	1,218	1,222	1,232
▨ Southern Group	501	487	434	418	437	445
▨ Northern Group	237	207	235	205	202	197
■ National	2,031	1,979	1,940	1,841	1,861	1,874

Figure 13.3 Primary school enrolment by region 2007–2012

Source: Cook Islands Ministry of Education (2012).

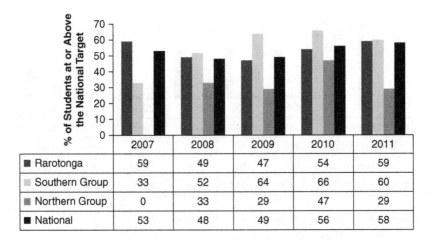

Figure 13.4 National Maori Literacy at Year 4 2007–2011
Source: Cook Islands Ministry of Education (2012).

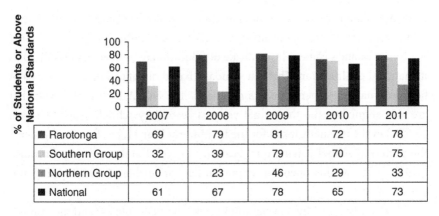

Figure 13.5 National English Literacy at Year 4 2007–2011
Source: Cook Islands Ministry of Education (2012).

Recent data shows progress towards achieving the Ministry's goals for improving literacy and the numeracy rates for primary school children in the Cook Islands. Refer to Figures 13.4 and 13.5.

The total enrolment for secondary school in 2012 was 1,796 students, reflecting a steady decrease in the enrolment number for secondary school from 1,951 in 2007 to the current enrolment (Cook Islands Ministry of Education, 2012). Refer to Figure 13.6. This trend is also evident in the decrease in the number of teachers at secondary school, which in 2007 were 133 teachers to 2012 with a

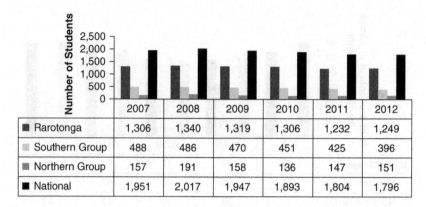

	2007	2008	2009	2010	2011	2012
■ Rarotonga	1,306	1,340	1,319	1,306	1,232	1,249
■ Southern Group	488	486	470	451	425	396
■ Northern Group	157	191	158	136	147	151
■ National	1,951	2,017	1,947	1,893	1,804	1,796

Figure 13.6 Secondary school enrolment by region 2007–2012
Source: Cook Islands Ministry of Education (2012).

total of 119 secondary school teachers. This has meant that the pupil–teacher ratio has averaged at 14 over the last 5 years.

Recruitment of secondary school teachers at senior level has been a challenge for the Ministry of Education. Since 2002, the Cook Islands Ministry has adopted the New Zealand's National Certificate of Educational Achievement (NCEA) as its national qualification. This is a standard-based qualification that consists of both internal assessment and examinations. The NCEA is in three levels that are also aligned to the three final years at secondary school, Years 11 to 13. NCEA Level 1 is usually taken for the first time at Year 11, but for most students the preferred school leaving qualification is Level 3 and University Entrance qualifications, as this opens up opportunities for further studies/training and employment.

The Cook Islands Ministry has put in significant effort to expand the number of subjects/courses being offered at secondary school, to ensure that students have increased access to a range of choices in both academic subjects and vocational and technical subjects. The Ministry has focused its current strategies for secondary school on expanding scope of subjects being offered, expanding Dual Pathways programmes (for both academic and vocational training) and for Alternative Pathways for students looking for non-traditional school courses. The Ministry has also been working on expanding and improving its services to the remote islands of the North through the development of a number of online learning courses. However, there are growing concerns with rate of retention at Year 12 and Year 13.

Technical and vocational education and training (TVET)

The Ministry of Education has been working hard to integrate the vocational and technical training programmes into the secondary academic programme. This is through the Dual Pathway programme, the Alternative Pathways programme and also with the expansion of technical subjects being offered at secondary school. These technical subjects have included: carpentry, hospitality, automotive engineering, graphics, material technology and recently traditional art.

Non-formal education (NFE)

NFE programmes available in the Cook Islands are through churches, youth groups, non-government organizations and cultural groups. NFE programmes range from religious instructions, to music, dance, drama and handicraft including carving and art.

Teacher development

The Cook Islands Teacher Training College (CITTC) had for a number of years trained teachers for the Cook Islands. However, by 2006, the college closed any further intake, due to an oversupply of teachers (Fua and Sanga, 2007). The Ministry, however, in 2011 had introduced a Fast Track Initiative for training of specialist teachers in the secondary school sector. The initiative required teachers to take subject specialist papers at university level including Ministry of Education courses that included assessment, curriculum and youth/child development courses. In the last 2 years, a total of 21 teachers have participated in this programme (Cook Islands Ministry of Education, 2012).

Priority issues

Cook Islands education system has done well in progressing towards the MDGs. By 1999, the country had achieved universal basic primary education and recorded a high adult literacy rate of 93 per cent (Fua and Sanga, 2007). Similarly, they have done well in achieving the strategic goals of the PEDF, particularly in ECE, primary school education, integrating TVET into the secondary school curriculum and investment in teacher professional development.

However, there are several priority areas that Cook Islands continues to find challenging in continuing the country's educational development.

Relevant curriculum

The close association with New Zealand has brought benefits as well as challenges for the Cook Islands. In early 1991, Sir Geoffrey Henry (prime minister of Cook Islands at the time) addressed a gathering in Rarotonga hosted by UNESCO on Education, culture and identity reiterated the same issue of a responsive education system. He stated 'I am aware not of balance but of imbalance. I feel that, in this community, education has yet to be relevant to whom we are'. He went on further to state that 'any hope of recovering what has been lost, any chance of attaining greater balance, surely depends on a greater commitment by everyone, parents, children, politicians and educators' (Teasdale and Teasdale, 1992: p. 13).

A decade later, the Ministry of Education Cook Islands continues to search for this balance in an effort to meet the educational needs of the country and at the same time meet New Zealand standards for quality education. The undertaking to ensure relevancy in the education system is most evident at ECE and Primary School level, with a strong emphasis on parental involvement, strong focus on Maori language and culture, long-term commitment to progressing literacy (in both English and Maori) and in numeracy. These efforts are certainly strengths of the current education system. The effort to meet New Zealand standards for quality education is most obvious at senior secondary school level, with the return to using the NCEA as the graduating qualification from high school. This has presented several challenges, particularly the increasing retention rate for Year 12 and Year 13. With NCEA, there is also the need for an increased number of specialist teachers at secondary school level. The Ministry, at its best, has set up several strategies in an effort to deal with these demands including the Fast Track Initiative for specialist secondary school teachers and widening the range of subjects available through the Dual pathway as well as through the Alternative pathway programme.

Education for sustainable development (ESD)

Although Cook Islands enjoy one of the higher levels of HDI in the region, it faces a similar challenge to other Polynesian countries, namely that of a decreasing population due to outward migration and negative growth rate. With easy access to New Zealand, there are now more Cook Islanders living in New Zealand than in the Cook Islands. In the last decade, resident population for Cook Islands are slowly decreasing so that the 2001 census recorded a population of 18,000 but by 2012 it was estimated at 10,777. This is also reflected in the decreasing enrolment rate at primary and at secondary school level. The decreasing population and the consequent decrease in the school population have several implications for financing education and in supplying teachers for remote schools. This has meant more classes in the outer islands offering multi-grade classes and in some cases the close down of schools.

The increasing number in outward migration has also meant that younger people of working age are leaving the Cook Islands. Thus the challenge for the Ministry is in offering an education system that meets the labour market of the country or the labour market demands of New Zealand, with the reality being that most of their school graduates will leave the country. The challenges faced by the education system of the Cook Islands in striving for relevancy and ESD are shared with other Polynesian countries.

Tonga

Background

Geographical location

Tonga is an archipelago consisting of 169 islands, 36 of which are inhabited. These islands are divided into three regions, with Vava'u, Niuafo'ou and Niuatoputapu to the north, Ha'apai islands in the central region and the southern region consists of 'Eua and Tongatapu. The capital of Tonga, Nuku'alofa is located on the southern island of Tongatapu. Tonga is located to the east of Fiji and north east of New Zealand.

Political status

Tonga is an independent constitutional monarchy, and the only remaining kingdom in the Pacific, currently headed by His Majesty King Tupou VI. Tonga government is headed by a prime minister, who is appointed by the King upon recommendation from the Parliament. Tonga has a unicameral parliament with House of Commons and House of Lords. Tonga's constitution has been in place since 1875, making it the third oldest constitution in the world.

Economic status

Tonga's economy depends on agriculture, fisheries and to a lesser extent on tourism. The economy has been suffering stagnant growth over the last 10 years. Foreign aid and remittances from Tongans living overseas have helped prop up the country's economy. The latest statistics show Tonga's Real GDP Growth at 4.7 per cent (Tonga Department of Statistics, 2012).

Social status

As a kingdom, Tongan society is still culturally ranked according to commoners, nobility and monarch. With modern economy, education and politics, a secondary classification cuts across the traditional ranking system, that in the last 30 years an emerging middle class has grown and with an elite middle class group being more and more evident in the early twenty-first century. The latest statistics show that Tonga has a population of 103,036 (2011 census) (Tonga Department of Statistics, 2012).

Education system

Overview

Education in Tonga is free and compulsory for ages 6 to 14 years old. Tonga Ministry of Education legally oversees all education systems in the country. However, provision for education at ECE, primary, secondary and tertiary are shared with the major church groups in the country. All ECE centres are privately owned, either by church groups or communities. Government provides 89 per cent of the primary schools, while church/private-owned educational systems operate 76 per cent of the secondary schools and 60 per cent of tertiary institutes are operated by the government (Tonga Ministry of Education, 2011). The government, with funding support from New Zealand and Australia, provides an additional school grant to each school, regardless whether it is private or government. All private educational systems are operated by their own governance systems and structures. Government schools are operated by the Tonga Ministry of Education.

ECE

ECE in Tonga is mainly operated by church and community groups. The growing interest in ECE is quite recent and it has been driven largely by private groups. At present, a Diploma in ECE is offered out of the Tonga Institute of Education. The USP through its Tonga campus also offers a Certificate in ECE. In the Ministry of Education's current policy framework, the ECE is featured as one of the key strategic goals of the Ministry. The Tonga Education Act is currently under review, and the amendments to the Act will include the expansion of the compulsory school age from age 4 to 18. With this new legal provision, it is

Table 13.1 ECE centres, school roll and number of teachers by major district as of 30 September 2011

Island	ECE centres		Pupils' roll				Teachers		Pupil/ teacher (P/T) ratio
	Number	%	F	M	Total	%	Number	%	
Tongatapu	40	56	566	693	1,259	70.57	112	64.37	1:11
'Eua	8	11	70	50	120	6.73	20	11.49	1:6
Ha'apai	6	8	45	56	101	5.66	12	6.90	1:8
Vava'u	13	18	120	113	233	13.06	23	13.22	1:10
Niuas	4	6	30	41	71	3.98	7	4.02	1:10
Total	71	100	831	953	1,784	100.00	174	100.00	

Source: Tonga Ministry of Education (2011).

likely that the interest and support for ECE will continue to grow in the future. Table 13.1 shows the latest enrolment figures for ECE in Tonga.

Formal school education (primary/secondary)

Primary education in Tonga is from Class 1 to Class 6 (Year 1–Year 6). The school entry age is normally 6 years. There is a secondary school entrance examination at the end of Class 6 of which all students sit a national exam in Mathematics, Science, Tongan Language and English. Total marks for each child determines the secondary school that the student will be accepted to enter. There continues to be a strong competition for students to gain high marks so that they can enter the better resourced government secondary schools. Unfortunately, the secondary school entrance examination and the competition for high marks has meant a large pool of student retention exists at the end of Class 6. This means that students who fail to gain the marks to enter their school of choice retake the entire Class 6 year again. This consequently impacts on resourcing teachers at this level and on the quality of teaching at this level. The Ministry in its strategic plan aims to phase out the Class 6 exam in the near future, extend the primary school years to include additional 2 years and with the possibility of a secondary school entrance exam at Class 7/Form 2.

The access rate to primary education is 100 per cent; this has come as a result of the government's long-standing policy on ensuring that no child shall have to walk more than 2 miles to a primary school. A total primary school enrolment of 17,033 students was recorded in 2011. Table 13.2 shows the latest enrolment figures for primary school students in Tonga, for 2011.

Table 13.2 All primary school enrolments by gender as of 30 September 2011

Age	Class 1		Class 2		Class 3		Class 4		Class 5		Class 6		IE		Total		Grand Total
	F	M	F	M	F	M	F	M	F	M	F	M	F	M	F	M	
4	9	11													9	11	20
5	535	563	13	8										2	548	571	1,119
6	764	867	435	459	8	9							3	1	1,210	1,337	2,547
7	57	69	809	916	418	389	9	11					2	1	1,295	1,386	2,681
8			47	77	847	896	397	411	10	13			1	1	1,302	1,398	2,700
9					70	87	727	886	382	367	16	15	1	2	1,196	1,357	2,553
10							73	114	765	892	331	342	1	1	1,170	1,349	2,519
11									79	137	913	925			992	1,062	2,054
12											224	339	1	4	225	343	568
13											24	51			24	51	75
14															0	1	1
16												1			0	1	1
Not stated	20	21	9	13	21	19	15	25	5	16	10	21			80	115	195
Total	1,385	1,531	1,313	1,473	1,364	1,400	1,221	1,447	1,241	1,425	1,518	1,694	9	12	8,051	8,982	17,033
Grand total	2,916		2,786		2,764		2,668		2,666		3,212		21		17,033		

Source: Tonga Ministry of Education (2011).

Table 13.3 Number of primary school teachers since 2007 by controlling authority

Year	Education system	Male	Female	Total	% Female	% Total
	Government	180	398	578	68.8	86.9
2007	Non-government	14	73	87	83.9	13.1
	Total	**194**	**471**	**665**	**70.83**	**100**
2008	Government	184	397	581	68.3	87.37
	Non-government	17	67	84	79.76	12.63
	Total	**201**	**464**	**665**	**69.77**	**100**
2009	Government	182	394	576	68.4	85
	Non-government	25	79	104	76	15
	Total	**207**	**473**	**680**	**69.56**	**100**
2010	Government	173	403	576	69.97	85.08
	Non-government	20	81	101	80.2	14.92
	Total	**193**	**484**	**677**	**71.49**	**100**
2011	Government	173	431	604	71.36	85.56
	Non-government	16	86	102	84.31	14.44
	Total	**189**	**517**	**706**	**73.23**	**100**

Source: Tonga Ministry of Education (2011).

Table 13.3 shows the latest figures for primary school teachers, showing a high number of female teachers at primary school level, reflecting a similar trend observed elsewhere in the region. Table 13.4 shows 129 primary schools spread across the archipelago; there is a school on almost every village and every island. Government-owned primary schools are provided with teachers but with limited teaching and learning resources. Although all government-operated primary schools are free from paying fees, each community plays a significant role in the development of their village schools. Parents are major local donors in giving financial aid for renovations, building of fences and supplying additional teaching materials for the children. The Tonga Education support programme provides school grants to all primary schools for renovations and purchase of school supplies. Nevertheless, the involvement and the financial contributions from parents continue.

In 2012, a new primary school curriculum was rolled out by the Ministry of Education for Class 1 to Form 2 at secondary school. Two key features of the new curriculum focus on strengthening Tongan culture and early access to creative technology. Other features of the curriculum include strengthening of sports and health. The new curriculum also marks a shift in thinking towards a more student-centred learning and an outcome-based approach.

Secondary education in Tonga is from Form 1 to Form 7 (or Year 7 to Year 13). Students normally enter secondary school at the age of 13 and if they do

Table 13.4 Number of primary schools in Tonga by managing authority and by district as of 30 September 2011

District	Controlling authority							
	Government	FWS	SDA	TOK	LAFALAFA	BAHA'I	ACT	Total
Tongatapu	51	6	2	2	1	1	1	64
'Eua	6	0	0	0	0	0	0	6
Ha'apai	19	2	0	1	0	0	0	22
Vava'u	31	0	0	1	0	0	0	32
Niuatoputapu	3	0	0	0	0	0	0	3
Niuafo'ou	2	0	0	0	0	0	0	2
Total	112	8	2	4	1	1	1	129

Source: Tonga Ministry of Education (2011).

Table 13.5 Number of schools, enrolments, and teachers in post at government and church secondary schools, 2010/2011

	Schools			Enrolment			Teachers		
	High	Middle	Total	High	Middle	Total	High	Middle	Total
Government	8	7	15	4,137	1,032	5,169	250	43	293
Church	24	16	40	8,572	1,097	9,669	624	69	693
Total	32	23	55	12,709	2,129	14,838	874	112	986

Source: Tonga Ministry of Education (2011).

remain until Form 7, they normally leave secondary school by the age of 18. Latest statistical records show that in 2011 there were a total of 14,575 students who were enrolled in secondary school in Tonga. Table 13.5 presents the total number of secondary schools, including middle schools, the total number of enrolment and the number of teachers working in the secondary school sector. It is worth noting that church systems operate 40 schools out of 55 secondary schools in Tonga, with a total enrolment number of students at church schools at 9,669 or 53 per cent of the student population (Tonga Ministry of Education, 2011). Teacher data is for 2010.

There are three external exams in secondary school: the Tonga School Certificate at Form 5, the Tonga Form 6 Examination and the Tonga National Form 7 Certificate at the final year. In 2012, the Ministry of Education introduced the Tonga Form 6 Certificate and National Form 7 Certificate, to replace the regional Pacific Secondary School Certificate and the Form 7 Certificate normally offered by the regional South Pacific Board for Educational Assessment (SPBEA). The Ministry of Education has plans to phase out the Form 6 exam at secondary.

The National Form 7 Certificate allows the student to enter university and other tertiary institutes, while the Form 5 and Form 6 certificates can allow students to enter most vocational training institutes. Similar to Primary school, there is an increased retention number at Form 5 and the enrolment number decreases as students' progress towards Form 7.

At present, the secondary school (Form 3–Form 5) is under review with the expectation that the new curriculum will roll out within the next 2 to 3 years. The current secondary school curriculum continues to be heavily in favour of academic subjects, such as English, Geography, Accounting and Science with minimal attention to technical, cultural and sports curriculum. The teaching approach also continues to be teacher-driven, mainly theoretical ideas and with heavy emphasis on examinations.

TVET

Through funding from New Zealand and Australia, there has been significant support given to the promotion of TVET. The first national TVET policy was launched in early 2013 to govern provision of this curriculum. Although Tonga's education system had encouraged vocational subjects, such as industrial arts and home economics in secondary school, it had suffered neglect in the previous years as increasing emphasis was given to academic subjects. With the current support for TVET and the increasing recognition that not all students wish to pursue academic oriented careers, the Ministry of Education is working hard to strengthen pathways towards greater participation in technical and vocational subjects. It does not help when most parents still push their children towards more academic subjects in the desire to pursue white-collar jobs.

TVET is now introduced as subjects in most church schools at Form 3 and Form 4, providing an alternative pathway for students to enter tertiary TVET institutes after high school. With an increasing number of TVET providers in Tonga, there are now more choices for students to pursue a range of courses, including maritime, agriculture, engineering, hospitality and fashion and design subjects.

NFE

NFE in Tonga is mainly provided by non-government organizations and church groups, usually on an ad hoc basis, depending on demand and funding support. The most traditional of the NFE is found in the churches, with Sunday schools and religious instructions for church members. Other forms of NFE evident at community level generally focus on the passing of traditional knowledge and skills in areas ranging from fishing, agriculture, handicrafts, weaving, cooking, traditional performing arts, music and traditional responsibilities for Tongan customary rituals.

Teacher development

Tonga Institute of Education, the government owned teacher's training college, has been training Tonga's teachers since the 1940s. Other teacher training providers, such as the church-owned Tupou Tertiary Institute, offer Diploma in Education and also USP through its Tonga Campus offer teacher education with certifications ranging from Diploma in Education to Master of Education and Master of Arts in Education.

The Tonga Institute of Education has recently been reviewed and is currently working on redeveloping its programme for 2015. The Institute offers a Diploma in Education for both primary and secondary teaching, Diploma in ECE and more recently Certificate in Teaching for untrained teachers and Postgraduate certificate in teaching for teachers with a degree but with no teaching qualification. The Ministry of Education plans to register all teachers; both government and private teachers, by 2015 and the minimal qualification for registration will be the Certificate in Teaching. There remain over 200 untrained teachers in Tonga who are mainly from the church and private education systems. The Certificate in Teaching is intended to process through the remaining untrained teachers in Tonga to reach the Ministry's target of full teacher registration by 2015.

Priority issues

Tonga has a long history of demonstrating its commitment to education, both at primary school and secondary school level. It has also enjoyed a very high literacy level in the past. However, in the last 10 years the performance of the Tonga education system has suffered series of setbacks as result of political changes in leadership and the impact of the national financial crisis.

Relevant curriculum

Although Tonga has been one of the few countries in the region who pioneered the introduction of Tongan studies in schools in the 1980s, its education systems continue to push for greater recognition of the Tongan language and culture. The recent review of the curriculum for primary school has seen the separation of Tongan language from Tongan subject, thus creating a second subject for teaching Tongan studies. It is yet to be seen whether the new curriculum for the secondary school will continue this trend. Although the creation of two subjects in the Tongan studies area is a step forward, much work remains to ensure that Tongan culture and language are taught across the curriculum rather than in these specific subjects.

The issue of relevancy of the curriculum to Tongan students remains a significant concern for educational development in Tonga. One of the most strategic approaches that can begin to resolve this issue is the offering of Tongan language and culture across the curriculum. It is only through a much more relevant curriculum, where Tongan students can recognize their world that they can begin to truly engage in learning, and to critique and apply the knowledge they have learned. The high retention rate at Class 6 and at senior secondary school, plus the number of students that are pushed out of the system at senior secondary level, all attest to the irrelevancy of the curriculum and the struggle to make sense of knowledge system are beyond their everyday lives.

ESD

For Tonga, the issue of relevant curriculum is directly link to the issue of ESD. For the last 10 years, Tonga has been struggling to raise its economic performance. Several political events, including a civil strike in 2005 that resulted in government raising the salary of civil servants against a weak economy; the riot of 2006 that destroyed a significant number of businesses in the capital of Nuku`alofa and the reduction in remittances from overseas Tongans due to the current global crises, have all contributed to a struggling economy. Tonga imports over 50 per cent of goods with export consisting mainly of agriculture products, fisheries and traditional handicrafts. Local manufacturing is limited and despite heavy investment in tourism, it has not really taken off like Cook Islands or Fiji. Tongans have always prided themselves in a good education and its people, as it continues to send rugby players, fruit pickers and working professionals overseas. It is remittances from these Tongans that help the local economy stay afloat.

The average Tongan continues to live a semi-subsistence livelihood, living off the land and from the ocean. However, impacts of climate change are already evident in certain small low lying islands in the Ha`apai group and in Vava`u and it has affected crops and catch from the ocean. Although the average Tongan continues to live a semi-subsistence livelihood, the skills needed to survive in these conditions continue to be lacking in the formal schooling system. The belief that academic and white-collared jobs are more desirable than farm work or fishing or traditional handicraft still remains steep in most parents' and teachers' thinking, thus Ministry's efforts to promote TVET subjects and Tongan language and culture are still met with resistance.

Most people in the farming, fishing and handicraft industry learn their trade from their parents and from their community through NFE processes, not through the formal education system. Although the formal education system focuses on subjects like Economics, Accounting, Computer and other formal subjects, after 12 years of schooling the average Tongan youth still struggle to find a formal employment. There are a high number of students who graduate from high school and are not able to either find a job or earn a livelihood for themselves. As the curriculum favours academic subjects and teaching methodologies remain abstract, students finish from high school with high aspirations of getting a white-collared job in a stagnant economy, simply struggle to find paid employment. This is compounded by the fact that students upon completing formal education lack the practical skills to earn neither a livelihood from traditional farming and fishing nor the entrepreneurship to create a livelihood for themselves using available natural resources of the country.

The Tongan education system continues its work towards an education system that will enable Tongans to live sustainably on their islands.

Tuvalu

Background

Geographical location

Tuvalu is an archipelago of six atolls and three coral islands with a total land size of 26 square kilometres, making it one of the fourth smallest country in the world. Southern Tuvalu is made up of Funafuti, Nukulaelae and Niulakita, and in the central region are islands of Nui, Nukufetau and Vaitupu. Northern Tuvalu is made up of the islands of Niutao, Nanumea and Nanumaga. Tuvalu is located north of Fiji and south of Kiribati.

Political status

Tuvalu gained independence in 1978 from the United Kingdom and is a parliamentary democracy under constitutional monarchy. The head of government is the prime minister, who is selected by members of a unicameral parliament. There are no formal parties, and elections are still closely linked to family ties and kinship groupings. Local governance is based on traditional structures of chiefs and family links. Tuvaluan society is fairly egalitarian, with a strong culture and democratic principles. Each island is governed by local governance council consisting of chiefs and elders.

Economic status

Tuvalu's main source of revenue is through the fishing and dotTV licences and interest from the Tuvalu Trust Fund and the Falekaupule Trust Fund. Tuvaluan seafarers are also internationally recognized for their skills and their remittances also contribute to the economy of the country. For most families in Tuvalu, their main income is from formal employment, fishing, agriculture and handicraft.

Social status

The latest census count, in 2002, showed that Tuvalu's population was at 9,359 with current estimated population now residing in Tuvalu at 11,000 (2012). Tuvalu has a significantly young population with 36 per cent of the total population younger than 15 years old. The 2002 census showed an annual growth rate of 0.5 per cent. The Tuvaluan population is spread across 8 inhabited islands, with at least 3,962 people living on the main island of Funafuti in 2002.

Education system

Overview

The Department of Education is responsible for ECCE, TVET, NFE, Primary and Secondary Education, Junior Secondary School and curriculum and assessment. The Education Act of 2008 and 1977 governs education in Tuvalu and outlines that parents are responsible for ensuring that their child is at school. Education in Tuvalu is free and compulsory from ages 6 to 15 years old. In Tuvalu, there are 18 ECE centres, 9 primary schools and 2 secondary schools. There are ECE centres and primary schools on each of the eight inhabited islands, with one government-owned secondary school on Vaitupu and one private secondary school on Funafuti.

Although government contributes more than one-quarter of its budget to education (26% in 2011), the spread of a relatively small population over a number of small islands makes financing education in Tuvalu very costly.

The government's contribution to the education system is mainly towards paying teachers' salaries, with minimal funds for operations, maintenances, procurement of furniture and teaching resources. Local island governance systems and parents teachers associations play significant role in supplementing the cost of primary education on each island.

ECE

Provisions of ECE in Tuvalu are under the Tuvalu National Pre-School Council, and are managed by communities, non-government organizations and private providers. ECE is not compulsory in Tuvalu and has yet to come formally under the Department of Education. However, the government does provide funding support for infrastructure, resources and professional development for teachers. The 2002 census showed that 90 per cent of children were enrolled in ECE. ECE in Tuvalu can take in children from ages 3 to 6 years old.

There is no formal national curriculum framework for ECE in Tuvalu and as a result each ECE centre provides their own curriculum programme and determines their own regulations and activities. There has been a 59 per cent increase in the number of qualified teachers for ECE in Tuvalu, an increase from 27 in 2007 to 43 in 2011 (UNICEF, 2011).

Formal school education (primary/secondary)

Primary education in Tuvalu is compulsory and it is offered from Class 1–6 and Form 1–2. There are eight government primary schools located on each of the islands with an additional private primary school on Funafuti, operated by the Seventh Day Adventist Church. Latest statistics from 2010 show an enrolment of 1918 students (UNICEF 2011). The 2002 census showed a 99.9 per cent of children of 6–13 years old attending school.

The Tuvalu Department of Education recently introduced a national secondary school entrance examination at Form 2, which unfortunately has resulted in high retention rate for students at this level. Although there are only two secondary schools in Tuvalu, there is a perceived difference in the quality of the two schools, in favour of the government-owned secondary school. Normal practice is that students will continue to retake the exam until they qualify to enter secondary school, or reach the school leaving age and exit from the education system. Current work programme of the Tuvalu Department of Education includes investigation into the problem of student retention at this level.

Secondary education in Tuvalu is compulsory at lower secondary (ages 14–15) and voluntary for upper secondary (ages 16–17). The private secondary school, Fetuvalu High School, offers the Cambridge curriculum. The government-owned secondary school Motufoua offers a combination of curriculum, borrowing from the Fiji Junior Certificate Program for Year 10, Tuvalu School Certificate for Year 11 and the South Pacific Board of Educational Assessment for Year 12. As evident in other Pacific countries with a similar array of curriculum and exams at senior secondary level, the enrolment numbers drop as students progress up to Year 12. Census from 2002 showed a significant decline in enrolment starting at age 14 and this is most evident among boys. The census for 2002 showed that by 15 years old only 88 per cent of girls are still at school compared to 67 per cent of boys. This further declines by 16 years old, as 27 per cent of boys and 41 per cent of girls were still in school. However, this trend levels off by the time the remaining students reach 19 years old, as a higher number of boys complete secondary school (37%) compared to girls (33%). The census also showed that more boys continue on to complete tertiary education. It is highly likely that with access to the Tuvalu Maritime Training Institute, boys have a better chance of entering tertiary education than girls. Tuvalu Maritime Training Institute normally enrols only boys. There are limited options for girls for further tertiary studies in Tuvalu.

TVET

There are several training providers in Tuvalu that offer skills training including Motufoua secondary school through the Fiji Junior Certificate, the Tuvalu Maritime Training Institutes, the Department of Public Works section for training, private and non-government training centres.

There is an absence of a national TVET policy framework to organize all the various TVET training providers and programmes.

NFE

NFE in Tuvalu is provided by a range of private and non-government organizations, including the USP Tuvalu campus, Tuvalu Association of NGOs, Tuvalu Overseas Seamens Unions and private providers. There is an absence of a national coordination mechanism to bring these trainings under a more structured system, as a result most NFE programmes are offered ad hoc and there is little mechanism to assess quality of each programme delivered.

Teacher development

The absence of a teacher training institute for Tuvalu presents several challenges, mainly the limitation in providing structured professional development for teachers, the upgrading of qualified teachers and ensuring common teaching standards for all teachers. Tuvalu teachers, at present, can enrol at the USP Tuvalu campus taking the Bachelor of Education programme through online mode until second year, and then they will still need to move to Fiji to the USP's main campus to complete their degree programme. Other teachers are often sent to Tonga, Samoa, Kiribati and Solomon Islands for teacher training.

Priority issues

Curriculum relevance

The Tuvaluan culture is one of the more resilient Polynesian cultures with strong ties to their language, their way of life and use of traditional governance systems in contemporary governance. However, the Tuvaluan world view is not evident in their curriculum nor in the way that Tuvaluan children are taught at schools. With a range of curriculum, Fiji Junior Certificate, Cambridge Curriculum, SPBEA, Tuvalu and others, being offered from ECE to secondary school, there is no sense of alignment nor is there coherency in a student's learning journey. Added to this is the number of examinations that students go through, from the National secondary school entrance examination to the Fiji Junior Certificate, the Tuvalu School Certificate, the SPBEA Form 6 and the Cambridge assessments, all are taxing on students' learning journey. Consequently, there is a growing number of students, mainly boys who are pushed out of the education system as they progress to senior secondary school.

It is not just the irrelevancy in the curriculum that is pushing Tuvaluan students out of school, it is also the quality of teachers and the lack of resources to provide students with an education that is relevant to their world. Limited budget and lack of access to teacher professional development programmes both contribute to the challenge of providing an education that is relevant in Tuvalu.

ESD

Tuvalu is one of the smallest island states in the region and unfortunately, one of the Pacific islands that is most affected by the global climate change. The average height of atolls is less than 2 metres above sea level and with climate change, Tuvalu faces several challenges, including coastal erosion, less rainfall and prolonged droughts, decreasing fisheries population and Pulaka pit salination as a result of saltwater. The issue of adaptation is addressed at government level, with efforts to work together with the local governance Kaupule and other stakeholders. However, the education system's curriculum remains far from addressing issues of climate change education and disaster risk management.

The impact of climate change on Tuvalu is similar to other Pacific nations that include Kiribati, Marshall Islands and Federated States of Micronesia. The very real threat to the livelihoods and future of these island states pushes the idea of ESD to its very core – an education for survival. For Tuvalu and other similar states, ESD is about the survival of the people and the culture, heritage and language that they are endowed with. The prospects of relocation and becoming environmental refugees are and will be a reality not only for Tuvalu but also for most other low-lying atoll countries in the region. An education system that is relevant for Tuvalu is one that prepares their people for survival in a changing climate.

Conclusion

The issue of quality for the region and specifically for Polynesian states is really an issue of relevancy. The search for quality, therefore, is all too often a search in the wrong places, heading in the wrong direction and missing what quality is really about in our region. All too often, the discourse over quality education in the region focuses on examination marks, number of students pushed out of the system, quality of teachers, but never really on the relevancy of the total system to the student's way of life and context.

The study of Cook Islands, Tonga and Tuvalu, has shown a story that is repeated in all other Polynesian states, that of searching for quality. The search for quality in the Polynesian states is often against the context of a country heavily influenced by a more developed nation, in the case of Cook Islands and Niue, it is the influence of New Zealand. Furthermore, the search for quality is also against the context of a struggling economy with evidence of hardship and challenges of earning a sustainable livelihood, such as the case of Tonga and other similar countries in the region, including Kiribati, Tuvalu, Nauru, Vanuatu and Solomon Islands. The case of Tuvalu demonstrates the challenge of searching for quality education in a small island states faced with threats of global climate change. Tuvalu's case is also evident in other Pacific states including Republic of the Marshall Islands, Kiribati and Federated States of Micronesia.

Given this context and the socio-economic and geographical climate, educators can easily be misled on where and how quality education may look like. To return to the region's educational vision as expressed in PEDF, there is 'quality education for all in Pacific island countries' (Pacific Islands Forum Secretariat, p. 5). This 'quality education' is further expressed as each Pacific person is able to make a meaningful contribution to the social, cultural and economic development of the region.

What we see from the case of Cook Islands, Tonga and Tuvalu is that access to education at ECE and primary level are near 100 per cent; however, in all three cases, the rate of school drop-out starts as early as 14 and accelerates by senior secondary school level. Evident in all three countries is the large pool of students who are retained at senior secondary school level to pass numerous external examinations. It is interesting to see that in all three countries, as students' progress to senior level, the influence of other curriculum takes a stronger hold, as in the New Zealand certificate, the Fiji certificate, the SPBEA regional certificate and the Cambridge programme. However, also evident in all three countries is the increasing number of unemployed youth.

The effort to incorporate TVET programmes into secondary education is also evident in all three countries, with the belief that this will provide an alternative pathway for students who are not succeeding with the more academic programme at senior secondary level. This is certainly a worthwhile effort, but much remains to be done to ensure that TVET programmes are tailored to the demands of the labour market for each country.

Similarly, the effort to incorporate traditional knowledge systems including indigenous languages and culture into the curriculum still remains incomplete. The pathway towards sustainable development for all three countries lies in the incorporation of traditional and contemporary knowledge systems into the curriculum, pedagogy and total school system. When students see their everyday lives reflected in the schools, they begin to be engaged, learn to critically reflect and apply their skills and knowledge. Here lies relevancy of the school system to that of the Polynesian child's world. And here, we will find quality education, when education offered is meaningful, worthwhile and useful for the Polynesian child.

Note

1 The PIFS is a regional body that coordinates economic, social and political development of member countries in the region that include Polynesia, Melanesia and Micronesia countries.

References

Cook Islands Ministry of Education (2012), *Statistics Digest*. Rarotonga, Cook Islands: Ministry of Education.

CIA (2013), *World Fact Book: Cook Islands*. Available at: www.cia.gov/libraray/publications/the-world-factbook/geos/cw.html (Accessed: 7 April 2014).

Fua, S. J. and Sanga, K. F. (2007), *Teachers and Education in the Pacific: A Desk Study Report*. Suva, Fiji: Institute of Education, University of the South Pacific.

Ministry of Education, Women's Affairs and Culture, Annual Report (2011), Nuku`alofa, Tonga: Ministry of Education.

Pacific Islands Forum Secretariat: Pacific Education Development Framework (n.d.), Available at: http://www.forumsec.org.fj/resources/uploads/attachments/documents/Pacific%20Education%20Development%20Framework%202009–2015.pdf (Accessed: 7 April 2014).

Sanga, K., Chu, C., Hall, C. and Crowl, L. (2005), *Re-Thinking Aid Relationships in Pacific Education*. Wellington, New Zealand: He Parekereke Institute for Research and Development in Maori and Pacific Education, Victoria University.

Sanga, K. and Taufe`ulunga, A. (2005), *International Aid Impacts on Pacific Education*. Wellington, New Zealand: He Parekereke Institute for Research and Development in Maori and Pacific Education, Victoria University.

Teasdale, B. and Teasdale, J. (1992), *Voices in a Seashell*. Suva, Fiji: Institute of Pacific Studies, University of the South Pacific.

Tonga Department of Statistics (2012), Available at: www.mic.gov.to (Accessed: 7 April 2014).

UNICEF (2011), *Achieving Education for All in Tuvalu*. Suva, Fiji.

Micronesia: An Overview of the Federated States of Micronesia

Robert Underwood, Robert Andreas and Unaisi Nabobo-Baba

A sense of indecisiveness about the purpose of education and whose values should be taught has created split personalities for many Pacific Island educators. While we are saying it is important to maintain our traditional values and skills, that is not reflected in what is taught in schools. The necessary grounding in cultural values that is so necessary for identity development is not prioritized in educational planning and policy developments. A balance has to be struck where education is supportive of culture and tradition but also stresses academic, technological and vocational skills to live and be competitive in the modern world. (Dr Hilda Heine, Minister of Education, Marshall Islands Today quoted in Heine, 2002: 87 – speaking on the on relevance of education in Micronesia)

Introduction

All nations and their education systems are shaped by their history and the physical, socio-cultural and political milieu in which they are situated. Context is then a pertinent feature in terms of addressing the challenges, priorities and prospects of education systems, and especially those in small Pacific Island Countries (Crossley, 2010). This chapter examines the nature of the education systems in Micronesian states focusing mainly on the challenges and priorities of the Federated States of Micronesia (FSM). It does this because the FSM's educational realities reveal many of the issues that are common throughout the sub-region. This chapter is written with the hope that by highlighting the challenges of education in the region, stakeholders and readers alike will be able to take stock of the priority issues that need addressing, with some measure of respect for the work that has been done and continues to be done. This chapter is written utilizing the textual analysis of data from recent official reports and the related research literature, as well as findings from 15 in-depth interviews with FSM educators and policy makers.

Context and background

The context of this chapter is Micronesia. Micronesia means tiny islands. All of the 2,100 tropical islands spreading across Micronesia in the Western Pacific are small. All are either volcanic or coral covered with dense foliage and faced with heavy rainfall and humidity (Thomas, 1984: p. 67). The Western Pacific region has experienced what Thomas has referred to as 'a confusing and often disastrous sequence of cultural encounters [with] European, Far Eastern and American powers' (ibid.). Colonialism brought heavy death tolls due to introduced diseases such as smallpox, venereal diseases and respiratory illnesses. For instance, by 1852 Pohnpei had two-thirds of its total population decimated by introduced diseases. At about the same time, from a population of about 100,000, only 3,000 were known to have survived in Palau. The Chamorro population in the Marianas and Guam suffered the same fate. Truk (now Chuuk) was the exception because they were feared and Westerners avoided their islands (ibid.: p. 68). Micronesians who are said to be a mixture of Melanesian and Polynesian stock therefore have over time experienced Spanish, German, Japanese and American colonial rule.

Spain had tight control of Micronesia until 1898 after the Spanish American War. By this time, Germany had also made inroads into Micronesia via trading stations in the Gilbert and Ellice Islands (now Tuvalu and Kiribati), Marshall Islands, Yap and the Caroline Islands.

Spain lost the Spanish American war of 1898 and lost the control of Guam and the Philippines to the United States, while Germany increased its control over the rest of Micronesia. Germany transferred people from one island to another as its labour needs dictated, and substituted communal ownership of land for individual ownership. This control lasted until World War One broke out and Japan entered the region with a different goal from that of Germany. Japan wanted an extension of the Japanese Empire unlike Germany that needed only trading stations.

By 1940, the Japanese population in the North West Pacific was more than 80,000, some 20,000 more than that of the native population of about 60,000

(Wenkam and Baker 1971: p. 28 in Thomas, 1984: p. 69). The Japanese stayed for a little more than three decades. After its loss in 1945 during World War Two, Japan transferred all of its territory to the United States as a United Nations trust.

On the different goals of colonization, Thomas (1984: pp. 69–70) wrote:

The American intention in the islands differed somewhat from the intentions of the three colonial predecessors. Spain apparently had seen the territory as a symbol of might and empire, a region in which to extend Catholicism in a modern way and a useful supply station for ships between Mexico and the Philippines. Germany had viewed the islands as both a symbol of empire and a setting for such commercial ventures as the copra industry. Japan had considered Micronesia a permanent extension of the Japanese empire, a military buffer to the east of her home islands, a resettlement area for an expanding population, a source for agricultural and mining products, and a market for Japanese goods . . . The Americans saw Micronesia as a key location for military installations – guarding against future surprise attacks from the West . . . Economically America regarded Micronesia as a liability rather than an asset . . .

The federated states of Micronesia and education

The FSM consists of the states of Chuuk, Kosrae, Pohnpei and Yap. These four States combined to form the nation that is FSM in a voluntary federation in 1982; they are semi-autonomous, with each retaining considerable autonomy. Each of the four states manages their own domestic affairs, resources and external relations as well as forming partnerships of their own choice except for defence (Thomas, 1984: p. 72). The FSM national capital is located in Palikir, Pohnpei. Palikir is also home to FSM's only postsecondary institution the College of Micronesia (COM); however, this has campuses in the four states.

The FSM has a Compact of Free Association (COFA) with the United States. The COFA has articulated a set of unique arrangements and relationship between FSM and the United States. This includes the US providing finance and other assistance to FSM, while FSM provides geopolitical rights and hence brings security to certain US defence-related concerns in the region. More than 98 per cent of all education funding comes to the FSM via COFA. Use of such COFA funding is guided by the FSM/US Fiscal Procedures Agreement (FPA) and the Joint Economic Management Committee (JEMCO) comprising three US and two FSM members. In addition to finance, FSM citizens enjoy free access to the United States for education and employment, and those interested may join the military.

There are a total of 192 schools (public and private) in the FSM. Of these, 34 per cent are located in the outer islands. These outer islands, most being isolated and far away from urban centres, are reachable only by boats and ships. These are at times infrequent and with erratic schedules. Small aircrafts are also available if afforded. The population of FSM based on the 2010 census is 102,143. Of this, 36,902 (36%) are of school age between the ages of 4 and 18. For the school year 2012–2013, 72 per cent of this school age population were enrolled (FSM NDOE, 2013).

Educational challenges in FSM and Micronesia

In this section, the main educational challenges faced by the FSM are examined in turn. These include challenges related to: islandness and small scale, indigenous education, languages and epistemologies, coordination between different levels of government, the quality of education and student achievement, teacher professionalism and leadership, data collection and reporting, community involvement and financial dependency.

Islandness and small scale

While it is a truism that all education systems face challenges, education systems in the small island states of the Pacific Islands, and especially its smaller constituent Micronesia, are distinctive in that they face overarching challenges of smallness and islandness. In terms of educational context, Bacchus and Brock (1987) recognized this when they outlined three main features related to smallness and islandness: scale, isolation and dependency. These core themes can be seen throughout the following analysis of education in the FSM.

Furnishing schools for all students, for example, continues to be a major challenge throughout Micronesia, especially in islands such as those of FSM, with very small populations. Thomas (1984) recognized this when he wrote: 'In 1953, there were 68 one-room schools out of the territory's 144 public primary schools'. In 2009, the National Department of Education's (NDOE) Focused Strategic Report for 2009–2015 noted: 'huuk and Yap States have many small schools on scattered outlying islands. This presents problems in communication, transport, management, monitoring and supervision' (FSM NDOE, 2009: p. 18). Shaw (1982) has written about this in-depth, and in 2014 efforts continue to be made to consolidate schools, joining them together with a view to maximize resource use and efficiency.

Smallness of scale as found in the FSM has further socio-economic implications that include: problems of development and over-concentration, limited population bases, open economies and overdependence, high public expenditure, vast distances, high costs per unit output given the small population sizes, the dominance of public sector employment, problems of finance and aid dependency, patronage and nepotism. All of these factors have significant implications for education and human resource development.

A limited population base also means that small states do not enjoy the advantages of economies of scale. For instance, for the purchasing or local production of textbooks, unit costs are far more expensive than compared to a bigger country with larger numbers of pupils/students in the population. Economies of scale are important for successful industrialization and economic diversification, hence the economies of small states are often over-concentrated to restricted internal markets.

For the FSM, national and state economies can be said to be open to outside integration and especially to the United States, and, increasingly, to the economies of tuna buying countries. This, together with a higher import dependence, makes for 'economic, political and cultural vulnerability' (Bacchus and Brock, 1987: p. 2). The costs of providing basic public services, including education and health, are high, and costs of running the public service can be disproportionately higher if compared to those of larger states. Further, large distances in the islands make costs disproportionately expensive and educational services as a result can be difficult to maintain (see, e.g. Nabobo-Baba et al., 2012). For the FSM, the COFA addresses some of these challenges; however, prioritizing resources for education remain problematic and contributes to ongoing dependency on external aid. While such aid may help to solve some problems, it can also prioritize donor agendas and create its own set of challenges (Sanga et al., 2005). Other studies, including Chapter 8 in the present volume, focus directly upon international aid and Pacific Islands education and explore such issues in greater detail (see Baba, 1987, 1989, 1992; Coxon, 1996; Hickling-Hudson, 2002; Bretton Woods Project, 2003; Coxon and Taufe'ulungaki, 2003).

Isolation and the close inter-personal relationships that characterize small states (Bacchus and Brock, 1987: p. 4) often generate administrative and other related challenges. This can be seen in the FSM, where interviews have revealed that one of the main challenges of working in the education system is nepotism, which at times may deter the making of appointments and other decisions based on merit. Local educators affirm this observation noting, for example, that the power of the traditional chiefs in Pohnpei and of the upper classes in Yap constitute important and influential elements in educational decision making and how a conservative attitude to work may see a lack of change as officials 'play safe'.

However, as Bray (1992: p. 38) argues, educational planners faced with issues of close personal contacts can also capitalize on their advantages and at the same time try to minimize their problems. This is because close proximity can enhance the personalization of educational leadership, planning and decision making. For instance, a long-time educator when interviewed said: 'It is not easy to hide in small places' and a locally based professor reported that 'it is easy to call meetings and coordinate participation in a book writing workshop for instance because everyone lives not too far off from each other'. Bray (1992: p. 34) points out that accountabilities, sensitivities, easy participation and ease of coordination can be strengths for small states. A further challenge closely associated with many small states is related to declining student numbers. This is associated in part with high migration rates in the FSM. 'Student population continues to decline . . . Migration out of the country is one of the primary reasons that contribute to the decline in student population . . .' (FSM NDOE, 2013: p. 2).

Indigenous education, languages and epistemologies

This section focuses more closely upon issues relating to indigenous education in the light of research that suggests that the place of indigenous knowledge, skills and values in the curriculum is one of the most pervasive challenges faced in Micronesian education. There are many examples that can be used to illustrate this, one of which relates to the potential for greater attention to be given to Pacific sailing traditions, experience and technologies in schooling. For example, much can be learned from 'long-distance voyaging – one of the most exciting features of the history of the Pacific is through the out-riggers and double hulls' (Quanchi, 1991: p. 69). Indeed, within Micronesia, a canoe sailed 2,800 kilometres from Satawal Atoll to Okinawa Island near Japan in December 1975 for an international marine expo (ibid.: p. 75). Again in 1976, as highlighted by Quanchi, 'an eight metre inter-island, out-rigger sailing canoe, the *Maharek Maihar*, left Pulawat Atoll in Truk (Chuuk) for Guam . . .' (ibid.).

The importance of indigenous knowledge is also revealed by discussions of land ownership and the terminology used to describe it. Ownership is often

Table 14.1 Major native language of the FSM

State	Languages
Yap	Yapese, Ulithian, Satalwalese, Ulithian (1), Woleian (1)
Chuuk	Chuukese, Mortlockese, Western
Pohnpei	Pohnpeian, Pinglapese, Mwoakilese (Mokilese), Sapwuafikese (Ngatikese), Nukuroan (2), Kapingamarangian (2)
Kosrae	Kosraen

Notes: (1) The areas where Ulithian and Woleaian are spoken are politically part of Yap, they have a basis in Chuukese. (2) Nukuroan and Kapingamarangian are descended from the Polynesian language group.

Source: Adapted from FSM NDOE (2009: p. 6).

understood in the local vernacular languages of Micronesia and the Pacific quite differently from that of the outsider or settler community. This is an issue that covers both intra-tribal and inter-tribal relationships as well as local vs. foreigner or as in the case of Guam's Pagat, the mother country, the United States and its unincorporated territory.

Closely related to the earlier are challenges related to vernacular or indigenous languages and cultures. These are some of the most important signifiers of a defined group of people. In FSM, the NDOE has developed National Curriculum Minimum Standards in Vernacular Languages to grade 12. However, as recently as 2009 it was reported that 'the curriculum is not widely implemented or resourced and there is little instruction in local language beyond grade 3' (FSM NDOE, 2009: p. 7). While there is scope for improvement in the future, this will depend on how educators and policy makers prioritize such developments. Concerted support by local traditional leaders and chiefs as well as politicians will help further vernacular language development and curriculum implementation.

Moreover, the FSM has over 13 major languages or dialects, with every state having their own language or a number of languages and dialects. The FSM languages are spoken nowhere else in the world and they are part of the Proto-Austronesian Language family (Table 14.1).

Ballendorf alerts us to related epistemological challenges concerning indigenous education in Micronesia which concern the closed nature and availability of knowledge. He cites Workman and colleagues and notes that:

> Traditionally, Micronesians view knowledge as private not public property. People possessing special knowledge hold it carefully and do not share it openly

or arbitrarily. . . . Other members of the society would not attempt to copy the experts but would defer to their expertise. The masters would never promote themselves or offer free vocational advice. (Workman et al., 1981 in Ballendorf, 1993: p. 34)

While young people today may think differently about how knowledge is treated traditionally, aspects of traditional knowledge remain present and influential in both education and wider FSM society. Ballendorf thus goes on to suggest that there is a residue of tradition throughout Micronesian societies and in educational decisions, learning styles and Micronesian psychology. In times when the possessor of certain knowledge had to pass it along to others because of illness or old age, a careful selection process was undertaken for a successor. The heir was selected by consensus decision according to clan and family status as well as ability. Even after the selection was made and the apprenticeship started, the master would not tell all. To do that would have been to die. Hence, there were always areas of innovation and discovery as well as creativity for the new expert. Of course, the expert would never exercise full authority until the old master died (Ballendorf, 1993: p. 35).

Coordination between different levels of government

In 2009, the FSM NDOE Report noted a need for more systematic alignment between the National Government and State mandates maintaining that, 'Unfortunately some policy handbooks are out of date and are no longer being used to guide the operation of the SDOEs' (FSM NDOE, 2009: p. 9). The NDOE in Pohnpei thus depends on the cooperation of its State Departments of Education (SDOE) in implementing change and maintaining standards. In Yap, a management audit report also noted that the SDOE was in compliance for only 15 out of the 122 criteria derived from the State constitution, State Code and its own policy handbooks. This is a compliance rate of about 12.29 per cent (ibid.).

The quality of education and student achievement

The NDOE Report for 2009–2015 highlights poor student achievement, under-qualified teachers and loss of staff as the first three challenges faced by the system. This is further related to a perceived lack of relevance of education – evident in the emphasis on academic education to the detriment of vocational skills. Over

Table 14.2 Underachievement in maths in FSM

Year	Sixth grade Lg Art	Sixth grade Math	Eighth grade Lg Art	Eighth grade Math	Eighth grade Science	Tenth grade Lg Art	Tenth grade Math
2005	34%	17%	49%	35%		40%	13%
2008	23%	11%	44%	27%		32%	17%
2006					11%		
2008					2%		

Source: Adapted from FSM NDOE (2009: pp. 12–15).

recent years, education reports in the FSM have consistently reported that poor student achievement remains the number one challenge across the four States. The FSM National Minimum Competency Standards-Based test (NMTC) 2012 on reading and maths attest to this. Indeed, underachievement for indigenous and other island children, especially in Maths and English, is a particular challenge in FSM as it is across the Pacific Islands (see, e.g. Pene et al., 2002). Percentage passes in selected subjects can be seen in Table 14.2 which shows underachievement, except for tenth-grade Maths which improved by 4 per cent in 2008.

English proficiency is clearly a major challenge because it is the official language of the FSM; however, less than perhaps 2 per cent of FSM students are able to speak this fluently and most have limited English proficiency (FSM NDOE, 2009: p. 6). There is also the related issues of curriculum relevance, and encouraging all personnel to align their teaching to federal, national and state standards and guidelines remains one of the biggest challenges. This points to further professional issues that are raised in the next section.

Teacher professionalism and leadership

The quality of teachers is rightly seen as important for the success of children, and Darling-Hammond (2010: p. 194) notes that 'nations that have steeply improved their students' achievement, such as Finland, Korea, Singapore and others have attributed their success to their focused investments in teacher preparation and development'. This is also true for the FSM where since 2008 there has been a Teacher Certification Policy in place. However, according to FSP (FSM NDOE, 2009) only a fraction of teachers are currently certified. The (FSM) Congress Committee on Education thus noted on 3 June 2009 that only 41 teachers from a total of 1,974 (3.4%) were certified (FSM Standing Committee on Education, 2009).

Related to this is the fact that opportunities for the professional development of teachers are limited. Yap State evidences this by noting that:

> An audit of Yap State Department of Education found that the department offered a total of 2 training Courses in the year 2007–2008: 72 hours of computer training for 16 teachers . . . and 30 hours of Oral English training for 49 Grade 1&2 teachers and Principals. This represents training for 65 of the state's 376 teachers (83% received no training). (FSM NDOE, 2009: p. 16)

The FSM has also over the years shown fluctuating numbers of teaching staff, and at times a dramatic loss is clearly evident. For instance, numbers dropped from 2,255 in 2008 to 1,974 in 2009. In the same period Chuuk reported a loss of 47 teachers while Pohnpei lost 234. In addition to the availability of appropriate training and qualifications, there is an urgent need for the FSM to rethink how teachers are identified, rewarded and retained.

Another related challenge in FSM concerns the lack of good leadership. All interviewees for this study highlighted leadership at school and district level as weak, and, reflecting points raised earlier, a former principal emphasized that 'management boards in private schools tend to be run sometimes like family affairs, there is so much intervention by non-school concerns and this impacts the school leadership'. He went on to note that in many cases, leadership ethics seemed wanting and mismanagement of school finances can result. Many interviewees thus raised the need for the improved training of school leaders, with one noting 'the unfair hiring practices that school leaders and other people of influence have shown'. All interviewees therefore agreed that school leaders need to be more effectively trained on all matters of leadership, highlighting ethics, educational finance and professional conduct.

Data collection and reporting

The JEMCO 2011 (FSM NDOE, 2011) report draws attention to the challenges created by inadequate data collection and reporting, and this has been identified as a consistent problem in almost all JEMCO reports since 2005. Missing data, unreliable data and untimely submission of data all thus affect how funding and system weaknesses are understood and resolved. Thus, two of the four states report both private school and public school data. The other two do not. Hence data sets become incomplete, inconsistent and therefore unreliable. Another common challenge concerns the reporting or transfer of data from state level to the national office.

Community involvement

Interview findings also draw attention to the need for greater parent and community involvement, especially in curricular decisions. This has been a longstanding challenge worldwide (see for instance Stefy, 1991: pp. 363–364) and in FSM many interviewees identified this as a major problem. Thus, one experienced principal noted: 'It is minimal . . . this is a big problem . . . to get community participation is hard. People don't seem to care . . . only a handful of parents and community members show interest'. Reflecting the magnitude of this, two Micronesian teachers conferences held in 2011 addressed this problem and this continues to attract significant attention. Finally, two broader community challenges that deserve focused attention are identified by Pene et al. (2002: p. 1). The first is the lack of ownership by Pacific peoples of the formal education process. While the churches have succeeded in becoming integrated fully with the Pacific ways of life, education remains an alien process and is viewed by many Pacific peoples as something that is imposed from outside: an instrument designed to fail, exclude and marginalize the majority, and therefore irrelevant and meaningless to their way of life. The second relates to the impact of externally defined visions and goals of education. This includes the ongoing influence of centuries of colonialism and neo-colonialism that have an impact upon every aspect of island life. Ballendorf (1993), for example, draws specific attention to the impact of the Pacific War experience on islanders, maintaining that for most part this was traumatic and must be addressed in schools and higher education institutions.

Financial dependency

The high dependency of FSM on US funding creates its own sets of challenges. In 2008 for example, the Gross domestic product for FSM was 238.1 million (Pacific Islands Training Initiative, 2009). Out of this 23.9 per cent was derived from education grants, including the Education Sector Grant (ESG) and the Supplemental Education Grant (SEG) (FSM NDOE, 2008). The ESG and SEG are two major education funding sources in FSM. The SEG is treated as a federal education programme by the United States. Both grants are reviewed by the Honolulu office of the US Department of Interior's Office of Insular Affairs

Table 14.3 Education spending as a percentage of GDP

Country	Education Spending as a percentage of GDP
USA	4.8
Marshall Islands	11.8
Palau	10.3
FSM	23.93

Sources: FSM NDOE (2009: p. 10) and Central Intelligence Agency (n.d.).

(OIA) and the US Department of Education. The Honolulu OIA office serves as a secretariat for JEMCO (FSM NDOE, 2009: p. 7).

Bray and Packer (1993) among others have explained how an over dependence on aid tends to perpetuate a cycle of dependence where self-reliance can become lost in the quagmire of attempts to maintain continued support from donors of all types.

Prospects for new sources of funds remain bleak for the future, although in the light of uncertainties around the sustainability of COFA, new external players are increasingly visible and new arrangements, with or without the United States, may be possible. Dependency can certainly create a sense of helplessness and much anxiety is apparent in the FSM since COFA is expected to wane by 2023, less than a decade away. This means that future long-term strategic planning in education may have to depend on the capacity of the states and the national FSM government to generate new sources of finance. A related financial challenge concerns the poor return on educational expenditure. The FSM spends a considerable amount of its GDP on education (see Table 14.3) compared to other countries. For example, in 2009 it used 23.93 per cent of its GDP on education.

Priorities for education in FSM and Micronesia

In the light of the earlier assessment of contemporary educational challenges, it is now pertinent to consider future priorities. In doing so, it is helpful to begin with the five articulated national education priorities that, in the light of influence from the Millennium Development Goals for Education, are articulated by the FSM NDOE (2009) Report for 2009–2015.

These are to:

- improve the quality of learning in FSM;
- improve the quality of teaching in the FSM;

- consolidate performance monitoring and data-based decision-making systems;
- strengthen participation and the accountability of the education system to communities and
- ensure that education is relevant to the life and aspirations of the FSM people, meets manpower needs, improves lifelong learning, enables students to complete postsecondary education and assists in the economic and social development of the FSM.

Given these five wide ranging priorities for the FSM, key strategic and focused developments that are being pursued include improvements to: accreditation, teacher certification and professional development, data management and reporting, development of a Statewide System of Support, with particular focus on the state of Chuuk and improving access to vocational education opportunities for all students (FSM NDOE, 2009: p. 5).

In addition, building upon the work of researchers such as Kiribati academic, Teweiariki Teaero (2002: p. 79) and Konai Helu Thaman (1992), Professor of Education and UNESCO Chair of Teacher Education and Culture at USP, on culture-based thought patterns, pedagogy and what effective learning means in the Pacific, the FSM NDOE Report of 2009 also argued that: 'To preserve the culture and traditions for its people and to prepare them for communication with the world at large, the FSM seeks to develop a bilingual society' (FSM, NDOE, 2009: p. 7). Vernacular languages are therefore used for instruction up to grade 3 and this is envisaged to continue up to grade 12. Pohnpeian is one of the few languages of Micronesia that has a dictionary and a reference grammar; thus the Pohnpeian–English dictionary project remains a priority for Pohnpei DOE. As such, it has funded a 3-year dictionary project for further lexical input, digital conversion of database and easy online access of the dictionary worldwide. There are many other priorities for indigenous education in Micronesia (see Heine, 2002; Teaero, 2002) but progress will depend on FSM leaders and policy makers providing the resources needed to make change a reality. But realistic priorities are essential if success is to be achieved.

It is, therefore, argued that future educational priorities for the FSM must not be too numerous or ambitious. Fewer priorities stand a better chance of successful implementation, and interviewees for this study have already reported that there are far too many programmes and reforms in the educational system, and they fear that educational officials are swamped by constant attention to the need for associated data reporting. This draws further attention to the multiple roles that workers and government officers in small island states like the FSM have to carry out (see, for instance, Bray and Packer, 1993: pp. 75–92).

Prospects for the future

Looking to the future, there are many possible developments that may take place in the cultures and the cultural industries of our peoples in FSM, and these may depend to a large extent on the policy priorities of the national government and the four member states.

The Pacific Bilingual Bicultural Language Association (PIBBA) Chapters of FSM offers one possible boost to efforts to revitalize FSM's cultural heritages, languages and values, and especially for the elements which give people a strong sense of self and identity. Native Canadian scholar Marie Battiste (2000), writing on the postcolonial spaces that must be created for indigenous peoples, especially those formerly colonized, emphasizes that such communities must reclaim indigenous voice and vision in their educational processes. Such reclaiming requires consistent effort by local leaders, supported by regional efforts and examples from elsewhere where indigenous peoples are doing well in schools. FSM educational policy makers and planners at every level may also contribute in enhancing the communal development of cultures, cultural industries and vernacular languages.

The school curriculum in FSM does incorporate aspects of Micronesian cultures in terms of content. What may still need to be promoted is greater research on the epistemologies and pedagogies of Micronesia as well as the improved documentation of traditional knowledge related to the heritages of the people.

Pacific educator and Minister of Education in the Marshall Islands, Dr Hilda Heine advises:

> . . . a critical process must begin that forces Pacific islanders to become more aware of how we have internalized, accepted, and succumbed to Western knowledge, processes, and standards in our education systems, irrelevant as they may be. Part of the struggle to reconcile relevant Western standards, knowledge and processes vis-à-vis our way of life is ensuring that teacher education focuses on enhancing teachers' exposure to, and respect for local knowledge and skills, processes, values, and standards. . . . (2002: p. 89)

The beginning of 2014 heralded the start for the tenth FSM National JEMCO Education Indicators' Report, within which the FSM will have to report on 21 progress indicators to the JEMCO.

One positive development is the improvement in data Compliance to Standards. Prospects for the improvement of state compliance and efficient reporting of standards in education have been erratic for sometime, but as the 2009 NDOE report for 2009–2015 shows, there is some promise that prospects will be or can be better: 'The NDOE currently lacks a range of sanctions, positive or negative, to apply to SDOEs in the event of their success or failure in applying standards' (FSM NDOE, 2009: p. 9). It is envisaged that new sanctions may improve compliance, and there is real prospect in seeing a marked improvement in FSM data collection and reporting after the joint meeting between the education directors of the four states and the COM President and the adopted Resolution (FR 12–04) 'to enforce the submittal of verified data and authenticated reports to the National Government on education matters . . ' (FSM NDOE, 2013: p. 3). JEMCO similarly passed a resolution on the same ensuring that there is independent verification of the 21 performance indicators (RESOLUTION JEMCO 2012-MT-3) (ibid.).

Interviewees have also argued that more positive steps, including workshops on state data collection and on analysis and reporting mechanisms for state DOE officers established by the national DOE, may help. New incentives for improvement are similarly endorsed as possible avenues for improvement, including opportunities for training abroad, offers of scholarships for official qualifications on data analysis and information processing and support for practitioners to attend appropriate conferences.

It would appear, therefore, that while policy via resolutions will encourage better prospects for data collection and reporting on time, DOEs may also look simultaneously at personnel training, retraining and improved communication links and resourcing for state DOEs. Bray and Steward (1998: p. 11) nevertheless point to the difficulties involved in training and retaining qualified personnel in small states, which may not be able to afford to have the full range of specialists that bigger states appoint. Moreover, they also note that they cannot control the out migration of personnel that they have trained. In this respect, the allowance provided by COFA for FSM citizen migration to the United States remains in essence a double-edged sword. Migration can deprive the FSM of talented and ambitious young people and qualified personnel, although it can also generate substantial domestic income from remittances.

There are also prospects for the overall improvement of teacher qualifications. Thus, the FSM JEMCO Report of 2013 (FSM NDOE, 2013: p. 6) shows a decrease of 12 per cent for non-degree teachers between 2010–2011 and 2012–2013. Teachers with AA/AS grades show a 14 per cent increase and BA/BSc degrees show a 29 per cent increase in the 3 years (2011–2013). While the trend is positive, there remains a need for a nation-wide comprehensive framework for strengthening teaching, generating new resources in the system and improving training opportunities for both pre-service and in-service teachers.

Prospects are also improving with the better coordination and merging of small schools in order to consolidate resources and enhance efficiency. The FSM JEMCO Report of 2013 (FSM NDOE, 2013: p. 5) thus notes that:

> The count of schools with 50 or less students dropped significantly from SY 2010–2011 to SY 2012–2013. . . . Chuuk had a 12% decrease (58 schools with 50 or less student in SY 2010–2011 to 7 schools in SY 2012–2013). This was due to mergers of ECE with elementary schools and elementary schools with junior high schools.

High drop-out rates may also continue to be an issue for all four states. However, with increased parent and other stakeholder participation and involvement, it is possible that attendance will significantly increase. Another avenue may be to look at the possibility of building more boarding facilities so as to reduce overcrowding and the need for outer island students to stay with relatives. This is identified by four of the interviewees for this study as a key priority for the FSM, especially for outer-island students staying in urban centres like Weno on Chuuk or Colonia in Yap and Pohnpei. Only Kosrae has no outer islands.

Good leadership, improved teacher education and finding ways of retaining excellent teachers are vitally important for Micronesia and FSM. Student achievement may then see a marked improvement if more teachers are trained to a higher level, and parents and the community become more involved in education. These education systems do have to improve the quality of data that they generate for systematic planning. The debate about curriculum relevance also points to the need to establish successful vocational alternatives as opposed to sending all such candidates abroad, some of whom may not return. One possible prospect is the further development of the College of Micronesia into a fully fledged university or polytechnic with the linking of courses and programmes to other related regional and overseas institutions of higher education.

Overall, it is argued that the long-term prospects of education in the FSM, like the nation itself, will depend in a major way on the long-term strategic interests of the United States in the region. In addition, the FSM will have to address ways of widening options in terms of its donor profile. Such diversification will need to be negotiated carefully, although there is some evidence of this now happening with, for example, the provision of more scholarships by China.

Conclusions

This chapter discusses how the historical background and the contexts of colonialism and neo-colonialism have influenced the development of education in the FSM and Micronesia. It then considers the influence of islandness and smallness as frameworks for the identification and analysis of the challenges, priorities and prospects for education in the FSM and wider region. An important argument is made by Heine (2002: p. 88) who points to a process of decolonizing the mind for Pacific leaders. Implied throughout this chapter is a missing link of sorts, something is not gelling in terms of people and formal education. She suggests:

> We need to review how [our] western education systems alienate pacific Islanders from ownership and participation in the education process; denigrate traditional knowledge, values, skills and ways of learning; and impose standards that make education irrelevant to anything more than living a western lifestyle . . .
>
> Communities must regain and reclaim education, the ownership of schools, educational programs and curricula can be reorganized to a) emphasize language development in both written and oral skills with a push toward multilingualism; b) stress indigenous understanding of culture and history; past and present and focus on ways to address current issues; c) put in place curricula which are grounded in self determination, cultural self esteem, personal vision and passion; d) promote development of indigenous programs and practices which will significantly improve academic achievement and critical thinking skills, reduce absenteeism, and attrition, and reduce social problems among children and youth.

The FSM has successfully remained as a nation, in part due to the goodwill and way things are conducted by the four states in terms of unifying the nation. Much of this is due to the Micronesian and Pacific way of relationships, with deep respect for kinship. This may also help in the long-term if leadership, policy and strategies are jointly decided and implemented by the States with support from the NDOE in Palikir. While the four different states take time to develop and implement policy through consensus building at the national parliament in Palikir, they do carefully navigate their differences and commonalities as they build the nation that is FSM. Extending that special relationship to those of other islands in the Micronesian region may also be a way forward for all in meeting the challenges of education.

References

Baba, T. (1987), 'Academic Buccaneering Australian Style: The role of Australian Academics in the South Seas', *Directions: Journal of Educational Studies* 9(1), 3–11.

— (1989), 'The Business of Australian Aid, Training and Development'. Marjorie Smart Memorial Lecture, St Hilda's College, The University of Melbourne.

— (1992), 'Higher Education and the Development of Small States'. Keynote Address, Small States Higher Education Meeting. 14–18 June, Brunei.

Bacchus, K. and Brock, C. (1987), *The Challenge of Scale: Educational Development in the Small States of the Commonwealth*. London: Commonwealth Secretariat.

Ballendorf, D. A. (1993), 'Observations on Regional History and Micronesian Students', *Micronesian Educator* 4, 27–38.

Battiste, M. (2000), *Reclaiming Indigenous Voice and Vision*. Canada: UBC Press.

Bray, M. (1992), *Educational Planning in Small Countries*. Paris: UNSECO.

Bray, M. and Packer, S. (1993), *Education in Small Sates: Concepts, Challenges and Strategies*. Oxford: Pergamon Press.

Bray, M. and Steward, L. (1998), *Examination Systems in Small States: Comparative Perspectives on Policies, Models and Operations*. London: Commonwealth Secretariat.

Bretton Woods Project (2003), 'Poverty Reduction Paper (PRSP): A Rough Guide'. Available at: http://www.brettonwoodsproject.org/2003/04/art-16298/ (Accessed: 8 May 2014).

Central Intelligence Agency (n.d.), 'Country Comparison Education Expenditures', *World Fact Book*. Available at: https://www.cia.gov/library/publications/the-world-factbook/rankorder/2206rank.html?countryName=Micronesia,%20Federated%20States%20of&countryCode=fm&regionCode=au#fm (Accessed: 7 May 2014).

Coxon, E. (1996), *The Politics of Modernization in Western Samoan Education* (unpublished PhD thesis). Auckland: University of Auckland.

Coxon, E. and Taufe'ulungaki, A. (2003), *Global/Local Intersections: Researching the Delivery of Aid to Pacific Education*. Auckland: Research Unit for Pacific Education, The University of Auckland.

Crossley, M. (2010), 'Context Matters in Educational Research and International Development: Learning from the Small States Experience', *Prospects* 40(4), 421–429.

Darling-Hammond, L. (2010), *The Flat World and Education: How America's Commitment to Equity will Determine Our Future*. New York & London: Teachers College Press.

FSM NDOE (2008), *Federated States of Micronesia National JEMCO 20 Education Indicators Report*. Palikir, Pohnpei: National Department of Education.

— (2009), *Focused Strategic Plan 2009-2015*. Colonia, Pohnpei: National Department of Education.

— (2011), *Federated States of Micronesia National JEMCO 20 Education Indicators Report*. Palikir, Pohnpei: National Department of Education.

— (2013), *Federated States of Micronesia National JEMCO 21 Education Indicators Report*. Palikir, Pohnpei: National Department of Education.

FSM Standing Committee on Education (2009), *Federated States of Micronesia Standing Committee Report*. Palikir: Federated States of Micronesia Congress. Available at: http://www.fsmcongress.fm/pdf%20documents/16th%20Congress/Committee%20 Reports/SCR%2016-09.pdf (Accessed: 5 May 2014).

Heine, H. (2002), 'A Marshall Islands Perspective', in F. Pene (ed.), *Tree of Opportunity: Rethinking Pacific Education*. Suva, Fiji: Institute of Education, The University of the South Pacific, pp. 83–89.

Hickling-Hudson, A. (2002), 'Revisioning for the Inside: Getting under the Skin of the World Bank Sector Strategy', *International Journal of Educational Development* 22(6), 565–577.

Nabobo-Baba, U., Naisilisili, T., Bogitini, S., Baba, T. and Lingam, G. (2012), *Rural & Remote Schools in Udu, Fiji: Vanua, Indigenous Knowledge, Development and professional Support for Teachers & Education*. Suva, Fiji: University of the South Pacific-FALE & Native Academy Publishers.

Pacific Islands Training Initiative (2009), *Federated States of Micronesia Fiscal Year 2008 Economic Review*, Palikir: US Department of the Interior Office of Insular Affairs. Available at: https://www.spc.int/PRISM/country/fm/stats/Economic/FSM_ EconReview_FY08_wStats.pdf (Accessed: 7 May 2014).

Pene, F., Taufeu'lungaki, A. and Benson, C. (eds) (2002), *Tree of Opportunity: Rethinking Pacific Education*. Suva, Fiji: Institute of Education, University of the South Pacific.

Quanchi, M. (1991), *The Pacific in the 20th Century – Pacific People and Change*. UK: Cambridge University Press.

Sanga, K., Chu, C., Hall, C. and Crowl, L. (eds) (2005), *Rethinking Aid Relationships in Pacific Education*. NZ: He Parekereke, VUW.

Shaw, B. (1982), 'Smallness, Islandness, Remoteness and Resources: An Analytical Framework', in B. Higgins (ed.), *Regional Development in Small Nations*. Japan: UN Centre for Regional Development, pp. 95–109.

Stefy, B. E. (1991), 'Community Participation', in A. Lewy (ed.), *The International Encyclopedia of Curriculum*, pp. 363–364.

Teaero, T. (2002), 'Old Challenges, New Responses to Educational Issues in Kiribati', in F. Pene (ed.), *Tree of Opportunity: Rethinking Pacific Education*. Suva, Fiji: Institute of Education The University of the South Pacific, pp. 72–82.

Thaman, H. K. (1992), 'Looking Towards the Source: A Consideration of Cultural Context in Teacher Education', in C. Benson and N. Taylor (eds), *Pacific Teacher Education Forward Planning Meeting Proceedings*. Suva, Fiji: The University of the South Pacific, pp. 98–105.

Thomas, R. M. (1984), 'The US Trust Territory of the Pacific Islands (Micronesia)', in R. M. Thomas and T. N. Postlethwaite (eds), *Schooling in the Pacific Islands: Colonies in Transition*, Oxford: Pergamon Press, pp. 67–107.

Wenkam, R. and Baker, B. (1971), *Micronesia. The Breadfruit Revolution*. Honolulu: East-West Centre.

Pacific Island Countries: Improving Educational Reach with Information and Communications Technology

Govinda Ishwar Lingam, Shikha Raturi and Kisione Finau

Introduction

Information and Communications Technology (ICT) is now regarded as an indispensable driving force in speeding up developments in all sectors of a nation's economy, including education. Over the years, developments in ICT have proliferated, with tremendous impacts. However, these development benefits apply unevenly in certain contexts, especially in Pacific Islands Countries (PICs). This chapter looks at the provision of ICT in improving educational reach in the PICs served by The University of the South Pacific (USP). It discusses both the opportunities and the challenges small island nations face in keeping abreast of escalating ICT developments. USP is used as a case study to illustrate its involvement, services and continuous efforts towards ICT integration in education. Finally, this chapter looks at the future possibilities for these island states to take advantage of ICT in improving educational access for as many students as possible regardless of their location and available time.

ICT growth and targets

The rapid progress in growth and development in ICT has contributed to a new global economy powered by technology, fuelled by information and driven by knowledge. To take full advantage of the power of ICT, people across the world, in particular in PICs, need to learn about, adapt to and embrace it. Commentators have highlighted the great potential of ICT and the many opportunities it brings with it to improve the situation of the populace, not through economic development alone but through its potential to transform the society in manifold ways. The buzzwords characterizing these fundamental changes in economic and social spheres include the *learning society* and the *knowledge economy* (OECD, 1999).

Trends in developing countries have clearly shown the potential of ICT for transforming the economy (Blurton, 1999; Larson, 2000; Africa Partnership Forum, 2008; Nwosu and Ogbomo, 2008; Ezell, 2012; UN Report, 2012; Menefee and Bray, 2013). Most users of ICT currently live in the United States, Europe and Asia with fewer than a quarter residing outside these regions, the Pacific included (Blurton, 1999; Larson, 2000; Khuong Vu, 2005). While the trend continues to grow globally, much remains to be desired in the Pacific (ITU Report, 2013). Human resources and training in ICT integration in education in the Pacific region also present a characteristically fluid situation.

Nabobo-Baba (2008) focusing on accessibility and Thaman (2001) on quality of distance education (DE) have highlighted two factors as crucial for improving these areas:

- human resource and economic development in the Pacific, considering the number who emigrate every year from, for example, Fiji (Baba, 1997), a continuing trend which has since 2008 stabilized (Bureau of Statistics, Fiji, 2013)
- integration of technology and training in schools and higher education (Horsley, 1984; UNESCO, 1993; Thaman, 2001; Bakalevu, 2005; Johansson-Fua, 2005; Puamau, 2005; Nabobo-Baba, 2008; Sharma, 2008, 2009; Whelan, 2008).

With reference to ICT and its impact in developing countries:

> [ICTs have great potential to] facilitate the acquisition and absorption of knowledge, offering developing countries unprecedented opportunities to enhance educational systems, improve policy formulation and execution, and widen the range of opportunities for business and the poor. One of the greatest hardships endured by the poor, and by many others who live in the poorest countries, is their sense of isolation, and to open access to knowledge in ways unimaginable not long ago. (Blurton, 1999: p. 9)

PICs look to two international reports to help them establish targets and goals for their ICT development. On the one hand, the first report, Core ICT Indicators (2010), is a joint effort by various international organizations led by the International Telecommunication Union (ITU) to develop a set of ICT indicators in a non-technical style to suit a broad audience. The report targets policy makers and official statisticians, especially from developing countries, highlighting the importance of using a range of technologies in the developing countries, which seems germane to the status of ICT in PICs. The indicators for ICT infrastructure and access, use of ICT in education are of particular importance to PICs. On the other hand, the World Telecommunication/ICT Development Report (2010) is a mid-term review focusing on monitoring the World Summit on Information Society (WSIS) targets. It highlights 'connecting universities, colleges, secondary schools and primary schools with ICT' as target 2 to be achieved by 2015. This target recognizes the multiple benefits of providing access to ICT infrastructure within the education system while acknowledging the need to have both old and new technologies in place for their effective potential for delivering educational content. It is noticeable that none of the PICs, except for Nauru, has contributed to this report, leading many to speculate that perhaps we are not doing enough ourselves, or we do not report our views clearly enough. This report rightly states:

> Setting targets and measuring progress in the area of ICTs in education involves a balancing act between identifying quantifiable information to monitor international goals, on the one hand, and taking into account the heterogeneity of national circumstances, on the other. (World Telecommunication/ICT Development Report, 2010: p. 40)

A sea of islands: The PIC context

PICs are made up of anywhere from one to hundreds of quite small islands, most of them with only limited resources for economic development. The island states, many of which receive detailed attention in this volume, include but are not limited to Cook Islands, Federated States of Micronesia (FSM), Fiji, French Polynesia, Guam, Kiribati, Marshall Islands, Nauru, New Caledonia, Niue, Palau, Papua New Guinea, Samoa, Solomon Islands, Tonga, Tokelau, Tuvalu, Vanuatu and Wallis and Futuna. In relation to land mass, all these states fall within the category of 'small states' or small island developing states (SIDS) (Matthewson, 1994; UNESCO, n.d.). On the one hand, Nauru and Niue have only one island each, Cook Islands has 15, Vanuatu 80 islands, Papua New Guinea and Fiji more than 300 each and Solomon Islands more than 400. Tokelau, on the other hand, consists of three atolls and Marshall Islands, 32. While Fiji's largest island is approximately 18,500 square kilometres, the total above sea-level area of

Tokelau is only 11.2 square kilometres. Yet even the largest islands are dwarfed by the immensity of the ocean over which they are scattered, about one-third of the globe's surface. The distances between islands in PICs can vary from 20 km to 3,500 km, and within the EEZs, national sizes belie the disproportionately tiny land masses, many of which barely emerge above the high-tide sea level. The linguistic profile is complex too, with hundreds of languages that are used in these islands; however, English as a second (or more) language is a common denominator for the majority of Pacific Islanders. Overall, the PICs covering the enormous body of ocean, are characterized by their wide-ranging diversity – not least, geographical, economic, social, cultural, linguistic, historical, political, and in educational development. Jenkins's description is apt:

> Vast tracks of ocean divided up into jigsaw-like geometric shapes and appearing to cover a sizeable proportion of the surface of planet earth. The many islands appear almost a scattering dot . . . a region so diverse and disparate in its communities and cultures, and [provision of any services in such a scattered geographical context is a mammoth challenge]. (Jenkins, 1993: p. 19)

The size (or lack of it) of most of these island nations means they face severe financial constraints in their efforts to make headway with any developments, ICT notable among them: dependence on foreign aid to help improve various sectors of the economy, including ICT provision and development, seems inescapable, and for most of them, constriction of financial resources ensures that development is aid-bound and aid-driven (Sanga, 2005).

ICT in PICs

Clearly, geography and small economies have greatly impeded PICs in their efforts to take full advantage of developments in ICT. On their own, it would be difficult for most of them to provide ongoing support for ICT development and spread its benefits to all people irrespective of where they live; yet various initiatives and efforts have been made to maximize the use of ICTs in education in the region.

Preparation for ICT

The Pacific ICT Outreach (PICTO) under the Economic Development Division of the Secretariat of the Pacific Community (SPC) has embarked on awareness of ICT as a national priority (Pacific News Centre, 2012). PICTO conducted workshops in Niue, Marshall Islands and Palau (SPC, n.d.) for the benefit of parliament members. Similarly, in Samoa PICTO, through the European Union-funded project 'Information and Communication Technology Access for the Poor: Improving Access to ICT by informing and engaging Pacific ACP Legislators' was able to train staff of the Legislative Assembly and also provided two computers, a printer and two uninterruptable power supply; small projects like this help too. Likewise, Tuvalu sought assistance from AusAID and under the Tuvalu Australia Education Support Project (TAESP) helped to improve ICT infrastructure. Tuvalu, like most other countries, continues to lag behind in capacity building in ICT.

Some countries have established ICT learning centres with the help of community and school partnerships. In Solomon Islands, the People's First Network (PFNet) and Youth First Computer Centre are shining examples of school–community collaboration in ICT development. The PFNet is quite successful and there are plans to replicate the idea in other countries in the region. One Laptop Per Child (OLPC),[1] a non-profit education project, has seen a range of results in its implementation process across the world; the same has happened in PICs too. Professor Nicholas Negroponte, the project's founder, with his team of experts from academia and industry, developed a robust and energy-efficient laptop 'xo' at media labs in Massachusetts Institute of Technology (MIT), USA. The project aims to empower the children of developing countries to learn by providing one connected laptop to every school-age child. The implementation of this project in PICs, though, has not followed the concept of OLPC; for instance, the schools in Fiji have one xo laboratory per school instead. OLPC donated xo between 20 and 500 laptops to each of eight island nations in 2008 (Cook Islands, Kiribati, Niue, Papua New Guinea, Samoa, Solomon Islands, Tonga and Vanuatu). Overall, Fiji, Marshall Islands and Solomon Islands have embraced the project far more than other countries; their MoEs made arrangements for teacher training on the xo machine, setting up xo computer laboratory and ensuring each class in the school gets an opportunity to learn with xo. This positive climate of technology adoption could also be attributed to strong collaboration between various stakeholders on the OLPC project.

Private sector initiative

In 2007, the Fiji arm of the Bank of the South Pacific (BSP) kick-started the OLPC project in Fiji by donating 800 xo laptops to the Ministry of Education

(MoE), Fiji for distribution to a selected group of primary schools; USP has joined hands with MoE Fiji by signing a Memorandum of Understanding (MoU) to assist with a pilot project with three schools. Under this MoU, the School of Education (SOE) in USP provided training to primary teachers on the xo laptop for a period of 6 months leading up to the launch of the project on 22 March 2013. A total of 33 primary teachers from three pilot schools (recipients in the first lot of 800 donated laptops) is now equipped with necessary pedagogical and technical skills to integrate ICT into their learning and teaching practices. There is an expectation that inclusion of an xo laptop in learning (each child gets an opportunity to work with xo twice a week in the school laboratory that hosts 30 xo laptops) will increase numeracy and literacy in the three pilot schools. It has been a historical undertaking for the MoE, for this will be the start of the technological era in primary education. The project has illustrated the importance of a good partnership (BSP, MOE and USP) in the successful implementation of a project. It is good to note that the MoE Fiji has rolled out a 5-year plan with the first round of purchase of laptops for FJD1.3 million ($800,000 approved by Cabinet and $500,000 will be sourced from within the Tuition Grant to Schools). This phase will extend the OLPC project by providing xo laptops to 30 primary school children and training their teachers. The 5-year plan speaks of reaching out to all the rural schools in Fiji (email correspondence with Narain Sharma, MoE, Fiji, 5 April 2013). This will surely be an interesting development to follow.

Prior to the Fiji launch, OLPC was officially introduced in the Republic of Marshall Islands (RMI) by the Minister of Education, Dr Hilda Heine, in January 2013. Delap Elementary School is the first school in RMI to receive and use the xo laptops. Once again overseas aid initiated the OLPC, Marshall Islands project; 1,000 xo laptops were purchased under the Compact Supplemental Education Grant Fund. In the case of Vanuatu, the MoE has requested the SOE at USP to facilitate training for their primary teachers: bachelor of education in-service primary teachers based at Port-Vila Campus are being trained on the xo-laptop for OLPC. At the time of writing, Tuvalu, Samoa and Kiribati are also looking to USP for teacher training to support their OLPC projects.

The introduction of OLPC laptops will no doubt enhance the learning environment in the classrooms. There is already evidence that three primary schools in OLPC Fiji Pilot project are beginning to see increased attendance, improved behavioural attitudes, from a state of euphoria in the first week to sustained levels of motivation and interest among the children (Raturi, personal observation). However, only time and research will tell if the xo intervention (one xo lab per school) will have an impact on the cognitive and behavioural domain of these students. A longitudinal research study to inform the stakeholders of the progress and challenges is currently under consideration for Fiji with an intention to extend to other PICs to generate locally grounded evidence for the region.

ICT-integrated pedagogies

Universities and MoEs acknowledge the need to support teacher training in ICT for its successful integration in education. This is already evident from USP and MoE Fiji's partnership for the OLPC Fiji project. Horsley (1988) was sounding the alert on the need for teacher training in the use of computers as early as 1988 and efforts are still being made in this direction. A UNESCO report also highlighted the role of teachers and students in the integration of ICT in education. This UNESCO Bangkok Report (2004: p. 104) on Asia–Pacific states, 'When teachers perceive ICT as a tool to meet curricular goals, they are more likely to integrate ICT in their lessons'.

The research study in 2004 (Williams et al., 2004) reaffirmed this, reporting that two-thirds of the teachers interviewed in the region had learnt to teach Computer Science on their own and 85 per cent of all the teachers wanted to learn online if opportunities were available. Williams and co-authors recommended initiating seamless use of ICT in all subjects in schools as well as use of ICT as a teaching aid to alleviate teacher shortages (ibid.). The UNESCO Bangkok Report (2004: p. 106) also says, 'Equipping students with ICT skills facilitates the effective integration of ICT in schools'.

Thus, the Pacific Regional Initiatives for the Delivery of basic Education (PRIDE) project with donor aid (EU) of € 8 million for a period of 5 years is credited with having achieved a number of outcomes: one of them is developing the curriculum in ICT and ICT-related professional development for teachers in the 12 member countries of USP along with some other PICs such as Papua New Guinea. Schools embracing ICT education in their curricula together with governments indicating interest by developing ICT plans (Thaman, 2001; Bakalevu, 2005; Johansson-Fua, 2005; Sharma, 2008 as cited in Raturi, 2010) are very important elements for the sustainability of ICT in education. Overall, the scenarios in PIC schools show promise but there is still a long way to go.

While all these initiatives are a clear indication of PICs incorporating ICT in learning and teaching practices for the good of children's education, they also spotlight the financial dependence on donors/overseas aid agencies and raise questions about the long-term sustainability of such projects. Most of the countries' support initiatives are funded by aid agencies but the countries themselves have not managed to sustain the momentum. Lingam (2010) reported the ICT situation in Vanuatu schools where teachers felt it was limited to only a few urban schools. In remote rural areas – all too typical in Solomon Islands and Vanuatu – lack of power supply is a major hindrance to ICT services such as the internet. Since this could widen instead of narrow the digital divide, there is a strong need to support viable ICT projects in rural parts of the PICs as well as in the main towns and cities. In the authors' work experience, even the urban areas in most of the PICS have intermittent supply of power and this affects their ICT services. For instance, this is quite common in Solomon Islands and the Honiara USP campus (the 'high end' of the Solomon Islands picture) has to depend on a local generator for power supply in order to keep the ICT services operational which in turn increases the overall cost of ICT implementation.

Country reports, such as 'ICT in Secondary Education in the Pacific Region: Status, Trends and Prospects' (2005) indicate many common problems faced by island nations in the Pacific, specifically, financing, lack of suitable infrastructure and lack of developed human capacity in ICT. Also, these challenges are further compounded by the lack of government initiatives and concerted effort in formulating policies for promoting and sustaining ICT development. In this regard, seeking help from various agencies offers one-way forward. The SPC together with other aid agencies has over the years been assisting regional countries in creating awareness and support for ICT development. In the majority of the PICs – including RMI, Niue and Tonga – ICT literacy programmes are available from a variety of ICT training providers, to up-skill students in their quest for ICT knowledge. At the same time, in countries such as Cook Islands, Fiji, Niue, Tonga and Vanuatu ICT programmes form part of the national curriculum at the secondary school level (ICT Capacity Building at USP Project, 2005).

The Asian Development Bank provided financial assistance to Tonga to set up a submarine cable system in 2011, and this provides high-speed internet access as well as improving accessibility to information and various ICT services. Overall, such an initiative will contribute towards economic growth and also allow ICT-based education to develop (Baselala, 2011). This project was launched by King Tupou VI on 21 August 2013 (Tonga Online, 2013).

ICT infrastructure

The ICT infrastructure varies across PICs with Fiji being the most developed in terms of access to tools and technology along with the technological experience.

Reddy (1989) reiterated the need for the use of relevant technology for education: considering the varied technological infrastructure across PICs, this remains a subject of much concern even today. The important debate is to what extent does technology mean utilizing radio (Reddy, 1989), or using the internet to enable online and blended modes of delivery (Raturi et al., 2011a) to educate students in isolated and distant islands, or all of these options combined retaining old technology (Johansson-Fua, 2005; Raturi, 2012a). A 2012 report (Internet World Statistics, 2012) on internet penetration and users in Oceania/Australia indicates considerable disparity among PICs and their population. The same report points out an increase in the number of internet users and penetration in all island nations. On the one hand, the smallest and least populated – Tokelau (1,331 according to December 2012 statistics) with only 66 internet users in December 2000 – had 800 internet users in June 2012. On the other hand, Fiji with a population of 890,057 (as of December 2012) had only 7,500 internet users in December 2000, which increased to 247,275 internet users (as of June 2012). This suggests that the increasing popularity of ICT in PICs will make it progressively easier and more necessary for educational institutions to integrate ICT into education.

The USP and ICT developments

The majority of the tertiary institutions across PICs are struggling with maximizing the ICT potential to improve their education accessibility and quality. However, USP is at the forefront in leveraging technology for tertiary education. All the tertiary institutions across PICs, in particular USP, have been transformed in their ICT integration in education. The USP serves as an excellent case study since it is a regional university that serves its 12 member countries (Cook Islands, Fiji Islands, Kiribati, Marshall Islands, Nauru, Niue, Samoa, Solomon Islands, Tokelau, Tonga, Tuvalu and Vanuatu), providing insights to the status of ICT in education across the region.

The complex and unique composition of USP enables it to make an impact that is even stronger and wider and goes beyond PICs to help connect the region to Australia, New Zealand and the international community. USP has so far been the key player tackling the varied infrastructure and human resource in ICT and education across the various PICs while offering its services to the island nations. It has long offered education to via distance mode (print-based) as well as traditional face-to-face mode. ICTs have been integrated not only in DE as a means to provide 'Education for All' (EFA) but also in the traditional face-to-face mode with the aim of increasing accessibility. However, the geographical diversity of island nations is such that catering to everyone's educational needs remains a daunting challenge. Although USP has made every effort to overcome this, more efforts are still needed in this direction. 'EFA' still remains an 'unfinished agenda' at USP just as it is for UNESCO (Qian Tang, UNESCO website, 2013). Understanding the context – the spread and diversity of the sea of islands and populations that USP serves – is critical for the strategies and tactics for optimizing the potential of ICT to contribute in meaningful ways to the educational development of PICs.

ICT and DE

USP started from humble beginnings in 1968 with technologies that assisted its various functions. On-campus teaching was face to face and print- (often photocopy) and library-based. DE (labelled extension services) was also print-based, with face-to-face tutorials in scattered local centres where feasible. The addition of satellite facilities to the armoury for audio meetings and tutorials was an exciting breakthrough in the 1970s. In the 1990s, USP centres were equipped with limited audio–video play back facilities and a satellite tutorial room for teleconferencing in order to provide an avenue for face-to-face interaction for DE students. However, this has limitations in terms of flexibility and moreover it can hardly provide quality interaction. It becomes imperative to tackle this issue considering the exponential increase in the DE enrolments (Wallace, 1990; Baba, 1997; Lingam and Burnett, 2008; Sharma, 2008; Rao et al., 2011). Traditional face-to-face classrooms at USP have undergone tremendous transformation along with the print-based DE. This includes a makeover from overhead projector to sophisticated multimedia systems, use of a home-grown Course Management System (CMS) such as Class Shares[2] to standard CMS such as WebCT, and Moodle 2.0, giving rise to the possibility of blended and online modes of delivery. ICT has played a critical role in USP's DE programme since it started in the early 1970s, transforming the educational quality year after year. This is evident in the fact that USP started with six print-based DE courses in 1971 and by 2011 the numbers rose to 330 out of which 29.6 per cent utilize Moodle (Rao et al., 2011).

Prasad (1993) made a point of cost given the average duty-free price for a small IBM computer (single disk drive) and dot-matrix printer at over FJD2500, while discussing financial, human and policy constraints as major obstacles in expansion of ICT-integrated education. Not only computers are much cheaper and more affordable now but the variety in computing machines has increased the options for students and teachers. The authors compare the scenario in 2007 when very few laptops were seen among students at USP Laucala Campus to 2012 when larger numbers of students own a laptop, netbook and even tablet. Just as netbook proved to be a cheaper option to laptops, cheaper versions of tablets are now seen in the market, which will undoubtedly capture students' attention. An increase in student numbers owning a mobile device is a rapidly emerging scenario. In a case study of postgraduate students at the SOE in USP, Raturi et al. (2011a) found that the majority of the students regardless of their age had access to a computer and very good experience with technology. It is noted that the participants in the study were professional and had been studying at USP for a few years. The participants in this study are termed 'digital adapters' (Raturi et al., 2011a) who have shown willingness to embrace technology and are at par with the 'net-generation'.

The use of ICT that was deemed essential for DE at USP has now become the backbone of the education system at USP right from administration to research, learning and teaching. However, reliable telecommunications infrastructure and ICT policies in all PICs will help USP and other tertiary institutions with the integration of ICT in education at all levels. The implementation of optic fibre cable (which has been in the planning stage for a few years now) with country policies in ICT will enhance progress in this direction. It should be noted that the USP Strategic Plan 2013–2018 (2013) has committed to ICTs as one of its seven priority areas, which should help greatly with the prioritization of ICT infrastructure, policies and its integration in education at the tertiary level in the South Pacific region.

USP is credited in the region for pioneering the use of satellite technology for student support, especially for the DE as well as for all other communication and information transfer through USPNet, and has made continuous effort since. This has been a remarkable ICT journey for USP. USPNet, the telecommunications umbrella of the university, has helped bridge the digital divide in the region. The Pan-Pacific Education and Communication Experiments by Satellite (PEACESAT) on Applications Technology Satellite-1 (ATS-1) is the first enterprise to assist USPNet with ICT support for their educational needs in PICs. According to the PEACESAT website: 'The Pan-Pacific Education and Communication Experiments by Satellite (PEACESAT) has been working to lessen the ICT divide in the Pacific Islands region for over 30 years' (PEACESAT 2013).

USP and other tertiary institutions in the region have made use of PEACESAT to increase their educational and administrative support. It is important to note that NASA, Carnegie Corporation and USAID provided vital support for this venture. After a brief breakdown of USPNet due to non-functional ATS-1, it recouped its services with the help of INTELSAT in 1986; support came from Project share signatories and Cable and Wireless Public Limited (Hong Kong). In the early 1990s, USPNet was able to connect Cook Islands, Fiji, Solomon Islands, Tonga and Vanuatu, giving them direct access to satellite space segment. On the one hand, these five countries got the support from their national carriers (Telecom Cook Islands, Fiji Post and Telegraph, Solomon Islands Telekom, Tonga Telecommunication Commission and Telecom Vanuatu) along with international carriers such as Cable and Wireless Public Limited, Fiji International Telecommunications Limited (FINTEL) and Telecom New Zealand. On the other hand, Nauru, Niue, Tokelau, Tuvalu and (Western) Samoa were connected with USPNet via HF radio relay. Marshall Islands and Kiribati, however, were not connected with USPNet during this period due to their poor infrastructure and lack of support from their national carrier.

USPNet, telephone and facsimile provided USP much needed support for its administrative tasks such as meetings with campus and centre directors/managers and extension studies and DE communications. The advances made by USPNet together with its point-to-point communication in the early 1990s helped DE students in the region in particular, providing opportunity to schedule meetings and classes at any time of the week. While radio broadcast and satellite tutorials helped deal with the 'isolation factor' to some extent, many communities in the region still could not receive radio broadcasts and lacked electricity, making USP's efforts even more difficult. It was a common practice to produce tapes of simulated tutorials with students as actors asking likely questions (a sort of video tutorial with FAQs) and distribute them to the remote places in the region to provide students some degree of 'interaction'.

A result of the Renwick Report (Renwick et al., 1991) that illustrated the challenges faced by DE in PICs was the formation of the Telecommunications Policy Group, which was responsible for pushing the agenda for a better upgraded communication system (Chandra, 2000). As a result, USPNet 2000 was launched on 30 March 2000 with support from Japan, Australia, New Zealand and the USP (Chandra, 2000). This began USP's move towards acquiring state-of-the-art ICTs suited for twenty-first century pedagogical styles. This comprises providing full internet services to all centres and campuses in the 12 member countries (initially via Fiji Commercial internet services and by 2005 via Australian

Academic Research Network (AARNET), integrated full-duplex voice, data and video capabilities, associated learning technologies and infrastructure at the campuses and centres, opening doors for live lecture transmission) (Evans and Hazelman, 2006; Chandra et al., 2011). The euphoria of testing and reaching out for greater frontiers such as audio–video conferencing slowly started diminishing due to insufficient management of bandwidth by the mid-2000s, and USP Council once again stepped in to look for more cost-effective and reliable solutions (Chandra et al., 2011).

During the process of writing this chapter, and with regard to costs, Kisione Finau (Director, Information Technology Services at USP) remarked, 'While employing of AARNet was an expensive exercise for USP (paying FJD120,000 per annum to Fintel and Telecom Fiji each up until 2011) but it helped break the monopoly in the telecommunication sector when the market was deregulated in 2012. A new contract was thus negotiated and USP then stopped paying this royalty from 2012 onwards'.

This helped, but not to the full extent: the internet costs in PICs are still expensive and the connection between USP and member countries is also not reliable:

> The undersea cable market has been developing. Fiji has been the best cable-connected ACP Pacific country since 2001 as one of the landing sites for the Southern Cross Cable, and undersea cable costs from Fiji to the US and to Australia are now less than a twentieth of what they were a decade ago . . . [but] cost of access to undersea cable infrastructure [in Pacific Islands] remains high by world standards. (ACP-Connect Pacific Report, 2012: pp. 25–26)

USPNet was converted into an Internet Protocol (IP)-based system in 2006 allowing all communication and data exchange through internet technologies (Whelan and Bhartu, 2007). Since 2010, USPNet has improved tremendously. It was designed to establish technical efficiency and platforms provide a regional server solution for five major regional campuses and launch a more reliable audio–video conferencing platform such as REACT[3] (Chandra et al., 2011). Even though the satellite network went through a major upgrade resulting in a faster, more stable and efficient USPNet with better quality service to the region, it was still not able to reach out to the remote islands; USP opted for Ku-band network in 2011 (which was otherwise not possible with its C-band service). This incremental improvement on USPNet has enabled USP to integrate ICTs in its learning and teaching since 2000 in a way that opened the door for elearning, online learning and twenty-first century ICT-integrated pedagogies at large.

The course material and notifications to students at USP now started making use of ICTs instead of a paper base. Since 2000, USP began to use the CMS Class Shares, allowing the teaching faculty to upload PowerPoint Presentations, Word documents and other course materials for lectures and tutorials, a test and exam papers repository and messages and notifications. The limitation of Class Shares was its one-way communication and inability to notify students via email, as materials were uploaded on it. The use of WebCT followed, opening doors for a variety of pedagogical techniques for teaching faculty to experiment with but it had to be discontinued in 2007 due to its high licensing costs. However, WebCT demonstrated the importance of synchronous and asynchronous modes of interaction, which soon generated debates and impressed upon educators the need to review their pedagogical practices (Menrad, 2004). The use of ICTs made teaching and learning processes at USP more transparent than before, uploading course materials and using discussion forums on the CMS. The *ICT Capacity Building Project* funded by the Japanese government (2002–2004) was instrumental in improving USPNet and starting the elearning era at USP. Japanese International Cooperation Agency (JICA) experts were brought in to develop a number of courses in Computer Science and Information Systems. This also had a significant impact on courses that were developed by the Centre of Flexible and Distance Learning (CFDL). CFDL courses started making use of multimedia technologies as they began converting print-based DE courses to elearning mode (Chandra et al., 2011).

The recent rise of elearning

All sorts of experimentation bubbled away in PICs and the stock pot of USP in mid-2000s. Moodle was selected and used, mainly by the School of Computing, Information and Mathematical Sciences in the early days, while the Faculty of Arts and Law (now the Faculty of Arts, Law and Education) utilized EDISON (a customized Plone-based Content Management System), and WebCT was hosting courses in education and other disciplines. With funding limitations, Free and Open Source Software (FOSS) seemed to be the most plausible solution and Moodle was adopted as the new LMS in 2007 (Rajneel Totaram, Centre for Flexible Learning (CFL), USP, personal Communication, 2013). This transformed the education scene at USP. By 2007, USP was leading the region in ICT-integrated pedagogies, offering courses in four delivery modes: online, blended, face-to-face and print-based DE. By 2008, the Senior Management Team (SMT) at the USP Chancellor's Office became very supportive of

ICT-integrated education. This is reflected in the Strategic Plan 2013–2018 and by a number of recent initiatives, including: new staff training opportunities in Moodle, the sole CMS since 2010, at which time USP phased out Class Shares; incentives for the development of fully online courses and investment in Ku-band satellite, REACT and other ICT-related areas (since 2008). The fact that USP had no course offered fully online in 2007, one fully online in 2009 and then an impressive rise to 60 courses fully online offered in 2012 (Varunesh Rao, CFL, USP, personal communication, 7 February 2013) says it all. Even face-to-face courses utilize Moodle for uploading lectures and making announcements, which has helped increase interaction in a face-to-face course, enhancing the quality of education to a certain extent.

As Whelan and Bhartu (2007) pointed out, Moodle proved to be best suited for USP for its overall usability, reliability and functionality. Post-2008, Moodle gained further momentum with increased online pedagogical practices that made use of various tools such as assignment drop box, discussion forums, quizzes and lectures uploaded in various formats (PowerPoint presentation, Word documents, audio files, videos, etc.). USP-SMT pushed to make use of Moodle as the platform to upload course content and resources for learning and teaching for nearly all courses regardless of the mode of delivery. Rao et al. (2011) reported that 72.9 per cent of USP courses were on Moodle in 2011 as opposed to a 5 per cent in 2007 and 12.6 per cent in 2008. The perception of students and USP teaching staff has also changed over the years, with an increase in the proportion of students and staff comfortable with or even preferring the use of ICT integrated pedagogies. Raturi et al. (2011b) reported that in a case study at USP, nearly 80 per cent of learners (at the postgraduate level) preferred the Virtual Learning Environment (VLE) that made use of Moodle to varying degrees (blended and online delivery modes). Interestingly, Raturi et al. (2011b) found in their case study that convenience and flexibility were given as the most common reasons for the preference for VLE, and Menrad (2004), in another case study at USP, also reported a similar preference. However, more research into pedagogical practices of online learning and elearning in PICs is still necessary, as the learning and teaching context is not only diverse across the Pacific region but also different from the rest of the world.

At USP, while innovative methods are being utilized in the areas of elearning and mlearning (mobile learning) to catch up with the rest of the world, progress has also been made on the research front and sharing of learning and teaching practices via forums such as the Vice Chancellor's Learning and Teaching Forum (VCL&T) since 2010. It has been noted that the VCL&T forum helps share

ICT-integrated pedagogical practices with a wider community as this forum is also live web-cast to all the university's regional campuses. Discussing innovations such as using smart boards to enhance classroom teaching, an early warning system to alert and monitor students in an elearning environment, introduction of an ipads project in Samoa, using web-conferencing as a tool across the region for group presentations has helped instructors realize the potential of ICTs for the region. At the same time, although, 'talks and papers' that raise and discuss the opportunities and challenges generated by such innovations in the wake of regional diversity help various stakeholders to become better prepared for future developments.

ICT skills training

Online training for students and staff involved has been an important agenda for USP since 2008 and a great deal has been achieved since then. The CFDL (now CFL) prepared a simple 'Getting Started' guide on Moodle, which has been delivered to students during their first week at USP (Orientation Week) since 2009 (Rajneel Totaram, personal communication, 2013). USP recognized a lack of ICT skills among some of the first-year students and started offering UU100: Communication and Information Literacy as a compulsory course for all students enrolled in the year 2010 and thereafter. UU100 focuses on developing knowledge and competence in the use of computers and information resources among students. Thus, the course has helped students to prepare better not only for their studies requiring use of ICT in their tertiary education but also to acquire the necessary skills to meet the changing demands of the twenty-first century work-place. The USP Learning Management Team and other staff are periodically sent overseas for training and experts in elearning, mlearning and ICT are invited to run workshops and give lectures to staff at USP. Within USP, too, there now prevails a strong culture of ICT-related training and the staff is encouraged to attend.

Teacher training in online pedagogical practices, yet another important area, is taken care of by the SOE in USP. ED403 – Teaching Online: Pedagogy and Practice is taken by tertiary institution staff aspiring to become online instructors or even to sharpen their pre-existing online teaching skills, instructional designers, educational technologists and even MoE staff. In the last year, this course has been taken one step higher, with students practicing the use of web 2.0 tools, for example, making short audio, video and screen capture presentations for a dummy lecture, and conducting final presentations making use of web-conferencing software (www.gotomeeting.com). The hidden curriculum in ED403 helps students realize how to manage online teaching with unexpected technology hiccups. The establishment of the 'Teachers' Resource and eLearning Centre' (based in the SOE) in mid-2012 has opened up the path for continuous professional development for teachers across the region. The SOE acknowledges the importance of ICT training for school teachers; the Teachers' Resource and eLearning Centre also provides workshops for in-service and pre-service teachers that will help them prepare to teach with ICT as a tool.

Looking to the future: regional achievements and challenges

The support from JICA has helped USP with the upgrading of USPNet, installation of Ku-band systems at the Laucala campus and eight remote centres in the region, in the implementation of a regional m-Learning (with 20 ipads) pilot project in Samoa and the setting up of the Pacific Computer Emergency Response Team (PacCERT) from 2010 to 2012 (News@USP, 31 January 2013). Overseas funding, especially from Australia and New Zealand, has also assisted USP in reaching its current status in ICT and its integration in education. With initial support from various organizations, USP is now leading the region in a number of technology-integrated educational initiatives such as the Early Warning System project (to alert learners to their unsatisfactory performance in the course), sms project and the edutainment project under 'mlearning', 'elearning', 'tablet project', 'smart classroom', all with the aim to enhance students' learning experiences.

While the developments at USP show tremendous promise, work on certain technical areas is needed to capitalize on its potential with its ICT reach in higher education. For instance, funding, together with speed, reliability and responsiveness of web-based technologies, still remain big issues for USP and PICs at large, despite all the support and efforts from various stakeholders. Different island nations have achieved different milestones despite various challenges.

Some of the significant milestones are:

- Framework for Action on ICT Development in the Pacific;
- ICT Policy for Fiji, Vanuatu and
- Roll-out of Ku-band in remote sites in Tonga, Solomon Islands, Vanuatu and Fiji.

Ongoing priority challenges are:

- the non-implementation of optic fibre cable, which remains an issue in the majority of PICs, except for Fiji and the French and American territories in the South Pacific region;
- issues of human resource development in the ICT sector, in part but not solely owing to migration and
- lack of an educational and general ICT policy framework in a number of PICs.

Many communities throughout the region also still lack electricity and telecommunication facilities and some communities have unreliable infrastructure for these. Despite the many efforts and visible successes, diversity and distance still constitute a formidable environment for all forms of teaching and learning.

Renwick and others aptly described DE in PICs in the closing decade of the twentieth century, and this still rings true today:

> There can be no other part of the world with as many challenges to the development of effective distance education as the region covered by the USP. That remains the case today, and it was even more so in the early 1970s, when the university took its first decision to develop its Extension Services. The problems which other institutions have to some degree, the USP has on a massive scale. (Renwick et al., 1991: p. 41)

It is sobering to see how many of the challenges from the 1990s still persist. Whelan and Bhartu were correct in highlighting the level of complexity and dilemmas in implementing a policy or plan at USP by pointing out that, 'the deployment of an LMS takes place across one institution (USP) but in a dozen very different contexts' (Whelan and Bhartu, 2007: p. 1055). This is an observation that can be reiterated no less for USP's efforts towards ICT integration in education at different levels today.

In concluding, Lingam (2010) has pointed out the continuous effort required, despite the provision of ICT, for the education sector to grapple with issues relating to student access and equity. He adds that owing to the remote locations of PICs, access to ICT is difficult for primary school teachers and therefore it is not easy to reach out to those who are in the remotest locations. Teachers are the only civil servants serving in many such contexts, because in a remote location there is usually one school serving a small student population. The remote, and sometimes even the less remote, parts of the Pacific region not infrequently face considerable difficulties in accessing email and internet services; in other parts, there may not even be an electricity supply (Lingam, 2010). These are challenges not only for the Pacific region but also for other jurisdictions (Matthewson, 2000; Gold et al., 2002, as cited in Lingam, 2010). Taylor (1999) cautioned that we are faced with the situation of technology haves and have-nots. Many communities in various countries in the region lack electricity or even broadcast radio (Matthewson, 1994, as cited in Lingam, 2010). Technology can clearly help but, if we are not careful, it can also further widen the gap in access to continuing education between those living in rural and urban areas (Lingam, 2010). However, the formulation and implementation of a systematic, and locally grounded, research agenda could do much to help to understand such complexities, and to attend to the barriers to the future integration of ICT in education at all levels.

On the one hand, PICs are looking ahead to ensure each island nation's ICT infrastructure improves. This is evident in the fact that FSM, Fiji, Guam, Marshall Islands, PNG, Tonga and American Samoa already have optic fibre cable, Vanuatu launched its optic fibre cable in early 2014 and Samoa and Solomon Islands are negotiating. On the other hand, O3b[4] solutions in the Cook Islands have paved the way for a different kind of technology in the region. A few National Research and Education Networks do exist in the Pacific Region, such as the Pacific Islands Universities Research Network (PIURN) established in November 2012, the USPNet Project of the USP and French-established networks for New Caledonia, Wallis and Futuna and French Polynesia. However, a need to establish a Pacific Regional Research and Education Network (PRREN) was deliberated at the ACP Connect – Connectivity in the Pacific Meeting in Apia, Samoa, 18–19 April 2013. Two of the resolutions from this meeting will in turn strengthen regional initiatives in educational quality with ICT:

> Pacific ICT Regulatory Resource Centre (PIRRC) and USP will provide some seed initiatives in Research computing, Education technologies, digital libraries etc. as starting points for participation. USP as the lead Council of Regional Organisations in the Pacific (CROP) agency for ICT will establish an information clearing house as part of the ICT Outreach initiative. (ACP-Connect Pacific Report, 2012: p. 5)

USP, being now the leading CROP agency for ICT, will be developing PRREN, which will have ripple effects in strengthening the research agenda in PICs. The development of RREN involves negotiating with PICs governments where the countries employ submarine fibre. Simply put, since the countries currently use only one-eighth of their cable capacity, each country will be requested to give one-eighth towards RREN, facilitating improvement of the internet capacity and hence of the quality of education and research.

USP is serving the Pacific region. Although technology has revolutionized the delivery of education, there are still clienteles whose remoteness renders them well-nigh unreachable. Online learning is a major challenge in a context such as this (Lingam, 2010; Raturi, 2012b). The assumption that technology enhances student learning and academic achievement needs careful assessment by all stakeholders including the higher education sector. The authors' extensive work experience in the Pacific region helps to reveal both the strengths and the limitations of ICT in reaching out to many students in remote locations across the region. However, a systematic research agenda with action research as an essential component has much to offer to better inform the higher education sector on ICT-integrated pedagogies and practices. It is appropriate to conclude that ICTs have been well integrated into PICs education systems at both school and tertiary levels and their use can be expected to rise exponentially in the years to come. The sporadic use and functionality of telecommunication systems in PICs, which Wah (1997) highlighted as the second millennium approached, has dramatically improved, yet this still needs to be strengthened further for successful penetration across the ocean swells of our region.

Finally, it is reassuring to note USP's commitment, in its Strategic Plan 2013–2018, to the use of ICT at different levels of education throughout the region. This emphasizes both the role ICT will play in building the knowledge economy and USP's effort to reach students in the remoter reaches of the region. The commitment to leverage ICT infrastructure and its integration in education is evident in the University's Strategic Plan: 'ICT and knowledge economy' is one of its seven strategic themes for the period 2013–2018:

> The University will play a key role in this area (ICT and Knowledge Economy) as well as develop a knowledge Hub and ICT-based pedagogies, making its knowledge creation both a regional resource and a means to developing and enhancing regional capacity to take advantage of the rapidly emerging ICT-based industries and environments. (USP Strategic Plan 2013–2018: p. 23)

The commitments being made by the ministries of education and other stakeholders throughout the region, such as the 5-year plan and funding earmarked by MoE, Fiji, are a further boost to the education sector. Acknowledging these opportunities and challenges, and with ongoing support from a wide range of national and international stakeholders, the use of ICTs to enhance accessibility to quality education is clearly a priority agenda that key players in the region are keen to advance throughout PICs, and across the wider Australia, New Zealand and Pacific Region as a whole.

Notes

1 www.laptop.org.
2 Class Shares was USP's home grown course management system that allowed only one-way communication, that is from lecturer to student.
3 REACT is a software, 'Remote Education And Conferencing Tool'; it allows for audio–video conferencing from a personal computer.
4 http://www.o3bnetworks.com/.

References

ACP-Connect Pacific Report (2012), 'Assessment Study of Needs and Identification of Options for Interconnecting Local Research and Educational Centres in the ACP Pacific Region', *ACP-Connect-2012-011-v5*. AETS Consortium.

Africa Partnership Forum (2008), *ICT in Africa: Boosting Economic Growth and Poverty Reduction. A Report for Africa Partnership Forum, 7–8th April, 2008*. Available at: http://www.africapartnershipforum.org/meetingdocuments/40314752.pdf (Accessed: 27 August 2013).

Baba, T. (1997), 'Higher Education and Human Resource Development in Pacific', *Directions* 19 (2). Available at: http://www.directions.usp.ac.fj.cache5.usp.ac.fj:2048/collect/direct/index/assoc/D770136.dir/doc.pdf (Accessed: 20 December 2012).

Bakalevu, S. (2005), 'Regional Perspective on Current Status and Trends of ICT Applications in Education', in ICT Capacity Building at USP Project, Fiji (ed.), *ICT in Secondary Education in the Pacific Region: Status, Trends and Prospects*. Available at: http://www.usp.ac.fj/jica/ict_research/documents/pdf_files/ICT%20in%20Secondary%20Education%20in%20the%20Pacific%20Region.pdf (Accessed: 20 December 2012).

Baselala, E. (2011), 'ICT Project to Link Tonga to the World', *Fiji Times*. Available at: http://www.fijitimes.com/story.aspx?id=178734 (Accessed: 27 March 2013).

Blurton, C. (1999), *New Directions in ICT-Use in Education*. Paris: UNESCO.

Bureau of Statistics, Fiji (2013). Available at: http://www.statsfiji.gov.fj/index.php/migration-a-tourism/10-migration-statistics/migration-a-tourism/117-movement-of-fiji-residents (Accessed: 30 September 2013).

Chandra, R. (2000), *From Dual-Mode to Multimodal, Flexible Teaching and Learning: Distance Education at the University of the South Pacific. Conference Proceedings.* Available at: http://www.col.org/SiteCollectionDocuments/2_conf_proc_Chandra. pdf (Accessed: 20 December 2012).

Chandra, R., Koroivulaono, T. and Hazelman, V. (2011), 'Leveraging Technology for Tertiary Education in the South Pacific', in M. Martin and M. Bray (eds), *Tertiary Education in Small States: Planning in the Context of Globalization.* Paris, France: International Institute for Educational Planning, pp. 215–232. Available at: http:// www.iiep.unesco.org/fileadmin/user_upload/Info_Services_Publications/pdf/2011/ Martin-Bray_Small_states.pdf (Accessed: 20 January 2013).

Core ICT Indicators (2010), *Partnership on Measuring ICT for Development.* Available at: http://www.uis.unesco.org/Communication/Documents/Core_ICT_ Indicators_2010.pdf (Accessed: 3 April 2013).

Evans, J. and Hazelman, V. (2006), *Hard Digital Realities: Teaching with Technology in the Pacific Islands.* Available at: http://pcf4.dec.uwi.edu/viewpaper. php?id=192&print=1 (Accessed: 31 January 2013).

Ezell, S. J. (2012), *The benefits of ITA Expansion for Developing Countries.* The Information Technology and Innovation Foundation.

Gold, M., Swann, J. and Yee Chief, I. (2002), 'Keeping It Flexible: Integrating Technology into Distance Education in the South Pacific', *Educational Technology and Society* 5 (1), 55–59.

Horsley, M. (1984), 'Some Perspectives on Computer Education in South Pacific Schools', *Directions: Journal of Educational Studies.* Available at: http://www. directions.usp.ac.fj.cache5.usp.ac.fj:2048/collect/direct/index/assoc/D769896.dir/ doc.pdf (Accessed: 20 December 2012).

— (1988), 'Training Teachers to Cope with Computers in Schools', *Directions: Journal of Educational Studies.* Available at: http://www.directions.usp.ac.fj.cache5.usp. ac.fj:2048/collect/direct/index/assoc/D769967.dir/doc.pdf (Accessed: 20 December 2012).

ICT Capacity Building at USP Project (2005), *ICT in Secondary Education in the Pacific Region: Status, Trends and Prospects,* ICT Capacity Building at USP Project (ed.). Fiji. Available at: http://www.usp.ac.fj/jica/ict_research/documents/pdf_files/ ICT%20in%20Secondary%20Education%20in%20the%20Pacific%20Region.pdf (Accessed: 20 December 2012).

ITU Report (2013), *Measuring the Information Society.* International Telecommunication Union. Available at: http://www.itu.int/en/ITU-D/Statistics/ Documents/publications/mis2013/MIS2013_without_Annex_4.pdf (Accessed: 7 March 2014).

Internet World Statistics (2012), Available at: http://www.internetworldstats.com/stats6. htm (Accessed: 5 January 2013).

Jenkins, D. (1993), 'Regional Collaboration in Teacher Education', *Pacific Curriculum Network* 2 (1), 19–20.

Johansson-Fua, S. (2005), 'Regional Workshop on ICT in Education: A Summation', *ICT in Secondary Education in the Pacific Region: Status, Trends and Prospects*, ICT Capacity Building at USP Project (ed.). Suva, Fiji. Available at: http://www.usp.ac.fj/jica/ict_research/documents/pdf_files/ICT%20in%20Secondary%20Education%20in%20the%20Pacific%20Region.pdf (Accessed: 20 December 2012).

Khuong Vu. (2005), *Measuring the Impacts of ICT Investments on Economic Growth*. Available at: http://www.hks.harvard.edu/m-rcbg/ptep/khuongvu/Key%20paper.pdf (Accessed: 28 August 2013).

Larson, A. (2000), *Remarks Delivered at the Sovereignty in the Digital Age Series*. Washington, DC: Woodrow Wilson Center.

Lingam, G. I. (2010), 'Continuing Education via Distance Learning: The Case of Primary Teachers in the Regional Countries Served by The University of the South Pacific', *International Journal of Continuing Education and Lifelong Learning* 2 (2), 89–99.

Lingam, G. I. and Burnett, G. (2008), 'Reaching the Unreached Primary Teachers: Distance Teacher Education at the University of the South Pacific', *Journal of Distance Learning* 12 (1), 16–25.

Matthewson, C. (1994), 'Distance Beyond Measure: A View from and of the Pacific', *Directions: Journal of Educational Studies* 16 (2), 29–35. Available at: http://www.directions.usp.ac.fj.cache5.usp.ac.fj:2048/collect/direct/index/assoc/D770092.dir/doc.pdf (Accessed: 20 December 2012).

— (2000), 'The South Pacific: Journeys of Navigation in Distance Education', in R. Guy, T. Kosage and R. Hayakawa (eds), *Distance Education in the South Pacific: Nets and Voyages*. Suva, Fiji: Institute of Pacific Studies, The University of the South Pacific, pp. 43–97.

Menefee, T. and Bray, M. (2013), 'Education in the Commonwealth: Towards and Beyond the Internationally Agreed Goals', A Report Commissioned for the 18th Conference of Commonwealth Education Ministers in Mauritius, 28–31 August 2012 based around the theme 'Education in the Commonwealth: Bridging the Gap as we Accelerate Towards Achieving Internationally Agreed Goals'. London: Commonwealth Secretariat.

Menrad, H. (2004), 'The Online Experience – The Students' Perspective', *Directions: Journal of Educational Studies* 26 (2), 27–40.

Nabobo-Baba, U. (2008), 'Education: "Increasing the Distance!" – Realities of E-ducation in the Developing World – The Case of The University of the South Pacific'. Paper presented at *'E-ducation Without Borders'* Conference 2003. Abu Dhabi Men's College, UAE, 22–24 February.

News@USP (2013), *Technical Project Drawds to An End*. Available at: http://www.usp.ac.fj/news/story.php?id=1220 (Accessed: 31 January 2013).

Nwosu, O. and Ogbomo, E. F. (2008), 'ICT in Education: A Catalyst for Effective Use of Information', *PNLA Quarterly* 75 (4). The Official Publication of the Pacific Northwest Library Association. Available at: http://unllib.unl.edu/LPP/PNLA%20Quarterly/nwosu-ogbomo75-4.htm (Accessed: 24 August 2013).

Organisation for Economic Cooperation and Development (OECD) (1999), *Knowledge Management in the Learning Society.* Paris: OECD/CERI.

Pacific News Centre (2012), *SPC: Pacific Islands will Benefit from ICT.* Available at: http://www.pacificnewscenter.com/index.php?option=com_content&view =article&id=26549:spc-pacific-islands-will-benefit-from-ict&catid=45:guam-news&Itemid=156 (Accessed: 20 December 2012).

PEACESAT website (2013), Available at: http://www.peacesat.hawaii. edu/10ABOUTUS/ProgramTimeline/index.htm (Accessed: 2 February 2013).

Prasad, B. S. (1993), 'Computer Education in Fiji Secondary Schools: A Critique', *Directions: Journal of Educational Studies* 29, 15 (2), 52–58. Available at: http://www. directions.usp.ac.fj.cache5.usp.ac.fj:2048/collect/direct/index/assoc/D770080.dir/ doc.pdf (Accessed: 20 December 2012).

PRIDE website. Available at: http://www.usp.ac.fj/index.php?id=pride (Accessed: 27 March 2013).

Puamau, P. (2005), *Rethinking Educational Platform: A Pacific Perspective,* A paper presented at the International Conference 'Redesigning pedagogy: Research, Policy & Practice' National Institute of Education. Singapore: Nanyang Technological University.

Rao, V., Bhartu, D. and Koroivulaono, T. (2011), Moodle@USP. *A Report Submitted to USP.*

Raturi, S. (2010), Learners' Satisfaction of, and Preference for, Different Instructional Delivery Modes: A Case Study from the University of the South Pacific, Master of Education (unpublished thesis). Fiji: University of the South Pacific.

— (2012a), ICT in Education, *ED250: Curriculum Studies I* [Online via Internal VLE]. Fiji: University of the South Pacific.

— (2012b), 'Enhancing Interaction in Online Learning: Challenges and Opportunities', VC L&T forum. Fiji: University of the South Pacific. Available at: http://www.usp. ac.fj/fileadmin/files/videos/2012/VCs_L%26T_Forum/Learning%20Technologies/ Emerging%20Issues/Shika%20Raturi%20ED400/Shika%20Raturi%20ED400.html (Accessed: 2 April 2013).

Raturi, S., Hogan, R. and Thaman, K. H. (2011a), Learners's Access to Tools and Experience with Technology at the University of the South Pacific: Readiness for e-Learning, *Australasian Journal of Educational Technology* 27 (3). Available at: http://www.ascilite.org.au/ajet/ajet27/raturi.html (Accessed: 24 December 2012).

— (2011b), 'Learners' Preference for Instructional Delivery Mode: A Case Study from the University of South Pacific (USP)', *International Journal of Instructional Technology and Distance Learning* 8 (6). Available at: http://www.itdl.org/Journal/ Jun_11/index.htm (Accessed: December 2012).

Reddy, S. (1989), 'Educational Radio: Directions in the Pacific', *Directions: Journal of Educational Studies* 3, 18–24. Available at: http://www.directions.usp.ac.fj.cache5. usp.ac.fj:2048/collect/direct/index/assoc/D769827.dir/doc.pdf (Accessed: 20 December 2012).

Renwick, W. K., King, St C. and Shale, D. G. (1991), *Distance Education at the University of the South Pacific, Commonwealth of Learning*. Vancouver, Canada. Available at: http://www.col.org/SiteCollectionDocuments/Distance_education_University_South_Pacific.pdf (Accessed: 25 January 2013).

Sanga, K. (2005), 'A Strategy for Rethinking Aid Relationship', in K. Sanga, C. Chu, C. Hall, L. Crowl (eds), *Re-Thinking Aid Relationships in Pacific Education*. Suva, Fiji: University of the South Pacific Institute of Education.

Sharma, A. N. (2008), 'ICT in Teacher Education: The USP Experience', in J. Dorovolomo, C. F. Koya, H. P. Phan, J. Veramu and U. Nabobo-Baba (eds), *Pacific Education: Issues and Perspective*. Fiji: University of South Pacific, pp. 165–179.

Sharma, A. (2009). 'ICT in Teacher Education: The USP experience, Turmoil and Turbulence in Small Developing States: Going Beyond Survival', *11th Annual Conference*, Sir Arthur Lewis Institute of Social and Economic Studies, University of West Indies, St Augustine Campus, Trinidad and Tobago. Available at: http://sta.uwi.edu/conferences/09/salises/documents/A%20Sharma.pdf (Accessed: 24 December 2012).

SPC (n.d.), *Improving ICT Capacity for Palau National Congress*. Available at: http://www.spc.int/edd/en/section-01/digital-strategy/147-improving-ict-capacity-for-palau-national-congress?&lang=en_us&output=json&session-id=1127a0860a91e3c5f46f732aeed9bec6 (Accessed: 2 April 2013).

Taylor, R. (1999), *Use of ICT in Education: University of Canterbury and EcoCARE Pacific Trust*. Available at: http://www.biol.canterbury.ac.nz/people/taylorr.shtml (Accessed: 11 August 2009).

Thaman, K. H. (2001), 'Open and Flexible Learning for Whom? Re Thinking Distance Education', *Directions* 23 (1), 3–22. Available at: http://www.directions.usp.ac.fj.cache5.usp.ac.fj:2048/collect/direct/index/assoc/D770198.dir/doc.pdf (Accessed: 20 December 2012).

Tonga Online (2013), *King Launches High Speed Internet Connecting Tonga to the World*. Available at: http://matangitonga.to/2013/08/21/king-launches-high-speed-internet-connecting-tonga-world (Accessed: 23 August 2009).

UN Report (2012), 'Boosting Development with Broadband and ICTs', *UN Department of Economic and Social Affairs*. Available at: http://www.un.org/en/development/desa/news/ecosoc/communications-4-development.html (Accessed: 26 August 2013).

UNESCO (n.d.), 'List of Small Island Developing States', *Small Island Developing States*. Available at: http://www.unesco.org/new/en/natural-sciences/priority-areas/sids/about-unesco-and-sids/sids-list/ (Accessed: 29 August, 2011).

— (1993), *Distance Education in Asia and the Pacific: Country Papers, New Papers on Higher Education, Studies and Research*. 3. Available at: http://www.unesco.org/education/pdf/53_23c.pdf (Accessed: 24 January 2013).

UNESCO Bangkok Report (2004), *Component: Curriculum, Pedagogy and Content Development, Integrating ICTs into Education: Lessons Learned*. Available at: http://www.unescobkk.org/fileadmin/user_upload/ict/e-books/ICTLessonsLearned/6.pdf (Accessed: 8 January 2013).

UNESCO website (2013), Available at: http://www.unesco.org/new/en/education/
     resources/online-materials/single-view/news/unescos_vision_of_education_
     after_2015/ (Accessed: 2 April 2013).
USP Strategic Plan (2013–2018), *Towards Excellence in Learning and Knowledge
     Creation, Office of the Vice-Chancellor and President.* Fiji: The University of the South
     Pacific.
Wah, R. (1997), *Online Teaching: The Basic Issues at the University of the South Pacific.*
     Available at: http://tcc.kcc.hawaii.edu/previous/TCC%201997/wah.html (Accessed:
     27 December 2012).
Wallace, J. (1990), 'Extension Studies at USP – An Agenda for Research', *Directions:
     Journal of Educational Studies* 29–36. Available at: http://www.directions.usp.ac.fj.
     cache5.usp.ac.fj:2048/collect/direct/index/assoc/D769987.dir/doc.pdf (Accessed:
     20 December 2012).
Wheelan, R. (2008), 'Use of ICT in Education in the South Pacific: Findings of the
     Pacific eLearning Observatory', *Distance Education* 29 (1), 53–70.
Whelan, R. and Bhartu, D. (2007), 'Factors in the Implementation of a Learning
     Management System at a Large University', *ICT: Providing Choices for Learners and
     Learning. Proceedings Ascilite Singapore 2007.* Available at: http://www.ascilite.org.
     au/conferences/singapore07/procs/whelan.pdf (Accessed: 20 December 2012).
Williams, E., Kato, M. and Khan, N. (2004), 'Evaluation of Computer Science
     Curriculum in Fiji Secondary Schools', *ICT Capacity Building at USP Project.* Suva,
     Fiji.
World Telecommunication/ICT Development Report (2010), *Monitoring the
     WSIS Targets – A Mid-Term Review.* Available at: http://www.uis.unesco.org/
     Communication/Documents/WTDR2010_e.pdf (Accessed: 2 April 2013).

Index